PRACTICAL COMPUTING

LYNN HOGAN

Calhoun Community College

PEARSON

Prentice
Hall

Upper Saddle River, New Jersey

Hogan, Lynn.
  Practical computing / Lynn Hogan.
    p. cm.
  ISBN 0-13-144133-7
  1. Electronic data processing. I. Title.
QA76.H586 2005
004--dc22

                    2003024801

Executive Aquisitions Editor: Jodi McPherson
VP/Publisher: Natalie E. Anderson
Acquisitions Editor: Melissa Sabella
Editorial Assistant: Alana Meyers
Developmental Editor: Christy Parrish
Assistant Editor, Supplements: Melissa Edwards
Senior Media Project Manager: Cathi Profitko
Senior Marketing Manager: Emily Williams Knight
Manager (Production): Gail Steier de Acevedo
Project Manager (Production): Vanessa Nuttry
Manufacturing Buyer: Vanessa Nuttry
Design Manager: Maria Lange
Interior Design: Pre-Press Company, Inc.
Cover Design: Steve Frim
Cover Illustration: Amy Vangsgard/SIS, Inc.
Manager, Print Production: Christy Mahon
Composition/Full-Service Project Management: Pre-Press Company, Inc.
Cover Printer: Phoenix Color
Printer/Binder: Quebecor World/Dubuque

Pearson Education LTD.
Pearson Education Singapore, Pte. Ltd
Pearson Education, Canada, Ltd
Pearson Education–Japan

Pearson Education Australia PTY, Limited
Pearson Education North Asia Ltd
Pearson Educación de Mexico, S.A. de C.V.
Pearson Education Malaysia, Pte. Ltd

10 9 8 7 6 5 4 3
ISBN 0-13-144133-7

Acknowledgments

My sincere appreciation goes to Jodi McPherson, executive acquisitions editor, for first believing in this project. She never wavered in her support and her belief that this textbook would be successful. Special thanks go to Christy Parrish, development editor, for her hard work and attention to detail. We worked with a tight timeline, and I know that she put in just as many sleepless nights as I did. The entire Prentice Hall team is to be commended for supplying the design and organizational expertise necessary to ensure the success of this textbook. Melissa Sabella and Alana Meyers kept us on schedule, while Gail Steier worked tirelessly with the design. All in all, the success of this textbook is due not to my efforts alone, but to the combined talent and direction of the Prentice Hall family, of which I am pleased to be a member.

Thanks to the reviewers of this text, whose comments and suggestions were invaluable in our attempt to produce the best possible textbook:

Nazih Abdallah, University of Central Florida
Lancie Affonso, College of Charleston
Gary R. Armstrong, Shippensburg University
Ita Borger-Boglin, San Antonio College
Jack Bresenham, Winthrop University
Judith C. Brown, University of Memphis
Cindy Buell, Central Oregon Community College
Debra Burhans, Canisius College
Debra Chapman, University of South Alabama
Dewey DeFalco, Jones College
Allen Dooley, Pasadena City College
Larry Dugan, Finger Lakes Community College
Mimi Duncan, University of Missouri, St Louis
Susan Fry, Boise State University
Marta Gonzalez, Hudson County Community College
Kurt W. Kominek, Northeast State Technical Community College
Richard W. Land, International Academy of Design & Technology
Daniela Marghitu, Auburn University
Cindi A. Nadelman, New England College
Tim Pelton, University of Victoria
Jennifer Pickle, Amarillo College
Pratap P. Reddy, Raritan Valley Community College
Steven Smith, El Paso Community College
Steve St. John, Tulsa Community College
Doug Yoder, Columbus State Community College
David L. Zagorodney, Heald College

Dedication

A dream becomes reality when you set your mind to it and when you have the support of people who believe in you. For me, those people are my husband, Paul, who first challenged me to write a book, and my daughters, Jennifer and Allison, who put up with a part-time mother for the duration of this project. I must also recognize the contribution of my parents, who supported this effort with tireless enthusiasm. It is to my family that I dedicate this book, for without them, it would certainly not have been possible.

About the Author

Lynn Hogan chairs the Department of Computer and Office Information Systems at Calhoun Community College in Decatur, Alabama, where she has taught for the past 22 years. She coordinates academic programs in microcomputer applications, office information systems, and programming. Active in distance education, she developed Calhoun's first Web-based class and continues to encourage expansion of distance education into other areas, such as programming, keyboarding, and microcomputer applications.

Lynn Hogan resides in Alabama with her husband, Paul, and daughters, Jennifer and Allison.

Preface

FOR THE INSTRUCTOR:
Why I Wrote this Book

We know the special challenges posed by the computer novice, and we are here to help you meet them! *Practical Computing* will help you ease your students into the world of computing with a user-friendly design and creative multimedia tools that make learning exciting. Designed with input from instructors who understand your needs, the lessons in *Practical Computing* address concepts in a disciplined, yet enjoyable way.

The inspiration for this book came from a computer literacy class I designed for adults who had very little computer background but a real eagerness to learn. The students' questions, interests, and suggestions helped shape the content of the class and, subsequently, this book.

The result immediately sparks student interest by focusing on the tasks they want to accomplish with their PCs as well as skills that they can apply at home or in the workplace right away. The sequence of topics is carefully set up to mimic the way new users would explore their computer.

Chapter 1 begins with what a computer does and the way it functions. Chapter 2 introduces software and how to run the programs, and Chapter 3 covers what Microsoft Windows does and how to work with it.

Because many new users are frustrated by lost or missing files, we address managing files and folders early on, in Chapters 4 and 5. Next, students move on to Chapters 6–8 where they explore the Internet, the ultimate goal of many students. In Chapters 6 and 7 they will master World Wide Web navigation, and in Chapter 8 they will learn the basics of e-mail and the ethical issues involved with its use. In Chapters 9 and 10 students will develop a basic knowledge of creating documents and spreadsheets.

This practical approach will get your students up and running fast.

What's Inside:

- Content that fits the level of your students
- Case studies that make sense of the content
- Examples that demonstrate the topic in a realistic way
- Explanation of the Why of Why am I doing this?
- **Hands On:** Projects that allow students to practice the material they have learned
- **In the Know:** Segments that go into more depth on particular issues and technologies
- **Web Watch:** Links to Web Sites related to the material
- **Quick Tips:** Tips and shortcuts for the practical use of the PC
- **Sanity Check:** Troubleshooting and help for students who are confused

For the Instructor

Instructor Resources

The new and improved Prentice Hall Instructor's Resource CD-ROM includes the tools you expect from a Prentice Hall Computer Concepts text, like:

- The Instructor's Manual in Word and PDF formats
- Solutions to all questions and exercises from the book and Web site
- Multiple, customizable PowerPoint slide presentations for each chapter
- Computer concepts animations
- TechTV videos
- Image library of all of the figures from the text

This CD-ROM is an interactive library of assets and links. It writes custom index pages that can be used as the foundation of a class presentation or online lecture. By navigating through this CD, you can collect the materials that are most relevant to your interests, edit them to create powerful class lectures, copy them to your own computer's hard drive, and/or upload them to an online course-management system.

TestGen Software

TestGen is a test generator program that lets you view and easily edit testbank questions, transfer them to tests, and print them in a variety of formats suitable to your teaching situation. The program also offers many options for organizing and displaying testbanks and tests. A built-in random number and text generator makes it ideal for creating multiple versions of tests that involve calculations, providing more possible test items than testbank questions. Powerful search and sort functions let you easily locate questions and arrange them in the order you prefer.

QuizMaster, also included in this package, allows students to take tests created with TestGen on a local area network. The QuizMaster Utility built into TestGen lets instructors view student records and print a variety of reports. Building tests is easy with TestGen, and exams can be easily uploaded into WebCT, Blackboard, and Course Compass.

Training and Assessment   **www.phgenit.com/support**

Prentice Hall offers performance-based training and assessment in one product Train & Assess IT. The training component offers computer-based training that a student can use to preview, learn, and review Microsoft Office application skills. Web or CD-ROM delivered, Train IT offers interactive, multimedia, computer-based training to augment classroom learning. Built-in prescriptive testing suggests a study path based not only on student test results but also on the specific textbook chosen for the course.

The assessment component offers computer-based testing that shares the same user interface as Train IT and can evaluate a student's knowledge about specific topics in Word, Excel, Access, PowerPoint, Outlook, the Internet, and computing concepts. It does this in a task-oriented environment to determine students' proficiency as well as comprehension of the topics. More extensive than the testing in Train IT, Assess IT offers more administrative features for the instructor and additional questions for the student.

Assess IT also allows professors to test students out of a course, place students in appropriate courses, and evaluate skill sets.

TechTV is the San Francisco–based cable network that showcases the smart, edgy, and unexpected side of technology. By telling stories through the prism of technology, TechTV provides programming that celebrates its viewers' passion, creativity, and lifestyle.

TechTV's programming falls into three categories:

1. **Help and Information,** with shows like *The Screen Savers,* TechTV's daily live variety show featuring everything from guest interviews and celebrities to product advice and demos; *Tech Live,* featuring the latest news on the industry's most important people, companies, products, and issues; and *Call for Help,* a live help and how-to show providing computing tips and live viewer questions.
2. **Cool Docs,** with shows like *The Tech Of...,* a series that goes behind the scenes of modern life and shows you the technology that makes things tick; *Performance,* an investigation into how technology and science are molding the perfect athlete; and *Future Fighting Machines,* a fascinating look at the technology and tactics of warfare.
3. **Outrageous Fun,** with shows like *X-Play,* exploring the latest and greatest in videogaming; and *Unscrewed with Martin Sargent,* a new late-night series showcasing the darker, funnier world of technology.

For more information, log on to www.techtv.com or contact your local cable or satellite provider to get TechTV in your area.

Tools for Online Learning

Companion Web Site   **www.prenhall.com/practicalcomputing**

This text is accompanied by a companion Web site at **www.prenhall.com/practicalcomputing**. Features of this new site include an interactive study guide, downloadable supplements, online end-of-chapter materials, additional internet exercises, TechTV videos, Web resource links such as Careers in IT and crossword puzzles, plus technology updates and bonus chapters on the latest trends and hottest topics in information technology. All links to Web exercises are constantly updated to ensure accuracy.

ONLINE Courseware for Blackboard, WebCT, and CourseCompass

Now you have the freedom to personalize your own online course materials! Prentice Hall provides the content and support you need to create and manage your own online course in WebCT, Blackboard, or Prentice Hall's own CourseCompass. Content includes lecture material, interactive exercises, e-commerce case videos, additional testing questions, and projects and animations.

CourseCompass   **www.coursecompass.com**

CourseCompass is a dynamic, interactive online course-management tool powered exclusively for Pearson Education by Blackboard. This exciting product allows you to teach market-leading Pearson Education content in an easy-to-use, customizable format.

Blackboard   **www.prenhall.com/blackboard**

Prentice Hall's abundant online content, combined with Blackboard's popular tools and interface, result in robust Web-based courses that are easy to implement, manage, and use, taking your courses to new heights in student interaction and learning.

WebCT   **www.prenhall.com/webct**

WebCT provides many course-management tools, including page tracking, progress tracking, class and student management, a gradebook, communication tools, a calendar, reporting tools, and more. GOLD LEVEL CUSTOMER SUPPORT, available exclusively to adopters of Prentice Hall courses, is provided free of charge upon adoption and provides you with priority assistance, training discounts, and dedicated technical support.

Preface

For the Student

Welcome to the exciting world of computers! *Practical Computing* was written with you, the beginner, in mind. It is carefully arranged to guide you through every step of learning how to use your PC, from the first plug in to the latest upgrades. When you have completed this book, you will have the skills to get what you want out of this versatile machine.

The inspiration for this book came from a computer literacy class designed for adults who had very little computer background but a real eagerness to learn. The students' questions, interests, and suggestions helped shape the content of the class and, subsequently, this book.

Using This Book

The book is carefully set up the way you would first explore a computer.

Chapter 1 shows you the basics of what a computer does and the way it functions. Chapter 2 introduces software and how to run the programs, and in Chapter 3 you will learn what Microsoft Windows does and how to work with it.

To prevent you from getting frustrated by lost files, we address managing files and folders early on, in Chapters 4 and 5. Next, you will move to Chapters 6–8 to explore the Internet which may be why you wanted to learn how to use a computer in the first place. In Chapters 6 and 7 you will master navigating the World Wide Web, and in Chapter 8 you will learn the basics of e-mail and the ethical issues involved with its use. In Chapters 9 and 10 you will get a basic knowledge of creating documents and spreadsheets.

With this practical approach, you will be up and running fast.

IN THE KNOW: These are segments that go into more depth on particular issues and technologies.

---

38   *Software*

In the Know

Steve Jobs and Stephen Wozniak were high-school friends who shared a vision. Jobs fully believed that science and technology were the route to a better future for humankind, while Wozniak cheerfully believed in the goodness of humanity. Combining human-interest skills, a focus on technology, and a firm foundation in electronics, the two friends developed a video teletype terminal, complete with video display, and then tried to market the product. Challenged by the lack of interest they found with computer companies, they began their own company, named Apple after their favorite snack food. That was in 1976.

The original Apple computer, built at Jobs' home, was sold as a partially assembled kit for computer hobbyists. The first slogan for the new company was "Byte into an Apple." Quickly moving to capture more of the professional market share, they redesigned the Apple computer and packaged it in an attractive plastic case. That was the Apple II, introduced in 1978. Marketing was expanded to include the home computer user.

The Apple II included a built-in BASIC interpreter (allowing users to write computer programs in the BASIC computer language) and a color display. With eight expansion slots, a cassette tape drive, and a full-size 52-key keyboard, the Apple II became the most popular computer of its time. Schools began to invest in Apple computers, purchasing inexpensive programs like Apple Writer for student use.

In 1980, Apple brought out the Apple III, which was an instant disappointment. It included up to 256 KB of RAM, a floppy disk drive, and an optional 5 MB hard drive. But the computer that was supposed to run Apple II programs had difficulty, ran hot, and often failed. Reintroduced in 1981, it was overwhelmed by the success of the IBM PC, which was designed to be a business machine and was sold by a trained fleet of IBM representatives.

Apple's next attempt was to develop a business computer, the Lisa. The system included a GUI, a mouse, a floppy drive, and an external hard drive. Costing $10,000, the computer never caught on. Only 10,000 units were ever sold. The company regrouped in its effort to make a low-cost computer that could be used by anybody. During the 1984 Super Bowl, the Macintosh was introduced to the world. Immensely successful, the Macintosh continues to be Apple's primary product.

Apple continues as a viable computer company but is definitely overshadowed by the larger market share of PC-compatible computers. Microsoft controls a huge segment of the software market, relegating Apple's operating system to only about 10 percent of all installations. Sometimes a high-quality product is just not enough!

which makes it ideal for managing activities of large computers, does nothing to endear it to the personal computer market. UNIX's strength lies in its capability to coordinate activities between a server and its clients (smaller computers in communication with a server).

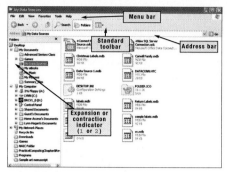

Figure 5.2 **Using Windows Explorer you can view computer resources, folders, and files.**

SANITY CHECK: If you are confused or lost, these will help you with troubleshooting and understanding the material.

◀▶ Other Ways

You can also work with My Computer in the Exploring view. Some people are more comfortable with the My Computer interface, and it is a little easier to get to because you don't have to travel the Start menu the way you do to access Windows Explorer. At the desktop or on the Start menu, right-click My Computer. Then click Explore. My Computer is displayed just like Windows Explorer, with a folders pane and a contents pane. Another way to get the same view is by double-clicking My Computer to open it, and clicking View, Explorer Bar, and Folders.

side. To open Windows Explorer, click Start, All Programs, Accessories, and Windows Explorer. In some older versions of Windows, you can access Windows Explorer by opening My Computer and clicking View, Explorer Bar, and Folders.

✓SANITY CHECK

Your view of Windows Explorer might show a tasks pane on the left instead of a folders pane. The tasks pane includes selections that are related to the item selected. For example, if the currently selected folder is *My Documents*, the tasks pane would include options to make a new folder, publish the folder to the Web, or to share the folder with others. Other options would appear if the selected item were a disk drive instead of a folder. You can easily toggle between the two views by clicking the Folders button on the Standard toolbar. If you don't see a Standard toolbar, click View, Toolbars, and click to bring the Standard toolbar into view.

Note that many items have a plus sign (1) before the title. Some might instead have a minus sign (2). The plus sign is an indicator that the item has additional folders beneath it in the folder structure. Click the "1" to expand the detail to another level. If any folders at the newly displayed level contain **subfolders**, you will see another "1" beside each of them, which you can click to display their contents. You will see that as each folder level is expanded, the display [...] so that you can easily determine which folders are on the same lev[...] are actually subfolders of others. After a folder is fully expanded, a m[...] will appear to its left. Clicking a minus sign removes the folder level [...] play. Please note that expanding and contracting folders affects only [...] the folder structure, not the physical arrangement of folders on the [...]

▶ Quick Tip

Some Web pages appear different or function better when viewed with an independent browser (either Netscape Communicator or Internet Explorer), as opposed to a commercial online service like AOL. You will know that only if the Web page displays a message letting you know that not all parts of the page will be visible, or if the view is distorted. If that should be the case, you can sign on to your service provider. Once connected, minimize the ISP window. That means that although you will still be connected to the Internet, the ISP's browser will no longer appear except as a button on the taskbar. If you have downloaded an independent browser, its icon should appear on the desktop. Double-click the icon to open the browser's window so you can work directly with the Internet using the browser itself.

QUICK TIPS: They provide tips and shortcuts for the practical use of the PC.

▼ Web Watch

As you work with the Internet, you will probably find a browser with which you are most comfortable and learn to use it well. Remember that a browser simply lets you view the Internet, allowing you to enjoy and customize your Internet environment. Visit **www.learnthenet.com/english/html/12browser.htm** to investigate the use of browsers and to get a few tips on browser selection.

WEB WATCH: These are links to Web sites related to material for your further learning.

a download from the Internet and have similar features, including a menu bar, toolbar, and address bar. Remember that if you are working with America Online or CompuServe, you won't need a separate browser. The browser is built into the interface of your service provider, making your Internet experience a little easier.

The Internet Explorer browser can be downloaded at **www.microsoft.com/ie**, whereas Netscape Communicator can be found at **www.netscape.com**. As with almost all software, new versions of browsers are periodically developed and made available. It is a good idea to download newer versions as they become available, because they normally include improved features for accessing Internet resources. You will learn to download programs in Chapter 7.

Accessing Web Sites

The World Wide Web (WWW) is definitely a commercial endeavor, with millions of Web sites offering products or services. Many other sites are informational or offer a public service. Virtual libraries are now available online, and professional organizations and nonprofit groups offer a wealth of consumer and medical information. With the abundance of information and entertainment on the Web, you will want to access interesting sites quickly and easily. That is the purpose of your browser.

A key element of the browser interface is the address bar, as shown in Figure 6.7. It is the long white bar toward the top of your browser screen, displaying a Web address that corresponds to the page that you are currently viewing. To move to another Web page, you can type the URL in the address bar. If you don't know the URL, you can search for specific sites using search tools described later in this chapter.

✓SANITY CHECK

When you type a URL and press ⏎Enter (or click Go), you expect to be directed to the new Web page. If, instead, you receive a message to the effect that the Web page cannot be displayed, it is likely that you typed the address incorrectly or that the Web page is no longer available. Check the URL to see if you made a typing error. If so, click in the address bar and retype the address, or simply make any corrections necessary to the address. If the Web page is no longer available, retyping the address won't help. The Web page is simply not there anymore. You can then use the search tools that you will learn later in this chapter to try to locate a similar Web page.

To type a URL and move to another Web page:

1. Click in the address bar where the current address is displayed. The address should become shaded, or selected.

✓SANITY CHECK

If the Web address is not shaded, but you see instead a blinking black bar (cursor), you can remove the current address by pressing Del to delete characters to the right of the cursor or ⬅Backspace to delete characters to the left of the cursor.

2. With the current address selected or deleted, type the new address. Be sure to press ⏎Enter or click Go after the address is typed.

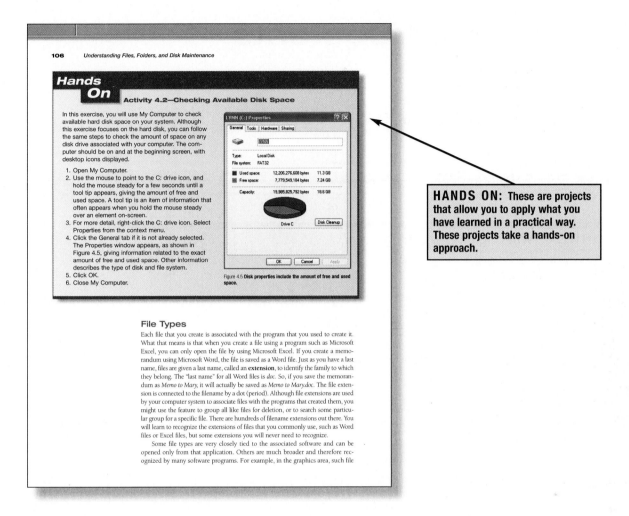

Hands On

Activity 4.2—Checking Available Disk Space

In this exercise, you will use My Computer to check available hard disk space on your system. Although this exercise focuses on the hard disk, you can follow the same steps to check the amount of space on any disk drive associated with your computer. The computer should be on and at the beginning screen, with desktop icons displayed.

1. Open My Computer.
2. Use the mouse to point to the C: drive icon, and hold the mouse steady for a few seconds until a tool tip appears, giving the amount of free and used space. A tool tip is an item of information that often appears when you hold the mouse steady over an element on-screen.
3. For more detail, right-click the C: drive icon. Select Properties from the context menu.
4. Click the General tab if it is not already selected. The Properties window appears, as shown in Figure 4.5, giving information related to the exact amount of free and used space. Other information describes the type of disk and file system.
5. Click OK.
6. Close My Computer.

Figure 4.5 **Disk properties include the amount of free and used space.**

HANDS ON: These are projects that allow you to apply what you have learned in a practical way. These projects take a hands-on approach.

File Types

Each file that you create is associated with the program that you used to create it. What that means is that when you create a file using a program such as Microsoft Excel, you can only open the file by using Microsoft Excel. If you create a memorandum using Microsoft Word, the file is saved as a Word file. Just as you have a last name, files are given a last name, called an **extension**, to identify the family to which they belong. The "last name" for all Word files is *doc*. So, if you save the memorandum as *Memo to Mary*, it will actually be saved as *Memo to Mary.doc*. The file extension is connected to the filename by a dot (period). Although file extensions are used by your computer system to associate files with the programs that created them, you might use the feature to group all like files for deletion, or to search some particular group for a specific file. There are hundreds of filename extensions out there. You will learn to recognize the extensions of files that you commonly use, such as Word files or Excel files, but some extensions you will never need to recognize.

Some file types are very closely tied to the associated software and can be opened only from that application. Others are much broader and therefore recognized by many software programs. For example, in the graphics area, such file

Please visit our Web site at **www.prenhall.com/practicalcomputing,** where you will find bonus chapters on the latest trends in information technology, an interactive study guide, online end-of-chapter materials, Careers in IT, TechTV videos, technology updates, crossword puzzles, and more.

Brief Contents

Table of Contents

Chapter 5   Working with Files and Folders **124**

Chapter 6   The Internet **147**

Understanding Your Personal Computer

A personal computer can offer a wealth of enjoyment to anyone who is willing to invest a little time in understanding how to work with it. Perhaps friends have told you how much fun it is to explore the Internet and keep up with family through e-mail. Others might be using a computer to create family trees, keep up with home finances, or maintain small business records. Those people on the computer commercials sure seem to think they need a computer! But what about you? Perhaps you have an interest but are just unsure of where to start. The first thing that you should do is carefully consider why you want a computer. Think about what you plan to do with it. Regardless of what you decide to use it for, owning a personal computer can open up a new world of activities and enjoyment.

The equipment that makes up a computer system is known as hardware. When you see an advertisement for a computer, you are reading about the computer's hardware. Such items as the keyboard, mouse, monitor, and printer are typical hardware

Objectives

When you complete this chapter, you will:

- Be able to identify types of personal computers.

- Understand how to power on a computer system.

- Become familiar with input, output, and processing components.

- Be aware of various categories of monitors and printers.

- Understand the concept of memory and how it relates to disk storage.

- Identify various forms of disk storage.

- Understand how to shut down a computer system.

- Know the steps to follow when setting up a new personal computer.

components. Anything related to a computer that you can pick up and hold is considered hardware. Knowing what hardware you will need to accomplish your computing goals is the first step toward making sure that you have all that you need to fully enjoy a computer.

Introducing the Personal Computers

The types of **microcomputers** on the market vary widely. One type of microcomputer, the **personal computer** (**PC**), is typically designed for individual use, providing access to the Internet and allowing users to work with programs of interest, for tasks such as word processing, editing photographs, or creating greeting cards. PCs can come in many sizes, from *desktop* models to *laptops* to *personal digital assistants* (*PDAs*) that are small enough to fit in the palm of your hand. Figure 1.1 shows a number of different personal computer options.

Most home computer users focus on getting the most capability for the lowest cost. A microcomputer system usually runs anywhere from $500 to $2,000, depending on manufacturer, speed, type, and other specifications. Before considering a computer for purchase, you should think about what you plan to do with it. A popular use of home computers is to create, edit, and print documents. You can maintain records on anything from business inventory to your book collection. It might be fun to learn to use a digital camera so that you can work with digital photos on a computer, printing them in various sizes. Many people enjoy recording family data and creating a family tree. Of course, connecting to the Internet

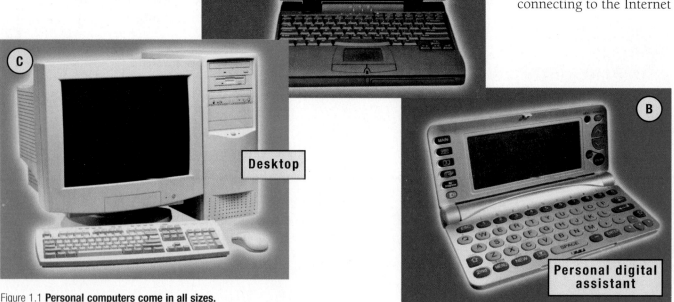

Figure 1.1 **Personal computers come in all sizes.**

In the Know

Who invented the computer? There is no simple answer to that question, because many inventors contributed to the development of the computer in many ways. Most researchers recognize Professor John Atanasoff and graduate student Clifford Berry as the developers of the world's first electronic digital computer around 1939. John Atanasoff recorded most of the early designs for the first computer on the back of a cocktail napkin.

The first to patent a digital computing device, the ENIAC computer, were Presper Eckert and John Mauchly. A subsequent patent infringement case involving Eckert, Mauchly, and Atanasoff voided the ENIAC patent and gave credit to Atanasoff. But as John Atanasoff told reporters, "I have always taken the position that there is enough credit for everyone in the invention and development of the electronic computer."

▣▶Quick Tip

When buying a computer, keep in mind that, although it is true that the newer, faster systems won't become obsolete as quickly as slower models, you will pay a premium for that technology. It is tempting to buy the fastest, most powerful computer system within your budget, but it isn't always necessary—or even advisable. Unless you have some heavy-duty applications requirements, such as graphic design, animation editing, or high-end gaming, you will be paying for capability that you simply won't use. Consider, instead, a midrange model that will support most typical applications. If you plan to concentrate on a particular area, such as graphics, you should put more money into hardware supporting that function than in other areas.

---

and using e-mail remain the most common reasons for purchasing a home computer.

Personal computers usually belong to one of two groups—PC or Apple Macintosh. The PC category hearkens back to 1981, when IBM released the first IBM PC, or "personal computer." The PC category used to refer to "IBM-compatible PC" but now simply means that the computer most likely runs the Windows operating system. The PC is by far the most commonly used desktop computer in both homes and businesses today. Typical PC systems include those made by Hewlett-Packard, IBM, Dell, and Gateway. Artists and graphic designers often prefer an Apple model, which runs the Mac OS operating system. Choosing which model to consider, the PC or the Apple, depends on what the computer will be used for and whether it needs to be compatible with other home or business computers.

A **desktop computer** is a personal computer in which all the components, including the keyboard, mouse, monitor, and system unit, easily fit on or under a desk. The CPU, or central processing unit, which is the large rectangular component, is either a *tower*, which sits upright underneath the desk, or a *desktop*, which lies flat underneath the monitor.

A **laptop computer** has just as much computing power as a desktop but comes in a much smaller package. Even smaller in physical size than a laptop, a **notebook computer** can fit inside a briefcase. Laptops and notebooks are handy tools for anyone who wants portable computer power, such as professionals who must make presentations or instructors who wish to grade computer assignments at home. Students might take notes on laptops or use them for gathering data from lab experiments. Some people simply don't want to be tied to a desk while working with the computer and like the freedom of movement that they get with a laptop.

In the Know

"I don't think it's that significant," was the comment made by Tandy president John Roach when IBM first introduced the IBM PC in 1981. Less than four months later, Time *magazine named the computer the "man of the year," due largely to the immense popularity of the IBM PC. The first operating system included with the IBM PC, DOS, was written by Microsoft, headed then, as now, by Bill Gates. The first IBM PC ran on a 4.77 MHz Intel 8088 microprocessor and had 16 kilobytes of memory, expandable to 256 KB. One or two 160 KB floppy disk drives were included, along with an optional color monitor. The cost? $1,565, which would be nearly $4,000 today! What really made the IBM PC different was that it was the first personal computer marketed by outside distributors, such as Sears.*

Like desktops, laptops include a microprocessor, memory, disk drives, input/output ports, and other standard components. Unlike desktops, laptops can run for a few hours on some type of rechargeable battery before being plugged back into an electrical source. Laptop displays usually range from 12 to 15 inches. To minimize space required, laptops generally forgo a mouse and instead include other types of pointing devices, such as a trackpoint or a touchpad. Laptops generally cost more than desktops, in the range of $800 to $2,500.

Another popular feature of laptops is the option of using a **docking station**, or **port replicator**. One advantage of using a laptop is that you can take the computer with you wherever you go. However, peripherals, such as a printer and scanner, are stationary devices that don't normally move with you. Consequently, when you return with your laptop and want to print a document, you must plug the printer cable into the back of the laptop. A docking station is a unit that remains on your desk with all peripherals, such as a mouse, printer, and scanner, connected. So instead of plugging and unplugging the printer into the laptop, you simply slide the laptop onto the docking station, locking it securely. At that point, the laptop functions much as a desktop unit, with quick access to the printer and other devices. When you need more portability, just remove the laptop from the docking station, and you're off!

Personal digital assistants (**PDAs**), sometimes called **handheld computers**, are among the fastest-selling consumer devices in history. More than 9 million have been sold, mostly from one company, Palm Computing. With the power of a notebook computer in a much smaller package, a PDA helps you manage your life, much as a daily planner might. You can store addresses and phone numbers, take notes, keep track of daily appointments, and communicate with other computers and PDAs. You can retrieve or send e-mail and download items from the Internet. You can play music and movies and run video games. Health professionals can keep track of patient information, technicians making service

In the Know

Alan Kay of the Xerox Palo Alto Research Center envisioned the first portable computer in the 1970s. He imagined a notebook-size computer called the Dynabook that would work with wireless network technology. However, William Moggridge of Grid Systems Corp. actually produced the first laptop computer in 1979. It had 340 kilobytes of bubble memory and a folding graphics display screen. By 1983, Gavilan Computer produced a laptop that weighed just 9 pounds, included a touchpad, and operated on an 8088 microprocessor. In 1986, IBM brought out the IBM PC Convertible, which came with its own application software, had two 3.5-inch floppy disk drives, and had space for an internal modem.

calls can record data, and parents can keep up with children's schedules. All of this is possible at an average cost of $400.

PDAs come in handheld or palm-size models. The palm-size model, as shown in Figure 1.2, can easily fit in a shirt pocket. They weigh anywhere from 4 to 8 ounces. Most handheld models feature a miniature keyboard for data entry, while the smaller palm units include a stylus/touch-screen technology in combination with handwriting recognition software.

PDAs are designed to communicate with your desktop or laptop so that you can transfer information from one to the other. Perhaps you record a phone number on your PDA and then later want to place that information in your permanent address book on your desktop computer. The communication between a PDA and a computer is called "data synchronization." PDAs can

Figure 1.2 **A PDA helps you manage your busy life.**

communicate with a computer through a cable or by way of an infrared connection, where information is beamed between devices using infrared light.

Powering On a Computer System

Getting a computer started isn't always as obvious an undertaking as you may think. The power button is in any of a number of places on different computer models. Current models usually have a round button on the front of the system unit. Some buttons click decisively and stay down when pressed, while others are more like a telephone button that hardly clicks at all. There is often a symbol that looks like a circle with a vertical line in it near the power switch. Turn on the system unit first, then the monitor (usually by pressing a small button at the front of the monitor), and then any peripherals, such as a printer.

Powering on your computer is called **booting**. "Boot" is actually short for "bootstrap," which means, "to pull yourself up by your bootstraps." When you press the power switch, several things happen. First the computer does some self-diagnostics, known as the **power-on self test** (**POST**). The POST determines whether components like the video card, mouse, memory, processor, and keyboard controller are operational. In short, it checks the health of your system each time you start the computer. The POST occurs without your involvement and without any obvious display.

✓ SANITY CHECK

You may at some point power on your computer and, instead of watching the display progress as usual, see a strange screen containing some text with an apparent error message. On a Windows-equipped computer, this often occurs when someone inadvertently leaves a disk in the diskette drive or a CD in the CD drive. During the boot process, the computer looks for operating system files in one or both of those drives before searching the hard drive, which is where Windows is installed. Try ejecting the diskette or CD and rebooting.

If the operating system loads correctly during the boot process, you will see a screen known as the **desktop**. Several icons, or pictures, will appear on the screen. It is from this display that you begin your computing session.

Taking a Tour

When you purchase a computer, it is helpful to understand the function of each component and know what to expect when you begin to work with the system. The equipment that comes with the system, including the system unit, monitor, keyboard, and mouse, is called **hardware**. At the most basic level, hardware is any part of a computer that can be touched. Let's take a tour of the basic hardware components that you are likely to find, and explore the purpose of each.

Input

A typical microcomputer system includes **input** devices, such as a keyboard and mouse. Input devices accept commands from a user and transform them into a form the computer can use. The modularity of current computer systems enables you to switch input devices at will. If you were not entirely pleased with the mouse that came with your system, you could visit a local office-supply store or general-purpose retailer and select an alternative mouse. Then, you could just disconnect the first mouse and connect the new one. The same flexibility applies to keyboards, scanners, and other input devices.

The **keyboard** (shown in Figure 1.3) is the primary input device for entering data into the computer. You may choose from a wide variety of keyboard models, from the most traditional to an ergonomic, possibly even cordless, model with added comfort features. Unless otherwise specified, most keyboards sold with desktop personal computers are the traditional 104-key models.

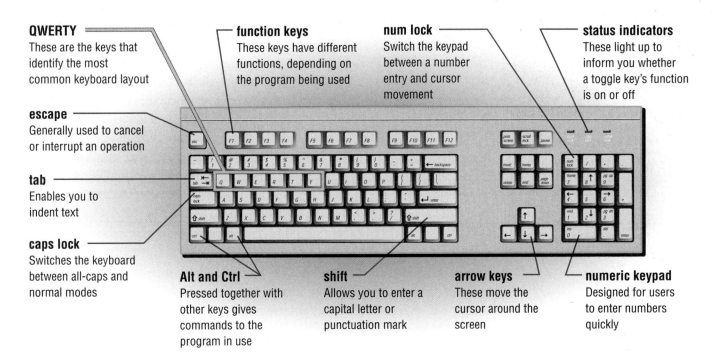

QWERTY
These are the keys that identify the most common keyboard layout

escape
Generally used to cancel or interrupt an operation

tab
Enables you to indent text

caps lock
Switches the keyboard between all-caps and normal modes

function keys
These keys have different functions, depending on the program being used

num lock
Switch the keypad between a number entry and cursor movement

status indicators
These light up to inform you whether a toggle key's function is on or off

Alt and Ctrl
Pressed together with other keys gives commands to the program in use

shift
Allows you to enter a capital letter or punctuation mark

arrow keys
These move the cursor around the screen

numeric keypad
Designed for users to enter numbers quickly

Figure 1.3 **Most computers come with a QWERTY keyboard.**

In the Know

The keyboard arrangement with which you are probably most familiar is the QWERTY, named for the top row of keys. When the typewriter was first developed, it was likely that a typist could type rapidly enough to cause the key mechanism to jam. The QWERTY arrangement was designed so that the most commonly used keys required a stretch, thus slowing down the typist. A little-known fact (or supposition) is that the keyboard was arranged such that salespeople could type the word typewriter (all letters found on the top row) without having to hunt and peck.

The Dvorak keyboard, on the other hand, places the most commonly used letters on the home row so that your fingers don't have to travel as far. The left hand has all of the vowels, and the right hand has only consonants. Therefore, no words in the English language can be typed with only one hand. If your keyboard is the QWERTY model, try typing the word "pumpkin." How many hands did you use?

Who would want to use a Dvorak keyboard? If you are already fairly proficient with the QWERTY keyboard, you are not likely to take the time to switch. Those new to keyboarding might be more inclined to give it a try. If you suffer from any wrist ailments or repetitive stress injury (RSI), the Dvorak keyboard may be for you, as it is much less stressful on muscles and tendons. Those who have made the switch to Dvorak report that it is much more comfortable to use.

Figure 1.4 **Ergonomic keyboards are designed to be more comfortable than traditional models.**

Ergonomics is the science concerned with the coordination of the workplace with the human body, assuring a high level of comfort and avoidance of certain health hazards. A quick glance at the keyboard aisle of a local office-supply store will reveal several keyboard models focusing on ease of use and conformity to the human hand structure. Because much of a computer user's time is spent at the keyboard, it is important that the keyboard help, not hinder, effectiveness. An ergonomic keyboard is shown in Figure 1.4.

✓ SANITY CHECK

A numeric keypad appears on most desktop-model keyboards just to the right of the letter arrangement. Suppose that you are familiar with the 10-key calculator and use those keys often to type numbers. This time as you type the numbers, they don't appear on-screen at all. What happened?

Historically, the numeric keypad keys were designed to serve a dual purpose. They represent numbers if you first press the NUM LOCK key (just above the numeric keypad), and they control cursor movement if you set Num Lock "off" by pressing the key one more time. So, if the numbers that you type don't appear, check for the green Num Lock indicator. If it is not lit, press the NUM LOCK key to set it "on."

Similarly, the CAPS LOCK key, when pressed once, causes all letters to appear in uppercase. If you find that your letters are appearing in uppercase although you didn't press the SHIFT key, check for the Caps Lock indicator. If it is lit, press the CAPS LOCK key one time to set Caps Lock "off."

The **mouse** (Figure 1.5) is the second most common input device. Moving the mouse over a flat surface simultaneously moves a mouse pointer on the display screen. Pressing buttons on the mouse allows you to select commands or objects on-screen. Pressing a mouse button is called "clicking." Unless otherwise specified, to *click* means to press the left mouse button, while to *right-click* means to press the right mouse button. To *double-click* means to rapidly press the left mouse button twice.

There are many different types of mouse devices. The most common device is a mouse that is connected by cable to the computer. However, there are several popular variations. One of the most popular new devices is the remote mouse. Such a cordless arrangement means that you don't have to work around cables that can become tangled or shortened by activity. The remote mouse, which is not connected to the computer, communicates with a battery-powered receiver that must be connected to the computer and placed within a few feet of the mouse. Another option is an optical mouse, which does not have a ball on the bottom, eliminating the need to clean the mouse periodically. Introduced in late 1999, the optical mouse can work on almost any surface and is quickly

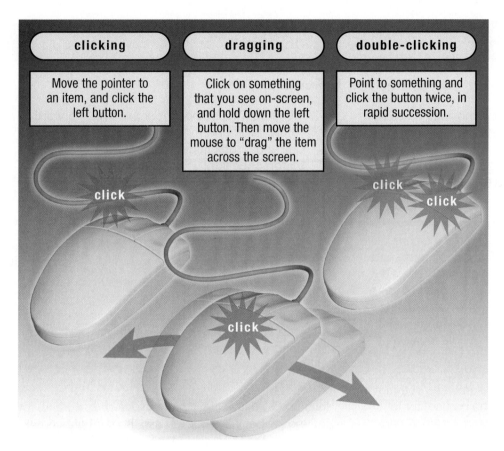

Figure 1.5 **A mouse is a common input device.**

becoming the preferred mouse option. A light-emitting diode (LED) transmits mouse movement, causing a corresponding shift of the mouse cursor on-screen. Some ergonomic mouse units are even arranged for foot movement instead of hand! Others allow you to maneuver with the thumb and fingertips instead of forcing a gripping action.

For those concerned with saving space, a **trackball** may be an attractive option. A trackball functions much like an upside-down mouse, with the ball on top. Moving the ball with your hand moves the mouse pointer on the screen. The trackball reduces hand movement and space requirements.

✓ SANITY CHECK

Are you left-handed? If so, you might find mouse movement and clicking somewhat awkward. You can make your mouse a "left-handed mouse." Open the Mouse Properties dialog box by clicking Start, and then Control Panel. Click Printers and Other Hardware. Click Mouse. Under Button configuration, click to select Switch primary and secondary buttons. Click OK. Then physically move the mouse to the left side of the computer and use your left hand. All clicks and double-clicks are done with the index finger of your left hand, and a right-click means clicking with your middle finger. *If you are working with a laptop with an alternate pointing device, you won't be able to change the mouse to left-handed.*

Hands On

Activity 1.1—Using the Mouse

In this exercise, you will practice moving and clicking with the mouse. To complete the exercise, you should be at a computer with a mouse attached. The computer should be on and at the beginning screen, with desktop icons displayed. (The following instructions apply to the mouse as a right-handed tool.)

1. The mouse should be to the right of the computer. Position the mouse comfortably on a mouse pad so that you don't have to reach too far for it.
2. Rest the heel of your hand at the base of the mouse. Hold the mouse between your thumb and little fingers. Place your index finger on the left mouse button and your middle finger on the right mouse button.
3. Practice moving the mouse. Watch the arrow move across the computer screen as you move the mouse. When moving the mouse, try to keep your wrist stationary on the mouse pad. As much as possible, use your fingers and hand to move the mouse.

4. Move the mouse pointer arrow over the word "Start" at the bottom left corner of the screen. Use your index finger to press the left mouse button once lightly. The Start menu (Figure 1.6) appears.
5. Roll the mouse pointer up to the words "All Programs." Roll directly to the right and up or down to the word "Accessories." Finally, roll directly to the right and up or down to the word "Paint." The sequence of menus is shown in Figure 1.7. Click once with the left mouse button.
6. You have opened the Paint program, which is a graphics program included with a typical Windows installation.

✓ SANITY CHECK

If you mistakenly click a program other than Paint, roll the mouse pointer up to the X in the top right corner of the window, and click once with the left mouse button. The window will close. Return to step 4.

Figure 1.6 **The Start menu provides several choices.**

Figure 1.7 **The Paint program is a handy tool for creating drawings.**

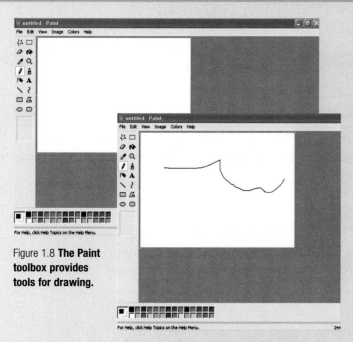

Figure 1.8 **The Paint toolbox provides tools for drawing.**

Figure 1.9 **Anyone can be an artist with Paint.**

7. Move the mouse pointer to the left side of the Paint window. You should see a grid of several "tools," as shown in Figure 1.8. Move to the Brush tool (second column, fourth down). Click the tool once with the left mouse button.
8. At the lower part of the Paint window, you should see a grid of colors. Click the red square once with the left mouse button.
9. Move the mouse pointer into the white area of the Paint window. Click and hold down the left mouse button while rolling to the right. Continue holding down the left mouse button while drawing an image, as shown in Figure 1.9.
10. At the top right corner of the Paint window, note the X. That is the close button, which you should click with the left mouse button now. When asked whether you wish to save the drawing, click No. The Paint program closes.
11. Find the Recycle Bin icon on the screen. Move the mouse pointer to the Recycle Bin icon, and click twice rapidly with the left mouse button. You have double-clicked, and the Recycle Bin window should open, as shown in Figure 1.10.

✓ SANITY CHECK

If the Recycle Bin window does not open after you double-click, you probably didn't double-click rapidly enough. Move the mouse pointer out to an empty area (one without an icon) and left-click once. Now move back to the Recycle Bin and try the double-click again.

12. Find the X at the top right corner of the Recycle Bin window. Move the mouse pointer to the X, and click once with the left mouse button to close the window.
13. Move the mouse pointer back to the Recycle Bin icon. With your middle finger on the *right* mouse button, click the *right* mouse button once. A menu will appear. Roll the mouse pointer down the menu and left-click the word "Properties." You will see the Recycle Bin Properties dialog box, as shown in Figure 1.11.
14. Find the X at the top right corner of the Properties window. Move the pointer to the X and click once with the left mouse button to close the window.

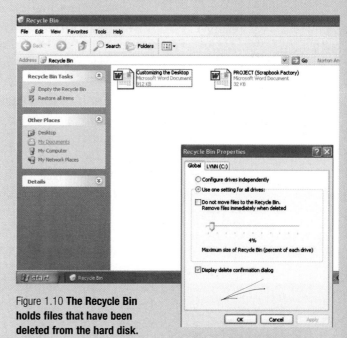

Figure 1.10 **The Recycle Bin holds files that have been deleted from the hard disk.**

Figure 1.11 **You can adjust Recycle Bin properties to reflect your preferences.**

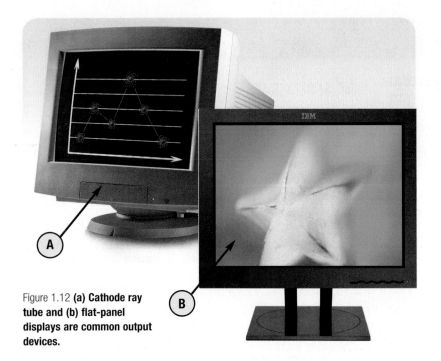

Figure 1.12 **(a) Cathode ray tube and (b) flat-panel displays are common output devices.**

Output

If you think about it, you only really use a computer because you wish to produce some form of output, whether it is printed, displayed on the screen, or in some other form. **Output** is the information that the computer produces, such as text, numbers, graphics, or even sounds.

The **monitor** is the primary output device. It is a televisionlike unit powered by pressing a button or flipping a switch. As you consider a computer purchase or upgrade, you can choose from two basic categories of displays—CRT and LCD, as shown in Figure 1.12. The typical monitor on a home computer is a CRT, or cathode ray tube. Newer technology flat panels, which were initially the standard with laptops, are actually liquid crystal displays (LCDs), gas plasma, or light-emitting diode (LED) displays. Flat panels are now available for desktop units, as well.

A CRT monitor, as shown in Figure 1.12, consumes a great deal of power, compared to other computer components—sometimes as much as 80 percent of total computer power consumption! The Energy Star program, initiated by the U.S. government in 1992, requires compliant monitors to suspend display and other noncritical processes after a period of user inactivity. When you move the mouse or tap the keyboard, the computer revives the display. If you have an Energy Star–compliant monitor, you will notice your computer occasionally "going to sleep" when you are not using it.

Even with Energy Star compliance, CRT monitors are still relatively power hungry. LCD monitors, on the other hand, are estimated to save $15 to $28 per year in energy costs over CRT monitors of the same size. Additional advantages are that a flat panel (LCD) gives a sharper image and requires less desk space. A slight disadvantage is that LCDs tend to have relatively narrow viewing angles, which means that someone seated to your side may not view the same clear image that you might, seated directly in front of the panel.

The specifications of monitors include the dot pitch, horizontal and vertical refresh rates, and viewable area, all of which directly affect the maximum resolution a monitor can display. **Resolution** is the number of individual dots of color, known as **pixels (picture elements)**, on a monitor's display. The higher the resolution, the sharper the image. The **dot pitch** is the measure of the amount of space between pixels. The smaller the dot pitch (preferably around .25), the better, because the closer the pixels are packed together, the higher the resolution.

The most common monitor sizes are 17 and 19 inches. The monitor size, which is a measurement diagonally across the glass face of the picture tube of a

CRT, is not the actual viewable space. The viewable area is the diagonal measurement (in inches) of the largest possible picture the screen can display, which on a CRT is never as large as the actual glass face. The LCD panels used in laptops and flat-panel monitors can display images all the way out to their edges, so their monitor size and viewable area measurements are the same.

Vertical refresh rate, the frequency at which images are redrawn on the display, is an important measure of how steady an image will appear on the monitor. A higher **refresh rate** gives better picture quality and less flicker. A vertical refresh rate of less than 75 Hz will most likely flicker. European law makes it illegal for an employer to force an employee to work with a monitor at less than 70 Hz vertical refresh rate. **Horizontal refresh rate** is the number of times per second that the monitor's electron beam travels along a line and returns at the start of the next. It is measured in kilohertz (KHz). When you see the refresh rate listed as part of a computer advertisement, it is most likely the vertical refresh rate, because that is what most professionals refer to as the "refresh rate."

The **printer** continues to be a very popular method of output for home computer users. The paperless office was once touted as a virtual certainty, given the capability to communicate and receive information electronically. However, human nature seems to suggest otherwise, as even the most sophisticated offices continue to print out many items. Especially in the home setting, you'll appreciate the ease with which you can print photographs, greeting cards, correspondence, Web page information, and creative projects. Figure 1.13 shows some popular printer choices for microcomputers.

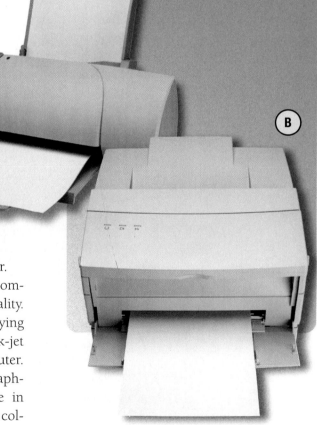

Typically, when you purchase a computer, the printer isn't included, although vendors do occasionally offer computer packages that include a printer and possibly a scanner. When purchasing a printer, you will probably choose between an ink-jet, a laser, or a **multifunction device**. If you have a laptop, you might also consider a portable printer.

Ink-jet printers are the most popular choice for home computer users, thanks to their affordable price and high quality. Almost all ink-jets include color capability, albeit in varying degrees of quality and resolution. The speed of an ink-jet printer is dependent in part on the speed of the computer. Graphics typically print very slowly, so, if you print many graphics or photographs, you will notice a significant decline in printer speed. Likewise, if you are printing many different colors, speed will suffer.

Figure 1.13 **Popular printer options for home computer systems are (a) ink-jet and (b) laser printers.**

Figure 1.14 **Multifunction devices are popular choices for home offices.**

Although the initial purchase price of most ink-jet printers is quite low, you should be aware that they can be rather costly to operate. Depending upon how much the printer is used, both black and color cartridges may need to be replaced often. You can purchase print cartridges wherever computers are sold, but they are certainly not cheap. Refilling your own cartridges or buying recycled cartridges are also popular options.

√**Laser printers** offer the highest print resolution and speed, which is measured in pages per minute. These printers, once priced out-of-reach for most home computer users, have become much more affordable. However, the lower-priced, low-end laser printers are usually not capable of color printing. Laser printer toner cartridges tend to last longer than ink-jet cartridges, so laser printers can be cheaper to operate. Laser printer technology is similar to that of a photocopier, and, like a photocopier, laser printers are typically large, requiring more desk space than ink-jet printers.

Multifunction devices (Figure 1.14) are popular in homes and small offices, as they offer such features as a printer, photocopier, fax, and scanner in one unit. Some multifunction devices include laser printing components, while others support ink-jet technology. Just as with stand-alone printers, the speed and resolution vary widely. If space is at a premium, a multifunction device may be ideal. The cost of the device, as well as the space savings, makes the purchase of a multifunction device attractive to a wide variety of users.

In the Know

Computer printers have been with us almost as long as computers. In 1953, Remington-Rand introduced the first high-speed printer, developed for use on the Univac computer. The IBM 3800 was the first high-speed laser printer, combining laser technology and electrophotography. The 3800 was installed at F. W. Woolworth's data center in 1976. Hewlett-Packard's LaserJet 4 came along in 1992, with a resolution of a whopping 600 x 600! Although the ink-jet printer was invented in 1976, it didn't become a home consumer item until 1988, with Hewlett-Packard's release of the DeskJet ink-jet printer. At that time, the cost of a DeskJet was $1,000!

System Unit

The **system unit** is the rectangular case that houses hardware components, such as the processor, memory, and disk drives. It provides protection for components and usually includes space to add additional disk drives later.

The **processor**, sometimes called the brain of the computer, is the hardware unit that controls all system activity. Without a processor, there would be no computer. In computer terminology, the processor is called the **CPU** (**central processing unit**). It actually consists of electronic circuits that accept, evaluate, and act on instructions found in software programs. It also communicates with input, output, storage, and memory devices. The CPU oversees everything done by the computer.

The CPU is found in the system unit. Its processing speed is measured in **megahertz** (**MHz**) or **gigahertz** (**GHz**). CPU speeds in personal computers get faster and faster each year. At this point it isn't unusual to find CPU speeds in excess of 3 GHz. The hardware unit that houses the CPU is called a **microprocessor**. Athlon and Pentium IV are examples of microprocessors. When you shop for a computer, you will consider both a microprocessor specification and a processor speed. Processors are manufactured by various companies, of which Intel is the most widely recognized. You might want to consider an Intel Pentium IV processor at a speed in excess of 2 GHz.

Data and programs are temporarily stored in an area called **memory** while they are being used. As you type a document, the text appears on the computer screen. This text is actually being stored in memory, which will hold it only *temporarily*. Memory requires a constant supply of electricity to retain its contents. If you want to recall the document later, you will need to save it to a disk or CD. Another term for computer memory is **RAM** (**random access memory**). RAM is *volatile*, which means that its contents are lost if there is an interruption of electricity.

Computer memory might be compared to a blackboard in a college classroom. After each class ends, the instructor erases the board. It only holds data or instructions pertinent to that day. It is "temporary memory." It is also limited in space; consequently, it can hold only a certain amount of information before it becomes full and must be cleared. Just as with computer memory, the blackboard contents change often, depending upon the focus of the class.

Memory is measured in a unit called a **byte**. To understand the concept of bytes, think about our own numbering system. Because we have 10 fingers, our numbering system is based on powers of 10. Think back to elementary school, when you might have experimented with an abacus. The abacus demonstrated the idea of positional notation, which means that each position was actually a power of 10. For example, the decimal number 101 means that you have one "hundred," no "tens," and one "one." It makes perfect sense, given our predisposition to units of 10.

A computer, however, doesn't work well on decimal numbers; rather, it is naturally disposed toward a binary number system, where each digit can have only two electronic states: on and off. One circuit might be open, while another might be closed. A computer, then, would work much better with the binary system, in

▶Quick Tip

Most PC-compatible computers contain an Intel CPU. In fact, the first IBM PC ran on an Intel 8088 microprocessor. IBM chose the Intel chip because it had already obtained the rights to manufacture Intel chips. That's one reason we are all so familiar with the Intel name.

Given that name recognition, you might wonder whether it's OK to purchase a computer without an Intel CPU. The fact is that, although Intel competitors like AMD and Cyrix might not have the marketing muscle of Intel, they should have just as much processing power. If microprocessors have similar CPU processor speeds, there is really no reason to prefer one brand name over another.

Hands On

Activity 1.2—Determining the Amount of Memory

In this exercise, you will determine the amount of memory (RAM) your computer has. The computer should be on and at the beginning screen, with desktop icons displayed.

1. Move the mouse pointer to the word "Start" in the lower left corner, and click once with the left mouse button. Move the mouse pointer up to the words "Control Panel," and click once with the left mouse button. The Control Panel window is shown in Figure 1.15.
2. A series of icons should appear in the Control Panel window. Click Performance and Maintenance. Click System.

3. The System Properties window appears, as shown in Figure 1.16. Click the General tab at the top of the window, if necessary. Take a look at the system properties, noting the amount of RAM. The amount of RAM shown in Figure 1.16 is 512 MB.
4. Move the mouse pointer over the X at the top right corner of the window. Click once with the left mouse button. The window closes.
5. Move the mouse pointer over the X at the top right corner of the remaining window. Click once with the left mouse button. The window closes.

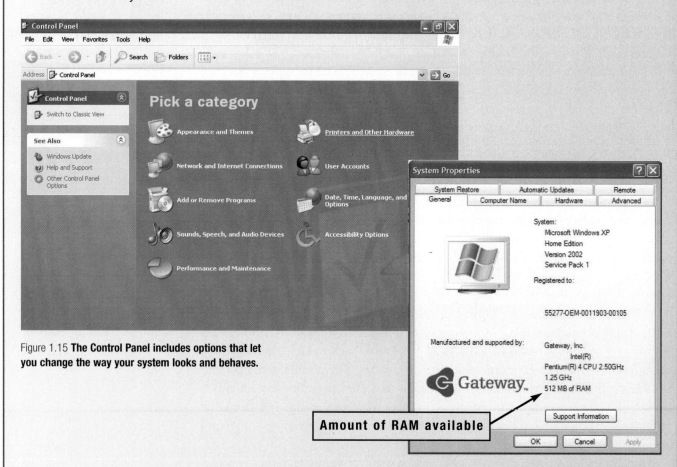

Figure 1.15 **The Control Panel includes options that let you change the way your system looks and behaves.**

Amount of RAM available

Figure 1.16 **You can check the amount of RAM in System Properties.**

In the Know

In a world of instant gratification, it is sometimes a little annoying to wait for your computer to go through the booting process when you press the power button. Why can't a computer work like a television, which comes on right away? IBM is currently working on a new memory technology that promises to eliminate the boot-up process. Magnetic random access memory (MRAM) *will be designed to store more data, access data faster, and use less power than current memory technologies. The goal is to have the new technology in computers, cell phones, and games by 2004. As the name suggests, MRAM will use magnetism to retain memory contents, rather than electrical power. MRAM may replace* dynamic RAM (DRAM), *which is the most common type of memory in use today, one that requires a continuous supply of electricity.*

which there are only two digits, zero and one. Just as our decimal system is based on powers of 10, the binary system is based on powers of two. Each digit in the binary system represents either a one, two, four, eight, or some power of two above that. Therefore, the number "10" in binary actually represents the decimal number 2, because the zero is in the "ones" place and the one is in the "twos" place.

The smallest binary component is the binary digit, or **bit**. A bit can hold one of two possible values: zero or one. It takes some combination of eight bits to represent what we consider a number or character on the keyboard. That combination is called a byte. As you consider bits and bytes, remember that all of the binary representation is internal. You won't be reading or working with data at the binary level. It is important that you understand the concept of bits and bytes only because that is the common measurement of memory.

Bytes are organized into larger groups, as well, called kilobytes, megabytes, and gigabytes. A **kilobyte** consists of 1,024 bytes, whereas a **megabyte** is approximately one million bytes, and a **gigabyte** is one billion bytes. The next time you peruse an advertisement for a personal computer, note the measure of RAM as something like 256 MB (256 megabytes). The byte is simply a measurement of capacity.

Also housed in the system unit are several **disk drives**. Those disk drives read data from a storage medium, such as a CD or diskette. You might think of such storage as being equivalent to a filing cabinet. It is a place where data, such as a document that you have just typed on the computer, can be saved. Storage can be magnetic, as in the case of hard disks, Zip disks, and floppy disks (diskettes), or optical, as with CD and DVD technology. A hard disk is shown in Figure 1.17a. A floppy disk and an optical disc are shown in Figure 1.17b. Some newer memory devices, like flash memory, are neither optical nor magnetic, but are considered solid-state storage devices, which means that there are no moving parts.

Figure 1.17 **(a) A hard disk is not removable. (b) Floppy disks and optical discs are portable.**

Magnetic Disk Storage

The most common disk storage device is the **magnetic disk**. The hard disk, floppy disk, and Zip disk are examples of magnetic disks. Although each of these categories has its own characteristics and storage capacity, they are all composed of one or more rotating disks or platters. The surfaces of the platters are coated with metal oxide and are read from and recorded to by electromagnetic heads. If you are familiar with a record player, the concept is much like the idea of the needle "reading" the record album.

A **diskette**, or **floppy disk**, is a magnetic disk, usually 3½" in diameter, enclosed in a plastic case. The disk drive in which you place a floppy disk for access is called an "A" drive. You can easily delete or change data on a diskette. Perhaps you wish to make changes to the document that you created and saved on a floppy disk last week. Using a program on your computer, just open the document, make changes, and save it back to the same disk.

The term *floppy disk*, while once descriptive of the rather flexible 5¼" forerunner to the current 3½" model, might not seem like an accurate descriptor of today's rigid diskette. However, inside the hard plastic casing is a very thin magnetically coated "floppy" disk. Although the packaging has changed, the nomenclature stands. We still refer to the small rigid disk as a floppy disk.

Floppy disks are usually preformatted in either an Apple (Mac) format or a Windows (IBM) format. The IBM notation doesn't mean the disk can only be used on IBM computers— simply that is formatted for use on a Windows-based computer. Floppy disks are usually designated high density (HD), which is simply a measure of the amount of data that can be stored on the disk.

Floppy disks are portable, or removable, so you can take the disk from the disk drive and carry it to other computers. They are also very limited in space and are not typically used for software storage. Consequently, some computer manufacturers are no longer including floppy disk drives as standard equipment.

Hard disks, another form of magnetic disk storage, have much more storage capacity than floppy disks. Just as the floppy disk is labeled the A drive, the hard disk drive default letter is "C." Although hard disks were originally available in sizes that started at 10 MB, today you would be hard pressed to find one smaller than 40 GB. That's 400 times the capacity! When deciding what hard disk size is adequate, you must consider that this is the location of most of your software, so it is important that the disk size match your needs. As home computers increase in storage space and power, software manufacturers develop software requiring ever more computer capacity. It's much like the old adage of which came first— the chicken or the egg!

A hard disk drive is not removable. It is a storage device in which the storage medium is not removed for use on another computer. Microcomputers

In the Know

The first "floppy disk" was introduced in 1971 by IBM. Unlike today's 3½" floppy, IBM's version was an 8" plastic disk coated with magnetic iron oxide. The name "floppy" came from the disk's flexibility. It was considered revolutionary because it was portable. In 1976, the 5¼" floppy appeared on the scene. Wang Laboratories developed it because the company wanted a smaller disk and drive to use in its desktop computers. Catching on quickly, the 5¼" floppy was produced by more than 10 manufacturers by 1978. Finally, in 1981, Sony brought out the 3½" floppy drive and diskette that we use today.

designed for home use invariably contain a hard drive. The size may vary, but the drive is always there.

A **Zip disk** (Figure 1.18) is a high-capacity floppy disk, capable of storing 100 to 750 megabytes of data. It is slightly larger in physical size than a normal floppy disk and at least twice as thick. A Zip disk can hold much more data than a floppy disk. For that reason, Zip disks are sometimes used for backing up hard disks and transporting large files between computers. In terms of the amount of time it takes to retrieve a saved file, Zip disks are faster than floppy disks but slower than hard disks. The cost of Zip disks is significantly higher than that of floppy disks, but the capacity and convenience of not juggling so many floppy disks makes a Zip disk an attractive option. However, due in part to the cost of Zip cartridges when compared with other media, such as a **CD**, many computer users are choosing CD or DVD drives over Zip drives when determining specifications for a new computer.

Iomega Zip 750MB USB Drive Photo courtesy of Iomega Corporation

Figure 1.18 **Zip disks can store up to 750 megabytes of data and are often used to back up hard disks.**

In the Know

You can become addicted to a computer activity that you enjoy. Learning to use that fantastic new genealogy software can cause you to sit in front of the computer for long periods of time. Be careful! Although scientists agree that there is no evidence that computer electromagnetic fields harm anyone, such intense periods of computer work can lead to tension and eyestrain.

Try these tips to maximize your enjoyment while minimizing strain:

Take eye breaks. You blink less often, exposing more of the eye surface to air, when you work at a computer. Every 15 minutes or so, look away from the screen at a more distant scene, perhaps out a window. Blink your eyes rapidly for a few seconds to clear dust and relax eye muscles.

Take rest breaks. At least once every 30 minutes, get up and move around. Walk, stretch, and get a drink of water.

Take minibreaks. When you are typing, you tend to do so in bursts, with stops in between. During those stops, rest your hands in a flat, relaxed manner. Open and close your fingers, and rotate your wrists.

Consider ergonomic software. It is very easy to become so engrossed in a computer activity that you remain at the keyboard for several hours. Although you might be having fun, such intense concentration can lead to eye and muscle strain. Ergonomic software is designed to run in the background, monitoring how long you've been using the computer. It prompts you to take rest breaks, and it suggests simple exercises.

Minimize glare on the computer screen. If lighting is too bright, the glare on the computer screen can be annoying. Try to move the screen, lower the light level, or purchase an antiglare screen. The computer monitor should not be placed in front of a bright window.

Optical Disc Storage

Some storage media, such as CD-ROM, CD R, CD R/W, and DVD, are categorized as **optical disc storage**. When you purchase a computer, it will probably be equipped with a CD drive or DVD drive in addition to a magnetic hard disk. A laser beam reads from and writes to an optical disc. Studies have shown that the life expectancy of a CD, housed in a normal home or office environment, is 100 years, while a magnetic disk might last a few decades. Be aware, though, that those statistics refer to disks that are recorded once and then put away. It does not mean that your hard disk, which is continually in use, will necessarily last a few decades.

Compact Disc–Read-Only Memory (CD-ROM) is a disc used to store programs and archival data that don't often change. CD-ROMs look like music CDs and are read by reflecting or refracting laser beams. In fact, they use the same physical disc format as music CDs, but special formatting allows them to hold computer data. If you have a CD drive on your computer, you can listen to music CDs as well as work with data and software files. A CD-ROM disc is shown in Figure 1.19.

Currently, CD-ROM technology is used extensively by software manufacturers as the medium of choice. After a CD is stamped by the vendor, it cannot be erased and filled with new data. CD-ROM technology allows the distribution of large quantities of information in a reliable package. In fact, some software is only available on CDs, which means that if your computer doesn't have a CD drive, you will lose out on a large segment of software.

Figure 1.19 **Desktop computers are often equipped with CD-ROM drives, capable of reading (but not writing to) CD-ROM discs.**

CD-ROM discs commonly hold approximately 650 megabytes of data, with some approaching 1 gigabyte. A single CD-ROM can store the equivalent of more than 500 floppy disks, or about 300,000 text pages. A single-speed CD-ROM drive can read a CD at the rate of 150 kilobytes per second. Faster drives are listed as multiples of that speed. If a CD-ROM drive is listed as 24x, that means that its maximum speed is 24 times 150 KB per second.

Compact Disc–Recordable (CD-R) is a type of compact disc that can be written to one time and read from many times. The CD-R medium requires a compatible CD-R disc drive. As with CD-ROMs, after data is written to a CD-R, it cannot be erased. You might use a CD-R disc to record digital family pictures or the huge family tree that you have developed. With evident compatibility issues with older-generation computers, and with the advent of CD-RW technology, CD-R storage is not as popular as it once was. However, most audio CD players, especially older models, can only read CD-R discs, so it is best to record music on a CD-R disc.

The speed of a CD-R disc drive is measured in terms of writing and reading speed. A drive designated as 8x/24x is capable of writing at 8 times 150 kilobytes per second (or 8-speed) and reading at 24-speed.

Compact Disc–Rewritable (CD-RW) is a type of compact disc that can be recorded, erased, and rerecorded. A CD-RW disc drive can read normal CD-ROMs and can write to and read both CD-R and CD-RW discs. A user can choose which medium is the best for a particular job.

DVD storage is very similar to a CD, but it has a much larger data capacity. The DVD acronym has progressed from "digital video disc" to "digital versatile disc," but most people today simply refer to it as "DVD" without worrying about what the letters stand for. DVD might ultimately bring home entertainment, computer storage, and business information into a single digital format, effectively replacing CD technology. DVD drives are also backward compatible, which means they can read CDs as well as DVDs.

A typical DVD can store up to 18 gigabytes of data, enough to record even full-length movies. Along with its cost-effective storage capacity, DVD technology

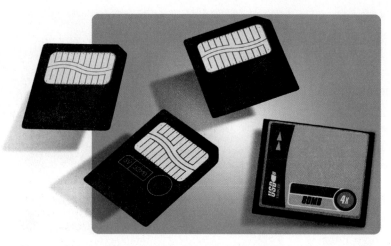

Figure 1.20 **Flash memory cards are found in digital cameras and other portable computer devices.**

facilitates very high-quality audio and video. **DVD-ROM** discs are designed for computer and multimedia applications, whereas **DVD-R** and **DVD-RW** are recordable and rewritable DVD formats. You can also purchase combo drives that combine features of CD and DVD technology.

Flash memory (Figure 1.20) is another form of storage that is neither magnetic nor optical and has no moving parts. Flash memory is often used with notebook computers because it uses little power, it is resistant to shock and vibration, and the size of both the storage device and media is small. Digital cameras and other portable computer devices also use flash memory in the form of sticks, cards, or drives.

Hands On   Activity 1.3—Identifying Storage Media

In this exercise you will identify storage devices on a computer system. The computer should be on and at the beginning screen, with desktop icons displayed.

1. Move the mouse pointer to the word "Start" in the lower left corner, and click once with the left mouse button. Move the mouse pointer up to the words "My Computer," and click once with the left mouse button. The My Computer window appears, as shown in Figure 1.21.
2. Look to the right and note the disk drives displayed. What disk drives do you see? In Figure 1.21 you see a hard drive, a floppy drive, and a DVD/CD-RW drive.
3. Close the My Computer window by moving the mouse pointer to the X in the upper right corner. Click once with the left mouse button.

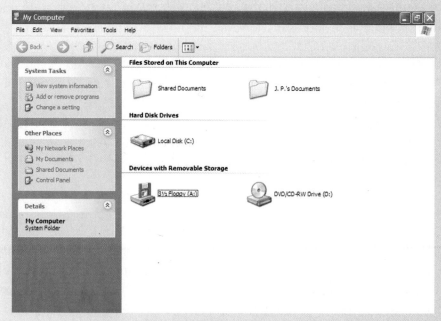

Figure 1.21 **The My Computer window displays disk drives.**

Shutting Down Your System

Correctly shutting down a computer system involves a little more than just pressing the power button. An orderly shutdown quits all software that you have not yet quit, prompting you to save any open files or projects. Always be sure to shut down the computer correctly so that you don't damage your computer or lose files that you are working on.

1. First, save your work and quit all programs.
2. Click the Start button.
3. Click Turn Off Computer.
4. Click Turn Off.

Watch the screen. Power to the system unit will be cut off. If there is any difficulty with the shut-down process, you should see a message on the screen. When the system unit powers down, you can shut off the monitor or leave it on to go into sleep mode. Some older computer models may display the message "It is now safe to turn off your computer," at which time you should manually press the power button.

Setting Up a New Personal Computer

Now that we have explored the pieces and parts of a typical microcomputer system, you might decide to go ahead and buy one! Whether this is your first computer or a replacement for one that you've outgrown, opening those boxes and pulling out that new machine is thrilling! Before you dive in, though, keep a few things in mind.

- *Don't throw anything away, especially the receipts and paperwork.* Warranties, instructions, vendor contact information, and checklists are all included somewhere in those boxes. Get a file of some sort to keep all these papers. In addition to having information close at hand, you'll be able to let the vendor know exactly what you received if you find something missing.

- *It is a good idea to fill out and mail all warranty cards.* It's true that you might wind up on a mailing list, but it is also important to document your purchase so that you can receive appropriate support should something go wrong later.

- *If possible, save those boxes for at least 30 days.* Assuredly, they will be big and bulky, but if you need to send anything back, repackaging will be a breeze.

- *Save all disks.* Although you might not intend to use them, or even know for sure what they are, you never know what the future holds. The software is most likely already installed, so the disks and CDs are your licensed copies for backup purposes, but you also need them close at hand for other reasons. Most important, identify and save the operating system CD. At a later time, when you are attempting to install a device or correct a

---

▓▶ Quick Tip

Should you turn the computer off when you are finished, or does this harm the system? You'll find much debate on the subject, with most computer technicians reporting that turning a computer on and off is hard on it. A continual on/off cycle may cause a computer to deteriorate over time as it heats up and then cools down. On the other hand, leaving a computer on consumes power, which you must pay for. You might try leaving the computer on until you are finished for the day. Then, in the evening, turn it off. You'll conserve a little power, while reducing wear and tear on the system.

▊▶Quick Tip

When purchasing a new computer, should you buy a nationally recognized name brand, or will a no-name brand work just as well? To a certain extent, you are likely to get what you pay for. That is not to say that the performance of some cheaper models might be less than that of the more expensive models. The real difference is in the service and support. Premier brands most often include superior telephone help without long wait times.

problem, you will be asked to insert the system CD, which you can do only if you have it filed away where you can locate it.

- *Understand your warranty.* It is a good idea to have a warranty that covers parts and labor for at least two years. If yours doesn't, you might want to extend the warranty.

Your new computer will come in several boxes. The largest box probably contains the monitor. Other components you will find as you unpack include the keyboard, the mouse, the speakers, the system unit, and the power cable. Set everything, including all documents, equipment, cables, and software, on the floor or desk. Along with an instruction manual, most vendors now include a "quick start" guide that leads you step- by- step through connecting all hardware. Read the quick start guide completely before beginning the set up. The instruction manual probably includes a "Getting Started" section, which you should read as well. Remember, if you get in a hurry, you get behind!

One of the best ways to protect your computer investment is to purchase an effective **surge protector**. Be sure that the surge protector includes phone line protection, as well. Some so-called surge protectors are basically just extension bars that minimally protect equipment but are likely to fail in the event of a serious electrical surge. What matters most is the voltage level at which preventive action takes place. Be forewarned: even the best surge protectors do not protect equipment from a direct lightning strike, resulting in a surge of millions of volts. During a lightning storm, you should unplug devices that could be damaged.

Before connecting any cables or plugs, make sure all components, including the surge protector, are off. Connect all devices to the system unit. Computer connections are usually color coded, so you can easily see that the purple cable plugs into the purple area on the back of the system unit. Never force a connection. If something doesn't fit easily, you probably have the cable upside down or you are making the connection in the wrong place. Plug all power cables into the surge protector, plug in the surge protector, and then flip the surge protector's power switch. Power on the computer first, then the monitor, and then any peripherals, such as a printer. Follow any screen prompts to complete the initial setup. File away all paperwork and software. You're ready to go!

✔ SANITY CHECK

You've plugged in your speakers, but when your computer boots, there is no sound. What is wrong? First, make sure the speaker cable is plugged into the correct area on the back of the system unit. There are several areas that will hold the speaker connector, but some are designed for other items, such as a microphone. Next, try adjusting the volume on the speakers themselves, or adjust the computer's volume by clicking the little yellow speaker in the lower right corner of the screen. Some computer models also have a volume dial on the back of the unit.

Chapter Summary

DON'T FORGET

- Computers designed for personal use include desktops, laptops, notebooks, and personal digital assistants.

- After you power on a computer, the computer performs self-diagnostics called the POST (power-on self test).

- The two most commonly used input devices are the keyboard and the mouse.

- The monitor is the primary output device. Monitor choices include the CRT (cathode ray tube) and the flat-panel display.

- Ink-jet printers are the most popular printer choice for home computer users, but laser printers and multi-function devices are becoming much more affordable.

- Common computer specifications include processor type, processor speed, hard disk size, monitor type and size, dot pitch, disk storage devices, and amount of memory (RAM).

- Memory (RAM) is the area where data and programs are temporarily stored while they are in use. It is volatile, depending on a continuous electrical supply to retain contents.

- Disk storage can be considered the computer's filing cabinet, where files are retained without regard to electrical supply. It is nonvolatile.

- Optical discs include CD and DVD formats, whereas magnetic media include the hard disk, floppy disk, and Zip disk.

- Shutting down a computer appropriately ensures that you will not damage the computer or lose open files.

- When setting up a new computer, it is important that you keep all paperwork, save all CDs and disks, and understand the warranty.

KEY TERMS

bit
booting
byte
CD
CD-R
CD-ROM
CD-RW
CPU
desktop
desktop computer
disk drive
diskette
docking station
dot pitch
DVD
ergonomics
flash memory
floppy disk
gigabyte

gigahertz *preminuts.*
handheld computer
hard disk
hardware
horizontal refresh rate
ink-jet printer
input
keyboard
kilobyte
laptop computer
laser printer
magnetic disk
megahertz
memory
microcomputer
microprocessor
monitor
mouse
multifunction device

notebook computer
optical disc storage
output
personal computer (PC)
personal digital assistant (PDA)
pixel (picture element)
POST (power-on self test)
printer
processor
RAM
refresh rate
resolution
surge protector
system unit
trackball
vertical refresh rate
Zip disk

TRUE/FALSE

Circle **T** if the statement is true or **F** if the statement is false.

T (F)   1. The correct way to shut down a computer system is to press the power switch.

(T) F   2. A Zip disk is a high-capacity floppy disk.

(T) F   3. The keyboard is the primary input device for entering data into a personal computer.

T (F)   4. The hardware unit that houses the processor is the microprocessor.

T (F)   5. Personal digital assistants (PDAs) have yet to catch on, still showing lackluster sales.

T (F)   6. A laptop is much smaller and less powerful than a desktop computer.

T (F)   7. RAM is nonvolatile, which means that contents are retained regardless of electrical supply.

(T) F   8. CD-R is a form of optical storage that can be written to one time and read from many times.

T (F)   9. Like a floppy disk, a typical hard disk is portable, allowing you to take it from one computer to another.

(T) F   10. The most popular printer choice for home computer users is the ink-jet printer.

MULTIPLE CHOICE

Circle the correct choice for each of the following.

1. This storage medium is not considered a form of magnetic storage.
   a. CD-RW
   b. hard disk
   c. floppy disk
   d. Zip disk

2. The primary output device for a personal computer system is a
   a. speaker
   b. monitor
   c. printer
   d. multifunction device

3. A pixel is
   a. another term for a flat-panel display
   b. the measure of the amount of space between picture elements
   c. a measure of the vertical refresh rate
   d. a dot of individual color on a monitor, otherwise known as a picture element

4. Which of the following groups shows order from lowest to highest?

   a. kilobyte, gigabyte, megabyte
   b. gigahertz, megahertz, hertz
   c. kilobyte, megabyte, gigabyte
   d. gigabyte, megabyte, kilobyte

5. Which of the following is not considered a printer choice for a home computer user?
   a. belt printer
   b. ink-jet printer
   c. multifunction device
   d. laser printer

6. The area where data and programs are temporarily stored while they are in use is
   a. CPU
   b. viewable area
   c. RAM
   d. CRT

7. The process of starting up a computer is sometimes called
   a. initiation
   b. booting
   c. opening the desktop
   d. clicking

8. A mouse that is not connected by cable to the system unit is a(n)
   a. wheel mouse
   b. optical mouse
   c. trackball
   d. remote mouse

9. Computer memory is measured in terms of
   a. bytes
   b. inches

c. hertz
d. cycles

10. The self-diagnostic procedure that occurs each time a computer is started up is the
   a. boot
   b. PDA
   c. RAM
   d. POST

PRACTICAL PROJECTS

1. Deciphering the Lingo

In this project, you will review a sample advertisement for a microcomputer system, identifying hardware specifications.

> 17" LCD Monitor
> Intel® Pentium® 4 Processor 2.40 GHz
> CD-RW Drive
> 40X CD-ROM Drive
> 512 MB DRAM
> 80.0 GB Hard Drive

a. In the ad above, how much memory is available?
b. What is the processor speed?
c. Is the monitor a flat panel or a CRT?
d. In the CD-ROM drive specification, what does the 40X mean? Be specific.
e. Does this computer include a floppy disk drive?

2. What Do I Want to Do?

Before selecting a computer for purchase, it is important that you evaluate your reasons for wanting a computer. What do you hope to accomplish? What do you think will be fun? Are there any projects that you have in mind?

Using the following checklist, select those areas that you would like to explore.

❑ E-mail
❑ Internet Research
❑ Games
❑ Word Processing
❑ Genealogy
❑ Graphics/Digital Photography
❑ Financial/Investment Analysis
❑ Desktop Publishing (greeting cards, calendars, brochures)
❑ Other (specify)

Having identified your computer goals, visit an office-supply store or general retailer and browse the software aisle to find products that might help you meet your goals. You can also check advertising inserts in a local newspaper. Find appropriate software and take a close look at the box to identify computer requirements. At a minimum, you should note the required operating system (OS), RAM (memory), and hard drive space. Do a little comparison shopping to find the same or similar products elsewhere.

You won't need to find any software to support the e-mail and Internet research categories, as those areas will be addressed when you contract with an Internet service provider.

In the table below, list your software selections. Which would you buy?

Software	Store/Vendor	RAM	OS	Cost

3. Identifying Computer Equipment

Now that you are aware of the hardware requirements for the software that you would like to purchase, it is time to find an appropriate computer. You should refer to the table from Project 2 for specific RAM and hard drive requirements.

Study computer advertisements in local newspapers and computer magazines. You can also visit office-supply and retail stores. Your goal is to find at least three affordable microcomputers, either laptop or desktop, that will support the tasks that you identified in Project 2.

List each of your choices, along with the hardware specifications, cost, and store that carries it.

4. Appearance Matters

As computers age, some components might begin to fail. Although monitors typically last a long time, it is possible that a monitor could fail, leaving you with a computer system in good shape, but no monitor. If that should happen, you could purchase a monitor to replace the old one. For this project, identify which monitor you would buy, giving its specifications and indicating why you chose it.

Your first task is to determine whether you will buy a flat panel or a CRT. Write a paragraph explaining how you made your choice and why you think it is appropriate. Provide monitor specifications in table format, listing such items as size, dot pitch, and refresh rate. Include the cost, as well.

5. Comfort Zone

With a new personal computer system in place, you are likely to spend a great deal of time using it. However, if the lighting is not right, the chair is uncomfortable, or the glare on the monitor is unbearable, you won't enjoy working on those computer projects. A well-designed work area will help you better organize your projects and work much more comfortably and safely.

Your goal in this project is to design a workspace for your new computer, selecting appropriate furniture, equipment, and lighting to maximize your comfort and productivity. Visit a library and peruse computer magazines and books for suggestions for ergonomically designed equipment and for tips on designing a comfortable work area. Take a look at advertisements for office furniture, noting those that are recommended for comfort and ergonomic design.

In your design, take into consideration your personal preferences and possible physical limitations. For planning purposes, consider the categories below. Provide a list of all furniture, accessories, and computer support tools, as well as suggestions for lighting, equipment positioning, and noise control. Give any other ideas or findings on work area design. Finally, list suggestions for minimizing discomfort and health risks while encouraging productivity.

Furniture and Accessories
Desk/work area
Chair
Storage

Computer Support Tools
Keyboard and keyboard supports
Wrist and palm rests
Mouse/pointing device
Mouse surface
Glare screen
Monitor blocks and risers
Cable management

Lighting
Task and work surface lighting
Overall room/window lighting

CHAPTER | 2

Software

Think about the reasons you want to use a personal computer. Perhaps you plan to track finances and chart your stock portfolio. Maybe you think it would be fun to create calendars, greeting cards, and newsletters. Even if all you have in mind is Internet surfing and e-mail, all tasks require you to use some form of software.

Software is the set of instructions that tells the computer how to accomplish a particular task. A computer without software is much like a car without gasoline. The car might be the fastest, most expensive car on the road, but it requires gasoline to move. No matter how fancy the computer hardware, you will need software to make the computer work the way you want it to. **Application software** is what makes it possible for you to accomplish your goals, such as typing documents or building a family tree. The next time you visit an office-supply store, browse the software aisle. Most of the packages that you see are for application software, each focusing on a particular

Objectives

When you complete this chapter, you will:

- **Understand the function of system software and application software.**

- **Describe major tasks of an operating system.**

- **Identify several types of operating systems used with microcomputers.**

- **List several categories of system utilities and describe the function of each.**

- **Describe software distribution methods.**

- **Identify legal issues associated with software development and distribution.**

- **Describe major categories of application software.**

job. You might recognize such titles as Microsoft Word, Photoshop, and Family Tree Maker. **System software,** *on the other hand, is concerned with the internal operations of the computer. Types of system software include the operating system and utility software. System software works in the background, taking care of basic computer operations and communication so that you can more fully enjoy your application software.*

Understanding System Software

A computer could not function at all without system software, which accepts directions from the user and manages internal computer operations. There are several categories of system software, but the one with which you will work most often is the operating system. The **operating system** (OS) works with application software to accomplish such tasks as saving documents and projects to a disk and recognizing input from the keyboard. An operating system also controls the computer's internal operations, keeps track of your files or projects, sends images to the monitor, and manages disk drives and memory. The operating system is the gateway to your application programs, working in the background to provide disk access, equipment coordination, and communication with the user. **Utility software**, another category of system software, performs such jobs as protecting your computer against computer viruses and backing up data onto other disks.

The Operating System

The operating system (OS) is the real software workhorse of your computer system. Every microcomputer must have an operating system to run other programs. The OS coordinates all system activities, from accepting and directing input to managing disk storage and memory allocation. When you work with application software, such as when you create a document, the operating system transparently serves as the interface between you and the application software, directing system activities and coordinating resources (Figure 2.1).

As the overall director of system requests, the operating system is the most important program that runs on a computer. The operating system assumes an expanded role on large computer networks, acting as a traffic cop to make sure that different programs and users working at the same time don't collide. It is also responsible for security, allowing only authorized access to the system.

Figure 2.1 **An operating system coordinates activities between the user, application software, and the computer's hardware.**

Although it is true that an operating system is a powerful piece of software that would require months to completely understand, it is comforting to know that you don't have to be an OS whiz to enjoy your computer. After all, what does it take to drive a car? You must minimally understand the way a car works, and it would help if you knew where the gas tank is and how to check the oil. Do you have to understand the intricacies of an internal combustion engine? No, you don't. As long as you can steer and brake, you're well on your way. Similarly, you don't have to understand every detail of a computer operating system before

In the Know

The IBM PC, introduced in 1981, was a revolutionary new product that changed the profile of both the computer and the typical computer user. No longer reserved solely for business and commercial use, computers soon became a mainstay of many homes. The most recognizable of the early microcomputer operating systems is **MS-DOS** (Microsoft Disk Operating System), which is a command-line OS adopted for the first IBM PC. Instead of having the graphical interface supported by current versions of Windows, MS-DOS required that users type DOS requests, using very specific commands and formatting. Memorizing commands and consulting a ready reference kept nearby were tiring and time consuming. Typing a command incorrectly might result in a cryptic error message like "invalid number of parameters," which to a typical home computer user left no clue as to the real problem. With little to compare it with, MS-DOS was readily accepted and mastered by computer users.

The history of MS-DOS began with IBM's search for a suitable operating system for the IBM PC. Prior to 1981, IBM executives approached Bill Gates, head of Microsoft Corporation, to explore partnership possibilities. Microsoft had never written an operating system, so Gates suggested that IBM contact Gary Kildall of Digital Research, who had written **CP/M**, the most successful operating system of that time. CP/M had effectively set the standard for operating systems. When they were unable to reach an agreement with Kildall, IBM executives returned to Gates and asked that Microsoft write a new operating system specifically for the IBM PC. Tim Paterson of Seattle Computer Products had already written an operating system called **QDOS** (Quick and Dirty Operating System). It was based on Kildall's CP/M but was different enough to be considered legal. Microsoft bought the rights to QDOS for $50,000. QDOS debuted as **PC-DOS 1.0** on the new IBM PC. IBM allowed Microsoft to market MS-DOS separately from the IBM PC product, which began Microsoft's rise to dominance in the software industry.

MS-DOS is not used by itself today, but it can still be accessed from some versions of Windows by clicking Start and then clicking Run. Type **command** or **CMD** and click OK.

tackling a computer task. Computer professionals might have a keen interest in the makeup of an operating system, but, those intent on enjoying specific computer applications probably want to know just enough about the operating system to make it work for them. Mastering those basic operating system activities will make working with application software much easier, and it's truly the first step toward enjoying a computer.

When you purchase a computer, it might be preloaded with an operating system. If you purchase a PC-compatible computer, the operating system is most likely a version of **Microsoft Windows**. Apple computers include Apple's operating system, **Mac OS**. Although those are the two most common operating systems found on microcomputers, you should be aware of other **operating system platforms**, such as **UNIX** and **Linux**, both powerful, well-designed systems used primarily in businesses and to support **servers** (computers designed to support other computer systems and to provide access to resources). Almost all PCs are sold with Windows installed; however, some distributors, such as Wal-Mart, ship computers with Linux preinstalled. Wal-Mart and other distrib-

In the Know

Although most people were enthralled with the command-line interface provided by MS-DOS, a smaller company was quietly working on a better design. Steve Jobs and Stephen Wozniak, the founders of Apple Computer, believed that the graphical user interface was the wave of the future. After a visit to the Palo Alto Research Center (PARC), to see Xerox's new graphical user interface, Jobs became intent on developing a similar interface for Apple's new Lisa—which stood for Local Integrated System Architecture—computer. The Lisa was introduced in 1983, carrying a new operating system with a graphical user interface. The cost? $10,000! Perhaps due in part to the cost, the Lisa failed to sell and was quickly replaced by the long-lived Macintosh, also based on a well-designed GUI. MS-DOS devotees spurned Apple's GUI, calling it "WIMP" (the Windows, Icons, Mice, and Pointers interface).

Around the same time, Microsoft became involved in the development of Windows, originally called Interface Manager (company executives wisely opted for the less intimidating title of Windows). Microsoft introduced Windows in 1985, a couple of years after Apple's GUI had appeared, and comparisons were immediately made. Most conceded that Windows was clumsy and less capable than the Mac OS (Apple's GUI operating system). Regardless of perceived quality, Microsoft has since far surpassed Apple in sales of operating systems.

Apple has never been able to overtake Microsoft and continues to hold only about 10 percent of the OS market. However, new versions of the Mac OS, most notably OS X, may help Apple solidify its consumer and business base.

utors also sell computers with no operating system at all, so that you can install your favorite.

Windows

It is very likely that you are working with a version of Microsoft Windows now. With well over 80 percent of the market share, Windows dominates personal computer operating systems. In a dramatic turn from the command-line MS-DOS interface, Windows focuses on communication through symbols, visual cues, and pointing devices, such as a mouse. Because of the reliance on graphic elements, Windows is called a **graphical user interface** (**GUI**), pronounced GOO-ee.

Windows was at first spurned by die-hard MS-DOS advocates, who were quick to criticize the Windows interface as bloated and bug-ridden (full of errors). Nevertheless, Windows quickly assumed a leadership position, due in part to Microsoft's compromise in making Windows **backward compatible** with MS-DOS. That means that MS-DOS users could still get to the MS-DOS interface even though they came in through Windows. Later Windows versions dropped the obvious connection with MS-DOS, focusing instead on improving hardware compatibility, simplifying file and program access, enhancing security and reliability, and introducing network options. Examples of command-line and graphical user interfaces are shown in Figure 2.2.

Figure 2.2 **Examples of (a) command-line and (b) graphical user interfaces.**

In the Know

Windows is the backbone upon which Microsoft built an empire, beginning with the first version of Windows in 1985. The Windows operating system has progressed through several versions, the most recent version of which is Windows XP. (Each time a software manufacturer brings out a new version of software, it is an improved or enhanced version.) By 1993, the number of licensed Windows users totaled more than 25 million!

November 1985—Windows 1.0 *was released. It allowed users to run several programs at the same time, although the programs couldn't be overlapped on the display. Windows 1.0 was not a huge sales success.*

April 1987—Windows 2.0 *made its entrance but was not very successful.*

May 1990—Windows 3.0 *finally paid off for Microsoft. With new features and significant improvements, Windows 3.0 sold 3 million copies in the first three months.*

April 1992—*With the release of* Windows 3.1, *Microsoft continued the effort to provide a more stable operating system. This version of Windows quickly became the most commonly installed operating system on microcomputers in the United States.*

May 1993—Windows NT *was introduced, providing a secure, stable environment for high-end microcomputers and servers. NT stands for New Technology, although critics nicknamed it Not Today, No Thanks, and Nice Try.*

August 1995—Windows 95 *sold more than one million copies in four days, due in part to an unprecedented frenzy of prerelease advertise-*ments. Windows 95 was the first Windows version that didn't require the user to first install MS-DOS. It was a significant improvement over earlier versions, with a much easier to use graphic display.

November 1996—*The first version of* Windows CE, *the operating system widely used in hand-held and palm computers, was introduced. Similar to desktop Windows versions, Windows CE was designed to run simplified versions of Windows programs.*

June 1998—Windows 98 *made its mark as the last major version of Windows running in conjunction with MS-DOS. Its interface was very much like Windows 95, so a user could easily switch from one to the other.*

February 2000—Windows 2000 *was a successful attempt to combine the strength and reliability of Windows NT with the flexibility required by consumers. While Windows 2000 is found on many home computer systems, it is positioned as a business OS.*

July 2000—Windows ME (Windows Millennium Edition) *was marketed specifically for the home user. Boasting enhanced multimedia features, Windows ME attempted to make the home computing experience easy and reliable. However, it was never a huge success and was quickly supplanted by Windows 2000 and Windows XP.*

October 2001—Windows XP *is an operating system unlike its predecessors. Although it incorporates features of Windows 2000 and Windows NT, its interface and operability make it just different enough to challenge even proficient Windows users. Two versions of Windows XP are available—Home and Professional.*

Many home computers now come installed with **Windows XP**, which is a new look for Windows, as shown in Figure 2.3. The GUI is somewhat similar to past versions, but there are many new features that make home computing more reliable and more fun. This single operating system integrates the stability of Windows 2000 with the consumer features of Windows ME. XP is very quick, booting and launching applications 36 percent faster than Windows 98 and remaining equivalent to Windows 2000 in performance. Windows XP comes in two versions—Home and Professional.

Windows XP includes a Product Activation feature that makes it difficult, if not impossible, to install a single copy on more than one computer. Recognizing that many homes now have several computers, possibly even networked, Microsoft offers discounts for multiple purchases of Windows XP.

Windows XP Home Edition introduces a new desktop, or interface. Frequently used features are found on the Start menu (the menu displayed when you click Start). For home users interested in music and recording, an en-

Figure 2.3 **Windows XP features a new graphical interface.**

hanced media player integrates DVD playback, music organization, and CD creation. You can enjoy video capture and editing, enhanced instant messaging (talking with someone on the Internet by typing messages), and easy switching between users on the same computer. With the Remote Assistance feature, technicians can take temporary control of your system to diagnose and correct problems. Windows XP Home also makes it easy for you to set up a home network for file, printer, and Internet connection sharing.

Windows XP Professional Edition includes features of the Home Edition, as well as additional capabilities that a business or large enterprise might require. Windows XP Professional is an effective replacement for Windows NT and

Web Watch

If you are considering moving from your operating system to Windows XP, you might want to visit **www.microsoft.com/ windowsxp/pro/ howtobuy/upgrading/ advisor.asp**. The Web site provides a tool called the Upgrade Advisor, which helps determine whether your system hardware and software are ready for Windows XP.

In the Know

Windows, like other software, requires a certain amount of system resources (processor speed, hard drive space, and memory). Before installing or upgrading to any Windows version, you should verify that your system has sufficient resources. Check the Microsoft Web site (www.microsoft.com) or simply read the system requirements on the Windows package to identify specifications. If you already have a version of Windows installed on your computer and wish to progress to a newer version, you might not need to purchase the **full version**. Instead, you could purchase the cheaper **upgrade**, which contains only those elements necessary to transition your older Windows version to the newer. Windows XP is upgradable from Windows 98/ME/2000 but does not support upgrades from Windows 95 or earlier.

Hands On

Activity 2.1—Identifying a Windows Version

In this exercise, you will identify the version of the Windows operating system installed on your computer (if your computer is a Windows-based PC). The computer should be on and at the beginning screen, with desktop icons displayed.

1. Click Start.
2. Click the Control Panel option, as shown in Figure 2.4.

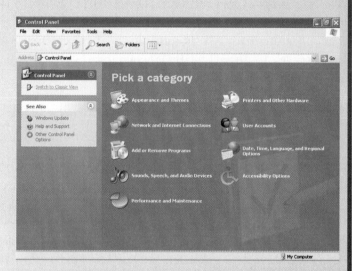

Figure 2.4 **The Control Panel is found on the Start menu.**

3. The Control Panel window (as shown in Figure 2.5) should open. Click Performance and Maintenance. Click System. You might have to scroll the screen slightly to see the System area. To scroll, click the downward-pointing arrow in the scroll bar to the right of the Performance and Maintenance window. If the window is already full size, you won't find a scroll bar to the right.
4. If the General tab (at the top of the window) is not displayed as shown in Figure 2.6, click General.
5. System Properties appears, as shown in Figure 2.6. In the center of the properties list, find the version of Windows.

Figure 2.5 **You can customize your computer system using the Control Panel.**

6. Click the X in the top right corner of the System Properties window to close it.

Figure 2.6 **Information about your system is displayed in System Properties.**

7. Click the X in the top right corner of the Performance and Maintenance window to close it.

Windows 2000. It includes a remote desktop, where computers can share desktop sessions, even if thousands of miles separate them. Tightened security and enhanced networking, even secure wireless networking, are also key features.

Mac OS

Mac OS was one of the first operating systems to incorporate a graphical user interface. Introduced by Apple in 1984, Mac OS was based on an interface developed by Xerox for use on the Alto computer. Since that time, Mac OS has undergone several revisions, culminating in **Mac OS X** (pronounced "OS ten"). The new operating system combines the stability of UNIX (a command-driven operating system), with the graphical user interface and ease of use of the Macintosh. Apple took great pains to make it easy for faithful users to migrate to OS X. The interface looks much like that of earlier versions, with the familiar menu bar, Apple logo, and even Apple's Finder. Mac OS X makes it possible to run applications in Classic mode, with the same look and feel of Mac OS 9. Don't be fooled by the familiar interface, though—OS X, as shown in Figure 2.7, is full of new features that easily rival Windows in both ease of use and technical specifications.

Figure 2.7 **Mac OS X is full of new features, improving its usability and reliability.**

UNIX

UNIX is an operating system developed by Bell Labs in the early 1970s. Although not often found on personal computers, UNIX (pronounced YOO-nix) provides excellent support for high-end workstations and corporate servers (Figure 2.8). UNIX, written in the C programming language, can run on any computer that has a C compiler. Universities embraced UNIX because of its portability and low cost. Antitrust regulations prohibited Bell Labs from marketing UNIX as a full-scale product, thus keeping the cost low.

UNIX was initially developed as a command-driven operating system. However, GUI interfaces have recently been developed for UNIX, improving its acceptance. Nevertheless, its complexity,

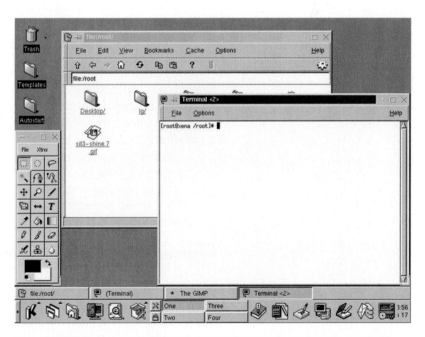

Figure 2.8 **UNIX is the operating system of choice for many larger computer systems.**

In the Know

Steve Jobs and Stephen Wozniak were high-school friends who shared a vision. Jobs fully believed that science and technology were the route to a better future for humankind, while Wozniak cheerfully believed in the goodness of humanity. Combining human-interest skills, a focus on technology, and a firm foundation in electronics, the two friends developed a video teletype terminal, complete with video display, and then tried to market the product. Challenged by the lack of interest they found with computer companies, they began their own company, named Apple after their favorite snack food. That was in 1976.

The original Apple computer, built at Jobs' home, was sold as a partially assembled kit for computer hobbyists. The first slogan for the new company was "Byte into an Apple." Quickly moving to capture more of the professional market share, they redesigned the Apple computer and packaged it in an attractive plastic case. That was the Apple II, introduced in 1978. Marketing was expanded to include the home computer user.

The Apple II included a built-in BASIC interpreter (allowing users to write computer programs in the BASIC computer language) and a color display. With eight expansion slots, a cassette tape drive, and a full-size 52-key keyboard, the Apple II became the most popular computer of its time. Schools began to invest in Apple computers, purchasing inexpensive programs like Apple Writer for student use.

In 1980, Apple brought out the Apple III, which was an instant disappointment. It included up to 256 KB of RAM, a floppy disk drive, and an optional 5 MB hard drive. But the computer that was supposed to run Apple II programs had difficulty, ran hot, and often failed. Reintroduced in 1981, it was overwhelmed by the success of the IBM PC, which was designed to be a business machine and was sold by a trained fleet of IBM representatives.

Apple's next attempt was to develop a business computer, the Lisa. The system included a GUI, a mouse, a floppy drive, and an external hard drive. Costing $10,000, the computer never caught on. Only 10,000 units were ever sold. The company regrouped in its effort to make a low-cost computer that could be used by anybody. During the 1984 Super Bowl, the Macintosh was introduced to the world. Immensely successful, the Macintosh continues to be Apple's primary product.

Apple continues as a viable computer company but is definitely overshadowed by the larger market share of PC-compatible computers. Microsoft controls a huge segment of the software market, relegating Apple's operating system to only about 10 percent of all installations. Sometimes a high-quality product is just not enough!

which makes it ideal for managing activities of large computers, does nothing to endear it to the personal computer market. UNIX's strength lies in its capability to coordinate activities between a server and its clients (smaller computers in communication with a server).

In the Know

Most of the software that you purchase is commercial, which means that you buy the right to use the software only and have no access to the **source code** used to create the product. If there is a problem with the software, you must wait for the software company to produce patches or fixes for it. You cannot modify the source code yourself.

Open source software, on the other hand, makes the source code available. Those users who want to do so are free to read and modify the source code. Anyone who finds a problem, or bug, in the software, can rewrite the faulty code. With so much revision possible, open source software tends to improve faster than commercial software.

Linux

Finnish college student Linus Torvalds created Linux to be an alternative to Windows. Although Linux is not derived from UNIX source code, its interface is intentionally similar to UNIX's interface. Linux is open source software. Several different organizations have developed variations of Linux, called *distributions*. Common distributions include Red Hat, Mandrake, SuSE, Caldera, Corel, and Debian. Linux has progressed into a powerful server and workstation system with a graphical user interface rivaling Windows (Figure 2.9). Linux can be downloaded from the Internet at no cost, but with no technical support.

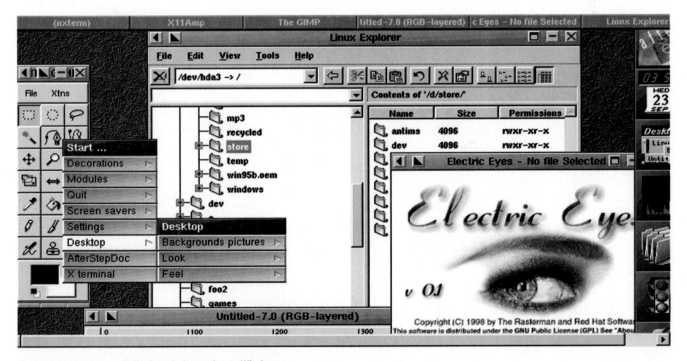

Figure 2.9 **Linux is a well-designed alternative to Windows.**

In the Know

Copyright protection is extended to computer software, making it illegal to reproduce software without authorization. But have you ever heard of copyleft? **Copyleft** is an outcome of the free, or open source, software movement. In general, a copyleft requires all modified and extended versions of a free software item to remain free. It is also called a GPL, or a General Public License. To copyleft a program, the developer must first state that it is copyrighted, and then add distribution terms to the legal document giving everyone the right to use, modify, and redistribute the program code or any derivative of that code. The distribution terms must remain unchanged, so that the program code and the freedoms are legally inseparable. In effect, a copyright prohibits copying commercial software, whereas a copyleft guarantees the freedom to copy an open source program code.

Alternatively, you can purchase Linux from a distributor, boxed with a CD, manuals, and technical support.

Why is such a powerful operating system free? Linus Torvalds believed in the power of collaboration. He made his Linux operating system available to anyone, with a challenge to make it better. Thousands of programmers took him up on his offer and helped build Linux into a sturdy, reliable operating system that can run on all types of computers. One reason Linux is not found more often on personal computers is that it is not sponsored by a recognized software company. In addition, since it is not a Microsoft product, it is not designed to run popular Microsoft software, such as Microsoft Office. Linux can, however, run comparable software packages, such as Star Office.

System Utilities

System utilities are programs that address such tasks as backing up (copying) disk files, scanning disk drives for errors, and eliminating computer viruses. Some system utilities are included with an operating system; others are purchased from third parties.

Antivirus Software

A **computer virus** is a malicious program purposely written to annoy you or to damage system files. The program can *infect* your system as it travels along a network or with a downloaded program, e-mail attachment, or portable diskette. Some viruses won't harm your system, but most are destructive. New computer viruses are written daily, so it is critical that you understand the threat and know what to do to protect your computer. **Antivirus software** is a type of system software that specifically protects your computer against known viruses.

Without adequate antivirus protection, it is easy to get a computer virus and not even know it. The most common way for viruses to pass is as e-mail attachments. The problem is that many viruses propagate themselves by infecting a system and then sending seemingly innocent e-mail to the addresses found in the user's e-mail address book. You might unknowingly receive an infected e-mail message from a friend. Without your awareness, the virus can "send" itself to everyone in your e-mail address file, making it appear that the e-mail came from you. Consequently, your friends and family won't hesitate to open the e-mail message. After all, it came from you. The virus then replicates on their system, and continues the process. It doesn't take long for hundreds of computers to receive the same virus.

Figure 2.10 **Norton AntiVirus is a utility that locates and eliminates computer viruses.**

The scenario played out above doesn't have to happen. You can purchase and maintain adequate antivirus software, such as Norton AntiVirus (Figure 2.10). Antivirus software scans your computer system, looking for programs identified in its database as viruses. If your antivirus software is up-to-date with the latest database, most viruses are caught and eliminated early. Updates to the virus database are available as Internet downloads. You will find much more information on viruses and antivirus software in Chapter 7.

Other System Utilities

If your computer experiences a power surge or hardware failure, your hard disk drive can be wiped out in a matter of seconds. You should never depend on only one copy of an important file or document. This is why it is important to make back-up copies of your hard disk data. A **backup utility** allows you to copy the contents of a hard disk to another form of storage, such as a Zip disk or CD. Hard disk sizes are increasing all the time. Many personal computers sport hard disk sizes in excess of 80 GB. With such a large amount of available storage space, you can easily save a great deal of data. If you don't make back-up copies of that data, however, you can lose it all with one hard disk failure. It is just as important to make copies of data saved on other storage media, such as floppy disks, Zip disks, CDs, or DVDs.

Many computer users enjoy creating graphics and working with digital photos. Graphics files, such as digital photos, are typically very large, requiring a great deal of disk storage space. One solution is to compress large files so that they don't require as much disk space and so that they are quicker to send by e-mail. **File compression** programs, such as WinZip and StuffIt, effectively reduce file sizes and are easy to learn to use.

The surface of a disk can become damaged, and sometimes errors occur as files are being saved. Windows includes an error checking utility (**disk scanner**) that scans a disk, determining whether the disk is reliable, while identifying any areas that are becoming unusable because of the way files are being arranged and recorded. Most disk problems are caused by software, sometimes when the operating system's internal record of file locations is damaged. The error checking utility can correct most software-related disk problems. However, if a disk is severely scratched or has experienced other physical problems, the disk scanner will not be able to make corrections. You will learn more about Windows' error checking utility in Chapter 4.

When you create a document, such as a report, you will want to save it to a disk for later access and printing. Theoretically, the document, or file, is being saved in a single unit. In reality, however, the file is probably broken up (**fragmented**) by the operating system and placed in various locations on the disk. With enough fragmentation, a disk can become slow and unwieldy. **File defragmentation** utilities rearrange the bytes on a disk to rejoin the pieces of files and programs and place them in adjacent locations, thus improving disk performance. You will find additional information on defragmenting in Chapter 4.

Understanding Application Software

The operating system might be the gateway to your computer, but application software is usually the desired destination. It is the reason you purchased a computer and why you enjoy it. Whatever your computer interest, it is probably supported by application software. If you are interested in designing a landscape, you can find application software dealing with the subject. Perhaps you have a digital camera and want to enhance digital photos. You can find plenty of image-editing application software to help you along.

Distribution Methods

You can obtain software by purchasing it from a store or downloading it from the Internet. Some software is even free.

Commercial

Sometimes called COTS (commercial off-the-shelf), **commercial software** is developed for and sold to the public. It is also copyrighted. When you purchase software, you don't purchase the right to modify or redistribute it, and you are not allowed to make multiple copies. Commercial software is the most common form of software and is what you see when you visit the software aisle.

Freeware

Freeware is software that is available at no cost. Although it is free, it is also copyrighted, which means that you can redistribute, but not modify, the program. Unlike open source, its source code is not available. Clip art (picture-type images) is one type of software that is often available as freeware. It might be copyrighted, but it is free in accordance with certain terms set by the developer. Technical support is not included with freeware. Many times, freeware is provided as the result of scholarly research or as part of a marketing study.

Shareware

You will often find software that is free to download and use for a trial period. The software developer hopes that after you try the software you will want to buy it. Such software is called **shareware**, which is **copyrighted**, and usually free only for a limited time (Figure 2.11). After the trial period, you are expected to voluntarily send payment

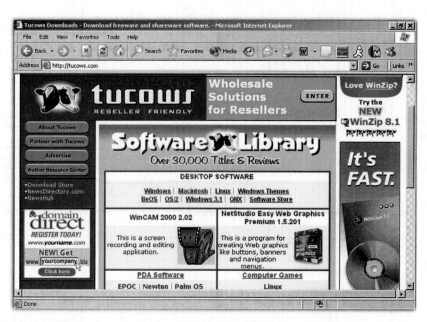

Figure 2.11 **Shareware is copyrighted software that is free for a limited time.**

to the software developer or uninstall the software. Some shareware contains a built-in expiration date, so that after a certain number of days, it is no longer usable. If, however, you would like to keep the software, sending payment to the developer entitles you to continue using it and usually provides you with additional benefits, such as manuals and technical support. Antivirus software is often available as an evaluation copy for a certain number of days. **Crippleware**, or **liteware**, is a variation of shareware in which software is available free of charge for a limited time. However, some advanced features or the ability to print are *crippled*, or unavailable, until you pay a fee to the author.

Public Domain

Public domain software is not copyrighted and has no terms of usage or conditions attached. You may copy it, sell it, or use it in any way you want. True public domain software is rare. Some clip art is considered public domain, but it is usually black and white and requires significant cleanup before it can be used. *Public domain* is a legal term that simply means "not copyrighted."

Installing Software

When you purchase or otherwise obtain software, you must **install** it on your computer system before you can use it. Installing software copies the software to your computer's hard disk and makes it available for use. During the installation, the program is configured so that it runs properly on your system. For example, let's say you've purchased a home computer and now want to use it to record and print your family records. You visit a local retail store and browse the software aisle. All of the software applications are packaged in boxes that list the required computer specifications. You note that there are several choices of software

Hands On

Activity 2.2—Checking System Specifications

In this exercise, you will check some of your system's specifications to verify that you have what is required to run a sample software program. For this exercise, assume that you plan to use your computer to create a scrapbook. You've decided on a scrapbook software package and found the following requirements listed on the box:

Windows 95, 98, NT, ME, or XP
Pentium® 133 MHz or Faster
32 MB RAM
CD-ROM Drive

Be sure the computer is on and at the beginning screen, with desktop icons displayed, before you begin.

1. Click Start.
2. Right-click My Computer. Click Properties, as shown in Figure 2.12.
3. The System Properties window should open, as shown in Figure 2.13. If the General tab (at the top of the window) is not selected, click General.

4. Find the version of Windows. You should also see the processor speed and the amount of RAM.
5. Click the X in the upper right corner of any open windows to close them.
6. Click Start.
7. Click My Computer.
8. Check for a CD or DVD drive. If you have one, it will be listed in this window.
9. Move the mouse pointer over the hard disk icon. Hold it steady to display a tool tip, giving hard disk free space, as shown in Figure 2.14.
10. Click the X to close the window.

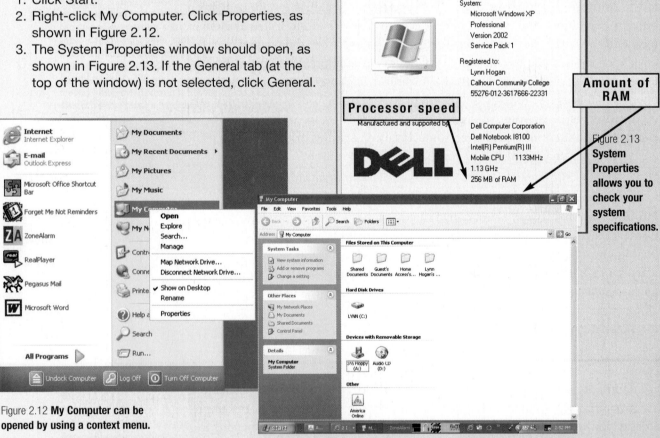

Figure 2.12 **My Computer can be opened by using a context menu.**

Figure 2.13 **System Properties allows you to check your system specifications.**

Figure 2.14 **Working with My Computer, you can find the amount of free space on a disk.**

geared to the preparation of family records. You select one that is within your price range and that meets the specifications of your computer system (operating system and amount of hard disk space and RAM). Returning home, you open the software box and find a CD-ROM along with some paperwork, perhaps an instruction manual or quick tips sheet. What next?

Most current commercial software is configured to begin installation automatically when you place the CD in the CD drive. Press the button to open the CD drive, place the CD-ROM shiny side down on the drive drawer, and press the button once again to close the drive. You won't need to do anything else for a few seconds, as the auto-install process begins. You will see a box appear on your screen asking whether you want to proceed with the installation. The box you are viewing is called a **wizard**, which is a series of guided screens that simplify a task by asking questions and allowing you to modify some settings. Usually, the settings that an Install wizard suggests are the most appropriate, so unless you have some reason to change the suggested settings, you should click the button titled "Next," or otherwise indicate your acceptance of the agreement. You will progress through several wizard screens before the installation process is complete.

During the installation process, you will probably be asked to register your product. Often, the registration can occur online. You can also mail in the registration. Although it is tempting to skip the sometimes time-consuming task of registering the software product, it is best to go ahead and take the time. By registering, you will receive information on software upgrades and might be given the opportunity to purchase additional products at a discount.

✓ SANITY CHECK

What if the auto-install process doesn't begin when you place the CD in the CD drive? Especially with older software, that is likely to happen. Some software is just not configured to install automatically. In that case, you must manually install it by locating the included installation files.

1. With the CD in place, click Start, and then click Run. The Run dialog box (Figure 2.15) appears.
2. At the next window, click Browse to locate the executable file. An executable file is a program file, usually called *install.exe* or *setup.exe*.
3. To check the CD for an executable file, click the small black triangle, or arrow, beside the Look In area (Figure 2.16). It is called a drop-down arrow.
4. Click to select drive D (or the letter given for the CD drive on your computer system).
5. In the subsequent list of programs, you should see one with a name that indicates it is an install or setup program, as shown in Figure 2.17. Click to select it.

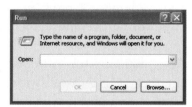

Figure 2.15 **Some software must be manually installed using the Run command.**

6. Click Open.
7. Click OK.

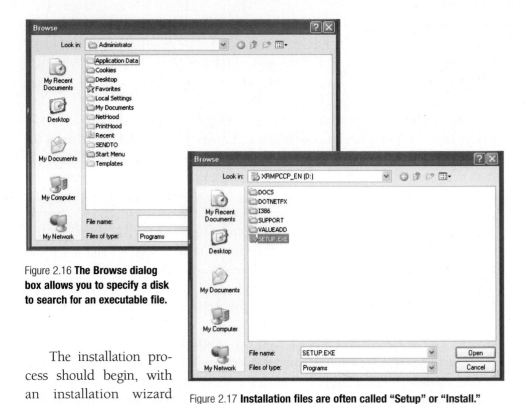

Figure 2.16 **The Browse dialog box allows you to specify a disk to search for an executable file.**

The installation process should begin, with an installation wizard leading you through the process.

Figure 2.17 **Installation files are often called "Setup" or "Install."**

After software is installed, you most likely won't need the CD anymore, except as a backup in case your hard disk ever fails. You should place the CD back in its case and put it in a drawer or cabinet for safekeeping. However, some software requires that the CD be present in the CD drive. That is most often the case with interactive computer games or data-rich encyclopedias. You might want to include some clip art in a document only to find that you need the original CD to obtain the clip art. Be sure to keep all software CDs handy so that you can use them if the software requires it.

Uninstalling Software

Although the hard drive on your system is likely large enough to hold quite a few software programs, the space available is limited. There will be times when you want to remove a program from your system. Removing a program is called **uninstalling**. An uninstall wizard is an automated series of steps that sometimes appears when you begin to uninstall a program. Depending upon the configuration of the software, you might work with an uninstall wizard, or the uninstall could proceed with no interaction with you beyond the initial command to uninstall.

Uninstalling a program removes all program components from a computer system. Uninstalling is not the same as deleting a program. During software installation, program files might be placed in a number of folders. The installation process might also make changes to the Windows Registry, which is a special file that keeps track of Windows and program settings. If you find what you think is the program folder and delete it, chances are you have removed only a small part of the complete program installation. Only a complete uninstallation will remove the program and all of its components.

To uninstall a program, follow this procedure.

1. Click Start.
2. Click Control Panel.
3. Click Add or Remove Programs. You will see a list of programs installed on your system, as shown in Figure 2.18.
4. To remove a program, click its title in the list, and then click Remove.
5. Respond to any prompts that might appear, perhaps through an Uninstall wizard.
6. Click the X in the top right corner to close any open windows.

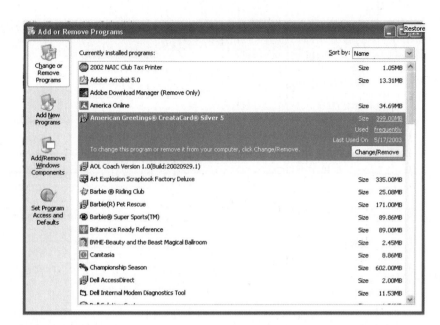

Figure 2.18 **The Add/Remove Programs window provides a list of programs installed on your system.**

Running Software

Running a program is called executing or launching. When a program is installed, its title might be placed in any of a number of locations on your computer. For example, you might see the program listed as an icon (picture) on your desktop (the screen that displays after a successful boot). If that is the case, double-click the program icon to run the program.

Most programs, however, appear simply as a title in a program list. To find that list and run the program, click Start and move to All Programs. A list of programs will appear, as shown in Figure 2.19.

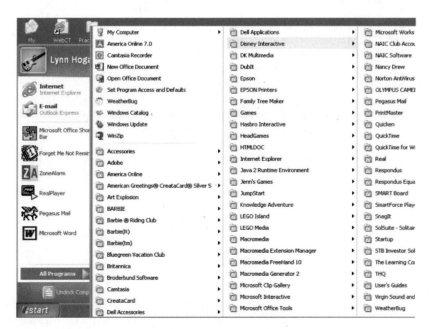

Figure 2.19 **You can choose a program to run from the program list.**

Hands On

Activity 2.3—
Running Software (Calculator)

In this exercise, you will run a small program called Calculator that is installed with Windows. The computer should be on and at the beginning screen, with desktop icons displayed.

1. Click Start.
2. Point to All Programs.
3. Move to the right, and up or down, to find Accessories.
4. Move to the right, and up or down, to find Calculator, as shown in Figure 2.20. Click Calculator.

5. If your screen doesn't look similar to that shown in Figure 2.21, click View (along the top of the calculator) and click Standard.
6. The Calculator is a handy tool that mimics a handheld calculator. You can enter numbers and calculations by clicking the calculator, or you can use the number keys and operators on your keyboard. Either way, the result is displayed on the screen. Try a few calculations.
7. Click the X in the top right corner of the Calculator to close it.

Figure 2.21 **The Calculator works much like a handheld calculator.**

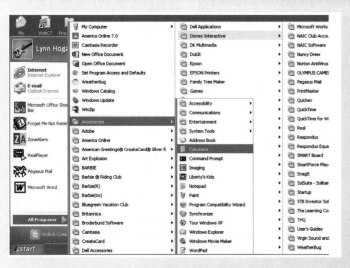

Figure 2.20 **The Calculator is found in the Accessories menu.**

Move to the list and progress up or down to locate the program you want to use. It is possible that yet another list will appear when you point to the program title. Proceed to the appropriate program name and click it to run the program.

Getting Help

At one time, software was packaged with lengthy and somewhat intimidating user manuals. The manuals included everything from how to install the software to the most obscure program functions. Now, when you bring home a new software application, you are likely to find only a slim manual with general information on program highlights. That is because manufacturers are now including extensive help built right into the software, available with a click of the mouse (Figure 2.22). You can also find assistance at the software manufacturer's Web site. In addition, a toll-free number is usually listed in the program documentation or at the software manufacturer's Web site. If you can't find the answer to your question elsewhere, you can always call for technical assistance.

Legal Issues

We have all heard that imitation is the sincerest form of flattery, but commercial software distributors find no truth or humor in that statement. The fact that they lose billions of dollars each year to illegal copying of software makes them very determined to address the problem head on. Like other works of art and literature, computer software comes under copyright protection, which makes it illegal to reproduce copyrighted software without authorization.

When you purchase commercial software, you purchase only the right to use the software. You do not own it. The accompanying **software license** agreement, called the **End User License Agreement (EULA)** specifies the terms of usage, and most certainly prohibits making more than one copy of the software. Legally, if you have more than one computer in your household on which you wish to place the purchased software, you must buy additional licenses. Businesses and educational institutions are bound by the same requirements, but software vendors usually offer **site licenses**, whereby a business can purchase the right to make a limited number of copies from a single software CD. Organizations can also purchase **server licenses**, which permit users connected to a server to access software installed on the server. Sometimes the server license specifies the number of users who can access the server software.

The Internet provides even more temptation to obtain software, written works, music, and graphics illegally. Although you would probably never consider stealing a laptop from a coworker's desk and taking it home, you might not have the same hesitation about collecting graphics or text from the Internet to include in a document that you are working with. Although some software is free to download from the Internet, it is usually accompanied by a license outlining terms of usage. Take the time to carefully read all licenses like the one

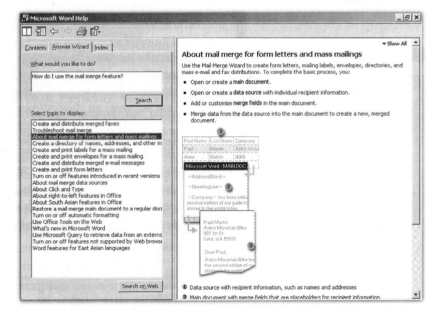

Figure 2.22 **Help is available with a click of the mouse.**

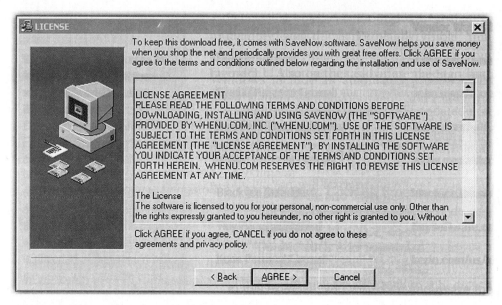

Figure 2.23 **A license accompanies most software, giving terms of usage. You should carefully read all license terms before installing software.**

shown in Figure 2.23, and study all items for evidence of copyright protection before collecting or downloading them.

Assume that a friend purchased a software package to assist with preparing tax forms. You are facing a short deadline with your own tax paperwork and have heard from your friend about how wonderful the software is and how much time she saved in getting the forms completed. She generously offers to let you "borrow" the software CD for a few days. It is her CD, right? So is there a problem with installing the software on your computer, only temporarily, until your taxes are complete? You aren't stealing anything—you are only borrowing the CD, much like checking out a book from the library. You can rationalize the situation until it seems harmless, but the truth is that making the copy on your computer is a violation of copyright, punishable by fines and/or jail time. Will you be caught? Probably not. But consider the development cost that went into the software product.

Reproducing copyrighted software without authorization is called **software piracy**. Such activities as making multiple copies of commercial software, counterfeiting and distributing software, and sharing software with a friend are all considered to be software piracy. Aside from being illegal, pirated software is a problem for consumers for several reasons. The software lacks documentation, and carries no warranty or upgrade options. Copied software could also be infected with damaging viruses. Another problem for consumers is that software piracy raises the cost of software. Think about the author's time and expertise. Think about the loss that occurs when 100 people like you copy the $25 piece of software. That's easily a $2,500 loss to the developer. They have to make that up by charging more for the product.

Some argue that a "pirate" is someone who attacks or kills others while stealing cargo. They maintain that the term "pirate" is too severe a description for a simple act of copying a piece of software for which the developer charges too much anyway. IDC, a world leader in analysis of information technology trends, doesn't agree, citing the fact that four of every 10 software products nationwide are pirated. It estimates that if the piracy rate dropped just 30 percent, economic growth could increase by $400 billion, creating 1.5 million jobs and generating $64 billion in taxes. Software piracy is no small thing, as evidenced by the No Electronic Theft Act of 1997 and the Digital Millennium Copyright Act of 1998.

In the Know

Following a 15-month undercover investigation by the United States Customs Service, with assistance from the Department of Justice's Computer Crime and Intellectual Property Section (CCIPS), John Sankus Jr. was convicted of conspiracy to commit criminal copyright infringement and sentenced in 2002 to the longest term ever imposed for Internet piracy—46 months in prison. Sankus was coleader of a group known as DrinkOrDie, the largest and oldest organized software piracy group ever prosecuted. Sankus' group illegally distributed copyrighted software, games, and movies over the Internet. DrinkOrDie is only one of many highly structured organizations that reproduce and distribute thousands of copyrighted works around the world.

Another case, prosecuted by the FBI, brought charges against Yaroslav Suris for reproducing and selling approximately $290,000 of pirated software through Yahoo! Auction. Pirated products included software from Adobe, Corel, and Macromedia. Suris pleaded guilty and was sentenced to two months of prison time and payment of $290,000 in restitution.

Both pieces of federal legislation augment U.S. copyright law, further defining and punishing acts of software copyright infringement.

The Software and Information Industry Association (SIIA) maintains a Web site providing information on piracy and copyright issues, including an area where instances of end-user, vendor, retail, and Internet piracy can be reported (**http://www.siia.net/**). *End-user piracy* is using multiple copies of a single software package on several different computer systems or distributing copies of software to others. *Vendor and retail piracy* occurs when a reseller distributes multiple copies of a single software package to others. That might happen if a retailer preloads computer systems with software without providing original manuals and CDs. *Internet piracy* is unauthorized electronic transfer of copyrighted software and material, such as music CDs. The Software Publisher's Association coordinates efforts to thwart software piracy (Figure 2.24).

Major Categories of Application Software

You probably have some definite ideas about why you want to use a computer. You can be certain that there is a type of software addressing just about every one of your ideas. Many computer users list word processing as one of the applications that they plan to use. Other major categories include spreadsheet, database, graphics, and presentation software. Collectively, those applications are called productivity software because they

Figure 2.24 **The Software Publisher's Association (SPA) is serious about preventing software piracy.**

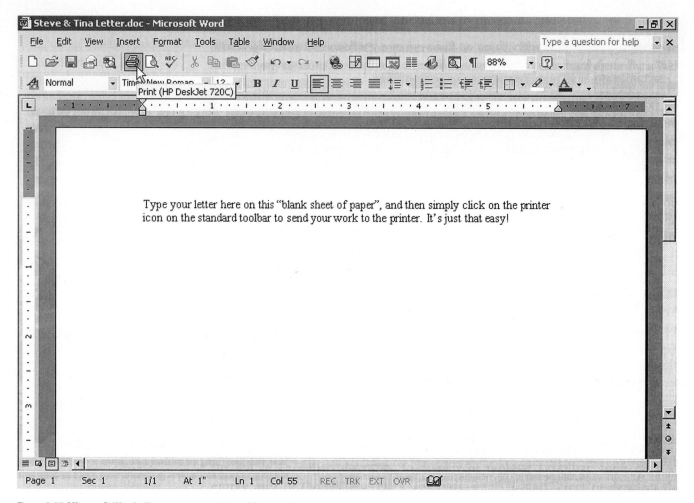

Figure 2.25 **Microsoft Word allows you to create and format documents.**

assist you in maintaining records, preparing written material, and producing projects that streamline your organization.

Word processing software—The most popular type of application software for home and educational use is a word processor, such as Microsoft Word (Figure 2.25). Previously considered merely a text manager, word processing software now allows you to create, edit, format, and print documents containing text, graphics, and even animation. You can store what you type on a disk and retrieve it later for additional printing or editing. Using a word processing software package, you can create letters, journals, reports, newsletters, mailing labels, and much more. You can also insert clip art and photographs into your documents.

Spreadsheet software—Spreadsheet software works with a sheet or workbook format consisting of an electronic grid of columns and rows, much like a teacher's grade book (Figure 2.26). You might use a spreadsheet for determining combinations of down payments and interest rates for the purchase of a home, for budget analysis, or for tracking progress in your walking program. A spreadsheet supports the display and manipulation of numbers in any meaningful way. Unlike a manually prepared spreadsheet, a computerized spreadsheet finds its

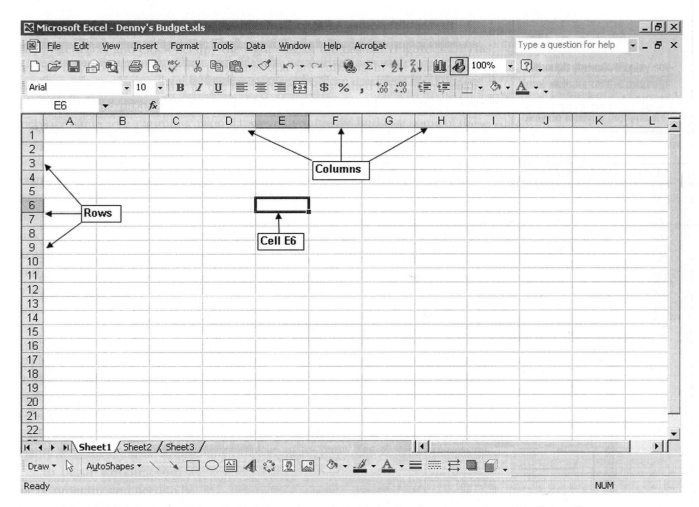

Figure 2.26 **A spreadsheet is an electronic grid of columns and rows. Each intersection of a column and a row is called a cell.**

strength in automatic recalculation. For example, you might design a spreadsheet to list all of your income and expenses for the month, with a net income figure calculated at the base. If the spreadsheet is set up correctly, a change in any expense figure will automatically adjust the amount of net income.

Database software—A database software package acts as an electronic filing cabinet. It allows you to list records in many different ways and to retrieve selected information on demand. With a database software package, you can store data, update it, retrieve it, and report it in printed form or on the monitor (Figure 2.27). Widely used in business for such diverse tasks as managing student records and promoting crime detection, it is also useful for the home computer owner. You can use database software for any task in which you want to store data, such as to keep a home inventory of appliances and electronic equipment, to keep records for your coin or stamp collection, or to keep attendance and membership records for a volunteer or church organization.

Graphics software—You can use graphics software to create or modify pictures and drawings. The simplest graphics programs are those referred to as image editors,

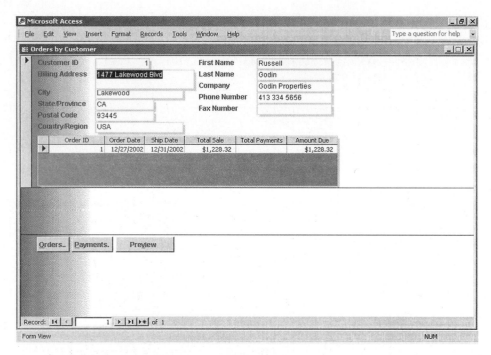

Figure 2.27 **A database application makes it easy to maintain records.**

which accept digitized photographs and provide editing and enhancement features (Figure 2.28). You can remove scratches from old pictures, enhance the color, and print the photographs in various sizes. Some graphics software also assists you in creating projects, such as greeting cards and calendars, featuring family pictures. Drafting and design programs are powerful graphics programs concerned with producing detailed construction plans.

Presentation software—Presentation software allows you to prepare computer slide shows, which are consecutively displayed screens of information. Businesses use presentation software to produce marketing slide shows (Figure 2.29). Many Web pages display slide shows prepared with presentation software. Churches rely on presentation slide shows for large-screen display of music and other activities. Any presentation made to a group where the display is to be projected on a large screen can be perfected with presentation software.

When you purchase a software package to accomplish a particular computer task, you are most likely purchasing what is called a **stand-alone program**, because it focuses on only one application. Packages such as those supporting personal finances, printing projects, and image editing are examples of stand-alone programs.

Another category of software, **integrated programs**, combines multiple functions, or activities, in one unit. The individual software components are not sold separately. Microsoft Works is an inte-

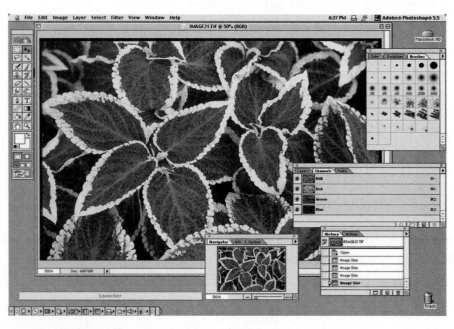

Figure 2.28 **An image editor is used to enhance photographs and graphics.**

Figure 2.29 **Presentation software is often used in classrooms.**

grated program that combines word processing, spreadsheet, and other common office tasks. It is often preloaded on personal computer systems because it is cheaper than an office suite but includes standard productivity applications helpful to a home computer user. In an integrated program, all components share a common interface, which simplifies the task of learning to work with the software because the menu structure and the way the components behave are very similar.

Office suites, sometimes called **software suites**, combine several individual software packages, sharing a common interface, into one unit. Although an office suite comprises multiple functions, the individual software components are also sold as separate software packages. Their combination into an office suite simply provides a complete package of productivity software at less cost than purchasing each component individually. Microsoft has dominated the office suite market with Microsoft Office, a package that includes a word processor (Word), a spreadsheet package (Excel), a database manager (Access), a presentation program (PowerPoint), and a personal information manager (Outlook). Each of those software applications is also sold individually, but, when packaged as a suite (Figure 2.30), the cost is much less than the collective individual prices.

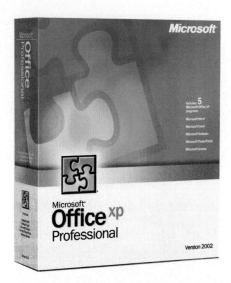

Figure 2.30 **Microsoft Office includes word processing, database, spreadsheet, presentation, and information management applications.**

It is important that the individual components of either an office suite or an integrated package work well together and be able to share data. For example, if you want to include a spreadsheet listing home inventory in a letter to an insurance company, the word processing package needs to be able to incorporate the spreadsheet. Most office suites include that functionality. Microsoft's component document technology is called **OLE** (**object linking and embedding**). If the Excel spreadsheet were embedded in the Word document, you could double-click the spreadsheet to launch Excel and modify the spreadsheet. Some applications include small programs, or **applets**, that are used to create objects. Microsoft Word includes a drawing tool applet (MS Draw) for formatting artwork.

With the huge variety of application software to choose from, you can have a lot of fun matching software to your interests. Knowing that the operating system will handle most machine-level activities without much involvement from you frees you to fully enjoy the applications for which you bought your computer. Now that you understand the connection between hardware and software, you are ready to delve into more specific coverage of operating system basics and to explore ways to use your computer to its full potential.

Chapter Summary

DON'T FORGET

- Application software includes programs that accomplish specific user tasks.

- Application software and system software work together to enable your computer to respond to your requests.

- The operating system directs internal system activities.

- Utility software is concerned with system tasks such as file compression and virus protection.

- Current operating systems include Windows, Mac OS, UNIX, and Linux.

- Most operating systems utilize a graphical user interface.

- There are various methods of distributing software, including shareware, freeware, public domain, open source, and commercial.

- Unauthorized copying of software is a primary legal concern for the software industry.

- Major categories of application software include word processing, database, spreadsheet, graphics, and presentation programs.

KEY TERMS

antivirus software	graphical user interface (GUI)	server license
applet	graphics software	server
application software	install	shareware
backup utility	integrated program	site license
backward compatible	Linux	software
commercial software	liteware	software license
computer virus	Mac OS	software piracy
copyleft	Mac OS X	software suite
copyright	Microsoft Windows	source code
CP/M	MS-DOS	spreadsheet software
crippleware	object linking and embedding	stand-alone program
database software	(OLE)	system software
disk scanner	office suite	system utilities
End User License Agreement	open source software	uninstall
(EULA)	operating system (OS)	UNIX
file compression	operating system platform	upgrade
file defragmentation	PC-DOS	utility software
fragmented	presentation software	Windows XP
freeware	public domain software	wizard
full version	QDOS	word processing software

TRUE/FALSE

Circle **T** if the statement is true or **F** if the statement is false.

T (F) 1. The operating system is an example of application software.

(T) F 2. Windows XP is available in two versions— Home and Professional.

(T) F 3. A computer virus is often transmitted through e-mail attachments.

T (F) 4. A disk scanner reduces file sizes so that they can be more easily exchanged.

T (F) 5. Shareware is copyrighted software that is developed for and sold to the public.

(T) F 6. System software is concerned with the internal operations of a computer.

(T) F 7. UNIX is an operating system that was developed by Bell Labs.

T (F) 8. The first operating system used by the IBM PC was Windows 1.0.   *was DOS*

T (F) 9. Linux is an operating system that is available only on large computer systems, not home computers.

(T) F 10. If a software program is copyrighted, it is illegal to reproduce it without authorization.

MULTIPLE CHOICE

Circle the correct choice for each of the following.

1. Copyrighted software that can be downloaded and used freely for a limited time is called
   a. freeware
   b. shareware
   c. open source
   d. commercial

2. Open source software is
   a. a variation of Windows
   b. what the OS stands for in Mac OS
   c. a type of freeware
   d. software that is distributed along with its source code

3. Which of the following is a command-driven operating system?
   a. MS DOS
   b. Windows
   c. Mac OS
   d. Linux

4. The legal protection given software, prohibiting unauthorized copying is based on
   a. patent
   b. trademark

   c. copyright
   d. logo

5. Software that allows a user to accomplish specific tasks is called
   a. application software
   b. operating system software
   c. utility software
   d. system software

6. Which of the following is *not* an example of a utility program?
   a. Microsoft Word
   b. backup
   c. file compression
   d. antivirus

7. When a version of software can access files and data created with an earlier version of the same software package, it is said to be
   a. reverse compatible
   b. multitasking
   c. Windows oriented
   d. backward compatible

8. An agreement with a software vendor that allows an organization to make multiple copies of a single software CD is a(n)
    a. server license
    b. multiple-user license
    c. site license
    d. EULA

9. After a software program is installed, it might be listed as
    a. a button on the menu bar
    b. a title on the status bar
    c. an icon on the title bar
    d. an icon on the desktop

10. A computer virus is
    a. a malicious program purposely written to annoy you or to damage computer files
    b. often transmitted by infected keyboards
    c. not always purposely written; some viruses occur naturally
    d. considered commercial software

PRACTICAL PROJECTS

1. Understanding Your Software

Your computer contains certain application software packages. Although some software might be listed as icons on the desktop (the screen that first appears when you turn on the computer), others will appear only on the program list. To become more familiar with your computer, you should be aware of what software you have.

For a complete program (application software) list, click Start, and point to All Programs. To the right, you will see a list of software. Some you will recognize, others you might not. Jot down the software by title. In the area below, list any software that you can identify as belonging to a general group (word processing, spreadsheet, and so on). For example, Microsoft Word is a word processor. Perhaps you see instead Microsoft Works, which is an integrated package, containing a word processing unit. If you can't identify the category for a software package you see, list it in the Other category.

Word Processor: _____
Spreadsheet: _____
Database: _____
Presentation: _____
Personal Information Manager: _____
Internet Service Connection (America Online, CompuServe, and so on): _____
Internet Browser (Internet Explorer, Netscape Navigator): _____
Other: _____
_____
_____

2. Curing a Virus

Unlike a human virus, there is usually a "cure" for a computer virus. Antivirus software developers, such as Norton (Symantec) and McAfee, are quick to produce virus definitions, or "cures" whenever new viruses are introduced. Look through computer magazines and scan the software aisle of your local office-supply center. How many antivirus software products do you find? Which would you buy?

To help make a purchase decision, look for software reviews in computer magazines, or online if you have an Internet connection. What features do you find most appealing? You might consider an integrated software package, perhaps containing an antivirus program along with other system utilities. After you settle on your choice, do a cost comparison to locate the best place (or Web site) to buy the product.

3. Taking a Look at MS-DOS

To fully appreciate the ease of navigation provided by a graphical interface such as Windows, you will take a quick look at MS-DOS. Most versions of Windows allow you to access the DOS interface. Remember that when the IBM PC appeared in 1981, it utilized MS-DOS as its operating system. MS-DOS is command driven, which means that you had to know commands to do everything from erasing a disk to displaying the contents of the hard drive. That's a whole lot more difficult than pointing and clicking!

Your computer should be on and at the desktop.

1. Click Start.
2. Click Run. Note the white bar beside the word "Open." If there is already an entry there, it will be shaded, or selected. Whatever you type will replace the entry. If there is no entry, you will see a blinking bar, which is called the cursor. *Don't click in the white area. If you make a mistake and click there, you can delete any existing entry by pressing the* Del *key (to erase characters to the right of the cursor) or the* Backspace *key (to erase characters to the left of the cursor).*
3. Type **command**.
4. Click OK.
5. The MS-DOS window appears. You will see a disk prompt (C:\>). That is called the "DOS prompt." The window is what the screen on an early PC looked like. If you didn't know what to type, you couldn't use the computer or any of its application software.
6. Type **dir** and press Enter. A rather cryptic display appears listing "directories," which are called "folders" in Windows installations. The display probably scrolls quickly, filling more than one screen.
7. To slow the display, type **dir/p** and press Enter. At each screen, the display pauses. Press any key to continue the listing. Continue paging through screens.
8. Type **cls**. Press Enter to empty the screen. The directory listing should clear.
9. Type **cld**. Press Enter. You should see an error message, because *cld* is not recognized as a command.
10. Click the X in the top right corner to close the DOS display. If presented with a Windows message, click End Now, or OK.

    Now, which would you rather work with, Windows or DOS?

✳ 4. It's All in the License

Assume that you just bought a software program to organize home finances. As you open the instruction manual that came in the software box, you find a license agreement just inside the front cover. A portion of it follows:

PLEASE READ CAREFULLY!

Home Finance, including without limitation the software's source code, object code, instructions, graphics, fonts, and other components, (collectively the "Software") is provided to you under license. No sale has occurred.

This license agreement defines the ways in which you can use the Software. Please read this Agreement as carefully as you would read any other legal document. If you find that its terms do not meet your needs or that you cannot agree to all of the conditions of this license, you may return the complete Software product with proof of purchase to ABC Development Corporation within 7 days for a full refund.

However, installing or using the Software will indicate your acknowledgement that you have read this Agreement and your acceptance of its terms.

1. **Copyright.** *The Software is copyrighted 2003 by ABC Development Corp. and its licensors. All rights reserved.*
2. **License.** *ABC Development Corp. grants you a nonexclusive license to use the Software and its contents in accordance with the terms of this license.*
3. **Use of Software.** *You may personally use the Software on only one computer at a time. ABC Development sells site licenses separately, should you desire to use the Software on multiple computer systems.*
4. **Copying the Software.** *You may not copy or reproduce any part of the Software, manual, or related materials, except as permitted by the Copyright Act of the United States, Title 17, United States Code. You may not copy, lend, lease, rent, decompile, reverse-engineer, disassemble, or alter the Software in any way or remove or alter copyright or other notices.*

The license is a legal document that specifies terms of usage for the software product. Based on the license, answer the following questions.

✳1. What kind of software is described in the license (shareware, freeware, commercial, open source, or public domain)?
2. Can you make a copy of the software product? What if your sister asks to use it temporarily? Is it OK for her to install it on her computer? Expand your answer to include reasons why she may or may not legally copy the software.
3. If you want to use the software on multiple computer systems, what does the license agreement suggest?
4. A license agreement is a contract between you and the software developer. However, unlike other con-

tracts, no signatures are involved. How do you acknowledge acceptance of the license terms?

5. What should you do if you don't agree with the license restrictions?

Some software is available as an Internet download. Called shareware, it is often free to try for a time before you are expected to pay for it. As you install the software, you will be presented with a license agreement. Indicating your acceptance allows the download to continue. A portion of a shareware license agreement follows:

This software is Shareware, which means that you can use it legally for 30 days free of charge to evaluate it. If during or at the end of that period you decide that you would like to continue using it, please register your copy.

Your single user registration will license you to use all current and future versions of the software; will support work on future versions, new features, and bug fixes; and will provide you with priority technical support via e-mail.

The software may be freely distributed, subject to, but not limited to, the following terms:

The software may not be sold or resold, distributed as a part of any commercial package, used or distributed in support of a commercial service, or used or distributed to support any kind of profit-generating activity, even if it is being distributed freely.

1. Are you allowed to make copies of this software product?

2. If the evaluation copy is free, why would you want to register it after 30 days?

3. Can you repackage the software and sell it?

5. Windows 2000 or Windows XP?

In your quest for a home computer, you might decide to "spec out" a system, which means that you plan to indicate your preferences and have a computer system designed specifically for you. Local computer shops will often build a computer according to your specifications, as will large manufacturers like Dell. Let's say you are at the point of selecting an operating system, and have narrowed your choice to either Windows 2000 or Windows XP.

Provide a comparison of the two systems, ultimately deciding which you would choose. Consider your home computer activities and the expectations you would have of an operating system. Find operating system reviews in computer magazines and other sources. Summarize your findings and conclusions in a tabular format.

CHAPTER 3

Working with Windows

Windows is the operating system of choice for most computer users. Every computer, no matter how large or how small, must have an operating system to coordinate system activities, including communication between the user and the application software. The nice thing about working with Windows is that, as a user, you don't have to read lengthy operating system manuals or spend days becoming familiar with the software. All you need to do is master a few basic skills that allow you to manage your computer better and get the most enjoyment from the time you spend running software.

You can think of the operating system as a doorway. The doorway provides access to a room where you can relax and catch up on the local news. Your focus is not on the doorway, but on the furniture and the television. However, without the door, you would not be able to enter the room. Likewise, your computer's operating system provides a stable, consistent environment in which you can enjoy your

Objectives

When you complete this chapter, you will:

- **Be familiar with basic elements of the Windows operating system, including icons, the Start menu, the taskbar, dialog boxes, and menus.**
- **Understand the desktop concept.**
- **Be able to manipulate windows, performing such operations as opening, minimizing, maximizing, restoring, moving, and resizing them.**
- **Understand how to create and modify user accounts.**
- **Be able to adjust display settings, including background, color scheme, and screen saver.**
- **Be able to adjust mouse settings.**
- **Be able to adjust the date and time settings.**
- **Be able to adjust speaker volume.**
- **Know how to get help.**
- **Know what to do if your computer fails to respond.**

favorite application software. It provides a link between your computer work and the supporting hardware, easing the task of saving files and coordinating input and output. Even when working with your word processing software or the program that you just bought to manage your business finances, you will be in communication with the operating system, whether you realize it or not. In effect, it is a transparent layer, but one that is critical for every activity of your computer.

The operating system is a complex set of software that would take a long time to fully master. However, the typical computer user only needs to be familiar with a few basic Windows skills to get plenty of enjoyment from a computer system. Although most microcomputers come installed with a version of the Microsoft Windows operating system, other operating systems include Mac OS (for use with Apple computers), UNIX, and Linux. Because Windows is the most common operating system, this chapter focuses on learning to function in the Windows environment. Most new PC-compatible computers are installed with Windows XP, which provides a new look and feel to the Windows environment. Even so, basic Windows operations are similar regardless of which version of Windows you work with.

Understanding the Windows Concept

A graphical user interface (GUI) is a visual environment where you make selections and give commands by clicking a mouse. It uses visual cues and pictures to interact with a computer user. You can make selections and move among applications by pointing and clicking with a mouse. A GUI is known as a **windowing environment**, where each window or screen box, gives you a view of a portion of your computer or application software. Within each window are **icons** (small pictures) representing programs, files, documents, or folders. Earlier command-driven operating systems, like MS-DOS and some versions of UNIX, accepted commands from a computer user in the form of typed statements. Those operating systems are now almost completely replaced by GUI interfaces, such as those used in the Linux, Mac OS, and Windows environments.

You will learn that most programs designed to run with Windows include common screen elements and behave similarly. They employ common methods of navigation and communication, with many menu selections appearing identically. Although program functions might differ, the way you access those functions is consistent. The most important thing is that you become comfortable with the Windows environment so that learning and using any Windows application comes easily. After you have mastered Windows, you should be able to move around in most applications with ease.

Knowing Your Way around the Desktop

The **desktop** is the background of the Windows display that appears after you turn on the computer and log on to your user account. The desktop is your "virtual" work environment, closely paralleling a typical office. Your desk is the place where you put paperwork and complete tasks. You often have several pieces of paper or projects on your desk at the same time. If you are not extremely organized, some of the paperwork can overlap or obscure other papers. Similarly, the Windows desktop arranges and displays your projects and other system activities. You can have several windows open on your Windows desktop at one time, and they can overlap or obscure one another. Thankfully, the Windows desktop makes it easy to access all open windows, even if some are hidden from view by others.

Your desk probably contains some personal effects, such as family pictures and items of interest that reflect your personality. Likewise, you can personalize the Windows desktop to better suit your needs and tastes by selecting the color scheme of various Windows components and including a background picture or graphic. You can also rearrange screen elements and create individual folders for programs and documents, creating a workspace uniquely designed for your interests and activities.

A typical Windows desktop is shown in Figure 3.1. Depending upon your version of Windows, as well as the programs and equipment included on your system, your desktop may appear different. However, you should at least see several icons and a colored or graphic background. Icons appear as graphic elements on the desktop, providing access to programs, folders, and files. You will learn to depend on the taskbar, another desktop element, for information on open windows and for quick access to programs, through the Quick Launch toolbar and the Start menu.

> **■▶Quick Tip**
>
> Even if you are working in another program, you can always get to the desktop by pressing and holding the ⊞ key and typing the letter Ⓜ. The desktop appears. To return to an open application or window, click the window's button on the taskbar. Another way to access the desktop is by clicking the Show Desktop icon, found on the Quick Launch toolbar.

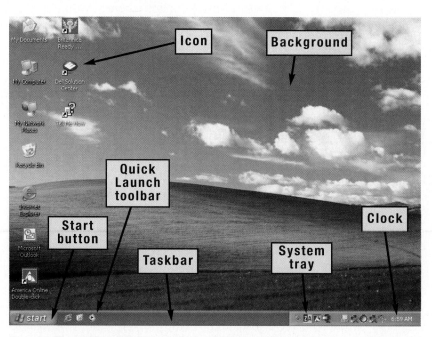

Figure 3.1 **The desktop contains icons and a taskbar, providing quick access to programs and system resources.**

In the Know

Windows XP includes a new tool to assist with keeping your desktop clean. The Desktop Cleanup Wizard checks for desktop shortcuts that haven't been accessed in a while and places them in one desktop folder so that your desktop is a little less cluttered. To use Desktop Cleanup, right-click an empty area of the desktop and select Properties from the context menu. Then select Desktop, and Customize Desktop. In the Desktop Cleanup area, be sure Run Desktop Cleanup Wizard every 60 days *is checked. In 60 days, Windows will check for any inactive shortcuts and will allow you to select the shortcuts that should be deleted. To activate the wizard, click Clean Desktop Now. Respond to all wizard prompts by clicking Next or Finish. All inactive shortcuts will be listed, but you can deselect (click the check mark) any shortcuts that you want to keep. The shortcuts that you leave checked won't actually be deleted, but will be placed in a folder on your desktop called Unused Desktop Shortcuts, which is created automatically. Click OK. Close all open windows.*

Icons

Icons are the small pictures that appear on the desktop. They are basic Windows elements that provide quick access to programs, documents, files, and folders. In a perfect world, an icon picture would give a clear indication of what it represents or leads to, but that is not often the case. Fortunately, more descriptive text is usually displayed directly under the icon, further identifying the icon's purpose.

✓ SANITY CHECK

Most desktops are configured to show standard elements, such as My Documents, My Computer, My Network Places, and Internet Explorer. If you notice that yours does not contain one or more of those elements, you can customize the desktop to include them. Right-click an empty area of the desktop. Click Properties. Click the Desktop tab. Click Customize Desktop. Click to place a check mark beside My Computer, My Documents, or any other element that is missing from your desktop.

To access the application or document represented by an icon on your desktop, double-click the icon. A double-click is accomplished by rapidly clicking the left mouse button twice. Single clicking an icon only *selects* the item so that it is available for moving, renaming, or deleting.

Taskbar

The **taskbar** is the horizontal bar usually found along the bottom of the desktop. It displays the folders, applications, and documents that are actually open

> **▶ Quick Tip**
>
> There is an art to double-clicking! Double-clicking is not the same as clicking the left mouse button twice at a normal rate of speed. To double-click, click the left mouse button twice rapidly. The trick is not only timing the speed of the clicks, but holding the mouse still. Any movement of the mouse during a double-click causes the action to be misinterpreted.

as *buttons*, or boxes, on the taskbar, so that you can always tell what is open in memory, even if it is not plainly visible. You can easily switch between open applications by simply clicking the program button on the taskbar, as shown in Figure 3.1. Also on the taskbar are the Start button (to the left), the clock (to the right), and other items that provide fast access to applications and system utilities.

Windows XP has a significantly updated taskbar that is easier to use than earlier versions. Instead of listing each open window as a separate button, as did previous Windows versions, Windows XP groups program buttons to show all

Hands On

Activity 3.1—Moving and Resizing the Taskbar

In this exercise, you will move and resize the taskbar. The computer should be on and at the beginning screen, with desktop icons displayed.

1. Move the mouse pointer to an empty part of the taskbar (one without any icons or features).
2. Click and hold the left mouse button while moving the mouse toward the top of the desktop. Such activity is called "clicking and dragging." The taskbar will not immediately "follow" the mouse pointer, but you should keep moving toward the top. As the mouse pointer approaches the top, the taskbar will pop into that area. Release the mouse button.

✓ SANITY CHECK

If the taskbar doesn't pop into the new location, it might be locked. Right-click an empty area of the taskbar and click Lock the Taskbar (if you see a check mark beside the selection). If the taskbar is not locked but still won't move when you drag it, you are probably clicking an occupied area of the taskbar. Reposition the mouse pointer to an empty area, and try the move operation again.

3. Move the mouse pointer to a blank area of the taskbar. Click and drag the taskbar to the right side of the screen. When the taskbar appears on the right, release the mouse button.
4. Click and drag the taskbar to the bottom of the desktop. Release the mouse button when the taskbar returns to the bottom.
5. Move the mouse pointer to the top border of the taskbar. Move the mouse pointer slowly, watching until it becomes a double-headed arrow. At that point, click and drag the taskbar border up, making the taskbar larger than before. Release the mouse button.
6. Once again, move the mouse pointer over the top border of the taskbar until it becomes a double-headed arrow. Click and drag the taskbar down to its original size. *Be careful not to make the taskbar too small, or it will disappear altogether!* If that should happen, you can resize it by dragging it from the bottom of the screen. Release the mouse button.

open documents when you click the button. For example, if you have six Word documents open, only one Word button is listed on the taskbar, followed by the number 6 in parentheses. When you click the Word button, you can choose from the list of six documents.

The Start Menu

The Start button is the beginning point for many Windows operations, such as running programs and accessing Windows components. Some Start menu items might have a right-facing arrow, which means that secondary menu choices are available. The Windows XP **Start menu**, as shown in Figure 3.2, has been redesigned to give quick access to all areas of the computer.

Taking a quick look at the Windows XP Start menu, you will see a definite left side and right side of the menu. Programs that you use often are automatically placed on the left side of the Start menu for easy access. The right side lists several Windows-specific items, including:

Figure 3.2 **Windows XP has completely redesigned the Start menu.**

- **My Documents**—displays a holding area for your documents and other files that you create.

- **My Recent Documents**—displays a holding area for recently accessed documents and files.

- **My Pictures and My Music**—provide quick access to your picture and music files.

- **My Computer**—shows all disk drives on your computer, including the hard drive, floppy drive, Zip drive, CD drive, and DVD drive. (You will explore features of My Computer in Chapter 4.)

- **My Network Places**—displays all the shared computers, printers, and other resources on a network to which your computer might be connected.

- **Control Panel**—allows you to customize the display settings (including background and color scheme), add new hardware devices, change mouse and keyboard settings, and make other system adjustments.

- **Connect to**—allows you to connect to the Internet through whatever connection your computer is configured for.

- **Printers and Faxes**—displays a dialog box allowing you to check the status of your printer and fax, along with any items being printed or faxed.

- **Help and Support**—provides a wealth of information, much of it updated online.

- **Search**—assists in locating files and folders on your system, along with Internet searches.

- **Run**—provides command-line access to programs and system information.

- **Log Off or Turn Off Computer**—allow you to disconnect from a network or user account or to power off a computer.

The usual way to access the Start menu is to click the Start button on the taskbar. You can also display the Start menu by pressing the ⊞ key (to the left of the space bar) or by pressing and holding the (Ctrl) key while pressing the (Esc) key.

✓ SANITY CHECK

A menu is displayed, perhaps the Start menu or some other program menu, but you don't want to make a menu selection. You just want the menu to disappear. What do you do? You have a couple of options. You can click a blank area of the desktop or application window. The menu should drop out of view. Alternatively, you can press the (Esc) key on the keyboard to make the menu disappear.

Toolbars on the Taskbar

Toolbars on the taskbar provide a quick way to access system resources and to open selected programs. The Quick Launch toolbar is usually displayed by default (when you first install Windows), but other toolbars are also available. They include the Address toolbar and the Links toolbar. A double arrow to the right of a toolbar indicates that there are icons that are not displayed. Click the double arrow to see those items. Clicking and dragging the vertical bar to the left of a toolbar resizes it. To display or remove a toolbar, right-click an empty area of the taskbar, click Toolbars, and click to select or deselect the toolbar.

Next to the Start button on the taskbar, you will find the Quick Launch toolbar. Icons on the Quick Launch toolbar (Figure 3.1) allow you to quickly access programs or the desktop with a single click. Although commonly accessed programs are listed on the Quick Launch toolbar, you might want to add others. Perhaps you often use Microsoft Word and would like the ease of single clicking its icon on the Quick Launch toolbar, but the program is not displayed there. If Microsoft Word is an icon on the desktop, you can click and drag the icon to the Quick Launch toolbar. The icon is copied to the toolbar so that you can access it with a single click from Quick Launch. To delete an item from Quick Launch, right-click the icon and select Delete from the context menu. Don't be alarmed when the Delete dialog box appears. Deleting the icon from Quick Launch simply removes the icon; it does not remove the program from your system. You can still get to the program through the Start menu or by double-clicking the program's icon on the desktop.

The Address toolbar lets you specify a Web page to visit. Type a Web address in the white text box, and click Go. The Links toolbar lets you add Web links by dragging them to the toolbar. The Desktop toolbar is used to place desktop items on the taskbar, although they will be so numerous that the toolbar will display them only if you click the arrow to the right of the toolbar title.

The System Tray and Clock

The system tray and clock occupy the right side of the taskbar (Figure 3.1). The system tray contains icons for programs that are running in the background. When a program is running in the background, it is called *resident in memory*. These programs probably started with the computer's startup and remain in memory while your computer is on. However, you might find that some of these programs do not necessarily need to be used on a regular basis; they are only needed periodically to perform important tasks. An antivirus program is an example of a program running in the background. You can access any of those memory-resident programs by clicking the program icon once. In a typical Windows installation, the clock is always visible in the lower right corner of the taskbar. When you move the mouse pointer over the clock and *hover,* or keep it steady for a few seconds, a tool tip pops up giving the current date and day. Later in this chapter, you will explore the clock more completely.

▶ Quick Tip

Although you can display several toolbars on the taskbar, you shouldn't overdo it. Displaying toolbars that you seldom use just takes up taskbar space, reducing the size of all others. If you must display multiple toolbars, you might consider moving a toolbar to a second line of the taskbar; you can do that by clicking the vertical bar just to the left of the toolbar heading and dragging it down to form a second row.

Working with Programs and Windows

Looking at the desktop, you will find several titled icons, including *Internet Explorer* and *Recycle Bin*. Each icon represents a window containing options for working with the various components and programs on your computer. Your desktop at home probably contains different icons from those on the computer desktop that you might use at a college computer lab or public library. That is because the combination of programs loaded on your system is not likely to be identical to the combination on any other computer system.

To begin working with a file or program, you need to be able to open, or access, the window in which it is stored. To open any program or file represented by an icon, double-click the icon. The window that appears contains several standard features, as shown in Figure 3.3. You will find a title bar at the top of the window, a menu bar, and one or more toolbars. An address bar identifies the current display location. To the far right of the title bar, you will find three small boxes, called window control buttons, each containing a graphic character. Those buttons allow you to manage the window by controlling its size or by closing it.

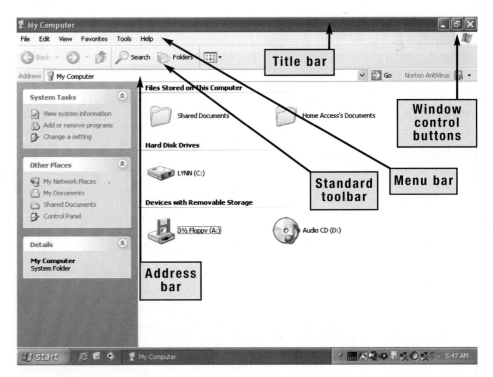

Figure 3.3 **All windows contain common elements.**

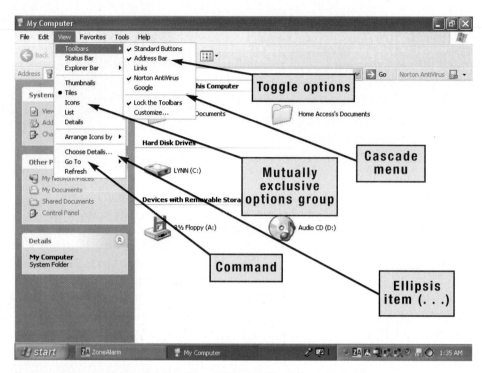

Figure 3.4 **A menu includes a list of options pertinent to the window or program.**

Menus

Most windows contain a menu like the one shown in Figure 3.4, which is a list of commands and options. Clicking a particular menu heading will give you access to a *drop-down menu* that contains specific selections. As you work in Windows and with Windows-based application software, you will learn to recognize various types of menu items. Note that when making a selection from a menu, you will always left-click once. There is no need to double-click a menu option.

◀▶ Other Ways

You can also open a program from the Start menu. Click Start, All Programs, and select the program to run by clicking its title.

◀▶ Other Ways

In a typical menu bar, all menu options contain one underlined letter. You can use the keyboard to access menu items by pressing and holding the (Alt) key on the keyboard and pressing the underlined letter. For example, most menu bars contain a Eile menu option. To access the menu item, press and hold down the (Alt) key and press the (F) key. The menu appears, just as if you physically clicked the File menu bar option.

- *Toggle options* are selections that are either "on" or "off." A check mark beside an option indicates that the option is enabled, or turned on. To disable the option, click the checked item. The check mark is removed.

- A *mutually exclusive options group* is a list of options that are alternatives to one another. Only one item in the group can be selected. To choose any item that is not currently selected, click the title and the first option becomes deselected. A bullet to the left of the menu item identifies the selected option.

- Some items have a small black arrow immediately to the right. Clicking one of those options causes a *cascade menu*—which is essentially a sub-menu of the first selection—to appear, containing even more selections.

- Some options are simple *commands,* not marked with any special symbols. Clicking a simple command causes the action to occur immediately.

- Finally, some options might be marked with an *ellipsis* (…). Clicking these causes a **dialog box** to appear. A dialog box is a special window that asks for some input from you.

In many menus, some of the menu options are gray, whereas others are black. You should be aware of what the different color shades mean. Gray, or dim, options are not currently available. That doesn't mean that they will never be available, but at this point you haven't done whatever is required to make those menu items available. Black selections, on the other hand, are immediately available.

Windows applications make broad use of another type of menu, known as a **context menu**, or **shortcut menu**, like the one shown in Figure 3.5. Context menus are completely dependent upon the object or area of the screen that a user right-clicks. Perhaps you want to change the background of your desktop. Move the mouse pointer to an empty area of the desktop and right-click. A context menu appears with several options, including Properties, which allows you to select a different background. If, however, instead of right-clicking an empty desktop area, you right-click a desktop icon, you will see a different context menu with selections related to that icon. In short, a context menu displays options that take into account the particular place you clicked on-screen, whereas a menu bar organizes options related to the entire application.

Figure 3.5 **A context menu displays options related to the object or screen area that you right-click.**

✓SANITY CHECK

You can rearrange icons on your desktop by clicking and dragging them to other locations. However, sometimes clicking and dragging an icon has no effect on it—it just remains in its original location. Why doesn't the click and drag work? Most likely, your desktop is set to "auto arrange" icons, which means that you cannot move them without first changing that setting. Many people like the auto arrange effect because it ensures an orderly desktop arrangement.

Right-click an empty area of the desktop, displaying a context menu. Click Arrange Icons By, and look at the Auto Arrange setting. Do you see a check mark beside the option? If so, your icons are locked in place and cannot be moved. To unlock the icons, click the Auto Arrange option. Now you can click and drag to move your icons.

Dialog Boxes

Sometimes, the application you are using requires some direction or precise instructions from you. For example, you might be preparing to print a document, but before the document prints, a box appears, allowing you to specify

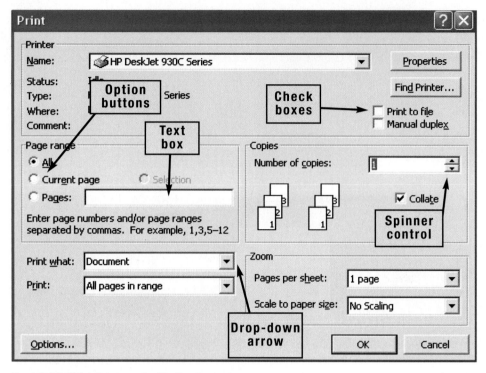

Figure 3.6 **A dialog box accepts direction from you.**

the number of copies and the specific pages to print. The boxes in which you can provide specific information or make specific selections are called dialog boxes. Dialog boxes appear almost any time you need to interact with the application directly. If you want your word processor to open a document, for example, you will need to indicate which document you wish to open and where it can be found. The word processor provides a dialog box to ask you for the information.

Windows dialog boxes often include several "pages," each identified by a file folder tab. Clicking a tab displays that page. Each page includes areas asking for your input or direction. Although a dialog box is a window of sorts, you will note that the familiar control buttons (maximize and minimize) are missing. Instead, you will see a close button and a question mark (?), which is a quick way to access help. At the bottom of the dialog box, you will find two, or possibly three, command buttons—typically *OK*, *Cancel*, and *Apply*. Clicking *OK* accepts any selections you have made and closes the dialog box. Clicking *Cancel* closes the dialog box without accepting any selections, and the *Apply* button executes any selections but doesn't close the dialog box.

Dialog boxes ask for input from you. To respond to that request, you must interact with such elements as text boxes, spinners, drop-down arrows, or option buttons, as shown in Figure 3.6.

- A *text box* is an item that is displayed as a white rectangular area in which you can type your selection. The text box in the print dialog box shown in Figure 3.6 allows you to type the range of page numbers to be printed.

- You will often find *drop-down arrows* in dialog boxes, which, when clicked, display a series of options from which you can choose.

- *Option buttons*, sometimes called radio buttons, are selections that are mutually exclusive. In the print dialog box (Figure 3.6), you can choose to print *all* pages, the *current* page, or a *series* of pages. Each of those selections is made by clicking an option button.

- *Spinners* are items that let you click an upward-pointing arrow to increase the item displayed beside the spinner or a downward-pointing arrow to decrease it. Alternatively, you can click in the text box beside the spinner and simply type the intended value.

Other Windows Elements

Most programs running in Windows display common screen elements, including a menu bar, one or more toolbars, a status bar, and a scroll bar. Figure 3.7 shows those common elements.

As you work with programs running under the Windows operating system, you will find that many menu items recur in various programs. For example, most programs include File, Edit, View, and Format menus. That makes your life a little easier, because having worked with the menu in one program, you will be familiar with the same selections in another program.

Programs also include one or more toolbars, which allow you to make changes and selections with a single click. Usually, the standard toolbar and the format toolbar appear automatically, but you can display other toolbars by clicking View, Toolbars and making a selection. Following the same set of steps, you can deselect any toolbar that you don't want to display.

A bar across the bottom of the program window, called the *status bar*, gives information related to the current settings of the program and, possibly, your position within a document. If the program window contains more space than can be displayed on the screen at one time, a *scroll bar* appears to the right or bottom (or both) of the window. You can click and drag the *scroll box* in the center of the scroll bar to display off-screen items.

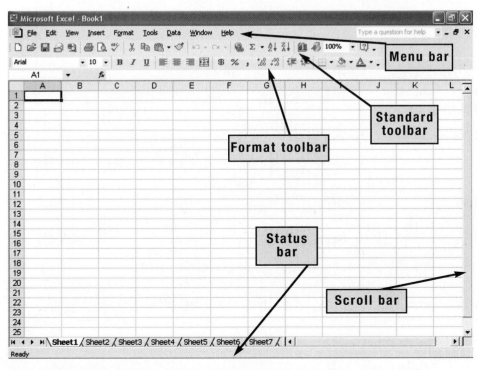

Figure 3.7 **Most program windows include a menu bar, one or more toolbars, and a status bar.**

Understanding User Accounts

When you install Windows XP, it automatically creates a **user account** for you with a user name and a password of your choice. A user account is a set of permissions associated with a user name. The account that Windows XP creates at installation is set at the administrator level, which means that this user has complete control of the system. You can install and remove software, delete files, and examine all system resources.

In addition to the administrator account, your system most likely includes a guest account, which provides access to the computer for anyone who does not already have an account. For more specific assignment of permissions and passwords for anyone else using your computer, you would need to create a separate account called a limited user account. Each account maintains its own desktop and system settings, so that a user can completely personalize the account environment. Users of one account cannot modify or read files housed in another account.

Creating a User Account

To create a user account, you must be logged in as an administrator. Remember that Windows XP created the administrator account during the initial installation, so to log in as an administrator, you simply turn on the computer and respond to the first screen asking for your password, if the account is password protected.

To create a user account:

1. Click Start.
2. Click Control Panel.
3. Click User Accounts (Figure 3.8).

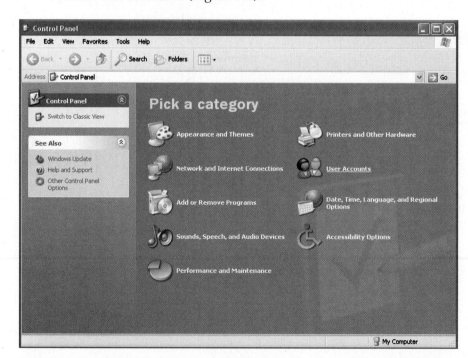

Figure 3.8 **You can protect the privacy and security of your computer system by creating user accounts.**

4. Click Create a new account.

5. Type a name for the new account, and click Next, as shown in Figure 3.9.

6. Click the access level, either Administrator or Limited. Click Create account (Figure 3.10).

7. The User Accounts screen immediately displays the new account.

8. Click the close button (X) in the upper right corner of the window.

9. Close any open windows by clicking the X in the upper right corner of a window.

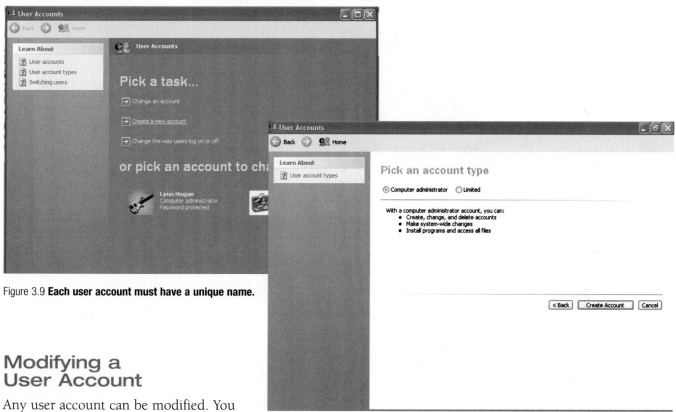

Figure 3.9 **Each user account must have a unique name.**

Figure 3.10 **Setting the access level of user accounts allows you to control the level of permission granted the user.**

Modifying a User Account

Any user account can be modified. You can create or change a password, choose a picture to associate with the user account, change the account name, change the permission level (administrator or limited), or delete the account. You can only make those changes, however, if you are logged on to an administrator account.

To modify a user account:

1. Click Start.

2. Click Control Panel.

3. Click User Accounts. A screen similar to that shown in Figure 3.11 will appear.

4. Click the user account that you want to change.

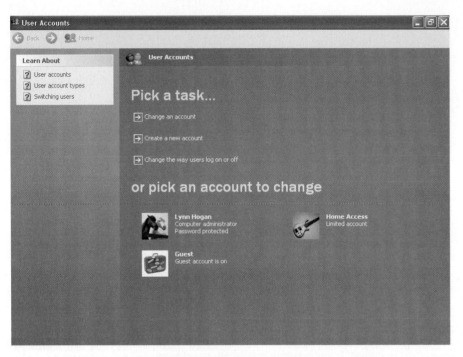

Figure 3.11 **You can change the settings of existing user accounts.**

5. Click the setting to be changed.
6. Follow all screen prompts to complete the changes.
7. Close any open windows by clicking the X in the upper right corner of a window.

Switching between Accounts

Windows XP allows you to switch between user accounts. You can click Start, Log Off, Switch User to change to another account. To log off the computer completely, click Start, Log Off, Log Off. You might log off an account when you leave your computer for an extended time so that your account remains private and secure.

Fast User Switching is a setting that allows you to quickly switch to another account without quitting any programs that are running. Suppose you are working on a mailing list when your son asks to check his e-mail. Without terminating your task, you can switch to his account, let him check his e-mail, and return to your work. Fast User Switching can be set only by an administrator account. With Fast User Switching on, you can quickly change to another account by pressing and holding down the ⊞ key while typing the letter ⓛ.

To set Fast User Switching:

1. Click User Accounts in the Control Panel.
2. Click Change the way users log on or off.
3. Click *Use Fast User Switching* if you want programs to remain open in one account when you switch to another. If you want programs to quit when a user logs off an account, clear the *Use Fast User Switching* box.

▶Quick Tip

You can copy files and settings from one account to another by using the Files and Settings Transfer Wizard. You can find the wizard by clicking Start, All Programs, Accessories, System Tools, and Files and Settings Transfer Wizard. Responding to the wizard prompts, you can copy the setup of an old account into a new one. This wizard is also useful for backing up your settings or moving them to a new computer.

Managing Windows

Using window controls you can manage desktop windows by maximizing, minimizing, restoring, or closing them. A **maximized** window takes up the entire screen. You might maximize a window to better view all the icons in the window or to provide more typing space. A **minimized** window is hidden from view but is not closed. A window can be **restored** back to its original size after it has been maximized. When you **close** a window, it is removed from memory.

Minimizing a Window

If you do not need to use a window for a while, you can **minimize** it to remove it from view. Your desktop can easily become cluttered with open windows. Although this doesn't confuse the operating system, coordinating multiple windows can be difficult for the user. It is important to remember that a minimized window is not *closed*, as it is still resident in memory. It is simply removed from view, much as you might put a calculator in a desk drawer when you are not using it. Then, later, you can readily retrieve the calculator when it is needed. Similarly, you can quickly redisplay a minimized window at any time by clicking its button on the taskbar. The window will reappear, and you will be able to resume work right where you left off.

To minimize a window, click the leftmost *button* at the top right corner of the window, as shown in Figure 3.12. The button is called the minimize button. The character on the button looks like a dash. After you click the minimize

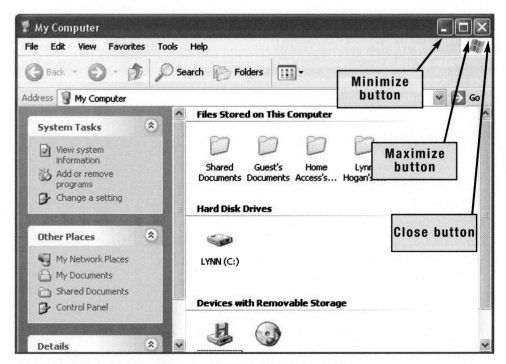

Figure 3.12 **Buttons at the top right corner of the title bar allow you to minimize, maximize, restore, or close a window.**

button, the window disappears from view. By looking at the taskbar, you can see that the window is still open. You will see a boxed area on the taskbar with the title of the minimized window. To redisplay the window, click its box, or button, on the taskbar.

✓ SANITY CHECK

What if you don't see a taskbar at all? That sometimes happens when the taskbar has been resized too small or when it has been purposely hidden from view.

First, check for size. Slowly roll the mouse pointer down to the bottom of the desktop. If a double-headed arrow appears, click and drag the taskbar back up into view. If you don't see a double-headed arrow, roll the mouse pointer to each side and to the top of the desktop, looking for the double-headed arrow. If it appears, click and drag out into the desktop to bring the taskbar back into view.

Some people prefer that the taskbar disappear from view when not needed, so they "hide" it. If the taskbar is hidden, it will appear when you roll the mouse pointer to the area where the taskbar would normally appear. Hold the mouse steady for a few seconds to see if the taskbar comes into view. When the taskbar appears, you can "unhide" it by right-clicking it in a blank area. Click Properties. The Taskbar Properties dialog box appears, as shown in Figure 3.13. (If you see a window other than Taskbar Properties, you probably right-clicked an occupied area of the taskbar, instead of a blank area. In that case, close the window and try the operation again.) If a check mark appears beside *Auto-Hide the Taskbar,* click the check mark to deselect it. Click OK. The taskbar should reappear and remain on-screen.

Figure 3.13 **The taskbar can be hidden from view by using the Taskbar Properties dialog box.**

Maximizing a Window

When you open most program windows, the window covers only about 75 percent of the screen. You can enlarge a window to fill your screen, which lets you view more of its contents. Unless you need to see more of the window than what is visible by default, you don't necessarily need to make it larger. It boils down to a matter of preference and workability. Some windows contain so many icons that you can manage them better if you maximize the window.

To **maximize** a window, click the middle button at the top right corner of the window, shown in Figure 3.12. The character in the button looks like a box. If, instead, you see what appear to be two boxes in the middle button, the window is already maximized, so you don't need to click the button. The maximized window should fill your screen.

Restoring a Window

If your window already fills the screen, the middle button on the right is called the **restore** button, shown in Figure 3.14. It looks like two overlapping boxes. Clicking it will cause the window to return to its previous size so that it takes up less than the full screen.

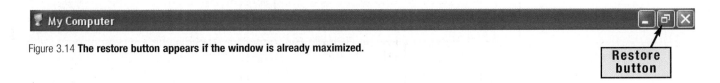

Figure 3.14 **The restore button appears if the window is already maximized.**

Restore button

✓ SANITY CHECK

Occasionally, a window will open in an awkward position, such that the three window control buttons to the far right of the title bar are not visible. This can make it difficult to maximize, minimize, and close the window. As a quick fix, simply double-click the title bar. The window will be maximized, displaying the three control buttons.

Closing a Window

When you close a window, it is removed from memory. Unlike a minimized window, a closed window does not appear on the taskbar. Click the rightmost of the

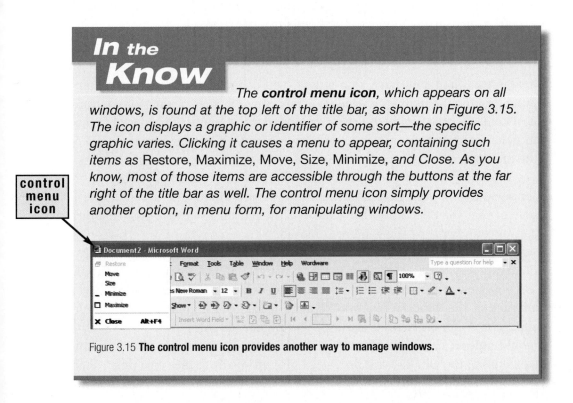

In the Know

The **control menu icon**, which appears on all windows, is found at the top left of the title bar, as shown in Figure 3.15. The icon displays a graphic or identifier of some sort—the specific graphic varies. Clicking it causes a menu to appear, containing such items as Restore, Maximize, Move, Size, Minimize, and Close. As you know, most of those items are accessible through the buttons at the far right of the title bar as well. The control menu icon simply provides another option, in menu form, for manipulating windows.

control menu icon

Figure 3.15 **The control menu icon provides another way to manage windows.**

Hands On

Activity 3.2—Opening and Managing a Window

In this exercise, you will practice managing a window. The computer should be on and at the beginning screen, with desktop icons displayed.

1. Double-click the Recycle Bin icon. The Recycle Bin window opens.
2. If the window is not already maximized, click the maximize (middle) button. The window should fill the screen.
3. The middle button now becomes a restore button. Click the restore button to shrink the window back to its original size.
4. Click the minimize button (leftmost of the three). The window disappears. Look at the taskbar to see where the window title appears as a button.
5. Click the minimized window's title on the taskbar. The window should return to the desktop.
6. Close the window by clicking the close button (to the far right). The window is closed and its title is no longer on the taskbar.

three window conrol buttons—the one with the X in it—to close the window, as shown in Figure 3.12. After you click the close button, the window is closed and removed from memory. To reopen a window, you must double-click the desktop icon or otherwise open the window from a menu.

Moving and Resizing a Window

Just as you often shift papers on a desk, you can shift windows on the computer desktop. Sometimes a window is positioned in such a way that you cannot see it all, or it may be covering an area of the screen that you need to see. In either case, you can move the window or resize it to gain better control of the desktop.

You know how to maximize and minimize a window, but sometimes you simply want to move the window slightly. To move a window, position the mouse pointer over the title bar of the window. Click and drag the window to another part of your desktop. The window is moved.

You can easily change the size of a window displayed on your screen. Enlarging a window lets you view more of its contents. Reducing a window lets you view items covered by the window. Position the mouse pointer over an edge of the window that you want to resize. The mouse pointer should change to a double-headed arrow. If you point to a corner of a window, the mouse pointer becomes a double-headed diagonal arrow. From that location, two sides of the window will be resized proportionally at the same time. Click

Hands On

Activity 3.3—Moving and Resizing a Window

In this exercise, you will move and resize a window. The computer should be on and at the beginning screen, with desktop icons displayed.

1. Open the Recycle Bin window (Double-click the icon).
2. If the window fills the screen, click the restore button to make it smaller.
3. Move the mouse pointer to a border of the window. The mouse pointer should become a double-headed arrow. Click and drag to make the window larger or smaller. Release the mouse button. The window should be resized.
4. Move the mouse pointer to the title bar. Click and drag the window to another location. Release the mouse button. The window should move.
5. Close the window.

and drag the window to the desired size. Release the mouse button. The window is resized.

Working with More Than One Window at a Time

Sometimes you need to have more than one window open at a time. While typing your investment club report in the word processing window, you might reach a point where you must calculate a cash balance. Instead of pulling out a hand-held calculator, you can open the Windows calculator, which appears in a window of its own. Both the word processor window and the calculator window are on-screen at the same time. After you complete the calculation, you might minimize the calculator so that you can quickly retrieve it later.

You can work in only one window at a time. The active window appears in front of all other windows and is identified by a brighter-colored title bar. To make another window the active window, click its button on the taskbar. Alternatively, you can click any part of the desired window to move it to the front.

If you have several windows open, you can hide some of them from view. The **Cascade** command lets you display, or layer, your open windows, one on top of the other. To cascade open windows, *right-click* an empty area of the taskbar. A context menu appears. Click Cascade (with the left mouse button). The windows neatly overlap each other.

To view some of the contents of all open windows at one time, in a horizontal or vertical fashion, you can use the **Tile** command. Right-click an empty area of the taskbar. From the subsequent context menu, click the desired tile option, horizontal or vertical. You will be able to partially view the contents of all open windows. Cascaded and tiled views are shown in Figure 3.16.

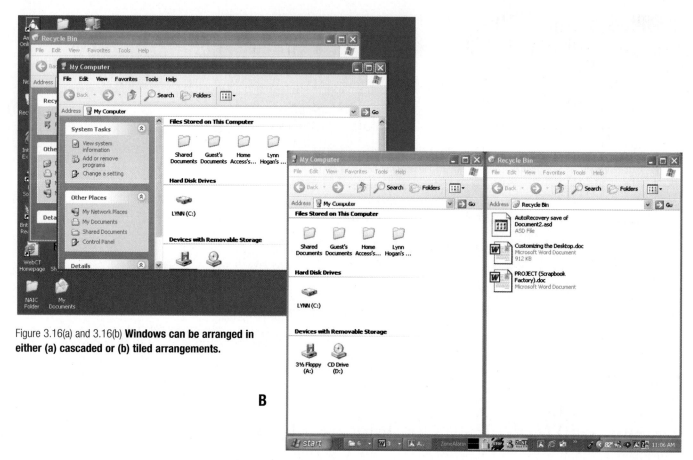

Figure 3.16(a) and 3.16(b) **Windows can be arranged in either (a) cascaded or (b) tiled arrangements.**

Hands On

Activity 3.4—Cascading and Tiling Multiple Windows

In this exercise, you will cascade and tile multiple windows. The computer should be on and at the beginning screen, with desktop icons displayed.

1. Open the Recycle Bin by double-clicking the icon.
2. Open the My Computer window by clicking Start and then clicking My Computer.
3. Cascade the windows by right-clicking an empty area of the taskbar. Click Cascade Windows. The two windows should be neatly overlapped.
4. Tile the windows by right-clicking an empty area of the taskbar. Click Tile Windows Vertically. The two windows should be displayed side by side.
5. Tile the windows horizontally. Right-click an empty area of the taskbar. Click Tile Windows Horizontally. The two windows should be displayed horizontally. Close both windows.

The taskbar displays the title of all the open windows, even those that are minimized and don't appear on-screen. Although the number of windows, or applications, that you can run at one time is limited only by your computer's memory and system resources, it is obvious that the taskbar is limited in size. As more windows are opened, the taskbar might begin to abbreviate the titles to allow more window buttons to appear. Eventually, the taskbar can become so cryptic that it is not easily understood. It just makes good sense to limit the number of open windows, if for no other reason than to make it easier for you to work.

Customizing Windows

Now that you are familiar with basic window controls, let's look at how to personalize your workspace. Many Windows settings can be adjusted to reflect your preferences. You can change the desktop background, select a screen saver (a moving screen display that appears when you are idle for a time), adjust the mouse double-click speed, set the clock, change the window color scheme, and control speaker volume.

Setting the Clock

The computer clock is displayed on the right side of the taskbar. If you move the mouse pointer over the clock and hold it steady, without clicking, the current date and day of the week pop up. To change the time or date, right-click the time. Look at the context menu. Click Adjust Date/Time. The Adjust Date/Time dialog box appears as shown in Figure 3.17.

Click the drop-down arrow beside the month area. You should see a list of months. Click the current month. If the year is incorrect, click the drop-down arrow beside that area and select the current year. The time is probably correct, but assume the minutes are off by a couple. Roll the mouse pointer over to the minute section of the time and double-click. The minutes should be *selected*, as shown by the shading that appears.

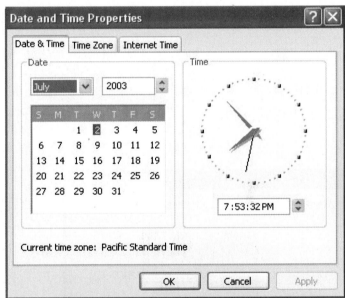

Figure 3.17 **Adjusting the date and time is easy when using the Adjust Date/Time dialog box.**

When an item is selected, or shaded, you can make changes simply by typing. *Without clicking anywhere else,* type the current minute. Although it is unlikely that you would need to adjust the seconds, let's do that just for illustration. Double-click the seconds area. Instead of typing the seconds, click the upward-pointing spinner. The seconds item will increase by one. Click the downward spinner. The seconds will decrease. Select the appropriate seconds by spinning up or down.

This dialog box has three buttons at the bottom: OK, Cancel, and Apply. Click OK. Remember that by clicking OK, you instruct Windows to accept your changes and close the dialog box. The dialog box will close, returning you to the desktop.

Changing Display Settings

The display is another way of saying "the way your screen looks." Unless you have made some changes, the **background** of your desktop is probably a shade of blue. When your computer is on but you haven't moved the mouse or touched the keyboard for a period, you might see an image or design continuously moving across your monitor. That is called a **screen saver**; it stops when you move the mouse or press a key on the keyboard. Screen **resolution** determines the sharpness of the display and the size of icons and other screen elements. Although it is important to have the display set in such a way that you can clearly see the applications you need to interact with, customizing your display is also a great way to add some personality to your workspace. Just as bringing a plant and a picture of your family to your office can help reduce your stress at work, customizing your Windows environment to better suit your personality can help make your time on the computer more enjoyable.

Selecting a Background

The background is the graphic, color, or picture that appears behind the icons on the desktop. The background will not appear in open windows or dialog boxes—only on the desktop. Selecting a background is a fun way to personalize your workspace. A typical Windows installation includes a set of backgrounds from which you can choose. As you become a proficient Windows user, you can even place a favorite photo in the background!

To select a background:

1. Click Start.
2. Click Control Panel. The Control Panel window opens.
3. Click Appearance and Themes. The Display window opens.
4. Click Change the desktop background. Your display should look like that shown in Figure 3.18.
5. Click the up or down scroll arrows beside Background to see additional choices.
6. Click any choice and notice that the preview screen just above the background area displays your current choice.
7. Click any other choice to preview it. Note that the first choice in the list is "None," which should be selected if you choose not to include a graphic background.

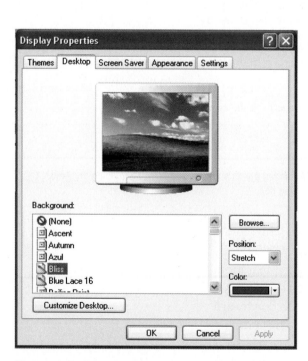

Figure 3.18 **Changing the background is a fun way to add some personality to your desktop.**

✓ SANITY CHECK

If you choose a background but the preview screen shows your choice only as a small block in the center of the display, check the Position selection. It should be set at Stretch for the background to fill the screen. If it is set at Center instead, the background image may appear only in the center. To change the position, click the drop-down arrow and make another selection.

8. When you have made your selection, click Apply if you have additional settings to adjust or OK to close the dialog box.
9. Close any open windows.

Selecting a Screen Saver

At one time, screen savers were necessary to keep static images from "burning" into the monitor. A college might have an accounting computer lab with a constant display of some sort of worksheet. After a time, the worksheet grid lines would appear on the monitor, even with the monitor turned off. Screen savers were developed to keep the monitor image changing constantly when there is no user activity.

With current display technology, the original purpose for a screen saver is no longer needed, but you might consider using a screen saver for another reason: it's fun! You might have seen a screen saver that looks like an aquarium, with fish swimming by. Perhaps you even heard some accompanying "glubs," and watched bubbles rise to the surface. Windows provides a set of screen savers, but you can also purchase or download free screen savers from the Internet. You can even learn to create your own screen saver, with family photos flipping in and out of view.

A more serious reason to consider using a screen saver is for system security. If you have selected a screen saver, it will appear when you leave your computer for a short time. Any work that you might have left on-screen is obscured by the screen saver. If you set a *screen saver password,* the screen saver won't disappear until you type the password. What that means is that no one else will be able to use your computer unless they know the password.

To select a screen saver:

1. Open the Control Panel, and click Appearance and Themes.
2. Click Choose a screen saver.
3. Click the drop-down arrow beside the screen saver item, and select a screen saver. You will see a preview of your selection in a preview box. Figure 3.19 shows the screen saver dialog box.

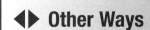

◀▶ Other Ways

For a quicker way to access Display Properties, right-click an empty area of the desktop. Choose Properties from the context menu. The Display Properties dialog box appears.

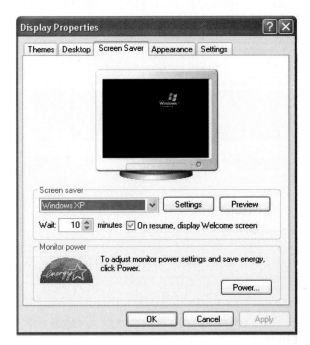

Figure 3.19 **A screen saver can add another level of security to your computer.**

4. The wait time is the amount of time that will lapse before the screen saver starts. You can adjust the wait time by using the spinner control.
5. Click Apply if you have additional settings to make or OK to close the dialog box.

To set a screen saver password:

1. Open the Control Panel, and click Appearance and Themes.
2. Click Choose a screen saver.
3. Select the *On resume, password protect* box. The next time the screen saver is activated it will remain on-screen until you move the mouse or type a key on the keyboard. You will then be prompted for your password, which is the same password that you selected when you created your user account. If you do not use a password to log on, you cannot set a screen saver password.

✓ SANITY CHECK

If you do not see the *On resume, password protect* box when you begin to set a screen saver password, Fast User Switching is on. You will, instead, click the box beside *On resume, display Welcome screen*. Instead of using a screen saver, Fast User Switching will put the computer on standby, unlocking it only when a user types the correct password.

> **▶ Quick Tip**
>
> Some application software, particularly computer games, might require a different *color* setting. Depending on your computer system, you probably have at least two choices: medium (16-bit) or highest (32-bit). You will find the color settings in the Settings area of the Display Properties dialog box. To choose another setting, click the drop-down arrow in the Color quality area, and make the selection.

Figure 3.20 **Screen resolution determines the sharpness of the display.**

Adjusting Screen Resolution

The display resolution determines the sharpness of images and the size of screen elements. The higher the resolution, the smaller the on-screen objects, but the sharper the detail. If you need to make objects larger, you should decrease the resolution. Some application software requires a certain resolution, so you should be aware of how to change it.

To change the resolution, click Appearance and Themes from the Control Panel. Click *Change the screen resolution*. Figure 3.20 shows the screen resolution settings. In the area titled Screen resolution, notice a slider, or continuum, that displays the current resolution. You might see 1024 by 760 or 800 by 600. Click and drag the slider to increase or decrease the resolution. The preview screen displays the effect. If you like it, click OK. Otherwise, return the slider to the original position or try another resolution. Of course, clicking Cancel will return the settings to the way they were before you changed them in the dialog box. After making a selection, you will have to respond to a few Windows prompts to accept the new setting. Before the new settings take effect, your screen may flicker slightly or you may be prompted to restart the computer.

In the Know

You are already aware that it is not a good idea to leave your computer running constantly. Normally, you should power down your computer when you quit for the day. If you often take breaks during the day, you might also consider setting your monitor to shut down automatically after a certain period of inactivity. If your monitor is Energy Star compliant, it is already set to automatically power down independently of the power management system. To check your monitor power options, right-click an empty area of the desktop, and select Properties from the context menu. Click the Screen Saver tab. Click the Power button, and check the monitor delay time. If you want, you can change the setting by clicking the drop-down arrow beside the Turn Off Monitor area and selecting a different delay.

Other options in the Power Management dialog box include System Standby, System Hibernates, and Turn Off Hard Disks. Standby mode means the computer is still on but is using significantly less power. A computer comes out of standby mode when the mouse is moved or a key is pressed. Whatever you were working on before the computer went into standby mode is redisplayed so that you can pick up where you left off. During system standby, the computer minimizes power usage by shutting down some noncritical systems

Hibernation occurs when a computer appears to go into a much sounder sleep than system standby, thus taking longer to "wake up." When you boot the computer from a complete off state, a full POST (power-on self-test) is performed, taking some time. In contrast, a computer coming out of hibernation skips the full boot process and simply loads a snapshot of the way the system

looked before the computer "went to sleep." In hibernate mode, the computer is fully powered off and is not consuming any power. To take a computer out of hibernate, press the power button. The computer displays what you were working with when it went into hibernate mode.

System standby and hibernation are similar, each with unique advantages. System standby responds more quickly to wake-up events, requiring only mouse movement to become immediately ready. With hibernation, you must press the power button to bring up the computer. If you're not sure whether your system is in standby or hibernation, first press a key or move the mouse. If nothing happens, press the power button. You are less likely to lose unsaved data or projects when a computer is in hibernation. Standby doesn't create a copy of RAM, whereas hibernation does. Therefore, even if you have not yet saved a copy of your project to disk, it can be retrieved from a computer in hibernation. Don't count on hibernation as the sole source of system power down, though. Go ahead and shut down the system completely each night so that all system resources are cleared and reset when the computer reboots in the morning.

A final setting allows you to specify the length of time a hard disk drive will wait to detect hard drive activity before powering down. Power automatically returns to the hard drive when it is accessed by the operating system.

Recommended power management settings are:

- *Monitor—20 minutes*
- *Standby—45 minutes*
- *Hibernate—90 minutes*

Adjusting Mouse Double-Click Speed

One of the biggest challenges for novice computer users is manipulating the mouse. Double-click speed often needs to be adjusted to the user's preference and can easily be made slower or faster. The rate at which you naturally double-click may be slower than what the operating system expects.

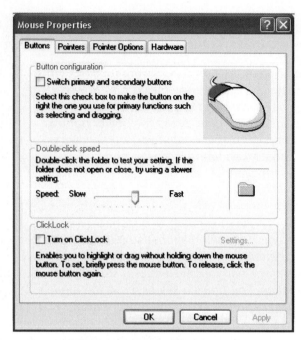

Figure 3.21 **Changing mouse properties allows you to customize the way your mouse responds.**

To change the double-click speed:

1. Click Start, and choose Control Panel.
2. Click Printers and Other Hardware.
3. Click Mouse.
4. Click the Buttons tab, if necessary. You will see a slider area titled *Double-click speed*, with a tab positioned somewhere near the middle, like the dialog box shown in Figure 3.21. If you think the speed at which you naturally click is too slow, you may want to click and drag the tab to a slower than average speed. After you have repositioned the tab, double-click the folder displayed to the right. If your double-click speed now matches the requirement, the folder will open. Double-click the folder again to close it. If the speed is still not right, make another adjustment to the slider and try the folder again. When the speed is just right, click OK. Close any open windows.

Adjusting Volume

Today's personal computers are truly multimedia, with full-featured sound, video, and interactivity. As a standard, computers come equipped with a set of speakers. One of the first things you might want to do is learn to control speaker volume. Many speakers have a volume knob, much like that of a television set, which you can adjust. Others, especially laptops, which normally have no external speakers, must be adjusted through Windows.

Check the system tray for a volume icon. You may have to expand the system tray by clicking the small arrow beside it to see all icons. Click the volume icon, which looks like a loudspeaker. Click and drag to adjust the volume slider.

Alternatively, you can use the Control Panel to adjust volume. Open Sounds, Speech, and Audio Devices from the Control Panel. Click Adjust System Volume. Under Device volume, drag the slider to increase or decrease the volume.

Getting Help

There will be times when you need assistance with some feature of Windows or some other aspect of your computer. There are several ways to get help.

- The built-in *Help and Support* feature of Windows provides answers to many questions and offers some helpful tutorials.

- *Windows XP newsgroups* allow you to ask questions of a community of users and experts.

- *Windows technical support* is a phone call away but may not be free.

Hands On

Activity 3.5—Changing Settings

In this exercise, you will practice making adjustments to the display, mouse, and time. The computer should be on and at the beginning screen, with desktop icons displayed.

1. To change the background, right-click an empty area of the desktop. Click Properties, and then click the Desktop tab.
2. Click the up or down scroll arrow beside the Background area to display more choices. Click any one that looks interesting. The preview screen displays your choice. Don't click OK or Apply.
3. Now click the Screen Saver tab. Click the drop-down arrow beside the Screen saver area, and make a choice from those listed. Your selection appears in the preview area. Change the wait time to 3 by clicking the spinner up or down. Don't click OK or Apply.
4. To change the screen resolution, click the Settings tab. Click and drag the slider tab to display 800 by 600. Notice how the sample display changes. Now drag to 1280 by 1024. Do you see the difference? Again, don't click OK or Apply.
5. Because you are just experimenting, you probably are not ready to make your selections permanent. Click the Cancel button to cancel all changes and close the dialog box.

6. Next we'll look at adjusting the time setting. Roll the mouse pointer to the clock on the right side of the taskbar. Hold it steady to see the current date and day.
7. Right-click the time. From the context menu, click Adjust Date/Time.
8. Change the seconds by double-clicking the seconds area of the time. Either type the new seconds or click the spinner control up or down to adjust. If you are at your home computer and are sure that you want to make the change, click OK. If you are working in a public lab, click Cancel to close the dialog box without accepting any changes.
9. Experiment with double-click speeds to find one that is most comfortable for you. Open the Control Panel window. (Click Start, Control Panel.) Click Printers and Other Hardware. Click Mouse. Click Buttons, if necessary. Click and drag the slider tab to increase or decrease the double-click speed. It is not a good idea to make the double-click speed as fast as possible! Hardly ever would you be able to double-click fast enough if you set the double-click speed at its fastest setting. Double-click the folder to check the new double-click speed. Make adjustments as necessary. Click Cancel to close the dialog box without accepting changes.

• If you know someone who might be of assistance, you can communicate with them online through *remote assistance,* which is a new feature with Windows XP.

Windows Help and Support is available from the Start menu. Click Start, Help and Support. The first Help page provides many useful links. Some links start tutorials and guided steps for various operations. An "Ask for Assistance" area starts the remote assistance task and allows you to join in some newsgroups.

If you know the exact term that you need help with, type it in the Search box and click Go. Results are categorized by *Suggested Topics* (those that are most relevant to your search term), *Pick a Task* (links to detailed procedures to complete a task), and *Overviews, Articles, and Tutorials* (links to articles that might give a basic understanding of the topic).

Another way to use the Help and Support feature is through the index or table of contents. At the Help and Support page, click Index. You will see a table of contents showing topics for which help is available. You can scroll through the list to find what you are looking for, or you can make your search quicker by typing your search term in the Index box. As you type your search term, Windows narrows the display according to what you have typed. If a topic looks interesting, click it and click Display to view related information.

Perhaps you are puzzled about the right way to print a document.

1. Click the Start button on the taskbar.

2. Click Help and Support. The Help Topics dialog box appears, as shown in Figure 3.22.

3. Because you have a search topic in mind, "printing," click Index.

4. Click in the Index text box, and type the word *printing*. As you type, Windows narrows the selections until you see the word "printing" as a choice. There are several subheads under the printing category. Click *overview*. Click Display.

4. Click *Print a document*. Click Display. To the right, you will see supporting information on the topic of printing.

Dealing with a stubborn computer problem is frustrating, especially if you don't feel that you have the knowledge or expertise to correct it. The remote assistance feature allows you to invite a person to help with your computer problem from a distance. You and your helper must both be online and must be using

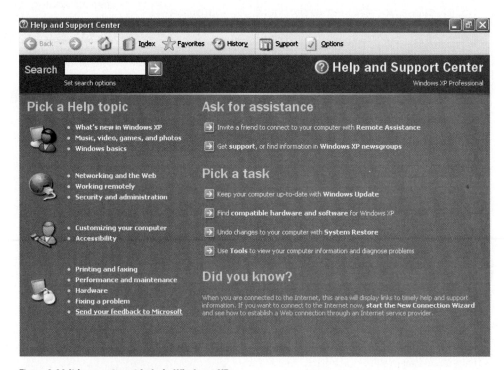

Figure 3.22 **It is easy to get help in Windows XP.**

compatible operating systems, such as Windows XP. You will both be able to see your computer screen, and to communicate. You might even want to share your mouse and keyboard! Besides both being online at the same time, the only other requirement is that you both use either Windows Messenger Service or an e-mail account through Outlook or Outlook Express. If you are working with a firewall (an access-restricting program), you might not be able to use remote assistance.

At the first page of Help and Support, click *Invite a friend to connect to your computer with Remote Assistance*. After that, click *Invite someone to help you*, as shown in Figure 3.23. Follow all prompts to initiate the session.

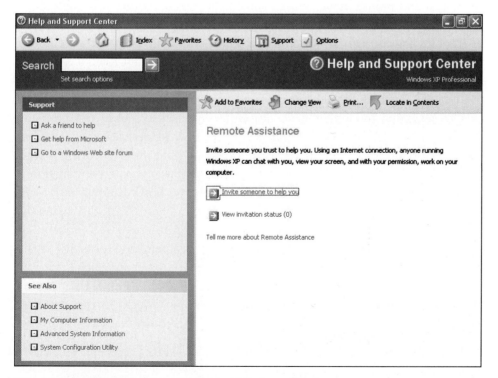

Figure 3.23 **Using Remote Assistance, you can get help from a friend.**

Hands On

Activity 3.6—Getting Help

In this exercise, you will seek assistance with a computer activity. The computer should be on and at the beginning screen, with desktop icons displayed.

1. Click Start. Click Help and Support.
2. Assume that you are not certain of how to restart a computer without shutting it down completely. Click Index. Click in the index text box and type *restarting*.
3. Click any displayed topic that looks appropriate. Click Display.
4. Supporting text should be displayed in the right pane. Click the close button (X).

Also at the Help and Support page, you can get help from Microsoft or join a newsgroup by clicking *Get support or find information in Windows XP newsgroups*. Make your choice of support and follow all prompts.

Working with a Computer That Fails to Respond

For various reasons, your system might occasionally freeze or lock up. All activity ceases, and mouse movement is halted. The first thing that you might do is wait a few minutes. Perhaps you are saving a lengthy document with a lot of graphics and formatting, which might take a little time. However, if you don't soon see any return to normalcy, it is likely that you will have to take corrective action.

Usually, a system locks up because a program with which you are working fails to respond. You might never know for sure what caused the problem, but the most important thing is that you know how to clear the program from memory and get the system going again. Press and hold the Ctrl key, then press and hold the Alt key, and then press the Del key (this keyboard combination is seen written as Ctrl+Alt+Del). Release all three keys. The Windows Task Manager dialog box appears, similar to the one shown in Figure 3.24, displaying the status of programs in memory. One of the displayed programs will probably be tagged "Not Responding." To shut down that program and possibly regain control of your computer system, click to select the program and click End Task. You might have to click End Task in yet another dialog box before the program terminates. Sometimes, pressing Ctrl+Alt+Del doesn't work, in that the Task Manager doesn't appear and the system remains locked. In that case, your only choice is to turn the computer off. Wait a few seconds before turning it back on. Occasionally, an error message will let you know that your system is busy or that a fatal exception has occurred. Although those messages at first glance appear alarming, they usually are not indicators of a serious problem. Just restart your system.

Figure 3.24 **Using the Task Manager, you can close programs that are causing problems.**

▮▶Quick Tip

Occasionally, your computer might fail to respond or might give symptoms of other problems. Most of the time, the difficulty is not critical and, in fact, there might be a simple solution. Before declaring it quits or investing in an expensive service call, try these steps:

1. *Restart the computer.* Many problems occur in memory so, by restarting your computer, you will clear memory and start anew.
2. *Check all connections.* Make sure all cables are plugged tightly into the back of the system unit as well as into the peripherals themselves (printer, scanner, and others).
3. *Call for help.* Check with a tech-savvy friend or other more experienced computer user. They might have suggestions or they might have encountered the same problem.

Chapter Summary

DON'T FORGET

- A windowing environment includes a GUI (graphical user interface).

- The desktop, Start menu, taskbar, icons, and menus are basic elements of the Windows operating system.

- The background of the Windows display that appears when a computer is first started is the desktop.

- Window controls include minimizing, maximizing, restoring, and closing windows.

- Open windows can be moved and resized.

- Several windows can be open at one time, and they can be cascaded or tiled for easy viewing.

- To personalize the workspace, you can adjust many settings, including the clock, the mouse settings, the display settings, and volume control.

- Windows XP allows you to create multiple user accounts, with different levels of permissions.

- If a computer locks up, you can press Ctrl+Alt+Del to open the Task Manager, from which you can close programs that are not responding.

KEY TERMS

background	icon	shortcut menu
cascade	minimize	Start menu
closing a window	maximizing a window	taskbar
context menu	minimizing a window	tile
control menu icon	resolution	user account
desktop	restoring a window	windowing environment
dialog box	screen saver	

TRUE/FALSE

Circle **T** if the statement is true or **F** if the statement is false.

T F 1. When you close a window, it is removed from memory.

T F 2. The background appears on the desktop, as well as in all dialog boxes and application windows.

T F 3. The horizontal bar usually located across the bottom of the desktop is the toolbar.

T F 4. You can have only one window open at one time.

T F 5. The cascade arrangement layers open windows one on top of the other.

T F 6. Linux uses a graphical user interface.

T F 7. Clicking the Apply button in a dialog box accepts all changed settings and leaves the dialog box open.

T (F)   8. You can resize windows but cannot move them.

T F   9. If a computer locks up, you can press Ctrl + Alt + Del to display the Task Manager.

T F   10. A context menu appears when you right-click a screen element, such as the desktop or the taskbar.

MULTIPLE CHOICE

Circle the correct choice for each of the following.

1. A graphic, color, or picture that appears on the desktop behind the icons is called the
   a. screen saver
   b. resolution
   c. background
   d. window

2. Items on a menu that are either "on" or "off" are called
   a. mutually exclusive options
   b. toggle options
   c. commands
   d. cascade options

3. Window control buttons include
   a. minimize, maximize, close, restore
   b. move, resize, maximize, close
   c. minimize, maximize, open, close
   d. open, close, restore, maximize

4. Small pictures that appear on the desktop are called
   a. diagrams
   b. windows
   c. tools
   d. icons

5. The Start menu has been substantially redesigned in
   a. Windows XP
   b. Windows 2000
   c. Windows NT
   d. Windows Millennium

6. Minimizing a window
   a. removes a window from view and from memory
   b. makes the window much smaller but still visible on the desktop
   c. returns the window to its original size before it was maximized
   d. removes a window from view, but not from memory

7. To make screen objects larger,
   a. increase the display resolution
   b. increase window size
   c. decrease the display resolution
   d. select a screen saver

8. A special window that asks for confirmation from you or allows you to make selections is called a
   a. menu
   b. dialog box
   c. GUI
   d. shortcut

9. The Control Panel
   a. allows you to customize the display settings, add new hardware, and make other system adjustments
   b. allows you to create shortcuts
   c. controls the keyboard and monitor
   d. is another name for the desktop

10. When a computer system locks up, the cause is often
   a. a faulty operating system
   b. a damaged area of memory
   c. poor disk access
   d. a program that fails to respond

PRACTICAL PROJECTS

1. Open Dialog

In this project, you will label areas of a dialog box. Give the term associated with each item in Figure 3.25.

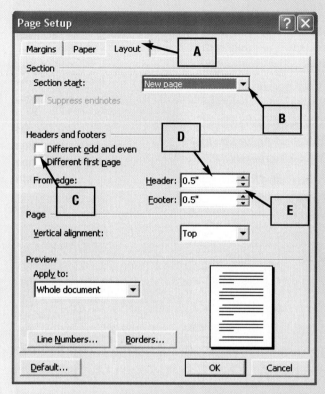

Figure 3.25 **A dialog box has several components that you should learn to identify.**

2. Moving Here and There

In this project, you will open multiple windows and practice moving and resizing them.

a. Open the Recycle Bin by double-clicking its icon on the desktop.
b. Open My Computer by clicking Start, My Computer. Make sure My Computer doesn't fill the entire screen. Click its restore button, if necessary.
c. Make the Recycle Bin the active window.
d. Minimize the Recycle Bin.
e. Drag My Computer to the center of the screen or to a corner.
f. Maximize My Computer.
g. Restore My Computer.

h. Resize My Computer to make it smaller.
i. Click the Windows button on the taskbar showing that two windows are open. Click to choose Recycle Bin from the subsequent list. The Recycle Bin window opens.
j. Close the Recycle Bin.
k. Close My Computer.

3. Adding On

Throughout the life of your computer, you will probably be adding devices, such as new mice, printers, scanners, and game controllers. Although connecting new devices used to be much more complicated, today you can usually just plug in the device without dealing with a lot of software or complex connections. That's all thanks to the USB (universal serial bus) port, which is a standard connector on the back of most computers produced since 2000. Most new systems come with several USB ports, so that you can plug in more than one device simultaneously.

Using Windows' Help and Support area, as well as any other resources, create a report on USB technology. Include information on the development and use of USB ports, the history of the device, and any advantages or recommendations for use.

4. Accessibility Options

Windows includes what are called accessibility options to assist those who need larger print or different keyboard management. Take a look at the accessibility options found in the Control Panel, and provide a summary of what is included. You might investigate other resources as well, to get some ideas on how to make the Windows environment even more flexible. In your findings, explain how to use any options and what purpose they serve.

5. Getting Help

In this project, you will use Windows Help and Support to get information on the product activation feature that is new with Windows XP. As a result of your search, answer the following questions:

a. Can you install a single copy of Windows XP on more than one computer?

b. What, exactly, is product activation?

c. How long do you have to activate the product after purchase?

d. What happens if you don't activate it within the allotted period of time?

e. What is a product key, where is it found, and why is it important in activation?

f. How do you register, or activate, your copy of Windows XP?

CHAPTER 4

Understanding Files, Folders, and Disk Maintenance

When you create a document, family tree, or financial spreadsheet, you are creating a *file*. Anything that you create and to which you assign a name is a file. For example, you might be working with a greeting card program, having just created a birthday card for your spouse. If you are not quite finished with the card but need to leave the computer for a while, you will need to save the card to a disk of some sort or you risk losing your work if a power outage occurs. At some point during the application's save process, you will be asked to name the card. You will also have the opportunity to specify to which disk drive the card project should be saved. It will help if you have a basic understanding of what it means to save the file and how to get a view of files that are saved on your disk media.

The hard disk is one of the most often used components of your computer system and, consequently, the one that is most important to maintain in

Objectives

When you complete this chapter, you will:

- Understand the difference between files and folders.

- Be familiar with My Computer.

- Be able to view the contents of a disk and check for available disk space.

- Understand how to clear unused or unnecessary files from your computer system.

- Be able to perform routine disk maintenance tasks.

- Understand the importance of backing up files.

- Be able to copy files to a CD.

good working order. By performing a few routine maintenance tasks peri-odically, you can keep your disks in top form, making sure disk compo-nents remain as responsive and as sturdy as possible. You will also want to occasionally back up (copy) files or entire disks, so that you don't risk losing important data.

Understanding File and Folder Concepts

Computer tasks that you enjoy might include word processing, investment analysis, home financial management, and photo manipulation. Most software applications allow you to create an item, such as a newsletter or scanned photo image, and save it to a disk with a name of your choice. A file is a collection of data, or a project, that has a name and that is placed on a computer storage device. Think about a file as a document, such as the bill that you received in the mail today. You probably have some system of organization to deal with bills. Perhaps you have a folder in a filing cabinet, marked "Bills to Pay." When you receive a bill, you place it in the folder for later mailing. A computer disk can have a similar arrangement of folders. The purpose of a computer **folder** is simply to organize files, much as you organize documents in folders in a filing cabinet. You might think of the filing cabinet drawer as the disk drive, with fold-ers in place to hold files. A computer folder is an area of a disk that you can name to indicate the nature of files that the folder is to hold.

Files

When you purchase a software package and install it on your computer, the files that make the program work (the **program files**, or **executable files**) are copied onto your hard disk. You cannot modify or edit those files. The files that you cre-ate, such as the greeting card, are sometimes called **data files**. After you save a data file, you can later open it, edit it, print it, and save it again.

You can save your data files to a storage device, such as a CD or hard disk. Saving to a CD, floppy disk, or Zip disk allows you to take the files to other com-puters (if those computers have disk drives that will accept your storage media). In most cases, you can open a data file only with the same software with which you created it. For example, suppose you create a picture project using Microsoft Picture It and save it to a CD. You take the CD to a college computer lab so that you can continue to work on it. However, unless the college computer lab has the same version of Microsoft Picture It that you installed, you won't be able to open the file. Now, there are some exceptions to that rule. A Microsoft Word document can be opened with WordPad (a Windows accessory program), and some files can be saved in such a way as to make them accessible to a wider range of programs. But, for the most part, you won't be able to open a file in anything other than the creating program.

You are already aware that disks vary widely in capacity. The size of a typical floppy disk is about 1.44 MB, whereas a Zip disk stores up to 750 MB of data. A DVD can hold up to 18 GB. The thing to remember is that when you save a file, you should consider its size when determining which disk to use. Graphics, such as a scanned photograph, take up much more space than text. If you are attempting to save a series of photographs from your digital camera, you could not hope to place them all on a floppy disk. You should probably use a CD or DVD for that task. Of course, the hard disk is always an option for saving photographs and other very large files, but most people opt for the more portable CD or DVD. Wherever you choose to save your files, be sure to clearly label the disk so that you can find the files later. You might also want to consider making duplicate copies of files that you can't afford to lose.

Folders

Disks, with the exception of floppy disks, contain a large amount of storage space. That large amount of space might be compared to a huge linen closet. Suppose that you have just had your house built and you decided to save money by not installing shelves in the closets until a later time. A linen closet is supposed to be used for linens and towels, so you begin to place such items in it. Little by little, the towels, tablecloths, and place mats begin to pile up on the closet floor. Some might topple over, only to be covered by still more items. Eventually, when you search for that special tablecloth, you will probably have an extremely difficult time digging through the mess to find it. If, on the other hand, you were very organized, you would place shelves appropriately in the closet. If you are extremely attentive to detail, you might even tape labels on all the shelves to remind you where each type of item belongs. You might label a towel shelf, a table linen shelf, a bed linen shelf, and a miscellaneous shelf. Stacked neatly, each item will always be easy to find.

Likewise, any computer disk can have multiple folders, similar to the shelves in the linen closet. Each folder is a labeled space in which you can store data or program files. A folder is actually just a holding location for files, holding documents electronically in the same way that paper folders hold documents in an office filing cabinet.

Just as a closet with no organization makes it hard to find items, a hard disk with very little folder structure is hard to work with and invites difficulty in locating saved files. Although some hard disk folder structure exists when you purchase a computer, you might want to create folders for files and applications specific to your interests. Suppose that you want to keep records related to several ongoing projects at work. You might create a folder labeled *Current Projects* on the hard disk or a CD and begin to save all related files there. Because you are keeping all the related information together in a logical, easy-to-locate space on the disk, it will be easy to find and retrieve any information you need.

Folders are organized in a hierarchical fashion, commonly referred to as a tree structure. Each folder can hold files and additional folders, so you quickly wind up with folders within other folders. The **root folder** is a disk drive itself. Some files might be stored in the root folder, but most will be stored within an appropriately named folder according to the contents of the files. A typical tree structure is shown in Figure 4.1 (on page 102). Note that the root folder has sev-

In the Know

One thing you will learn is that working with computers requires a new vocabulary. Listed below are a few terms related to the study of files and folders:

Folder   *Previously known as* a directory, *a folder is a holding area for files. Folders can be found on any disk storage device. The terms* directory *and* folder *are synonymous.*

Default folder   *When saving a file, you are given the opportunity to indicate on what disk and in what folder you want the file to be saved. Instead of specifying a location, though, you can accept the folder that the computer suggests, called the default folder. The default folder for Microsoft Office products, such as Word and Excel, is the* My Documents *folder on the hard drive.*

Current folder   *The current folder is the location in which you are working at a particular time. For example, let's say that you save your English assignments in a folder called English 101. When you open a file from the* English 101 *folder, your current folder becomes* English 101.

Root folder   *The root folder is another name for the disk drive itself. It is the doorway to all other folders. You don't usually find many files in the root folder, just other folders.*

File   *A file is a collection of data. You might consider a file to be a computer project, such as a worksheet showing recent household expenses.*

Hierarchical structure   *The organization of folders on your system is in a hierarchical structure, with some folders containing additional folders (sometimes called subfolders) beneath them.*

Path   *The route you would follow to reach a file or folder, if tracing along the hierarchical structure, is called the path. If a folder on the C: drive is labeled* Recipes, *the path would be indicated as* C:\Recipes. *If the Recipes folder contained another folder within it, labeled* Main Dishes, *the path to the Main Dishes folder would read* C:\Recipes\Main Dishes.

eral "branches," causing the tree structure to look like an upside down tree. One of the folders (branches), titled *Family Records,* contains two folders beneath it, one for each family name researched. A **path** is the route followed to move from the root folder to a lower-level folder. For example, the path to get to the *Hale* family folder is *C:\Family Records\Hale Family*. Each backslash represents a folder division. You will hardly ever need to state the path in that fashion, but understanding the path concept helps when you are interpreting some system commands, perhaps during installation of software.

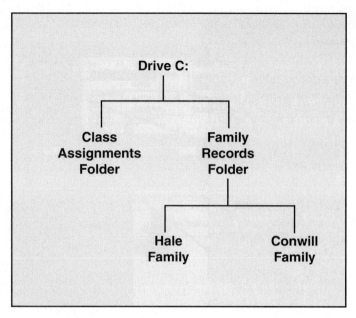

Figure 4.1 **Folder structure helps keep files and records organized.**

Using My Computer

Each of the storage devices (disks) on your computer can be used to store multiple files and folders. A typical personal computer might have a hard disk drive, typically referred to as the **C: drive**, a floppy disk drive, usually known as the **A: drive**, and a CD or DVD drive, which is probably the **D: drive**. If you have additional disk drives, such as network drives that are available to computers connected to a network, they will each be referenced by a letter. Given the immense popularity of CDs and DVDs, coupled with the much larger storage capacity of those units, manufacturers are beginning to stop including a floppy disk drive as a standard system component. It will be years to come, though, before the floppy disk drive ceases to exist, so it is still a viable storage option for some files.

You can view the contents of your disk devices, including any network drives using My Computer. You can find My Computer on the Start menu of Windows XP. My Computer is the easiest way to search for and open files and folders.

Viewing Contents of a Disk

You will often want to view the contents of your disks and check to see how much space remains for additional files. You will find My Computer on the Start menu, if you are using Windows XP, or on the Desktop in other Windows versions. Windows XP has added several new features to My Computer, so it looks different when compared with older Windows versions.

Using My Computer, you can get a picture of the folders and files that are currently saved on any disk drive on your system. However, don't expect to understand or recognize every file and folder. The operating system created many files during installation, and still more came along with other software applications. Although you won't recognize some of the folders, many of those folders and files serve a critical function in keeping your system running, even without your awareness. Don't worry if you don't understand all of what you see.

The View Menu

The My Computer window can be viewed in several formats. The icons shown in Figure 4.2 are called *tiles*. You can change the view by working with the View menu selection in the My Computer window. To access the View menu, click the Start button and click My Computer. Click View in the menu bar. You will see several options on the menu, as shown in Figure 4.3 (on page 104).

▮▶Quick Tip

No matter what your skill level, you can find a lot of information and answers to your questions in Windows XP's Help and Support area. If you are new to Windows, you might want to check *What's new in Windows XP,* found on the first page of Help and Support. Access help by clicking Help and Support from the Start menu. From there, you can take a tour or tutorial and learn all about what to expect from your operating system.

Hands On

Activity 4.1—Viewing Disk Contents

In this exercise, you will view the contents of your hard disk. The computer should be on and at the beginning screen, with desktop icons displayed.

1. Click Start (on the taskbar) and then click My Computer.
2. A window appears, as shown in Figure 4.2, listing all of your disk drives. Depending upon your computer system resources, you might see more or fewer icons than what is shown here.
3. Double-click the C: drive to view its contents. You might have to click *show contents of this folder* before the contents of the C: drive are displayed. You are at the root folder. Notice the icons that look like file folders. Those icons represent folders that are housed on the C: drive.

4. Double-click any folder to open it. You are likely to see a list of the folders and files that are housed within that first folder. You can recognize a file by the absence of a folder icon. Files are designated with an icon representing their *type*, which simply indicates whether they are word processing files, graphic files, or some other category.
5. Look for a horizontal or vertical scroll bar. If the folder that you selected does not have enough items stored in it to require additional space to display all icons, you won't see a scroll area. However, if you do see a scroll bar, click the scroll arrow (pointing down or to the right), to see the additional folders and files contained within the current folder.
6. Close the My Computer window.

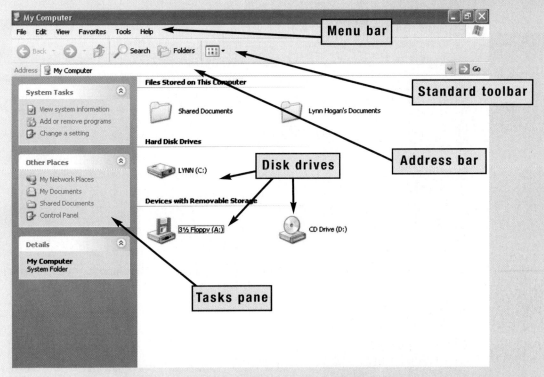

Figure 4.2 **Using My Computer, you can get a view of your computer resources.**

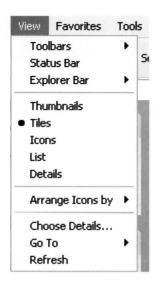

Figure 4.3 **Working with the View menu, you can change the way screen elements appear.**

From the View menu, you can open or close toolbars and change the way icons appear. The following list describes each of the options on the View Menu.

- **Toolbars**—allows you to turn the Windows toolbars on or off. Toolbars are those bars that appear at the top of the My Computer window, providing easy access to various operations, such as displaying the folder structure or changing the view. When you click the Toolbars options, you will see a list of toolbars. At least one should have a check mark beside it, indicating that it is already "on." To turn it off, click the item to remove the check mark. A feature that you can choose to turn on or off is called a toggle, and you make your selection by clicking the item. Usually, the Standard toolbar and the Address toolbar are displayed. The Standard toolbar contains areas that will be helpful as you navigate among folders in My Computer. You will also find a Views button (with a grid of squares), which provides quick access to all My Computer views. The Standard toolbar is shown in Figure 4.4.

- **Status Bar**—toggles the status bar at the bottom of the window on and off. You should leave this selection checked so that the status bar remains visible. The status bar provides information related to the items that are highlighted.

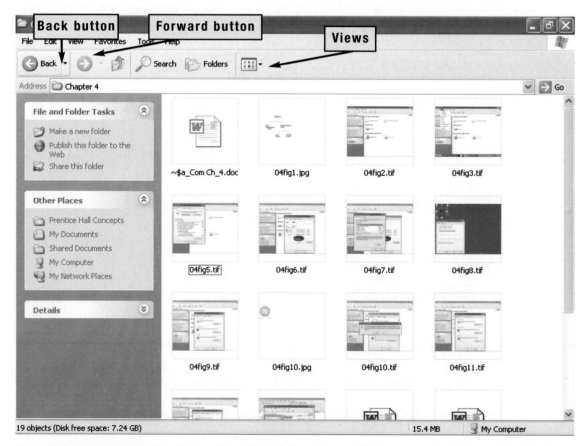

Figure 4.4 **The Standard toolbar is a feature of almost all windows. You can display or remove toolbars through the View command found on the menu bar.**

- **Thumbnails**—displays not only the folders, but also some images (pictures) that a folder might contain, so that you can quickly identify folder contents.

- **Tiles**—displays files and folders as large icons.

- **Icons**—displays files and folders as smaller icons than in Tile view.

- **List**—displays file and folder names preceded by small icons. This view is helpful if you are viewing a long list of files and folders and want to place as many as possible on-screen so that you can quickly scan the list.

- **Details**—displays files and folders with such information as file size, file type, and date created or modified. This is the only view that allows you to sort a folder's contents directly.

- **Arrange Icons by**—displays the Arrange Icons submenu, which allows you to sort the contents of a window differently. The following options are included in the Arrange Icons submenu when you are viewing the contents of a folder. If, however, you are viewing the first My Computer window, in which disk drives are listed, the contents of the *Arrange Icons by* submenu will be slightly different because it also includes Total Size and Free Space selections.

  Name—arranges contents alphabetically, with folders listed first, then files.

  Type—arranges contents by type, with folders listed first, and then files. Files are arranged in groups according to the type, which is the program with which the file is associated. All Word files are listed together, all Excel files are together, and so forth.

  Size—arranges contents by size, from smallest to largest.

  Modified—arranges contents in order of date saved, from latest to earliest.

  Auto Arrange—arranges contents in a straight line if you are using the Large Icons or Small Icons view. Selecting the menu item toggles the selection on and off.

  Align to Grid—is another toggle selection, with which you can cause icons to automatically align to a transparent grid.

- **Choose Details**—allows you to choose the details that you want to display in Details view. Almost any level of detail is possible, from name, type, and date created to author, status, and file attributes (whether a file can be modified).

- **Go To**—allows you to browse backward or forward through visited windows. The Standard toolbar buttons provide a quick method of browsing as well.

- **Refresh**—redraws the display to give an up-to-the-minute picture of system status. This is necessary in cases where things might have changed since the last view. For example, you might have just viewed the files on a floppy disk, but now that you have replaced that disk with another one, you want a current (refreshed) view of the new disk's contents.

Hands On

Activity 4.2—Checking Available Disk Space

In this exercise, you will use My Computer to check available hard disk space on your system. Although this exercise focuses on the hard disk, you can follow the same steps to check the amount of space on any disk drive associated with your computer. The computer should be on and at the beginning screen, with desktop icons displayed.

1. Open My Computer.
2. Use the mouse to point to the C: drive icon, and hold the mouse steady for a few seconds until a tool tip appears, giving the amount of free and used space. A tool tip is an item of information that appears when you hold the mouse steady over an element on-screen.
3. For more detail, right-click the C: drive icon. Select Properties from the context menu.
4. Click the General tab if it is not already selected. The Properties window appears, as shown in Figure 4.5, giving information related to the exact amount of free and used space. Other information describes the type of disk and the file system.
5. Click OK.
6. Close My Computer.

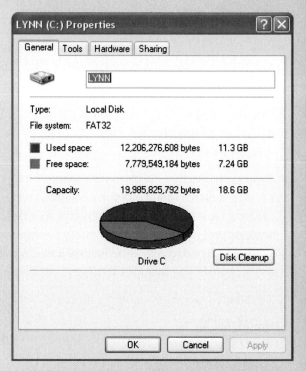

Figure 4.5 **Disk properties include the amount of free and used space.**

File Types

Each file that you create is associated with the program that you used to create it. What that means is that when you create a file using a program, such as Microsoft Excel, you can only open the file by using the same program. If you create a memorandum using Microsoft Word, the file is saved as a Word file. Just as you have a last name, files are given a last name, called an **extension**, to identify the family to which they belong. The "last name" for all Word files is *doc*. So, if you save the memorandum as *Memo to Mary*, it will actually be saved as *Memo to Mary.doc*. The file extension is connected to the filename by a dot (period). Although file extensions are used by your computer system to associate files with the programs that created them, you might use the feature to group all like files for deletion or to search some particular group for a specific file. There are hundreds of filename extensions out there. You will learn to recognize the extensions of files that you commonly use, such as Word files or Excel files, but some extensions you will never need to recognize.

Some file types are very closely tied to the associated software and can be opened only from that application. Others are much broader and therefore recognized by many software programs. For example, in the graphics area, the file types *bmp* or *jpeg* can be opened using any variety of image editing software or browser software. On the other hand, a file created and saved using your new scrapbook software most likely can be opened only by that particular software.

The default My Computer view (the one that appears when you first open My Computer), is not likely to display file extensions along with the files.

To display file extensions:

1. Open My Computer, click Tools on the menu bar, and click Folder Options, as shown in Figure 4.6.
2. In the Folder Options window (Figure 4.7), click the View tab. Click to deselect the box next to *Hide extensions for known file types* (if a check mark appears).
3. Click OK to close the Folder Options dialog box.
4. Close My Computer.

To see how files appear when they are listed with the file extension:

1. Open My Computer.
2. Double-click the C: drive.
3. Double-click Documents and Settings.
4. Double-click Owner, or the icon listed with your name.
5. Double-click My Documents. Several files should appear, with extensions.
6. Close My Computer.

Figure 4.6 **You can display file extensions by changing the folder options.**

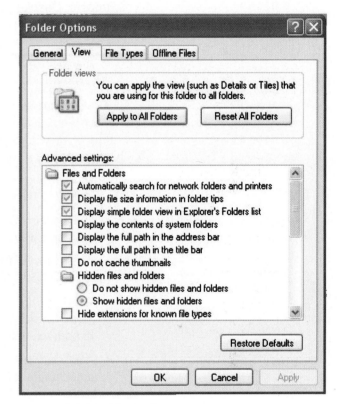

Figure 4.7 **The Folder Options dialog box allows you to change several file and folder settings.**

Maintaining Disks

Your hard disk holds not only your operating system, but all of your application software, as well. You might also save your data files there. Although most hard drives are sturdy and reliable, they will probably fail at some point if you keep your computer long enough. Just as you take a car in for routine maintenance to help it last longer, your hard disk requires some attention, too. There are several things that you can do to prolong the life of your hard disk.

The best way to fix problems is to prevent them from happening. Most disk problems are caused by software and can be corrected with software. Windows includes several disk maintenance utilities that you can work with to streamline the organization of the hard disk and to check for errors. As long as you perform those maintenance tasks regularly, you should avoid many problems.

Do not attempt any disk maintenance tasks on a public computer, as in a college or library lab. Those systems are most likely networked with security

In the
Know

One of the most frustrating problems for a computer user is dealing with a computer that is malfunctioning. Some glitches are a result of human error, but many times the problem is due to an environmental factor, such as dust buildup, static electricity, power surges, or excessive heat. Computer viruses are also a possible source of trouble. Despite your best intentions, sometimes a computer will just give you trouble. Fortunately, you can do the following things to lessen the possibility of having major problems.

- *Always use a surge protector. Never plug the computer directly into a wall outlet.*

- *Occasionally use compressed air to blow dust away from the keyboard and out of any obvious collection areas. Don't blow air directly into a disk drive, however, as it may cause dust to lodge in the drive.*

- *Don't place a computer in front of any direct heating or cooling source, and avoid placement beside water sources that might splash, including beside an open window.*

- *Leave room for a computer to "breathe," and don't back it directly against a wall. That might obstruct airflow to the vents.*

- *Avoid moving the computer excessively. If you have to move it, use extreme caution, as you can easily dislodge internal system components.*

- *Keep all original software, along with any documentation. You are legally allowed to make one backup copy of software as well, in case of software failure.*

- *Avoid saving files in the root folder. Keep all program and data files in appropriate folders. Make it a practice to save data files in folders separate from the application software. That way you are less likely to delete or overwrite program files.*

- *Keep a file of all documentation that came with your computer, including any warranty agreements.*

- *Keep backup copies of any data files that you can't afford to lose.*

- *Install a virus scan program and keep it current. Set the virus scan to scan for viruses automatically when the computer boots. Scan all downloaded files and e-mail attachments.*

privileges that will prevent you from modifying the hard disk. There are people employed to perform these maintenance tasks. The disk maintenance described here is intended for home computers only.

Using Disk Cleanup

It is all too easy to accumulate unnecessary files on your hard disk. The more bogged down a system is with files, the more slowly it might access those files for you. One thing that you can do to cut through the clutter is to run **Disk Cleanup** occasionally. Disk Cleanup calculates and displays the amount of space you can save by emptying the Recycle Bin (the temporary holding area for deleted files), deleting temporary Internet files, and possibly compressing old files. You can choose which of those deletions to allow, then let Disk Cleanup remove them from your system. There is no recommended interval of time to wait between cleanups, but if you are active on the Internet, thereby collecting a lot of temporary Internet files, you might run Disk Cleanup at least once a month.

To access Disk Cleanup:

1. Open My Computer.
2. Right-click the C: drive, and select Properties from the context menu.
3. Click the General tab, if it is not already selected, as shown in Figure 4.8.
4. Click Disk Cleanup (at the lower right corner of the Properties dialog box).
5. The utility calculates how much space can safely be cleared from your system. It might take several minutes to make that determination, particularly if you haven't performed this function in a long while. Select categories for deletion by clicking the check box beside each, as shown in Figure 4.9. Several categories will be selected by default (automatically). Unless you have some reason to want to retain files in any of those categories, accept the default settings and click OK.
6. Click Yes to confirm the deletion. The cleanup process might take a few minutes.
7. Click OK.
8. Close all open windows.

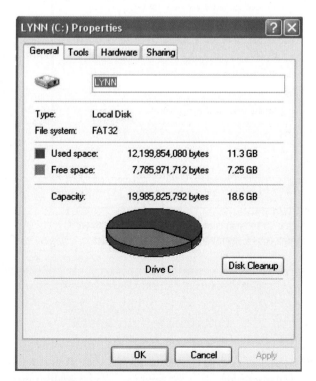

Figure 4.8 **The Disk Cleanup maintenance task helps keep your disk uncluttered.**

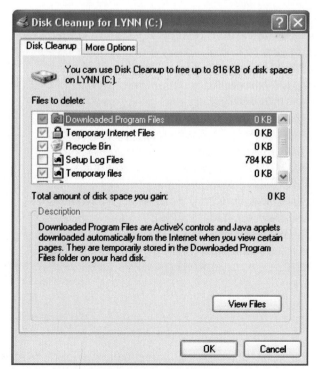

Figure 4.9 **You will usually want to accept Disk Cleanup's suggestions for file deletions.**

In the Know

When you delete a file, the file may appear to be removed, but the file actually remains on the disk until it is physically rewritten by other files. The file entry in the **file allocation table (FAT)** is removed so the computer no longer recognizes the file. The file allocation table is much like a book index, referencing files and their locations on disk. It is used by the operating system to retrieve files when you ask for them.

Although you might not mind the files remaining on your system until they're overwritten, you might think twice about it when you consider giving your computer to a charity and purchasing another. Do you really want your personal data, perhaps identifying tax numbers or credit card information, to be available to others who know how to retrieve such "deleted" items? Medical offices who keep patient information on a hard disk are legally bound to permanently remove data when the computer is taken from the office. All of this begs the question, how do I permanently delete data?

1. When you delete a file from the hard disk, it is placed in the Recycle Bin, which is simply a holding area on the hard disk. It remains there for a time in case you decide you made a mistake by deleting it and want to retrieve it. The Recycle Bin is set to occupy a certain percentage of your hard disk space. If that allotted space should ever become full of deleted files, some will automatically be removed permanently to make room for others. To keep files from making their way to the Recycle Bin when you delete them, first right-click the Recycle Bin at the Desktop. Select Properties. Click the Global tab. Click to place a check in the box that reads Do not move files to the Recycle Bin, as shown in Figure 4.10. Click OK. Now when you delete files, they'll be deleted immediately, not placed in the Recycle Bin.

2. You will need special software to permanently delete, or wipe, files from your hard disk. You might try Disk CleanUp 2000 or File Assurity. When the software asks how many times to overwrite the data, allow it to overwrite at least three times.

3. Because disks are magnetic, running a magnet over the surface should scramble the information as well, but don't try that on a hard disk unless you have no intention of using it again. The disk won't be destroyed, but all of the data will be a mess.

4. After the selected files are permanently deleted, you might want to go back to the Recycle Bin properties and remove the check mark beside Do not move files to the Recycle Bin so that in the future deleted files are placed in the Recycle Bin.

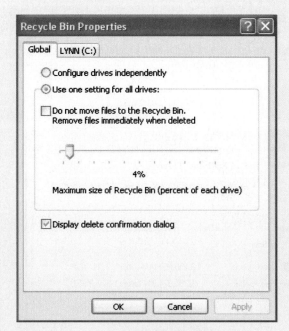

Figure 4.10 **You can customize the Recycle Bin to your preferences by modifying Recycle Bin properties.**

Routine Disk Maintenance

Some maintenance tasks should be scheduled so that you don't forget to perform them occasionally. You can use the Scheduled Task Wizard to automatically perform certain tasks. A couple of maintenance procedures—error checking and disk defragmentation—are too important to the health of your system to over-look.

Before beginning your exploration of maintenance utilities, be forewarned that the procedures might take an inordinate amount of time, so begin them only when you have plenty of time to let your computer work on its own. If you haven't defragmented your hard disk in quite some time, the defragmentation might take several hours, even overnight!

Error Checking

The Windows **Error Checking** utility examines a disk for data storage errors, from physical defects on the disk surface to weakened areas that might cause that space to be unreliable. An area that cannot be used due to a physical flaw is called a bad sector and is partitioned off by the error checker so that it is not available for data storage. Many identified errors can be corrected by the Error Checking utility before any data is lost. Be sure to check your disk for errors at least once every six months. Windows versions earlier than Windows XP use a utility called ScanDisk to check for disk errors.

To run Error Checking:

1. Open My Computer.
2. Right-click the C: drive, and select Properties from the context menu.
3. Click the Tools tab, as shown in Figure 4.11.
4. Click Check Now in the Error Checking box.
5. Click the check boxes beside Automatically fix file system errors and beside Scan for and attempt recovery of bad sectors.
6. Click Start. You will most likely see a message similar that shown in Figure 4.12, indicating that Windows needs exclusive access to the disk volume.
7. Click Yes if you want the error check to take place the next time you start Windows. If you don't see the message, the check will proceed, displaying a summary of any errors found. When the error check is complete, close all open windows.

Figure 4.11 **If you suspect a disk problem, you can run the Windows Error Checking utility to assess and possibly correct any disk errors.**

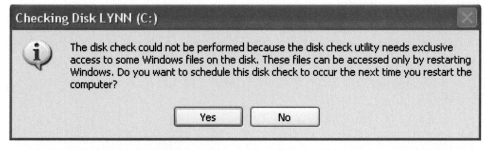

Figure 4.12 **This error message should not be alarming. It simply means that the computer must be restarted before the error check can proceed.**

Other Ways

Although some computer experts might argue that the only way to permanently remove all traces of a deleted file is to use specialized deletion software, you might be satisfied to send deleted files to the Recycle Bin and then empty the Recycle Bin. You can empty the Recycle Bin by right-clicking the Recycle Bin on the desktop and selecting Empty Recycle Bin. After the Recycle Bin is empty, run the disk defragmenter (covered in the next section of this chapter) to rearrange disk contents, effectively writing over the deleted files.

Disk Defragmenting

When you save a file on your hard disk, it seems as though the entire file is saved in one location. When you later call for the file, the operating system retrieves it and displays it on your screen as a single unit. However, in reality the file might be broken apart as it is being saved, with units clearly labeled and placed in areas called **sectors**. A disk is circular, with a series of concentric **tracks** on the surface. The disk is further divided into sectors, which in theory are shaped like pieces of pie on the disk surface. When a file is saved, the operating system notes the location of its pieces by track and sector numbers. If a file is not saved in one unit but instead separated into a series of sectors, it is said to be **fragmented**. A file is separated into pieces (fragmented) by the operating system as it attempts to fill every available disk area, no matter how small. When you call for the file later, the operating system just puts the pieces back together to display on-screen, although the file actually remains in pieces on the disk.

The problem with fragmented files comes later, when the fragmentation is so severe that the amount of time it takes for your computer to retrieve and display a file (**access time**) is bothersome. Another problem with fragmentation is that the operating system might not even be able to find enough large spaces in which to place a file. If a disk becomes too fragmented, it might fail completely. Although fragmentation can occur on other disk media, the hard disk is particularly vulnerable due to its large size and intense activity. If you periodically defragment your hard disk, at least twice a year, you should not experience any major fragmentation problems.

Defragmenting a hard disk is also called optimizing. When you optimize a disk, you rearrange the files so that the various portions of a file are placed closer together. The access time is reduced so that the file appears more quickly when you call for it. It is not unusual to see a disk operate up to five times faster than it did before you optimized it.

Although optimizing software packages, such as SpinRite (from Gibson Research) and Speedisk (from Symantec), are available, you can also use Windows' built-in disk defragmenter. Be certain to allow plenty of time for the defragmenting process; it might take several hours if you have not optimized your hard disk lately. Also, make sure that all programs and windows are closed before defragmenting.

To run Disk Defragmenter:

1. Open My Computer.
2. Right-click the C: drive, and select Properties from the context menu.
3. Click the Tools tab, as shown in Figure 4.11.
4. Click Defragment Now in the Disk Defragmenter area.
5. Click Defragment, as shown in Figure 4.13. The process may take several minutes or hours.
6. Click OK.
7. Close all open windows.

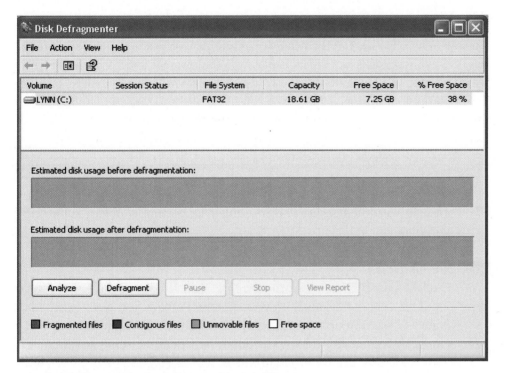

Figure 4.13 **Defragmenting a hard disk can take several hours.**

In the Know

Some programs are configured to start when your system is booted. Those programs might include your antivirus program or your firewall (software that prevents unauthorized access from the Internet). Defragmenting your hard disk might go a little faster if all background programs are closed. To check on what background programs are running, click Start, Run and type **msconfig** in the text box. Click OK. Click the Startup tab. All background programs are listed. Click the check box beside any that you want to close, or just click Disable All. For purposes of defragmentation, it should be safe to close all background programs. Click OK. Click Restart.

After the computer restarts and you log on, you will see a System Configuration Utility message, letting you know that your startup settings have been changed. Click OK. Click Cancel to remove the dialog box. Defragment the hard disk. When defragmentation is complete, you should enable all background programs. Click Start, Run, and type **msconfig** in the text box. Click OK. Click the Startup tab. Click Enable All. Click OK. Click Restart.

The Scheduled Task Wizard

You are now fully aware of the necessity of routine disk maintenance, but it is still easy to let those tasks slip by. Fortunately, Windows XP and earlier versions of Windows include an automated process whereby you can schedule tasks to occur without your involvement. You can fit the tasks to your schedule, but you should know that your computer must be on at the time the tasks are scheduled. Windows XP calls the automated scheduler the **Scheduled Task Wizard**.

To use the Scheduled Task Wizard:

1. Click Start. Click All Programs. Click Accessories. Click System Tools. Click Scheduled Tasks. The Scheduled Task window opens, as shown in Figure 4.14.
2. Double-click Add Scheduled Tasks.
3. Click Next.
4. Select a maintenance task to schedule. Your choices include the system utilities that are installed on your system. Perhaps you want to schedule a Disk Cleanup to run weekly. Scroll down in the Application window by repeatedly clicking the downward-pointing scroll arrow. Watch for the Disk Cleanup program title to appear (Figure 4.15).
5. Click Disk Cleanup.
6. Click Next.

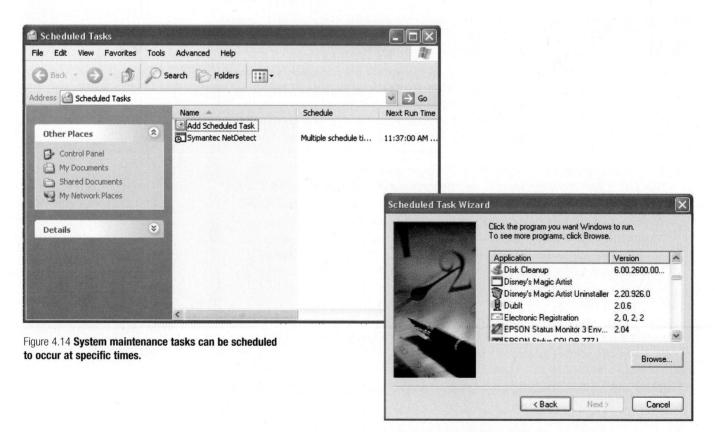

Figure 4.14 **System maintenance tasks can be scheduled to occur at specific times.**

Figure 4.15 **The Scheduled Task Wizard guides you through scheduling automated tasks.**

7. Click the option button beside Weekly. Tasks can be scheduled to run daily, weekly, monthly, or at a specific time, such as when the computer is booted.

8. Type a name for the task.

9. Select a run schedule for the tasks.

10. Click Next, and select a date and time to run the scheduled task. If you are working on a password-protected computer system, you will have to enter your password as well. Click Next.

11. Depending on when you scheduled the task to run, you might see another dialog box. Respond to it, and click Finish.

12. Close any open windows.

Backing Up (Copying Files)

In the blink of an eye, a disk can fail, causing you to lose all the programs and data stored there. Although this doesn't often happen, the fact that it could should be enough to convince you to make copies of important files. It would be easy to blame all computer problems on a malfunctioning computer, but the truth is that it is easy to get in a hurry and make simple mistakes that have major consequences, like deleting an entire folder and then emptying the Recycle Bin. When these mistakes happen, there is no one to blame but the computer operator! Your best bet is to keep a backup of your important data. A **backup** is simply a copy of one or more files. A backup can be as complete as copying your entire hard disk or as simple as making a copy of a few key data files.

When you install software, a copy is placed on the hard disk, so you can place the original software CD in a cabinet for safekeeping. With that in mind, losing application software from your hard disk is not usually disastrous, because you can reinstall it from the original CD. Data files are another matter. Data files are those projects that you personally create, such as the letters you have typed or your stock portfolio worksheet. If you don't have a copy of those items and the disk on which they are stored fails, they will most likely be gone forever. You can easily back up individual files and folders from the hard disk by copying them to a CD, Zip disk, or floppy disk. This chapter introduces a quick way to copy files from a hard disk to a CD.

When you make a copy of the entire hard disk, everything is copied, including the operating system, all application software, and all data files. The only problem with a complete disk backup is having a storage medium on hand that is large enough to hold the entire backup. You might consider a tape backup unit, available at office-supply stores, or purchasing a second hard drive. Although Windows XP includes a Backup utility, you can buy software like PowerQuest's Drive Image or Stomp's BackUp My PC, both of which include additional features, like the capability to save files across multiple CDs.

In a perfect world, you would learn to back up your hard disk and do so often. However, the fact is that you are more likely to be concerned with maintaining copies of your personal projects and pictures. In that case, you will want to focus more on learning to copy files to CDs and other media.

▣▶Quick Tip

Instead of indicating a specific day of the week and hour of the day for a scheduled task to occur, you can set the task to run when the computer is idle. After a task has been scheduled, it will appear in the Scheduled Task List. To set the task to run when the computer is idle, right-click the task and click Properties. Click the Settings tab. In the Idle Time area, select *Only start the task if the computer has been idle for at least.* Enter the length of time (in minutes) for which the computer must be idle before the task will run.

In the
Know
You might have noticed that a CD is often referred to as a disc, whereas a hard disk or floppy disk is spelled disk. Why the difference? Although you might sometimes note the different spellings, most software documentation settles on the single term "disk." However, to be technical about it, the word disk refers to magnetic storage media, such as hard disks, Zip disks, and floppy disks. Discs are optical media like CDs and DVDs. A probable reason for the distinction is that the CD was invented by Philips, a European company—hence the British spelling disc, whereas the hard disk was invented by IBM, an American company. Another possibility is that the CD evolved from the music industry, which typically uses the spelling disc to refer to CDs or albums.

Copying Files to a CD-R or CD-RW

As most new computers are equipped with a CD-R or CD-RW drive, you might find that copying files to a CD is an easy way to make sure you have backups of important files. The CD is becoming the medium of choice, given its low cost and high capacity. The minimum capacity of a CD is 650 MB. Copying to a DVD is a viable option as well, but most home computers do not come with a recordable DVD drive. So we will focus on the more common recordable CD technology. Windows XP includes a handy feature that allows you to easily copy files to a CD.

Just because your computer includes a CD drive does not necessarily mean that you can record CDs. A recordable CD drive works with either CD-R discs or CD-RW discs. The difference between the two is that a CD-R drive allows you to record only once. It is ideal for recording music CDs and for maintaining archival records (those that don't change). A CD-RW drive is more versatile, in that you can record to the CD any number of times, deleting at will and rerecording. Older computer models include a CD-ROM, which allows you to read CDs but not to record to them.

Before recording to a CD, consider these things:

- First, make sure that you have enough hard disk space to hold a temporary copy of all files to be copied. Windows might reserve up to 1 GB of space to hold files waiting to be copied.

- Be sure you have the correct disc for the job. A CD-R drive will only record to CD-R discs. When you purchase a package of CDs, you will need to be sure the label reads "CD-R" if you have a CD-R drive. A CD-RW drive will record to both CD-Rs and CD-RWs.

- You cannot copy more files to the CD than what it can hold. If your CD capacity is 650 MB, the files that you are copying cannot require more than 650 MB. Check the label on your container of CDs to determine their capacity.

- Consider running Disk Defragmenter and checking your hard disk for errors before recording CDs. Those operations assure that the hard disk is optimized and prepared to assist with the recording operation.

To copy files and folders to a CD:

1. Insert a blank recordable CD into the CD drive.
2. Open My Computer.
3. Browse to find the files that you want to copy. For example, suppose that you saved all of your digital photographs from a recent vacation in a folder on the hard disk labeled "Spring Break." The folder is one level removed from the root folder, with the path C:\Spring Break. To locate the pictures, double-click the C: drive icon. Click the Spring Break folder *once* to select it (Figure 4.16).
4. Check for File and Folder Tasks in the left screen area. If you see the heading, but no detail beneath it, click the words *File and Folder Tasks*. Under File and Folder Tasks, click Copy this Folder.
5. In the Copy Items dialog box, click the CD recording drive (usually the D: drive), and then click Copy.
6. At the My Computer window, respond to the prompt directing you to click a system tray icon to display all files to be copied. Windows displays a screen showing files that are waiting to be written to the CD. Confirm that the folder or files that you want to copy appear under *Files Ready to be Written to the CD* (Figure 4.17).

▮▶Quick Tip

When Windows finishes recording to a CD, it automatically opens, or ejects, the CD drive. You might prefer that the drive remain closed. To prevent the automatic eject, open My Computer. Right-click the CD drive, and select Properties. Click the Recording tab. Click to deselect *Automatically eject the CD after writing.*

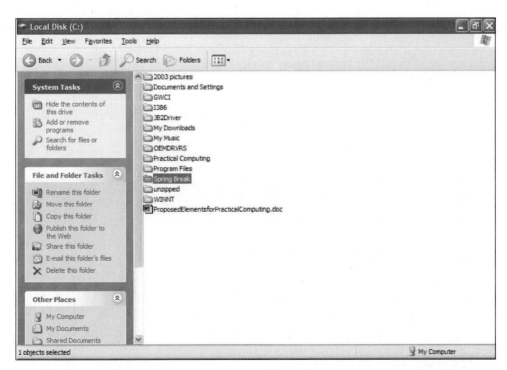

Figure 4.16 **You must select the folder or files to be copied to a CD.**

7. If there is no detail beneath CD Writing Tasks, found in the left pane, click the heading. Under CD Writing Tasks, click *Write these files* to *CD*.

8. The CD Writing Wizard will begin. Follow all instructions in the wizard.

9. When the wizard completes the task, it will display a check box allowing you to create another CD of the same folder. If you do want to make another copy, click Yes to write these files to another CD. Insert another recordable CD, and follow wizard instructions. Otherwise, click Finish, and remove the CD from the drive, labeling it appropriately.

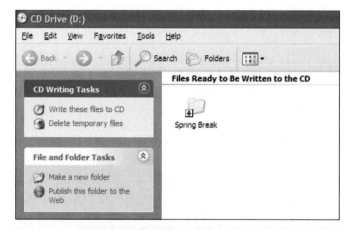

Figure 4.17 **Files are held temporarily until you confirm that they should be written to the CD.**

To view the CD to be sure files were copied:

1. Close all open windows. Close the CD drawer if it popped open after copying files.

2. In a few seconds, all copied files and folders should display, as shown in Figure 4.18. If they don't appear, open My Computer and double-click the CD drive icon.

3. Verify that the files or folders are there, and then close all open windows.

Figure 4.18 **Using My Computer, you can view all files and folders stored on a CD.**

In the Know

Although the floppy disk will most likely become obsolete in a few years, your computer probably still includes a floppy disk drive. It is true that the floppy disk is extremely limited in storage capacity, but it is still a good choice for backing up small files or for transporting files from place to place. Suppose that you have just saved a computer class assignment to a floppy disk. You are required to submit the disk to your instructor but don't want to give up your only copy in case you need to refer to it later. Here are the steps you would follow to make a copy of the floppy disk:

1. *Place the original floppy disk in the A: drive. That disk is your source disk.*
2. *Have another disk handy to act as the target, or destination, disk. The target disk will receive the copied information.*
3. *Open My Computer.*
4. *Click the A: drive icon once. Don't double-click it because that will open the disk drive window, when all that you want to do is select it.*
5. *Click File in the menu bar.*
6. *Click Copy Disk (Figure 4.19).*
7. *A dialog box appears, suggesting that the copy take place from one 3¹/₂" disk (floppy disk) to another. Click Start, and then click OK.*

8. *The copy begins with a message letting you know the source disk is being read. A progress indicator displays the status of the read process.*
9. *Activity stops and you are prompted to place the target disk in the drive (Figure 4.20). Replace the source disk with the target disk.*
10. *Click OK.*
11. *Activity begins again, with the progress indicator moving across the bar. When the copy is complete, click OK.*
12. *Be sure to label the new disk appropriately and place it in a safe place for later retrieval.*

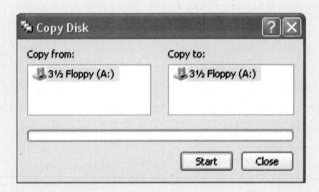

Figure 4.19 **Contents of a floppy disk can be copied onto another floppy disk.**

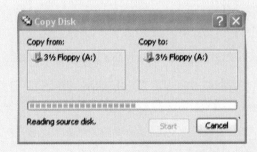

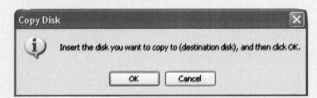

Figure 4.20 **You will be prompted to replace the source disk with the target disk.**

Chapter Summary

DON'T FORGET

- A file is an item that you create and name. A folder is a holding area for files on a disk.

- Files that make up a software application are called program files. Files that you create are often called data files.

- Using My Computer, you can view the contents of disk devices, checking for available disk space.

- Disk Cleanup is a utility that removes temporary and Recycle Bin files from your computer, clearing up disk space.

- Routine disk maintenance tasks include checking a disk for errors and defragmenting a disk.

- The Scheduled Task Manager allows you to automate certain disk maintenance procedures.

- It is imperative that you routinely back up (copy) files that you cannot afford to lose.

- Using Windows XP, you can easily copy files from the hard disk to a CD.

- To copy files to a CD, you must have either a CD-R or CD-RW disc drive.

KEY TERMS

A: drive	error checking	path
access time	executable files	program files
backup	extension	root folder
C: drive	file	Scheduled Task Wizard
D: drive	file allocation table (FAT)	sector
data files	folder	track
disk cleanup	fragmented	

TRUE/FALSE

Circle **T** if the statement is true or **F** if the statement is false.

T F   1. Data files can only be saved on a CD.

T F   2. Using the Scheduled Task Wizard, you can designate a time when disk cleanup will occur.

T F   3. Disk Cleanup checks a disk for errors.

T F   4. Sectors are concentric circles on the surface of a disk.

T F   5. The purpose of a file is to hold folders.

T F   6. If a disk is severely fragmented, it could become inaccessible.

T F   7. Another name for a program file is an executable file.

T F   8. Fragmentation can only occur on hard disks.

T F   9. If you plan to record data to a CD, you must have either a CD-R or a CD-RW drive.

T F   10. The My Computer feature allows you to check for available disk space.

MULTIPLE CHOICE

Circle the correct choice for each of the following.

1. Which of the following removes unnecessary temporary files from your system?
   a. Auto Arrange
   b. Disk Cleanup
   c. Disk Defragmenter
   d. Backup

2. Which of the following is a true statement?
   a. A CD-R drive can record to both CD-R and CD-RW discs.
   b. A CD-RW can be recorded to only once, but read from many times.
   c. A CD-R can only be read from—you cannot record to a CD-R.
   d. A CD-RW drive can record to both CD-R and CD-RW discs.

3. The disk utility that rearranges a disk so that pieces of files are placed as close together as possible is the
   a. Disk Defragmenter
   b. Disk Cleanup
   c. Disk Scanner
   d. Disk Reorganizer

4. The identifier that is automatically assigned to a filename when the file is saved, associating it with the software program that created it, is the
   a. identifier
   b. file group
   c. extension
   d. suffix

5. Which of the following is not an item in the View menu of My Computer?
   a. toolbars
   b. thumbnails
   c. details
   d. edit

6. In Windows XP, My Computer is found
   a. as an item on the Start menu
   b. as a program on the Program List
   c. on the Taskbar
   d. in the Quick Launch toolbar

7. The route followed to move along the hierarchical structure from the root folder to a destination folder is called the
   a. path
   b. route
   c. trail
   d. progression

8. Before recording to a CD, you should
   a. run Disk Cleanup
   b. clean the CD with a soft clean cloth
   c. make sure you have enough space on the CD for temporary files
   d. check to be sure the CD capacity is large enough for the files to be saved

9. The item that keeps up with where files are saved, acting much like a book index, is called the
   a. path
   b. disk index
   c. root folder
   d. file allocation table

10. Most disk problems are caused by
    a. software
    b. hardware
    c. human error
    d. computer malfunction

PRACTICAL PROJECTS

1. Be a Designer

In working with a computer, you will occasionally want to create one or more folders to better organize your projects. One way to do that is simply to plan the structure by drawing it before you begin to create the folders on a disk. Such a drawing is called a tree structure, because it looks like an upside-down tree. The root is the disk itself, with each additional level branching out below.

For this project, assume that you are using your computer primarily for word processing and have accepted several volunteer assignments. You plan to work with your church in preparing the weekly newsletter and church program, as well as designing all mail correspondence and other documents for Vacation Bible School. In addition, you are organizing a family reunion and will be producing several documents for it. You are enrolled in college this semester and are taking two computer courses: Introduction to Computers and Microcomputer Applications. Each class will require reports and other assignments, so you would like to place them on your disk where you can quickly find them.

Draw a hierarchy of folders, beginning with the root (assume that you are using the C: drive to save your projects). Develop as much structure as you think necessary to best organize your work. Remember a folder is simply a holding area for projects, not the projects themselves. Your structure should show only folders, not files.

2. Putting the Pieces Together

You know that file fragmentation is a common occurrence, but one that can lead to computer slowdown or even bigger disk problems. Write a few paragraphs describing what file fragmentation is, why it occurs, and what you can do to minimize any related problems. Use the Windows Help and Support area to find additional information. Include at least one graphic to support your summary. Along with your description, include some information about how you can tell that a disk is becoming badly fragmented.

3. Backing Up

Every organization should have a backup strategy to prevent loss of computer data. Perhaps every home should, too. Although you might not be running a multimillion dollar corporation, it can still be devastating to lose projects, pictures, and documents that you have worked on for days. Develop a personal backup strategy for your home computer. Keep in mind the types of data that you plan to work with, as well as where you will save your work—to a CD or DVD, the hard disk, or floppy disks. You might investigate the Windows Help and Support section, along with computer periodicals. Your plan should be detailed enough to provide specific directions on how to back up, what to back up, and how often to back up, and should be understandable by anyone, even a computer novice.

4. Look It Up

You can use the Windows Help and Support feature to obtain additional information on just about any Windows topic imaginable. Select a topic from the following list, and write a few paragraphs, giving specific examples and directions that would explain the concept to a beginner.

- Managing Power Options to Conserve Battery Life of Portable Computers
- How to Use Help and Support Features (Be specific about how to conduct searches, what features are available, and how a beginner could seek assistance.)
- Using Windows Media Player (a general overview of the program and how it interacts with CDs)
- How to Modify the Windows XP Interface (how to make it appear more like Windows 98 and Windows 2002)

Figure 4.21 **All files are identified by a file type.**

5. It's All in the Name (And the Icon)

As you learn to work with the My Computer feature, you will become comfortable with identifying files and folders. You will also understand how to list them with varying levels of detail and to recognize at least a few of the more commonly used file types.

a. Study the screen shot shown in Figure 4.21. Which items are folders? Which are files? Of the files, which are Word files? Take a guess as to which files are picture files. Sometimes file types and icons are self-explanatory, and sometimes they are not.

b. Open My Computer. Open the window representing C:\Documents and Settings\your name (or owner)\My Documents. You have just followed a path to display folder contents. Change the view to Details. Print the screen by pressing the PrtSc key found on the keyboard. Now change the view to Tiles, and print the screen again.

CHAPTER 5

Working with Files and Folders

Y ou can use folders to organize your records or files so that you can find them easily. Depending on the level of detail desired, folders can include subfolders at several levels of depth. Throughout this chapter, we will build an organization of folders for a fictitious rental property. Suppose that Jennifer has a folder on her computer related to rental records for properties that she rents to others. Within that folder, she has another folder with records of her lake home rental. An additional folder at the same level might include records pertaining to a mountain home rental. One or more levels of subfolders are possible, as diagrammed in Figure 5.1, organizing records of a certain topic at any level of detail. Although many folders are created automatically upon installation of software, you can work extensively with your own folders, creating, deleting, moving, and renaming them at will.

In this chapter, you will learn to work with **Windows Explorer**, which is a Windows feature that allows you to view and manage all the folders on

Objectives

When you complete this chapter, you will:

- **Understand how to view folders and files using Windows Explorer.**

- **Be able to expand and collapse folder views.**

- **Be able to create folders.**

- **Understand how to delete and rename files and folders.**

- **Be able to create a file and save it to a selected folder.**

- **Be able to select multiple files and folders.**

- **Be able to delete folders and files.**

- **Understand how to use the Recycle Bin.**

- **Understand how to find a file stored on a disk medium.**

your system. In one window, you can see the contents of all disks and expand folders to show any level of detail. Because Windows Explorer makes it easy to copy files from one disk to another or from one folder to another, it is a handy tool for making back-up copies. Using Windows Explorer, you can also move, delete, rename, and open files.

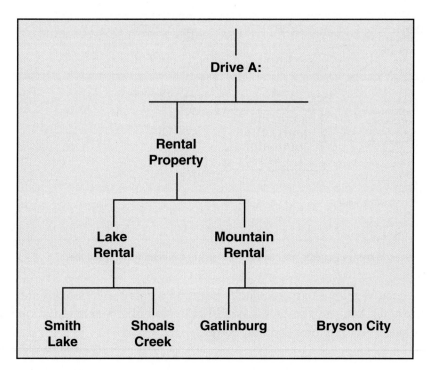

Figure 5.1 **Folders can be arranged according to purpose.**

Introducing Windows Explorer

To view folders and files, you can use either Windows Explorer or My Computer, both of which come with a typical Windows installation. This chapter introduces Windows Explorer, which, although similar to My Computer, provides a slightly different interface and method of displaying files and folders. The My Computer interface—that you worked with in Chapter 4—opens only one disk drive or folder at a time, displaying the contents. On the other hand, Windows Explorer displays more information at one time, showing all disk devices and folders, allowing you to move quickly from one folder to another. Figure 5.2 shows a typical Windows Explorer screen.

The Windows Explorer display is arranged into two distinct panes, a **folders pane** on the left and a **contents pane** on the right. The folders pane shows drives, folders, and other resources on your system. When you select a folder in the folders pane by clicking the folder title, its contents will appear to the right, including all subfolders and files. A folder icon identifies the item as a folder, whereas a file includes an icon related to the program used to create the file. Be aware that *files* do not appear in the *folders* pane, they only appear on the contents

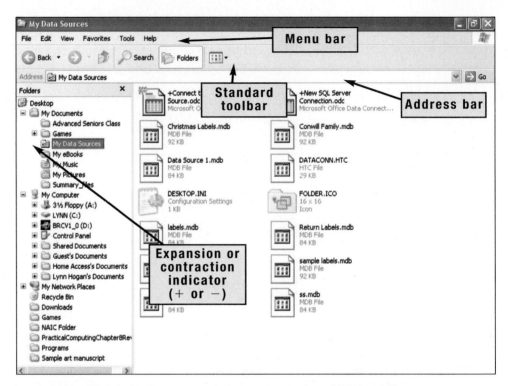

Figure 5.2 **Using Windows Explorer you can view computer resources, folders, and files.**

side. To open Windows Explorer, click Start, All Programs, Accessories, and Windows Explorer. You can also access Windows Explorer by opening My Computer and clicking View, Explorer Bar, and Folders.

✓ SANITY CHECK

Your view of Windows Explorer might show a tasks pane on the left instead of a folders pane. The tasks pane includes selections that are related to the item selected. For example, if the currently selected folder is *My Documents,* the tasks pane would include options to make a new folder, publish the folder to the Web, or to share the folder with others. Other options would appear if the selected item were a disk drive instead of a folder. You can easily toggle between the two views by clicking the Folders button on the Standard toolbar. If you don't see a Standard toolbar, click View, Toolbars, and click to bring the Standard toolbar into view.

Note that many items have a plus sign (+) before the title. Some might instead have a minus sign (−). The plus sign is an indicator that the item has additional folders beneath it in the folder structure. Click the "+" to expand the detail to another level. If any folders at the newly displayed level contain **subfolders**, you will see another "+" beside each of them, which you can click to display their contents. You will see that as each folder level is expanded the display is indented, so that you can easily determine which folders are on the same level and which are actually subfolders of others. After a folder is fully expanded, a minus sign (−) will appear to its left. Clicking a minus sign removes the folder level from the display. Please note that expanding and contracting folders affects only your view of the folder structure, not the physical arrangement of folders on the disk.

A menu bar appears at the top of the Windows Explorer window, with one or more toolbars underneath. The screen in Figure 5.2 shows a menu bar, standard toolbar, and an address bar. The *menu bar* might look familiar to you. This is because it contains many of the same features that you saw when you worked with My Computer in the last chapter. Each menu selection contains options that allow you to manage folders and files. The contents of the *File* menu vary, depending upon the item selected in the folders pane. The *Edit* menu contains many features for working with files and folders; however, you might find that many of the actions are easier to accomplish using a drag-and-drop method or the keyboard shortcuts that we will discuss later in this chapter. The *View* menu is identical to that of My Computer, which was described in Chapter 4. The *Favorites* menu provides a place to keep track of your favorite places to visit on the Internet. With the exception of Folder Options, you probably won't use many of the choices found on the *Tools* menu. As you learned in the last chapter, the Folder Options feature allows you to hide or display file extensions. As always, the *Help* menu can answer many of your questions and provide assistance with understanding the Windows Explorer interface.

The *Standard toolbar,* as displayed in Figure 5.2, offers shortcuts for several of the more common menu selections. As you learned in the preceding chapter, the *Back* button and the *Forward* button allow you to return to previously visited views. The *Up* button displays the folder that is positioned immediately above the current folder in the folder hierarchy. *Search* is a handy tool that helps you find files and folders if you can provide some sort of identifying information, such as when the file was created or some of the text that is included in the file. The *Folders* button toggles the left pane from tasks to folders. The *Views* button, which appears as a square icon, provides a quick way to change the way the screen icons are displayed.

The *Address bar* (Figure 5.2) not only displays the currently selected device or folder, but it also allows you to select another folder to view. You can click the drop-down arrow to the right of the address bar to make another selection. However, you will probably find that you prefer to make your folder selections by working within the folders pane. The most common use of the address bar is for a quick confirmation of the current folder.

The *Status bar* appears at the base of the Windows Explorer window, just above the taskbar. If it is not displayed, you can click View, Status Bar. The status bar gives information related to the selected folder, disk drive, or computer resource, such as how many objects are in the folder, how much space the folder requires, and how much free space remains on the disk.

> **▣▶Quick Tip**
>
> You might have noticed that the desktop appears in the folders pane of Windows Explorer. Although you might not have thought of the desktop as a folder, it actually is a folder on your hard disk, just like any other. It is located at the top of the folder listing and contains files, folders, and shortcuts. It is a good place to temporarily store e-mail attachments and newly downloaded files from the Internet so that you can easily find them later.

✓SANITY CHECK

Planning to check the contents of a particular folder, you might click the folder in the folders pane of Windows Explorer and see that nothing appears to happen to the right pane (contents side); the contents don't reflect what you thought was contained in the selected folder. What went wrong? You probably clicked the "+" or "−" displayed to the immediate left of the folder name instead of clicking on the name itself. In doing that, you expanded or contracted the folder view but made no change in the selection of the current folder. Be sure to click the name of any folder if you want to make it the current folder and check its contents.

Creating Folders

Creating folders is a simple process, but one that can become frustrating if you are not careful about the placement of those folders. If you don't notice or specify the location of the folder, it can become lost in a hurry. It will be housed somewhere on your system, but probably not at all where you intended it to be. This is one of those occasions when you should take your time and not rush through the process.

Let's explore how this works in real life. Assume that Jennifer, from our fictitious rental company, plans to organize her rental records. She plans to have a major folder, labeled *Rental Property*. Beneath that, she wants two additional folders, both at the same level, labeled *Mountain Rental* and *Lake Rental*. See Figure 5.1 for a diagram of the folder arrangement. By using Windows Explorer, she can create her folder structure and then begin to place rental records where they belong.

Before creating any folder structure, it is imperative that she correctly select the drive or folder under which the new folder is to appear. If the selection is not correct, the folder will be created, but it will not be placed in the intended location in her folder structure. For example, if she intends to create a folder on the floppy disk, but the currently selected disk drive is the C: drive, the folder that

Hands On

Activity 5.1—Creating Folders

In this activity, you will create new folders on a disk in the A: drive. You should have a blank floppy disk. Your computer should display the desktop.

1. Place the disk in the A: drive.
2. You plan to store dessert recipes on the disk and want to create a folder structure so that you can arrange the recipes. You will create a folder called Desserts, with two folders housed within it—Cakes and Pies. Open Windows Explorer, if it is not already open.
3. Begin your work in the folders pane (left side). Expand My Computer, if necessary, by clicking "+." Figure 5.3 illustrates a folders pane in which My Computer needs to be expanded.
4. Click 3½" Floppy (A:). Be sure to click the drive name, not the "+" to the side. If you don't see the A: drive listed in the folders pane, you might need to shift the listing up or down using the scroll bars. To shift the listings, click and drag the scroll box (found in the scroll area to the

Figure 5.3 **My Computer must be expanded to show more detail.**

right) or click the scroll up or down arrow repeatedly. Your screen should look like that shown in Figure 5.4.

she creates will be placed on the C: drive, and she may have a difficult time finding it later. If she wants to create the rental folders on the A: drive, she must click to select 3½" Floppy A. To create and name a folder, she must click File, New, Folder and type a name for the folder, perhaps *Rental Property*. Other folders are created in the same manner, with the only difference being the selection of the folder under which a new folder is to appear. Because the *Mountain Rental* folder is to appear as a subfolder of *Rental Property,* Jennifer must click to select *Rental Property* before creating the new folder.

✓ SANITY CHECK

During the process of creating a new folder, you might find that, instead of allowing you to type a new folder name, Windows simply names the folder *New Folder* and then deselects it. What happened? Before you typed the folder name, you probably clicked in the folder name area or pressed ↵Enter. By doing so, you accepted the suggested name. To correct the mistake, click the *New Folder* icon to select it. Click File, Rename. Without clicking anywhere, type the folder name as you would like it to appear. Press ↵Enter. The folder is renamed appropriately.

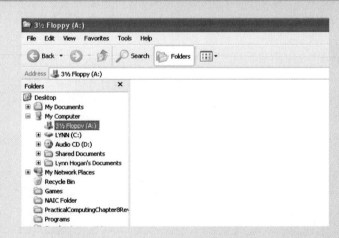

Figure 5.4 **If the contents pane is empty, there are no files or folders in the selected area.**

5. Click File, New, and Folder. *Without clicking anywhere*, type the new folder name— **Desserts**. Press ↵Enter.
6. Now, you will create a subfolder of *Desserts*, called *Cakes*. Click the "+" to the side of 3½" Floppy (A:) (in the folders pane) to expand the view. Remember that before creating a folder, you must select the folder or disk under which

the new folder is to appear. With that in mind, click the *Desserts* folder (in the left pane) to select it. Click File, New, and Folder. Type **Cakes** and press ↵Enter.

7. Check the address bar to make sure *Desserts* is still selected. Click File, New, and Folder. Type **Pies** and press ↵Enter.
8. Expand the Desserts folder by clicking the "+" to the left. Do you see two folders underneath, each indented equally, as shown in Figure 5.5?
9. Close Windows Explorer.

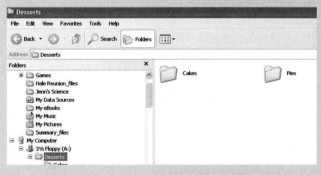

Figure 5.5 **Folders that are indented equally are on the same level.**

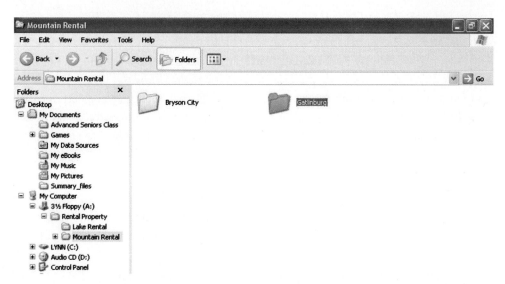

Figure 5.6 **A folder structure containing several levels of subfolders can easily be managed in Windows Explorer.**

Now let's take the case one step further. Suppose that Jennifer actually has two pieces of mountain property, one in Bryson City and one in Gatlinburg. She will need two folders within the *Mountain Rental* folder to hold records pertaining to both properties. She would first select the *Mountain Rental* folder and then create a folder for *Bryson City*. Similarly, she would select the *Mountain Rental* folder and create the *Gatlinburg* folder. Her final folder structure is shown in Figure 5.6.

✓ SANITY CHECK

What do you do if you find that you placed a folder in the wrong place? Perhaps a folder that should be at the same level with another one appears as a subfolder. You can simply click and drag the folder to the intended location. An alternative solution is to delete the subfolder and then recreate it in the right place. Be aware, though, that when you delete a folder, the folder is deleted *along with any files housed within it*. Be sure to check the contents of a folder that you are considering deleting to be sure that it doesn't contain files you don't want to delete. Click to select the subfolder that is incorrectly placed, and press (Del). Respond affirmatively when asked if you want the deletion to proceed. Click to select the folder under which the subfolder should have appeared. Click File, New, Folder. Type the folder name and press (↵Enter). The folder appears correctly in the folder structure.

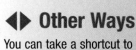 **Other Ways**

You can take a shortcut to renaming folders. Right-click the folder you want to rename. You must be sure that the mouse pointer is positioned directly on the folder name before right-clicking. From the subsequent context menu, click Rename. Type the new folder name, and press (↵Enter).

Renaming Folders

Folders can easily be renamed by using Windows Explorer. To rename a folder, you must first select the folder. One of the easiest mistakes to make is to be in a hurry and have the wrong item selected before you make changes, so take your time! Perhaps Jennifer prefers the name *Alabama Lake Rental* for her lake rental folder. She can easily rename the folder with just a few steps. After selecting the folder to be renamed, she would click File, Rename, type the new name, and

Hands On

Activity 5.2—Renaming Folders

In this activity, you will rename a folder. Place the same disk that you used for Activity 5.1 in the A: drive, if necessary. Your computer should display either Windows Explorer or the desktop.

1. You decide to include only one group of cake recipes—pound cakes. Therefore, you want to rename the *Cakes* folder to *Pound Cakes*. Open Windows Explorer if it is not already open.
2. Expand My Computer, if necessary, by clicking the "+." Expand 3½" Floppy (A:). Click the *Desserts* folder to select it (in the left pane).
3. To the right, you should see the two folders that you created in Activity 5.1—*Cakes* and *Pies*. Click *Cakes* to select it. *Cakes* should be shaded.
4. Click File, Rename. Type **Pound Cakes** and press ⏎Enter. You should now see two folders in the right pane—*Pies* and *Pound Cakes,* as shown in Figure 5.7.
5. Close Windows Explorer.

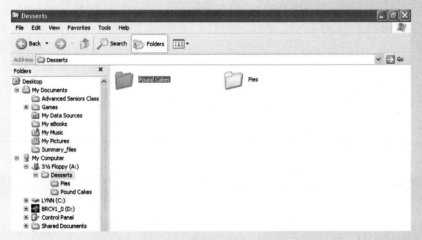

Figure 5.7 **A folder displays its new name immediately after you rename it.**

press ⏎Enter. When selecting a folder, be careful to click only once. A double-click *opens* the folder instead of merely *selecting* it.

After you have selected a folder and clicked File, Rename, the folder name should be shaded. With the name shaded, you can simply type a new folder name, without deleting any of the existing characters. If, on the other hand, the name is not shaded, but a cursor (small black bar) appears in the name, you will have to delete the existing characters before typing a new name. Pressing Del removes characters to the right of the cursor (blinking bar), whereas pressing ⬅Backspace removes characters to the left of the cursor.

Creating Files

Files are created using application programs. You might create a brochure using Microsoft Word, or you could use Microsoft Excel to create a spreadsheet showing household expenses. Working with Windows Explorer, you can create folders, but you cannot create files.

Assume that Jennifer wants to create a list of household furnishings for the Gatlinburg rental property. She already has a folder titled *Gatlinburg,* but the folder contains no files. Folders serve one purpose, that of providing a holding area for files. So all files (documents, spreadsheets, and so on) pertaining to the Gatlinburg rental should be placed in that folder. She will use Microsoft Word to create the list of furnishings. Word is usually found on the All Programs list (from the Start menu). Jennifer's furnishings list might appear something like Figure 5.8.

To save the document to a disk, she would click File, Save As. A dialog box similar to that shown in Figure 5.9 appears. There are two areas of concern on the dialog box—the save location and the filename. The save location is the

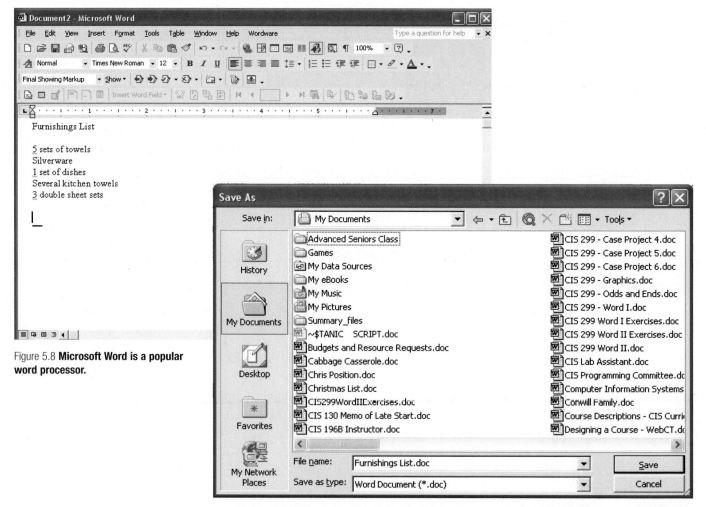

Figure 5.8 **Microsoft Word is a popular word processor.**

Figure 5.9 **When saving a file, you should note the save location as well as the filename.**

drive and folder in which the document should be placed. It is shown in the white box beside "Save In." Most applications indicate the *My Documents* folder as the suggested save location, but in this case, she plans to save this document on the floppy disk (the A: drive).

She will change the save location by clicking the drop-down arrow beside the Save In area and selecting 3$^1/_2$" Floppy (A:). Once the folder structure of a selected disk device is displayed, double-click a folder to select it as the save area. She will then double-click *Mountain Rental,* and double-click *Gatlinburg.* She will probably also want to make the filename more descriptive, perhaps calling it *Furnishings List.*

Although creating files might not be quite as straightforward as creating folders, it is relatively easy because most software applications designed to run with Windows contain a similar menu structure. In most cases, you can save a file that you have created by clicking File, Save As. Always remember to consider two areas in the Save dialog box—the area to which the file will be saved and the filename. That way, you are assured that the file is placed where you can find it and that you will recognize the file by name when you see it.

Renaming Files

You can rename files just as you rename folders. However, because files are identified not only by a filename but also with an extension, you must be careful to

Other Ways

You can also save a file using an icon on the standard toolbar if it is displayed in your word processor. The standard toolbar is the long bar at the top of the screen that contains several icons. One of the icons might look like a floppy disk. Move the mouse pointer to the disk icon and hold it steady without clicking. If your word processor is set to display tool tips, a short description of the icon appears. It is the "Save" icon. Clicking the disk icon is the same as selecting Save from the File menu.

Hands On

Activity 5.3—Creating Files

In this activity, you will create a pie recipe and save it in the *Pies* folder. Place the same disk that you used for Activity 5.2 in the A: drive, if necessary. If Windows Explorer is open, close it. Your computer should be at the desktop.

1. Open Word by clicking Start, All Programs, Microsoft Word (or open WordPad by clicking Start, All Programs, Accessories, WordPad).
2. Type a pie recipe. Make one up!
3. Click File, Save As.
4. Click the drop-down arrow beside the save location and click 3½" Floppy (A:). From the subsequent folder list, double-click *Desserts*. Next, double-click *Pies*.
5. The filename probably includes the recipe title if that's the first line of text you typed. If not, click in the filename area and then type the recipe name.
6. Click Save.
7. Close Word or WordPad.

maintain the extension when renaming. The first thing to do is to display both filenames and extensions. In Windows Explorer, click Tools, Folder Options. Click the View tab. If a check mark appears beside the "hide file extensions for known file types" option, click it to remove the check mark. If there is no check mark, just leave it as is. Click OK.

Let's say that Jennifer has decided to rename the furnishings list file to indicate that it includes only kitchen items. Using Windows Explorer to display the rental property folder structure, she can navigate to the *Furnishings List* file by selecting the *Gatlinburg* subfolder of *Mountain Rental*. She can rename the file by clicking it once to select it, then clicking File, Rename. The furnishings list will show an extension of either *doc* or *rtf*. Word files carry the *doc* extension, whereas WordPad typically saves files with an *rtf* extension. After typing the new filename, including the extension, and pressing ⏎Enter, the file is renamed.

✓ SANITY CHECK

Although you intended merely to select a file so you could rename it, the file opened instead! You must have double-clicked the filename instead of clicking it only once. There is a big difference between *selecting* and *opening*. When a file is selected, its filename is shaded, and you can then rename, delete, or move the file. However, when you double-click a file, it is opened in the software application so that you can continue to work with the contents. Simply close the application and try the selection again.

Deleting Folders and Files

Windows Explorer allows you to easily delete both files and folders. Simply click the file or folder that you want to delete and press Del. If a file or folder is deleted, it is removed from its original location and placed in the Recycle Bin, so that you can later recover the item, if necessary. However, files and folders deleted from other disk media, such as a floppy disk, are not sent to the Recycle Bin. You should be absolutely sure that you don't need an item before removing it from a floppy disk or CD. When you delete a folder, that folder and all its contents, including any subfolders and files, are removed.

Jennifer has sold the mountain property, so she no longer needs the *Mountain Rental* information. (If she had any files saved in that folder, she would probably want to print the information before deleting the folder.) Using Windows Explorer, she would expand the folder structure in the left pane to display the *Mountain Rental* folder. After selecting the folder, she would press Del to remove it. Windows gives you an opportunity to rethink your deletion by asking you if you are sure the deletion should continue. When you respond affirmatively, the folder is immediately removed. Files are deleted in exactly the same manner— click to select a file and press Del.

Assume that Jennifer no longer has any rental property and wants to remove all folders from the floppy disk so that she can reuse it for another purpose. She would select the floppy disk in the left pane (3½" Floppy A:), and then click to select an item (file or folder) in the right pane. After she presses Del, the item is removed. Later in this chapter, you will learn to select several items for deletion at once.

Hands On

Activity 5.4—Deleting Files and Folders

In this activity, you will delete a file and a folder. Place the same disk that you used for Activity 5.3 in the A: drive, if necessary. Your computer should display either Windows Explorer or the desktop.

1. Open Windows Explorer, if it is not already open.
2. Expand My Computer and 3½" Floppy (A:), if necessary.
3. You decide that you don't want to include any cakes, so you are going to delete the *Pound Cakes* folder. Expand the *Desserts* folder, if necessary, so that the *Pound Cakes* and *Pies* folders are shown.
4. Click the *Pound Cakes* folder in the folders pane (left side). It should be shaded, indicating that it is selected.
5. Press Del. A dialog box appears, asking if you are sure about the deletion. Click Yes. The *Pound Cakes* folder should disappear from your screen.
6. Close Windows Explorer.

Understanding the Recycle Bin

When you delete a file or folder from your computer, it is not permanently removed. Instead, it is saved in the **Recycle Bin**, which is actually a folder on the hard disk. If you need the file later, you can retrieve it from the Recycle Bin. When you delete a file from another disk, such as a CD or floppy disk, the file is immediately removed and is not placed in the Recycle Bin. If your goal is conserving disk space, you should empty the Recycle Bin occasionally.

Sending Files to the Recycle Bin

The Recycle Bin appears as an icon on the desktop. It is also listed in the folders pane of Windows Explorer. There are several ways to delete a file or folder and send it to the Recycle Bin:

- Using My Computer or Windows Explorer, click to select the file or folder and press (Del).

- Right-click a file or folder and select Delete from the context menu.

- Click and drag a file or folder to the Recycle Bin. This method only works if you can see both the file that you are deleting and the Recycle Bin.

If you send a folder to the Recycle Bin, the folder and all files contained within it are stored there. If the folder is later retrieved, all files are recovered along with the folder.

Managing the Recycle Bin

It might be a good idea to check the Recycle Bin occasionally so that you can see what files are stored there. Periodically cleaning out your Recycle Bin can help keep your system free from clutter. To open the Recycle Bin, double-click its icon

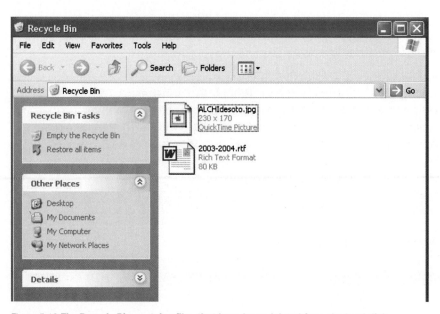

Figure 5.10 **The Recycle Bin contains files that have been deleted from the hard disk.**

on the desktop. You can also click the Recycle Bin in the folders pane of Windows Explorer. The Recycle Bin will appear, similar to that shown in Figure 5.10.

To retrieve a file from the Recycle Bin, open the Recycle Bin and select the file. Click File, Restore. This puts the file back where it was when you deleted it. Alternatively, you can right-click the file and choose Restore from the context menu.

Sometimes it's best to simply empty the Recycle Bin completely. You can do this at any time by right-clicking the Recycle Bin icon and selecting Empty Recycle Bin from the context menu. You can also open the Recycle Bin window and click File, Empty Recycle Bin. Either approach removes all files from the Recycle Bin, freeing some space on the hard disk.

Customizing the Recycle Bin

The Recycle Bin is configured to occupy a certain amount of space on your hard drive and to house files that have been deleted from the hard drive. However, you can change the amount of space reserved and cause files to be permanently deleted from your system, without stopping in the Recycle Bin. To customize the Recycle Bin, right-click its icon on the desktop, and select Properties. The Properties window appears, as shown in Figure 5.11. The first setting that you can change is the amount of space reserved for the Recycle Bin. Click the Global tab. The maximum size of the Recycle Bin is displayed as a percentage of the hard disk size, and is usually set at 10 percent. You can lower or raise the space reserved by clicking and dragging the slider. You might want to lower the space reserved so that more hard drive space is available for other applications. The other item of interest on the Properties window is *display delete confirmation dialog*. You can deselect the setting to keep the delete dialog box from appearing during a delete operation.

Copying and Moving Files and Folders

In the last chapter, we stressed the importance of making back-up copies of files. Here, you will learn how to copy files from one disk or location to another. In some cases, you might want to actually move the files instead of copying them. You can move files and folders from one folder to another, or from one disk to another. Although there are several methods of moving and copying (which we will describe in Other Ways), we will focus on only one method, but one that is almost foolproof!

Before attempting a move or copy, you must first select the items to be affected. If you are moving only one file, use Windows Explorer to view the file and then click to select it. When you move or copy folders, all subfolders and all files within the selected folder are moved or copied at one time. To move or copy a file or folder by clicking and dragging, you must be able to see both the sending area and the receiving area in the folders pane. At that point, with the file or folder selected, simply right-click and drag from the original location to the receiving folder or disk drive in the left pane. From the subsequent context menu, indicate whether you want to move or copy the item. Then you're finished!

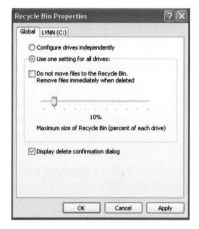

Figure 5.11 **You can change Recycle Bin Properties.**

◀▶ Other Ways

To copy or move a file or folder, open Windows Explorer. Click in the right pane to select the file or folder to copy. Display the tasks pane, if it is not already open, by clicking the Folders button. Under File and Folder Tasks, click *Copy this file* (or folder) or *Move this file* (or folder). In the Copy Items dialog box, select the drive or folder that you want to copy to, and click Copy or Move.

Another way to copy or move files and folders is to open Windows Explorer and right-click the file or folder to copy. Select Copy (or Cut) from the context menu. Right-click the drive or folder to which you want to copy. Select Paste.

Hands On

Activity 5.5—Copying a File

In this activity, you will copy a file from a floppy disk to the hard disk. Your computer should be at the desktop. The disk that you used in Activity 5.4 should be in the A: drive. You will copy the pie recipe from the A: drive to a folder that you create on the hard disk.

1. Open Windows Explorer.
2. Create a folder on the hard disk. Expand My Computer in the folders pane. Click to select Drive C. Click File, New, Folder. Type the new folder name, Pie Recipes, and press ⏎Enter.
3. Check to be sure the *Pie Recipes* folder was created. Expand Drive C, if necessary. In the left pane, scroll down to find the *Pie Recipes* folder. Click to select it. The right pane is empty, which means that there are no files in the folder yet. Your display should appear similar to Figure 5.12.
4. To copy the pie recipe, you must see both the pie recipe file and the folder to which you want to copy it (*Pie Recipes*). Expand 3½" Floppy (A:) in the folders pane. Expand the *Desserts* folder. Click *Pies* to view the contents of that folder. To the right, you should see the pie recipe that you created in Activity 5.3, which is the file that you plan to copy.
5. In the left pane (folders), you should see the *Pie Recipes* folder. You might have to scroll

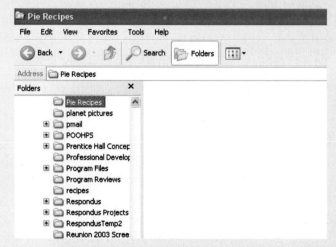

Figure 5.12 **The right pane will be empty if there are no files or folders contained in the selected folder.**

the folders pane up or down to see the folder. The contents pane remains stationary, displaying the pie recipe found on the floppy disk (Figure 5.13).

6. When you have positioned the folders pane to display the *Pie Recipes* folder, you are ready to begin the copy operation. Move the mouse pointer to the pie recipe in the right pane, and right-click and drag the file over to the *Pie Recipes* folder. Keep holding down the right mouse button until you are directly over the *Pie*

Selecting Multiple Files and Folders

There will be occasions when you want to move, copy, or delete several files or folders at once. Although you could deal with each item individually, it is much more efficient to treat them as a group. Imagine deleting 50 files individually. For each deletion, you would click to select the file, press Del, and agree to the deletion. Fifty times! On the other hand, if you knew how to select all 50 files at once, you could make that selection, press Del once, and respond affirmatively, but do it only one time.

Recipes folder. The folder should be shaded before you release the mouse button. A context menu appears, from which you should select *Copy Here*. The file is copied. Of course, if you had intended to move the file instead of copy it, you would have selected *Move Here* from the context menu. The only difference between moving and copying is that when a file is copied, it is duplicated in the new location, but

when it is moved, it is removed from the original location and placed in the new.

7. Check to see if the file is still in the original location. Select the *Pies* folder. Do you see the recipe in the right pane? Now see if it was indeed copied. Select the *Pie Recipes* folder. To the right, you should see the pie recipe.

8. Close Windows Explorer.

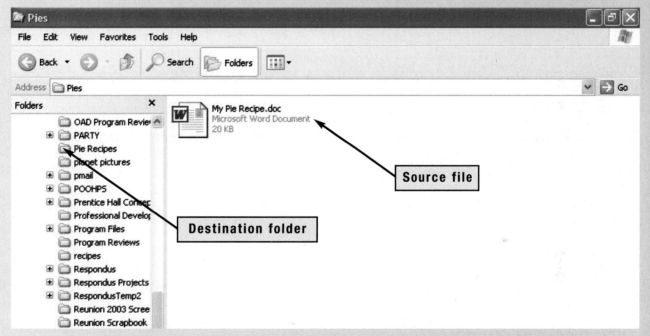

Figure 5.13 **When you copy a file or folder, you should be able to see both what you are copying and the area to which it is being copied.**

Using Windows Explorer, you can select multiple files and folders. If the files for selection are consecutively listed, you can click the first file, press and hold ⚓Shift, and click the last file. If the file list covers more than one screen, you will have to scroll the display down, while holding ⚓Shift, to find and click the last item in the list. On the other hand, if you are selecting several nonconsecutive files, click any file in the list, and then hold down Ctrl while you click every other item to be included. Continue holding down Ctrl until all files to be included are selected. After you have selected all items, you can proceed with the intended move, copy, or delete action.

In the Know

You can also move and copy files to a formatted CD or DVD, just as you can to a floppy disk. A formatted disc has been prepared for data storage. If you have a recordable CD or DVD drive on your computer system, you probably also have some disc creation software installed. Many computer systems include Roxio Easy CD Creator software. Check your program list to see what software you can find related to CD creation. When you open the software, you will probably see several options, one of which is to format the CD. After following all software prompts to format the CD, you can use the CD just like a floppy disk—you can click and drag files and folders to the CD, and you can save files to the CD.

▶ Quick Tip

For quick access to Windows help, press F1. It is found along the top of the keyboard, next to Esc. Pressing F1 displays a Search box, where you can type questions or keywords for which you need information.

Finding Files and Folders

It is almost too easy to lose track of files, especially if they are saved on the hard disk. When you download files, you copy them to your system, usually from the Internet or as an e-mail attachment. (You will learn to download files in Chapter 7.) However, you should know that although you can successfully save a downloaded file or program, you might have difficulty locating it when you want to open or install it. Such a situation is common if you rush through a download procedure and don't take note of the download location or filename.

Regardless of how you lost a file, you want to be able to find it again. That is easier if you have some idea of the filename. Assume that you downloaded a pie recipe, sent to you by e-mail attachment. You are sure that the downloaded file contained the word "pie" in the filename, but you're not sure of the entire filename. You also don't know where it was saved, except that it is somewhere on your hard disk.

Here's what you can do. Windows provides a handy Search Companion, found on the Start menu. You can also access it directly through Windows Explorer and My Computer by clicking *Search* in the menu bar. The folders pane becomes a task pane, displaying some options for your search. Because you know that the item is a document, click *Documents*. Although you could refine the search by indicating when you think the file was saved, you are not sure, so click Don't Remember. Then just type the word **Pie** in the search box (Figure 5.14). You might have to scroll down slightly to find the search box. Click *Search*. In a few seconds, at least one file appears in the right pane, the pie recipe that you created earlier in this chapter. If you want to see the recipe, double-click the file to open it. After viewing it, close Word or WordPad. Close the search pane by clicking the X in the top right corner of the section. Click *Folders* to redisplay the folders pane.

If you know any part of the name, you can include that information in the search box of the Search pane, just as you did in the preceding example.

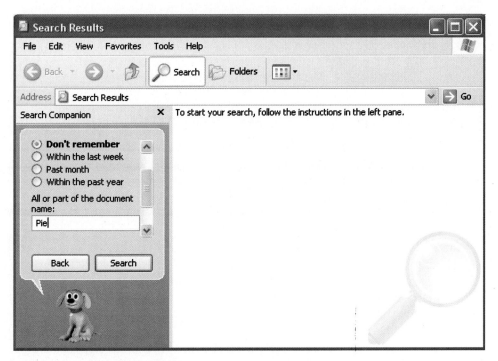

Figure 5.14 **Windows' Search Companion makes it easy to find files.**

Windows also includes wild cards—* and ?. The asterisk (*) can represent any character or characters. For example, if you are looking for all Word files, regardless of filename, your search item could be phrased ***.doc.** All Word files (files with a *doc* extension) are displayed as a result of the search. The question mark (?) wild card represents any one character. You might be looking for any files containing the words "Conwill" or "Conwell" in the filename. Your search could be phrased "Conw?ll," which would find either occurrence of the spelling in filenames.

Unless you specify otherwise, the Search Companion conducts searches of the hard disk. If the item you seek could be on another disk medium, you must redirect the search. If you clicked the category *all files and folders* in the search pane, you can redirect the search to another disk drive at the next screen. If you clicked any other category, you should click *use advanced search options*, and select another disk drive to search. You can also search for a file by size or by some text contained in the file itself (not just the filename).

Windows Explorer is your view of storage media and system resources that support your computer. In conjunction with My Computer, it allows you to completely manage the organization of any disk. Understanding how to copy files assures that you can make backups of important files, and knowing how to delete files is important as you maintain and reuse disks. You can even access Windows' Search feature through Windows Explorer, whereby you can find lost or misplaced files or folders. It is an invaluable tool as you continue exploration of your computer system.

Hands On

Activity 5.6—Finding Files

In this activity, you will conduct several file searches. Your computer should display either Windows Explorer or the desktop.

1. Open Windows Explorer, if necessary.
2. Click the Search button on the standard toolbar. You will find all Excel files (those with an extension of *xls*) on the hard disk.
3. Click Documents. Click in the search box and type `*.xls`. You might have to delete any previous search terms before typing the new search. Click Search.
4. You will see all Excel files found on the hard disk displayed in the right pane. Click *yes, finished searching*.
5. Assume that you are looking for a particular file, but remember only that it contains the word *First* somewhere in the filename. Click the Search button.
6. Click all files and folders.
7. In the box beneath "*all or part of the file name*," click and type the word `First`. You might first have to delete search terms from a previous search. Click Search.
8. Click yes, finished searching.
9. Click the Folders button to return the view to Folders.
10. Close Windows Explorer.

Chapter Summary

DON'T FORGET

- Both Windows Explorer and My Computer allow you to view folder structure and to access files on any disk associated with your computer system.

- Using the folders pane of Windows Explorer, you can expand folders to view more detail. You can also contract them to reduce the level of detail displayed.

- Windows Explorer makes it easy to create folders as subfolders of other folders or disk devices.

- You can delete folders and files by selecting them and pressing Del.

- When creating files, you work with application software, not Windows Explorer.

- You can rename both files and folders. When renaming files, be sure to include the file extension.

- You might select multiple files or folders if you want to work with an entire group at one time, perhaps deleting or moving it.

- The Recycle Bin contains files and folders that have been deleted from the hard disk. You can recover those items later if you need to.

- Windows includes a Search feature that helps you find files or folders if you have any information, such as part of the filename.

KEY TERMS

contents pane	Recycle Bin	Windows Explorer
folders pane	subfolder	

TRUE/FALSE

Circle **T** if the statement is true or **F** if the statement is false.

T ~~F~~ 1. To expand a folder's view, click the "+" to the left of the folder.

T ~~F~~ 2. My Computer is another name for Windows Explorer.

T ~~F~~ 3. The Recycle Bin holds files deleted from the hard disk.

~~T~~ F 4. Windows Explorer's standard toolbar contains icons that serve as shortcuts to many menu commands.

T ~~F~~ 5. Windows Explorer allows you to create both files and folders.

~~T~~ F 6. If you have selected multiple files, you can move or copy them all at once.

T F 7. A folder name must be two words.

~~T~~ F 8. The asterisk wildcard represents one or more characters.

T F 9. When moving a file from one disk to another, you can right-click and drag the file to the receiving disk or folder, then respond to a context menu.

T ~~F~~ 10. Folders cannot be deleted or renamed.

Expand all folders on the floppy disk. Are they all in order? Can you find the document that you created? If so, double-click the file to open it. Close the word processing program. Close Windows Explorer.

4. Moving Right Along

For this project, you will need a blank floppy disk labeled with your name and class title.

Working in Windows Explorer, create a folder on the floppy disk titled *Home Construction*. As subfolders of the *Home Construction* folder, create two more folders. One should be named *Interior Furnishings* and the other *Landscaping*. In those two folders you plan to keep records of expenditures related to the new home you are moving into.

Using Word or WordPad, create a document giving information on the landscaping plan, cost, and schedule. Save the file in the *Landscaping* folder and call it *Landscaping Plan*. To give more definition to the *Landscaping* folder, rename it *Front Yard Landscaping*. Rename the *Interior Furnishings* folder as *Back Yard Landscaping*.

The landscaping plan that you developed is actually for the back yard, so you need to move it to the correct folder. Expand the view of all folders on the floppy disk. Click *Front Yard Landscaping* to select it. You should see the landscape file listed in the right pane. Right-click and drag the *Landscaping Plan* file to the *Back Yard Landscaping* folder in the folders pane. Release the mouse button and select *Move Here* from the context menu. Check the view to be sure the file was moved.

You eventually decide that you can't afford to have all landscaping done at once, so you don't need the *Front Yard Landscaping* folder. Delete the folder.

5. Find It

In this chapter, you learned how to search for files that you might have misplaced. Consider this: You think that you received a document as an e-mail attachment at some point during the last two weeks. You have no idea of the filename or type. Can you find all files saved on your hard disk during the last two weeks? You might find some information in the Help and Support area. Expand your research, and give a written summary of the Search process, outlining how to find files by date, type, and file content.

CHAPTER 6

The Internet

By connecting to the **Internet**, you can enjoy a wealth of information and entertainment. You can plan a vacation, get news and weather updates, take a college class, search family records, pay bills, and research almost any topic. You can communicate with coworkers and friends through electronic mail (e-mail) and instant messaging ("talking" with others who are on the Internet at the same time). Stores that at one time offered goods only to walk-in customers have found the Internet to be an effective and relatively cheap way to sell those same items. To say the least, the Internet has revolutionized the way we access information and conduct business, and it has yielded almost unimaginable benefits for people of all ages.

Although it might at first glance appear to be rather complicated, the Internet is easy to work with and inexpensive to access. All you need is a computer that is configured for some sort of Internet connection, as described later in this chapter, and a contract with an **Internet service provider (ISP)**. In *addition, you will need to spend a little time learning to navigate the Internet, gather information, and enjoy Internet activities, such as e-mail. As you work with the Internet, you should be aware that it is not owned or regulated by any one organization, so anyone who has access to an Internet host server (a computer that is used to display pages of information on the Internet) can place anything they like there, regardless of whether the information is true or in good taste. Other issues of concern include protecting your privacy while you are online (connected to the Internet) and keeping your computer secure from viruses and unauthorized access. Chapter 7 explores the use of antivirus software and software designed to restrict access to your computer.*

Introducing the Internet

The Internet is actually a group of interconnected networks that span the world. Host server computers in every country are connected through over a million computer networks 24 hours a day. Estimates place the number of people using the Internet at millions, moving toward a billion. Although there are many ways to access information on the Internet, the one that most computer users enjoy is the World Wide Web.

The **World Wide Web** (WWW or the Web) is a subset of the Internet that displays pages of information in a way that is easy to navigate and understand. It was designed to be a graphical (point and click) medium, so you can make most choices and move from page to page by clicking areas on the screen known as **hyperlinks**—more commonly referred to as just **links**. Because it is so visual and user friendly, the World Wide Web is typically the most accessible and interesting part of the Internet for a home computer user. It contains a wealth of useful information, all of which is accessible to you at home through an Internet connection. It actually contains billions of documents, or pages, with thousands of new documents appearing every day. It is easily the fastest-growing component of the Internet.

The Internet originated in 1969 when a small group of computer scientists created a network to assist in the sharing of research and ideas from coast to coast. The Department of Defense's Advanced Research Project Agency (ARPA) sponsored the project and named it **ARPANet**. At the first demonstration of the network, there were no reporters, no photographs, and no records. No one remembers the first message; they remember only that it worked. The Department of Defense had an interest in the network as an installation that would withstand nuclear attack, allowing continual transmission of information and plans.

At first considered only a full-featured research and information distribution method, the Internet really boomed when commercial interests recognized its potential for marketing and sales. By that time, the network had progressed from ARPANet to a new organization called **NSFNet.** Although ARPANET was a

In the Know

Although many people think of the Internet and the World Wide Web as the same, the World Wide Web is actually only a component of the larger Internet. The Internet is a massive networking infrastructure, connecting millions of computers globally. Communication along the Internet can occur in a variety of languages, or **protocols**. The Internet is a huge conglomeration of networks and communication. Using the Internet, we can research almost any subject imaginable, download programs and files (bring them to our computers and save them), entertain ourselves, participate in online discussions (or chats), and take part in many forms of distance learning.

The World Wide Web, on the other hand, is a component of the Internet designed to share information, but in a much more standard and simple manner. The Web transmits data through the **HTTP** protocol, which is only one of the languages supported by the Internet. The Web makes full use of browsers, such as **Internet Explorer** and **Netscape Communicator**, to access Web pages. A browser is software used to locate and display Web pages. Hyperlinks and the use of graphics are also standard Web elements. In short, the World Wide Web is but a segment of the Internet, one that focuses on commercial interests, easy access, and general research.

secure, defense-funded network with limited access, NSFNet emerged in the 1980s as an academic enterprise, characterized by more open access. It was managed not by the government, but by contract with a private firm.

In 1989, the world was finally revolutionized with the advent of the World Wide Web. The Web made information and resources available to everyone, not just defense workers or academicians. With the introduction of graphical browsers, users who would not be at all comfortable with a command-driven system are able to navigate the World Wide Web by simply clicking links and entering recognizable address names.

Although the amount of information available on the Internet is staggering, it is important to remember that the Web is not regulated by any authoritative agency or group. Recognizing the lack of regulation, you will be aware that not all the information that you find there is correct or even in good taste. The Internet was designed in such a way that there is no central computer that acts as a regulator of communications. Each independent network makes its own rules and policies about what to publish and how to present information. Coordination occurs only through volunteer organizations from various countries that set standards for the global operation and that develop technical aspects of the network. The **World Wide Web Consortium (W3C)** is the leading organization that creates Web standards and develops specifications, guidelines, software, and

In the
Know

What do the Information Superhighway and the interstate highway system have in common? They were both created in 1957 as a direct response to the Russian launch of the Sputnik! President Dwight Eisenhower created both the interstate highway system and the Advanced Research Projects Agency (ARPA) as the United States dealt with the threat of communism and struggled to maintain a lead in satellite and communication technology. The ARPA organization brought together some of the most brilliant people in America, who began to focus on computer networking and communications. The result was the ARPANet, finalized in 1969, which was the forerunner of today's Internet, commonly referred to as the Information Superhighway.

tools. The Internet backbone, the main network connections through which traffic flows, is privately owned by various companies.

Connecting to the Internet

To connect to the Internet, you must consider four main components—computer equipment, connection type, Internet service provider, and software. You have undoubtedly seen commercials for **America Online** and **CompuServe**. They are two of the most recognizable commercial Internet service providers, but they are by no means the only ones. You have also probably heard about a modem but might not be certain of what it is or how it applies to your Internet connection. You will find answers to those questions and more in this chapter. To make the right choice of connection equipment and service provider, you must first consider what you expect from your Internet connection in terms of speed, reliability, and cost.

Computer Equipment

Most home computers sold today are configured for Internet access. That means that they have the necessary hardware to enable them to connect to the Internet through a telephone line or local area network. Because many Web pages employ a full range of audio and video effects, your computer should also be equipped with a sound card and speakers. Although there are no absolute minimum requirements, it does help if your computer has at least 128 MB of RAM and a processor speed of 400 MHz or faster. If you plan to access the Internet through a telephone connection, your computer should include a modem, at a speed of 56 Kbps (kilobytes per second) or faster. It is true that a faster processor and more RAM should enable you to travel the Internet more quickly, but you should remember that the speed of your travel is determined not only by your computer equipment, but by other factors that are beyond your control. The speed of the equipment utilized by your Internet service provider (the company with which you contract to provide Internet access) can slow you down, and you will find that if you are accessing the Internet at a time of day when many others are doing the same, you might experience a significant reduction in speed.

Connection Type

Many home computer users continue to rely on a dial-up account using a telephone line for accessing the Internet. Although this is generally the cheapest alternative, it is certainly not the only choice. In terms of speed, dial-up is far outpaced by other alternatives, including **cable modem**, **ISDN**, **DSL**, **wireless**, and, in some cases, **Internet TV** connections. Let's take a moment to look at each of those choices.

Dial-Up Modem

A **dial-up modem** is used to send digital data over a phone line. The term *modem* is a contraction of the words *modulate* and *demodulate*. The modem on your computer *modulates* data into a signal that is compatible with the phone line, and the modem on the receiving computer *demodulates* the signal back into digital data (as shown in Figure 6.1). If you are using a modem connection, you simply connect one end of a telephone line into the phone jack on the back of your computer's system unit, while connecting the other end into a wall phone jack. As mentioned earlier, most new computer systems are equipped with a 56 Kbps (short for 56 kilobits per second) modem. Most Internet service providers support 56 Kbps modems; however, some no longer support the 28.8 Kbps or 14.4 Kbps modems that are found on older systems. Consequently, if you have an older computer, you might find it difficult to connect to the Internet.

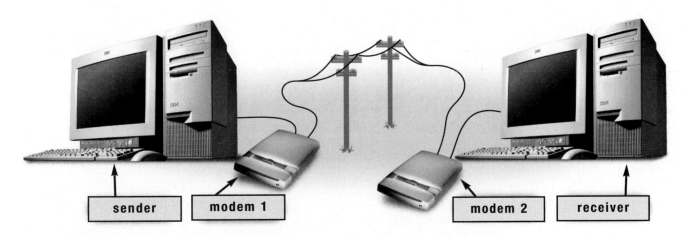

sender   modem 1   modem 2   receiver

Figure 6.1 **A dial-up modem translates digital signals into analog for transmission over a telephone line.**

Cable Modem

The connection that brings cable television to homes can also be used to provide high-speed Internet connection. A television cable carries television programming but has more than enough extra bandwidth for other purposes, such as connecting to the Internet. With a cable modem, installed by your local cable company, you are ready to take advantage of the high-speed connection. Whereas a typical dial-up modem speed is 56 Kbps, a cable modem easily transmits at more than 1 Mbps (million bits per second), which is at least 20 times faster. A small cluster of homes shares each Internet cable connection, but even so, hundreds of users can usually be online without any loss of speed. Home computers can be networked with a cable connection so that each computer can be online at the same time, even visiting different Web sites. With a cable modem, you are always online when your computer is on, which is an attractive thought from the standpoint of quick access, but which might pose a security risk if you are not adequately protected with a firewall to block out unauthorized access to your computer. (Chapter 7 explores firewall software along with other methods to protect yourself and your computer.)

Integrated Services Digital Network (ISDN)

Integrated Services Digital Network (ISDN) is a digital telephone service that allows you to simultaneously send and receive voice, video, or data transmissions. ISDN transmission speed can be as high as 128 Kbps for a typical home computer installation. There are several categories of ISDN, including **Basic Rate Interface (BRI)** and **Primary Rate Interface (PRI)**. Small businesses and home computer owners are more likely to benefit from BRI, which routinely reaches speeds of 128 Kbps. If a phone call comes in, the speed drops back to 64 Kbps. PRI, on the other hand, is geared to larger organizations, combining 30 channels of 64 Kbps transfer. Given its cost and special wiring requirements, PRI is not practical for the home computer user. To connect through ISDN, you need to contact your local telephone company and inquire about connection and rates. Be forewarned, though, there are still many areas where this service is unavailable.

Digital Subscriber Line (DSL)

Digital Subscriber Line (DSL), a high-speed telephone connection, is an attractive option because of its connection speed and the fact that you can be online without tying up your phone line. **Asymmetric DSL (ADSL)** is a type of DSL that uses existing phone lines but is much faster than even ISDN. Typical ADSL upload speed is 1 Mbps, whereas you can download files at up to 7 Mbps. Uploading is the process of sending a file from your computer to another computer. Downloading is when you copy a file or program from another computer to yours. The disparity between upload speed and download speed is evident in all connection technologies; typically downloading takes place with greater speed than uploading. Using a router that is available at most office-supply stores, you can network several home computers so that they can all be online at the same time, even accessing different Web sites.

In the Know

*The term **broadband** refers to a transmission type that carries several data channels over a single cable. DSL services combine separate voice and data channels over a single telephone cable. Cable modems also rely on broadband transmission.*

Many telephone companies offer DSL and can install the service on your computer; however, you must be within a certain distance of a phone company's central office to be eligible for DSL connection. As part of the installation, the telephone company usually provides a DSL modem. In some cases, you can even install your own DSL service by using a kit provided by the phone company. You must also pay a subscription fee monthly for the service as well as an account activation fee. To determine whether you are eligible for DSL service, call your local phone company.

The table shown in Figure 6.2 compares methods of connecting home computers to the Internet. Other methods of Internet access are better suited for larger organizations.

Wireless

A wireless ISP (WISP) is an alternative that provides a maximum bandwidth of 11 Mbps. An Internet signal is broadcast from a tower to individual home receivers. You will need a special modem to bring the signal to your computer. Both lightning and storms can affect the reliability of the wireless connection, but improved wireless technology is overcoming many weather-related problems. Wireless technology also allows you to be much more mobile when used with laptops, cell phones, and PDAs.

Internet TV

Accessing the Internet is only a small part of what you can do with a computer, but surfing the Internet and working with e-mail is all some people want to do. For them, such Internet access is enough. They don't plan to use other features common to a home computer, such as word processing or application programs. For that group of people, Internet TV, also called **Web TV** or **MSN® TV**, might be worth exploring. It is a service that displays the Internet on your television instead of a computer system, allowing you to visit Web sites and to send and receive e-mail (Figure 6.3). To enjoy the service, you must buy a set-top appliance, which you can get online, by phone, or from a local retailer. Connect the appliance to your television and to a telephone line. When you first turn on the set-top unit, you are automatically connected and are provided an opportunity to sign up for online service. From the convenience of your couch, you can navigate the Web using a remote control and a wireless keyboard.

Web Watch

Visit **www.business.com/ directory/internet_and_ online/internet_service_ providers_isp/wireless/** for additional information on wireless providers and services.

Internet Connection	Speed	Advantages	Disadvantages
Dial-up Modem	56 Kbps or less	1) Usually included with a new computer 2) Cost for ISP service ($0–$25 per month) 3) Easy to connect	1) Slow speed compared to other technologies 2) Wait time for modem to dial a connection
Cable Modem	Greater than 1 Mbps, but the speed does vary, depending on the number of users on the same cable connection. Download speed is faster than upload speed.	1) Leaves telephone line open for calls 2) Fast, reliable data transfer 3) Internet connection is always available (always online), so you don't have to wait for a dial-up to occur	1) Cost ($30–$50 per month) 2) Security risk because the computer is always online 3) If the television cable is disrupted, so is your Internet connection
ISDN	Up to 256 Kbps	1) Reliable 2) Leaves telephone line open for calls 3) Supports data transfer rates up to 128 Kbps	1) High cost of digital telephone connection (averaging $200 per month) 2) ISDN is not available in some areas 3) Installation can be difficult and time-consuming
DSL	1.5 Mbps download (copying files to your computer from a distant computer) and 640 Kbps upload (sending files from your computer to a distant computer)	1) Independently configured so that temporary loss of DSL connection doesn't cause a loss of telephone service 2) Each subscriber is on a separate network, so security risk is low 3) Fast Internet access and data transfer 4) Internet access is always available because the computer is always online	1) No current standardization, so if you move to another city, the DSL modem may be useless 2) High installation cost (as much as $750) 3) Connection is dependent upon how far you live from a telephone switching station 4) Security risk because the computer is always online
Wireless	Up to 11 Mbps (190 times faster than a standard dial-up connection)	1) Secure data transmission 2) Mobility (you can walk around with a laptop and not lose the connection)	1) Possibility of some weather-related transmission problems 2) Equipment installation can be time-consuming
Internet TV	Depends on the connection type, whether cable or dial-up	1) Easy to set up 2) All installation done at home, with no need for a technician 3) No need for a computer; the display is your television set	1) Initial cost of approximately $99 for set-top box 2) Limited Internet access 3) Can only access the Internet and e-mail; no other computer applications are possible

Figure 6.2 **There are several ways to connect a home computer to the Internet, each with unique advantages and disadvantages.**

Figure 6.3 **Your television set can serve as a gateway to the Internet if you subscribe to MSN® TV.**

Internet Service Providers

After you settle on a connection type, you must consider an Internet service provider (ISP). An ISP is a company that allows you to connect to the Internet through its host server. Some ISPs are full-featured, including specialized services. Others simply provide an Internet connection, without any special content. The cost for ISP service varies and is dependent upon the level of service provided as well as the number of hours per month included in the contract. Providers can include local phone companies, long-distance carriers (AT&T, MCI, Sprint), national online services (America Online, CompuServe, Microsoft Network), and locally owned firms.

Some ISPs, such as America Online, Microsoft Network, and CompuServe, provide a wide array of services attractive to a home computer user. They could be considered *Internet on training wheels* because they are easy for a beginner to install and understand, and they simplify Internet travel. In fact, they are often called **online services**, because they include so much more than a simple Internet connection. You will find all sorts of special features, such as America Online's *keywords*, that allow you to visit certain Web sites by simply typing a key term. Often, these online services will schedule online chats with celebrities and will offer discounted products for purchase online. Such full-featured ISPs are usually national providers handling a large volume of calls and connections. You might experience connection delays and higher prices with those subscription services but, in general, their ease of use makes them an ideal best choice for computer novices.

Web Watch

The MSN® TV Web site (**www.msntv.com**) explains how to use the service and how to install it in your home.

Web Watch

For more information on ISP services and costs around the world, check out **thelist.internet.com**. There, you can view ISPs by area code, state, or country.

In the Know

The term ISP is a well known abbreviation for Internet service provider, but did you know that there is also such a thing as an **IAP (Internet access provider)**? The two terms are often used interchangeably, but to be technical about it, IAPs are considered subsets of ISPs. A true IAP offers only Internet access with no additional services, whereas an ISP might also include leased lines and Web page development. Online services, such as America Online and MSN, provide proprietary content and many special features in addition to Internet access.

Web Watch

Some ISPs offer free services, which means that you don't necessarily have to pay for Internet access. You can look into some of those free options at **www.dailye deals.com/free_internet/ access.htm**. Keep in mind that although the access might be free, somebody is paying for the service—most likely advertisers—so you will have to live with advertisements as you use the service. Carefully research any "free" option. You might just get what you pay for, because some free services might be overburdened by user access, underpowered, and lacking in technical support.

Local providers are usually more interested in offering sleek, streamlined Internet service without any fluff. They don't usually offer special content or online activities. However, you will probably pay less for such service than you would pay to contract with a national provider, and if all that you are interested in is an entry point to the Internet, the service might be all that you need.

Software

To access the Internet, you will need two types of software—a **communications program** and an Internet **browser**. Communications software allows you to make the connection between your computer, the modem, and the ISP's computer. A browser is software that locates and displays Internet pages. It allows you to read and manage the information found on the Internet. Each ISP provides its own communications software, so when you install the software included on the online service CD, you are installing the necessary communications software. Major providers, like America Online and Microsoft Network (MSN), also include browsers with their products, so you don't have to deal with getting a separate browser. With one installation, you get both the communications software and the browser. Other ISP services might require that you use a separate browser, such as Internet Explorer or Netscape Communicator, two of the most popular browsers, both available as free downloads from the Internet. Internet Explorer is also included with a typical installation of Windows XP and appears as an icon on your desktop.

✓ SANITY CHECK

Just because you find Internet Explorer as an icon on your desktop doesn't mean that you have a connection to the Internet. The browser gives you a view of the Internet only after you are connected through an ISP. If you double-click Internet Explorer without first connecting through your ISP, you will see a message similar to "Page not Found." If you are using AOL or another full-service provider, you won't need to work with Internet Explorer at all, as a browser is included with AOL's installation. If you are working with a less full-featured provider, you might have to connect through the ISP service and then open Internet Explorer from your desktop.

Creating an Account with an Online Service

Before contracting with a service provider, you should decide what type of connection and ISP are best for you. The easiest and cheapest alternative, and one that many home users continue to select, is a dial-up modem and an online service, such as America Online. If your computer is equipped with a dial-up modem (which most are), you can plug a telephone cable from the modem connection on the back of your PC into a regular telephone wall jack.

The next step is to select an ISP. Your new computer probably came with an online service installation CD. If it didn't, or if you want to try an alternative service, look for online service CDs at local retailers, office-supply stores, and post offices. (These CDs are generally free to customers.) Although there are other choices, many new computer users opt to use a national online service because they are familiar with the name and trust the product to be easy to use.

To install the online service CD-ROM:

1. Place the CD in your CD drive, and follow the instructions that appear on-screen.
2. At some point during the installation, you will be asked to select a telephone access number, which should be a local telephone call for you. You should choose more than one telephone number so that if one number is busy or unresponsive, another might be available.
3. During the installation, you must create a **user name**. Often, the first user name that you create will not be accepted because it is already in use by another subscriber. In that case, you will be given a list of suitable alternatives. You can accept one of those, or you might create another unique user name.
4. A **password** is necessary, as well. Your password should definitely be easy to remember. Avoid the temptation, however, to select something as obvious as a pet's name. Instead, create a password of some combination of letters and numbers.
5. You might be required to enter a credit card number, although many online services allow Internet access for a certain number of hours before charging for the service. Such arrangements vary and are dependent upon existing programs from online services. Most home Internet users who spend a considerable amount of time working with e-mail and the Internet should opt for unlimited access plans.
6. When installation is complete, you will probably see an icon on the desktop for the new connection. To get to the Internet, simply double-click the icon. If you don't see an icon, check the program list (Start, All Programs).

> **▌▶Quick Tip**
>
> When creating a user name, you will probably find that your first choice is rejected if you include only letters. Although it might be tempting to create a user name made up of your first and last name, there might be many people in the world with the same name as yours, so a user name comprising those elements will most likely already be taken. Instead, try creating a user name with some combination of letters and numbers, such as your last name followed by the last four digits of your telephone number. Most ISPs require that there be no spaces in a user name. Above all, create a user name that is easy to remember.

Contracting with a specific Internet service provider is your choice, but you should make sure the contract allows you to discontinue the service at any time. Competition in the online services area is stiff, and you will want to keep your options open in case another company buys out your ISP or you simply find a better deal with another service and want to switch.

You might receive Internet connection CDs in the mail offering new online services or new versions of a service that you are currently using. If you want to change services, you might need to install the new CD, uninstall the old, and notify the company of your cancellation. If the CD is offering a new version of your current service, you might install it just as you did the original. Although you do not have to uninstall the original version of the service, you will probably want to do so to free up hard disk space. Versions are usually numbered sequentially, so it is generally safe to remove all versions with a lower number than the one just installed.

Understanding Web Addresses

Any person, group, or organization can post a **Web page** on the Internet. All it takes is a set of information designed with a **Web authoring tool** or **Web scripting** program and an Internet server (a computer with direct connection to the Internet) upon which to publish the page or set of pages. A Web page is based on a set of instructions, coded in a Web scripting language, such as **html**, JavaScript, or Java. Web authoring software simplifies Web page programming by allowing Web page developers to specify design without actually writing the supporting code. Each Web page has a unique Internet address, called a **Uniform Resource Locator** (**URL**), comprising a string of characters.

Taking a closer look at a typical URL, as shown in Figure 6.4, note that there is a standard way to designate exactly where and on what server a Web page is found. The access method, or protocol, listed as *http://* in the address, tells your communication software how to access that particular page. **Hypertext Transfer Protocol** (HTTP) is a type of communication protocol that uses hyperlinks, which are images or text on a Web page that you can click to move to other Web

In the
Know You can register a domain name by using the services of a domain name registrar. The **Internet Corporation for Assigned Names and Numbers (ICANN)** is the organization responsible for certifying companies as domain name registrars. The registrar determines the cost for registering a domain name, often in the form of a yearly fee.

Cybersquatting is a term that means registering or using a domain name in bad faith, with the intent to profit from the name at the expense of another person or company. What that means is that domain names reflecting the names of existing businesses or organizations can be bought early by an individual and then sold back to the businesses for a profit. Victims of cybersquatting include Panasonic, Hertz, and Avon. The Anticybersquatting Consumer Protection Act (ACPA) provides an avenue for victims of cybersquatting to sue the offenders. International arbitration is managed by ICANN.

Figure 6.4 **A URL is a Web page address that includes standard identifiers.**

locations. When typing an Internet address, you usually don't have to type the *http://* part of the address. If there is nothing typed there, your browser will automatically assume that the page is an http page.

The **domain name**, which follows the double slashes, is the address of the Internet server on which the Web page resides. The domain name will always have at least two parts, separated by a dot. Following the domain name and a slash is the directory, which refers to a folder on the host computer (Internet server). The page indicated in the URL shown in Figure 6.4 is found in the *pressroom* folder. Any additional folders, separated by slashes, continue to narrow the focus. Finally, the specific filename of the page requested is listed, followed by an extension.

The **top-level domain** name—the "*com*" in Figure 6.4—represents the purpose of the organization. You will often see URLs ending in *com*, which means that they are published by *commercial* entities. Many URLs include a two-letter, top-level domain name that indicates the country of origin, such as *us* (United States) or *ca* (Canada).

In the Know

Have you ever wondered about the meaning of the suffixes that are attached to URLs? Such items as .com, .gov, and .edu actually do mean something. Each suffix represents the top-level domain (TLD) to which the Web page belongs. The top-level domain is simply a category of Web pages. Here are a few examples:

.edu	Educational institutions
.com	Commercial businesses
.gov	Government agencies
.mil	Military
.org	Nonprofit organizations
.net	Network organizations
.ca	Canada
.us	United States

Not all URLs include all of the parts just described. For example, you can get to Intel's **home page** (the top-level page from which you can travel to others on the same Web site) by going to **www.intel.com**. (A Web site comprises several Web pages, much like a textbook contains pages.) At that point, you might click the *Business Computing* link, followed by *Desktop PCs*. In that manner, you could move to various Web pages without typing the entire URL of a specific file. Hyperlinks are unique to World Wide Web pages and make moving among sites no more difficult than pointing and clicking. You can usually identify a hyperlink on a Web page when the mouse cursor changes into an arrow, or a hand with a pointing finger (Figure 6.5).

So how do you begin viewing Web pages? First, you must have contracted with an Internet service provider, and you must have connected your computer to the Internet by means of a telephone line or other connection method. You should either see an icon on your desktop noting the service provider or get to the connection program by clicking the Start button on the taskbar, followed by All Programs, and then the provider name. You might also see the ISP listed in the Quick Launch toolbar on the taskbar.

After you open the ISP program, you will probably have to click Sign On or Connect. Depending on how the program is configured to start up, it might need your user name and password, although you don't always have to provide that information. Although your service provider might remember your user name

Figure 6.5 **A hyperlink can be graphic, as shown in this figure, or text. When you move the mouse pointer to a hyperlink, it becomes an arrow or a hand with a pointing finger.**

and password each time you log on, you should make a note of those items, as you might be asked for your password if you ever access your account from a remote computer or need to contact the ISP for support. The ISP program will confirm your identity and take you directly to the Internet. A browser will probably be displayed; however, some ISPs require that you open a separate browser, such as Internet Explorer.

Online services update their software periodically. When that happens, you have the option of either downloading a new version or installing the new version from a CD. Neither approach requires that you immediately uninstall the original program. New versions appear every couple of years, and it is your choice as to whether to switch to the new version. Although you will want to upgrade to the new version eventually so that you can take advantage of new features, it is perfectly all right to remain with the current version for a few more months.

Understanding Browsers

A **browser** is a software tool that enables you to travel the Internet. The browser is your window to the Internet, including a graphical interface and features that allow you to customize your Internet screen, as shown in Figure 6.6. The two dominant browsers are Netscape Communicator and Internet Explorer. Internet Explorer is a Microsoft product that is included with each installation of Windows. Both Internet Explorer and Netscape Communicator are available free as

 **Web Watch**

As technology progresses, so does our English language. The difficulty lies with being certain of how to spell new words and whether to capitalize or hyphenate them. The fact is, there is often no documented "correct" way to work with many such words. Is it "e-mail" with a hyphen or without? And must the word "Internet" always be capitalized? For an exploration of Internet grammar, visit **www.webopedia.com/ DidYouKnow/Internet/ 2002/InternetGrammar.asp**.

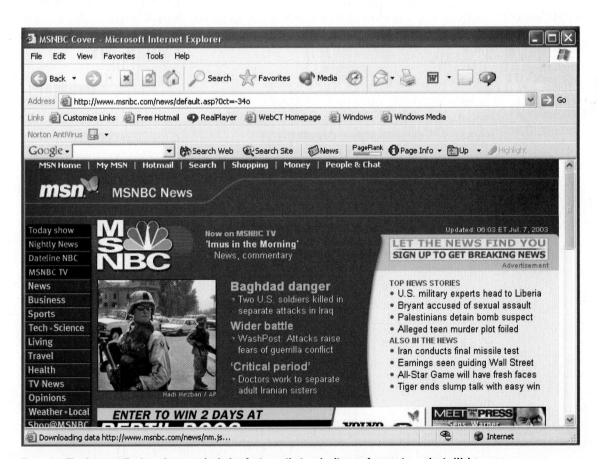

Figure 6.6 **The Internet Explorer browser includes features that make it easy for you to navigate Web pages.**

▶Quick Tip

Some Web pages appear different or function better when viewed with an independent browser (either Netscape Communicator or Internet Explorer), as opposed to a commercial online service like AOL. You will know that only if the Web page displays a message letting you know that not all parts of the page will be visible or if the view is distorted. If that should be the case, you can sign on to your service provider. Once connected, minimize the ISP window. That means that although you will still be connected to the Internet, the ISP's browser will no longer appear except as a button on the taskbar. If you have downloaded an independent browser, its icon should appear on the desktop. Double-click the icon to open the browser's window so you can work directly with the Internet using the browser itself.

Web Watch

As you work with the Internet, you will probably find a browser with which you are most comfortable and learn to use it well. Remember that a browser simply lets you view the Internet, allowing you to enjoy and customize your Internet environment. Visit **www.learnthenet.com/ english/html/12browser.htm** to investigate the use of browsers and to get a few tips on browser selection.

a download from the Internet and have similar features, including a menu bar, toolbar, and address bar. Remember that if you are working with America Online or CompuServe, you won't need a separate browser. The browser is built into the interface of your service provider, making your Internet experience a little easier.

The Internet Explorer browser can be downloaded at **www.microsoft.com/ie**, whereas Netscape Communicator can be found at **www.netscape.com**. As with almost all software, new versions of browsers are periodically developed and made available. It is a good idea to download newer versions as they become available, because they normally include improved features for accessing Internet resources. You will learn to download programs in Chapter 7.

Accessing Web Sites

The WWW is definitely a commercial endeavor, with millions of Web sites offering products or services. Many other sites are informational or offer a public service. Virtual libraries are now available online, and professional organizations and nonprofit groups offer a wealth of consumer and medical information. With the abundance of information and entertainment on the Web, you will want to access interesting sites quickly and easily. That is the purpose of your browser.

A key element of the browser interface is the address bar, as shown in Figure 6.7. It is the long white bar toward the top of your browser screen, displaying a Web address that corresponds to the page that you are currently viewing. To move to another Web page, you can type the URL in the address bar. If you don't know the URL, you can search for specific sites using search tools described later in this chapter.

✓SANITY CHECK

When you type a URL and press ↵Enter (or click Go), you expect to be directed to the new Web page. If, instead, you receive a message to the effect that the Web page cannot be displayed, it is likely that you typed the address incorrectly or that the Web page is no longer available. Check the URL to see if you made a typing error. If so, click in the address bar and retype the address, or simply make any corrections necessary to the address. If the Web page is no longer available, retyping the address won't help. The Web page is simply not there anymore. You can then use the search tools that you will learn later in this chapter to try to locate a similar Web page.

To type a URL and move to another Web page:

1. Click in the address bar where the current address is displayed. The address should become shaded, or selected.

✓SANITY CHECK

If the Web address is not shaded, but you see instead a blinking black bar (cursor), you can remove the current address by pressing Del to delete characters to the right of the cursor or ←Backspace to delete characters to the left of the cursor.

---

2. With the current address selected or deleted, type the new address. Be sure to press ↵Enter or click Go after the address is typed.

Figure 6.7 **By typing a URL in the address bar, you can move to another Web page.**

Hands On

Activity 6.1—Accessing Web Pages

In this exercise, you will move among Web sites by typing addresses in the address bar.

1. Connect to the Internet. If you are in a computer lab, you will probably need to double-click Internet Explorer at the desktop. If the lab uses a browser other than Internet Explorer, double-click that instead, or connect by signing on to your Internet service provider.
2. You are going to access the MSNBC Web site to catch up on some current national news. Click the current address in the address bar. The entire address should be shaded, or selected. If not, just click in the address bar at the end of the current URL and hold down the mouse button while sliding the cursor to the front of the bar. This should highlight the text.
3. With the current address shaded, type the new address: **www.msnbc.com.** Press ⏎Enter or click Go.
4. You should now be at the MSNBC news Web page.
5. Move your mouse pointer over elements on the page. A hyperlink is any area where your mouse pointer becomes a hand. Click any hyperlink to proceed to a new page of the Web site.
6. You can use the Back button on your browser to return to the Web page viewed just before the currently displayed page. The Back button is normally found at the top left of the browser in a toolbar, as shown in Figure 6.8. If you don't see the word Back, look for a left-pointing arrow. Click Back now. You should return to the MSNBC home page.

✓ SANITY CHECK

If you don't see the Back button on your browser's toolbar, click View, Toolbars, and check to be sure that a check mark appears beside Standard Buttons. *Note: The View Toolbar is available only in Internet Explorer or Netscape Communicator. If you are using an online service, like America Online, you will not have a View menu selection.* If you see no check mark, click Standard Buttons to select that feature.

Similarly, if you see no address bar, check to be sure the feature is selected. Click View, Toolbars, and click address bar if no check mark appears beside that selection.

7. Close your Internet connection by clicking the close (X) button at the top right of your browser window.

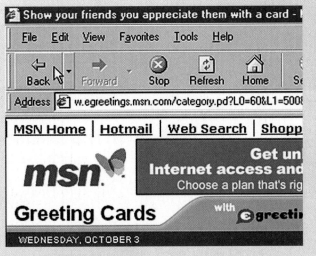

Figure 6.8 **Click the Back button to return to the most recently viewed page.**

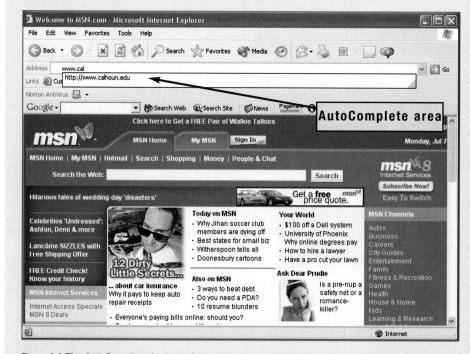

In the **Know** Although you can move to any Web page by typing the complete address of the desired Web page in the address bar, you might be able to use the AutoComplete feature of your browser, as shown in Figure 6.9. When you begin to type a Web address, the browser might suggest previously visited sites that include the same characters in the same order as what you are typing. Suggested addresses will appear in a list beneath the address bar as you continue to type. If one of those addresses is in fact the one that you are typing, you can click the address listed to immediately move to the site. If your browser doesn't support AutoComplete, or if a suggested address is not what you are typing, you will need to continue typing to enter the address as usual.

Figure 6.9 **The AutoComplete feature of some browsers suggests recently accessed sites that are similar to what you are typing.**

Introducing Web Sites

The Web brings a world of possibilities to your desktop. From the comfort of your home, you can now shop, bank, research topics of interest, and even find employment (as shown in Figure 6.10). Let's take a look at what you might find out there!

Online shopping is now a reality, to the relief of those shoppers who don't like to travel to malls and shopping areas! The percentage of customers shopping online is increasing each year, causing states to reevaluate the way they collect sales tax. Currently much of what you buy on the Web is not taxed. Stores with

In the Know

Is it safe to shop online? That is a question often asked by people considering making online purchases. The truth is that in many cases shopping online might be even safer than paying by credit card at your favorite restaurant. Using a credit card for online purchases is certainly no more dangerous than handing your credit card to a waiter or giving your credit card number to a sales representative over the phone. In fact, because reputable Web sites encode your transaction, online transactions are most often more secure than traditional face-to-face transactions. Encoding, or **encryption**, is technology used by Web servers to code the transaction so that outside parties won't be able to read it if they should intercept it.

A technology called **SSL (Secure Sockets Layer)** is a set of rules that guards against interception, protects data integrity, and assures clean data transmission and authentication. To be sure that a site uses SSL, check the URL, or Web address. If an "s" is added to "http," making it "https," you can be sure that SSL is in effect on that server. Depending upon your browser type and version, you might also see a padlock on the status bar at the base of the browser window. Such a symbol indicates the use of SSL.

Figure 6.10 **The Web provides information on just about any subject imaginable.**

both a storefront and an online presence are called *click-and-mortar* stores, and they are winning consumer confidence with on-time delivery of goods and ease of returning merchandise. Many consumers shop for groceries and even order pizza online!

Government agencies offer information online and encourage awareness of current events and federal holdings. The Library of Congress (**www.loc.gov**) includes electronic versions of many exhibits and encourages children's interest through a children's area. The White House site (**www.whitehouse.gov**) includes transcripts of radio addresses, a virtual tour of the White House, and other government information.

Hands On

Activity 6.2—Touring Web Sites

Have you ever wondered what historical event might have happened on your birthday? Look at a couple of sites that will give you such information.

1. Connect to the Internet. If you are in a computer lab, double-click Internet Explorer icon at the desktop, or if the lab uses a different browser, double-click that instead. Otherwise, connect by signing onto your Internet service provider.
2. Click in the address bar. With the current address selected, or shaded, type **www.historychannel.com/today/.** Press ⏎Enter or click Go. The home page of the History Channel will be displayed.
3. View the Web page and identify the area where you can enter your birthday. You might have to scroll down slightly to find the area. You will need to click a small black drop-down arrow beside the month and date locations to select your birthday. Click Go.
4. You should see a summary of a historical event that occurred on your birthday.
5. The Library of Congress supports a similar page that gives information on events that happened today. Click in the address bar to select the current address. Type **memory.loc.gov/ammem/today/ today.html.** Press ⏎Enter or click Go.
6. Go to the home page of the Library of Congress (type **www.loc.gov** in the address bar). Search the page for a link to "America's Library." Click the link.
7. Find a link titled "Jump Back in Time." You might have to scroll down slightly to find the link. Click it.
8. You should see a space on the page where you can enter your birthday. Do that now. As before, you should click the drop-down arrow beside the month arrow and click to select your birth month. Do the same for the date. Click Go.
9. Close the Internet connection by clicking the close (X) button in the top right corner of the window.

News agencies sponsor sites that include live video and audio broadcasts of news programs. All of the major television news areas sponsor an accompanying Web site. Newspapers and magazines are available online as well. Informational sites include map finders, yellow pages, and industry reviews.

Through online banking sites, you can check your bank balance, transfer funds, and pay bills or loans. Online banks should function in a secure mode, which means that the browser uses encryption to communicate with the bank's server.

Online stock trading is one of the fastest-growing applications in consumer-based electronic commerce. Investors are able to buy and sell stock without the assistance of a broker. Many discount brokerages are now online, including TD Waterhouse, AmeriTrade, and E-Trade.

Several states have virtual libraries, available to the state population through a password-protected site. If such a program exists in your state, you can probably get a virtual library card from any public library. The card and accompanying literature will direct you to the virtual library site. Most virtual libraries maintain full text or summaries of periodicals, newspapers, and scholarly journals, as well as transcripts from documentaries and radio broadcasts. Dictionaries and encyclopedias are also included.

Searching the Web

Browsing, sometimes called *surfing,* is fun and easy, but it is not the most efficient method for finding specific information. When you browse, you visit Web sites without direction, following interesting links as you find them. Just as you wouldn't flip aimlessly through a book to find specific information, neither would you leisurely browse the Web. When working with a book, you would more likely move to the index or table of contents to determine the location of information. When dealing with the Web, you would more likely use a **search tool.**

The Web includes major portals, which are Web sites that offer a broad array of services. Some portals provide resource discovery tools, called search engines or subject directories. In most cases, a search site can locate information for you once you have typed in one or more keywords. For example, if you want to find information on diabetes, you might use that term as your keyword to initiate the search for corresponding Web sites. Perhaps you are looking for information on car insurance. You can use the keywords *car insurance* to begin your search. Remember that the more specific you are in your choice of keywords, the more focused the search, and the more likely that you will quickly find the information you desire. After your search has returned a list of Web sites, you can visit any of them, following hyperlinks to find the information you seek. Expect to be disappointed with your first query, as it often takes several tries to express exactly what you are searching for with keywords. It is not unusual for an initial search to return thousands of matching sites.

Search Engines and Directories

Think carefully about your search topic before attempting a search. With experience, you will learn to analyze your information needs, select concise search

---

Web Watch

The FDIC sponsors a Web site containing tips for safe online banking. To review its suggestions, visit **www.fdic.gov/ bank/individual/online/safe .html**.

terms, and evaluate search engines so that you take full advantage of Internet information resources. Searching can be a complex process, one that is as scientific and thorough as you want to make it. It can also be simple and rewarding.

There are basically two types of search services: **subject directories** and **search engines**. Both offer similar services, with the dividing line between them often blurring. For example, the search engine AltaVista offers the LookSmart directory, which is a subject directory. Similarly, Lycos includes directory contents from the Open Directory Project.

A subject directory, as shown in Figure 6.11, offers links that are organized into subject categories. Both Yahoo! (**www.yahoo.com**) and LookSmart (**www.looksmart.com**) are popular subject directories. Subject directories are best used when you have a broad topic or idea to research. You might use a subject directory when conducting a search on the Civil War, for example. They are also helpful when you want to retrieve a list of sites relevant to your topic, rather than individual pages contained within those sites.

Search engines are useful when you have a narrow or obscure topic to research or when you want to search the full text of pages. Using a search engine, you will likely retrieve a large number of documents, not all of which will be directly related to your topic. A search engine is actually a database of Internet files collected by a computer program sometimes called a **spider**, **worm**, or

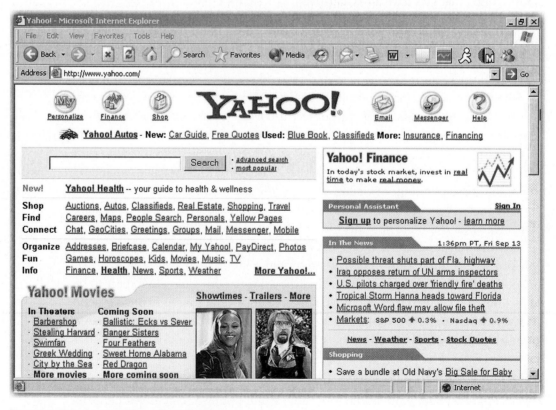

Figure 6.11 **Yahoo! is a popular subject directory.**

crawler. Results of a search engine query are indexed by title, full text, size, and URL. Although the results might be prioritized in order of relevance, the returned sites often contain few references to the searched keywords.

General search engine sites include AltaVista (**www.altavista.com**), Infoseek (**www.infoseek.com**), Lycos (**www.lycos.com**), as shown in Figure 6.12, Google (**www.google.com**), Dogpile (**www.dogpile.com**), and Mamma (**www.mamma. com**). Google is the preferred choice for many people, due to its fast, accurate, and comprehensive search results in order of keyword frequency. It has won numerous awards, including *PC World*'s Internet Product of the Year (2002). Both Dogpile and Mamma are referred to as multisearch search engines because they search more than one search engine at a time. As you become comfortable with a particular search engine, you will gravitate to it each time you conduct a search. Because each search engine reviews different lists of Internet content, each might return different results for the same search terms. Therefore, you might need to visit several search engine or subject directory sites before feeling that you have an exhaustive list of resources.

Figure 6.12 **Although there are many search engine sites, Lycos is one of the most well known.**

In your list of search results, you are likely to find a mix of at least two categories. Some results might be those of advertisers who have paid the site sponsor. Others are simply links to Web sites for additional information on the subject. Each search engine displays search results a bit differently; some search engines clearly label paid links, whereas others are less open. A recent study conducted by *PC World* magazine suggests that Google delivers exceptionally relevant matches, while at the same time clearly identifying ads.

If you don't get the results you need with one search or if you get too many sites, don't be discouraged. Either narrow your search, or try another search site. Choose your search keywords carefully, as they are critical to the success of your search. Try to be as specific as possible when wording your search terms. Persistence and advance preparation pay off!

Phrasing the Search

Each search site has its own set of rules; however, you will find that most interfaces are similar and that it is not difficult to adapt to individual site strategies. Regardless of which search site you begin with, it is a good idea to read the search rules, which vary among sites. Some search sites include a *Help* link that provides search details, such as how to include or exclude search terms.

Web Watch

Search Engine Watch is an organization focusing on evaluating and reporting about search engine sites. Visit the site at **www.search enginewatch.com/links/ article.php/2156221** to view a list of the top search engines and a discussion of each of their features.

To narrow a search, you might plan to use several keywords. For example, if looking for information on a scholarship in biology, you wouldn't want to simply specify *scholarship* as your keyword. Imagine the number of sites that search would return! Instead, you might begin with *biology scholarship* and work to narrow your search, if necessary, from there.

An inclusion operator, usually the plus (+) sign, is recognized by most search sites as an indication that connected terms must all be present in any results. If you type **biology+scholarship** as the search term, the results would only include sites containing both terms.

As the Internet is a vast computer database, you have to follow the rules of computer database searching. That process is based on principles of Boolean logic, which recognize the logical relationship between search terms. Simply put, it relies on three logical operators, OR, AND, and NOT. Most search sites have adopted a standard by which a space between multiple search terms defaults to AND. When using the keywords *Monarch Butterflies*, most sites will return only those site matches containing both words.

✓ SANITY CHECK

Make sure that you recognize the difference between the keyword area of a search engine and the address bar of a browser. Perhaps you know the address of a Web page, but instead of placing the address in the address bar, you put it in the keyword area of a search engine site. You might see a message similar to "Sorry, no information is available for URL . . . ." The problem is that although the Web address is valid, you placed it in the wrong location on the page. You should not place Web addresses in the keyword area. The keyword area is reserved for words that define your search.

A rule of thumb that usually works is to place your keyword phrases in quotation marks to force recognition of the keywords as a phrase. If searching for information on monarch butterflies, you might include the search terms in quotation marks, as "monarch butterflies," so that search results are for sites containing both words in that exact order but not one or the other singly.

If your search is more advanced, you should check the rules for advanced searches found at the search site. Depending on the rules of the search sites, you can include the NOT or OR operators. For example, if you are looking for all monarchs (kings and queens) but not butterflies, you might phrase your search "monarchs NOT butterflies." In some cases, as in the Google search site, it is even easier to phrase such searches—use the Advanced Search link to complete a form giving your preferences, without concern to exact phrasing.

Each search site works from a predefined set of rules concerning phrasing of multiple keywords. Working with Google, you can enclose all terms in quotation marks so that only sites containing those keywords *in that order* will be displayed. Including multiple keywords without enclosing them in quotation marks will return only sites with all keywords present but in any order.

If your search is successful, you will be presented with a list of linked sites. Clicking on any of those links will take you directly to the corresponding document or site. After reviewing the site, you might want to return to your search area. You might do so by clicking the Back button at the top of your browser window. If you receive a message similar to *Page Not Found* when you click a linked area, it means that the page is no longer available, or that the host server has some technical difficulty.

To enter keywords and conduct a search:

1. Click in the white area beside the search prompt. Usually, that area is titled "Search," "Look for," or "Search for." *Be certain to note the difference between the address bar of your browser and the keyword area of your search site.* The address bar acts only on Web addresses, whereas the keyword area is more free-form, allowing the entry of multiple keywords.

2. After typing your search terms, either press ⏎Enter or click the button beside the search area indicating that the search should proceed.

3. In a few seconds, you will see a listing of identified sites, as shown in Figure 6.13. You might have to scroll down slightly to see the results list. Each of the site listings will include a link, which, when clicked, will take you directly to that page.

Searching the Internet methodically yields a wealth of information on most topics. Consequently, it is important to remember that the Web is not regulated and that there is no guarantee that posted information is accurate. Critically evaluating sites, with regard to purpose, accuracy, objectivity, author, and currency of the subject, will help you determine whether a document is relevant.

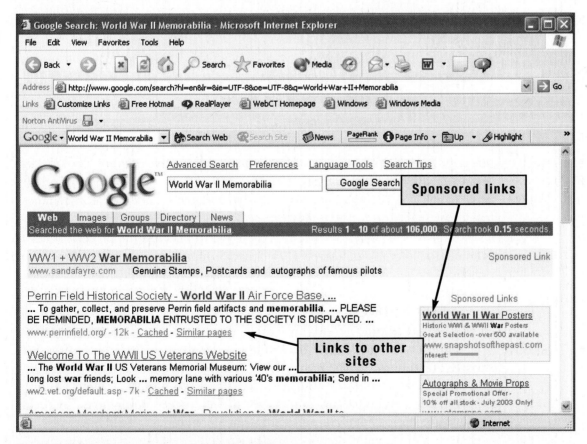

Figure 6.13 **The results of a search are listed as hyperlinks.**

Hands On

Activity 6.3—Conducting a Web Search

Suppose that you are enrolled in an English literature class and must find the full text of the poem "Snowbound" by John Greenleaf Whittier. You find yourself without access to a textbook but at a computer. Using a search engine, conduct a search for the poem.

1. Connect to the Internet. If you are in a computer lab, double-click Internet Explorer or another browser at the desktop. Otherwise, connect to your Internet service provider.
2. Click in the address bar. With the current address shaded, or selected, type **www.google.com**. Press ⏎Enter or click Go.
3. At the Google page, click in the Keyword area, just above the "Google Search" button. Type **Snowbound**. Click Google Search.
4. Looking at the results, you can see that there are many more sites related to the term "Snowbound" than simply the poem. Perhaps you need to narrow your search.

5. Click in the keyword area again, just to the right of the word "Snowbound." Press ⌫Backspace repeatedly to delete the current entry. See what happens if you type **"Snowbound Poem"** within quotation marks. Click Google Search. Note the results. Do you see the difference between the two searches?
6. To narrow your search even further, you might include the author's name in the keyword area. Connecting the keywords with a "[+]" assures that all terms are in the results, though not in any particular order. Click in the keyword area just to the right of the last entry. Press ⌫Backspace repeatedly to delete the current entry (all keywords). Type **Snowbound+Poem+Whittier**. Click Google Search.
7. From the results list, click an appropriate link to find the entire text of the poem. Were you successful?

Using Favorites (Bookmarks) and the History List

As you travel the Internet, you will undoubtedly find favorite sites to which you want to return often. Typing the URL each time you want to access a particular page, however, can get tiring and time-consuming. **Favorites**, or **bookmarks**, tag selected sites so that you can return easily. The process of setting a favorite is easy. When you are viewing a page that you want to mark for later reference, click Favorites, Add to Favorites (Internet Explorer) or Favorites, Add Top Window to Favorites (America Online). Figure 6.14 illustrates the process of using Internet Explorer to add a favorite. Netscape Communicator calls the tagged area a bookmark, allowing you to create it through the Bookmarks menu. The next time you want to visit the page, you won't have to type the URL in the address bar. Instead, just click Favorites and scroll down the list to find the name of the page to visit. Click the link to move to it.

Your browser also keeps a list of the pages you have visited, called the **history list** (Figure 6.15). The history list is handy if you want to revisit a page but can't remember the URL. Of course, clicking the Back button is the quickest way to get to a recent page from your current online session, but perhaps you want to find one that you saw yesterday or last week. Depending on the browser settings, the history list can keep a list of visited sites going back a month or more. To view the history list, click the History button on the Internet Explorer toolbar, or click View, Explorer Bar, History. Click to expand a time interval (such as two weeks ago), and click any listed Web site link to immediately return to that site.

Not quite as extensive as the history list, but still handy, is the list of the last 25 or so visited sites, available as a drop-down list from the address bar (Figure 6.16). You can check that list by clicking the drop-down button to the right of the address text box. If you want to go to any of the listed sites, simply click the site name.

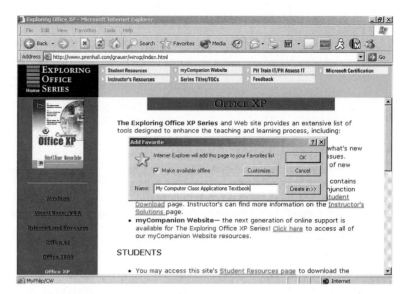

Figure 6.14 **Internet Explorer simplifies the process of setting a favorite.**

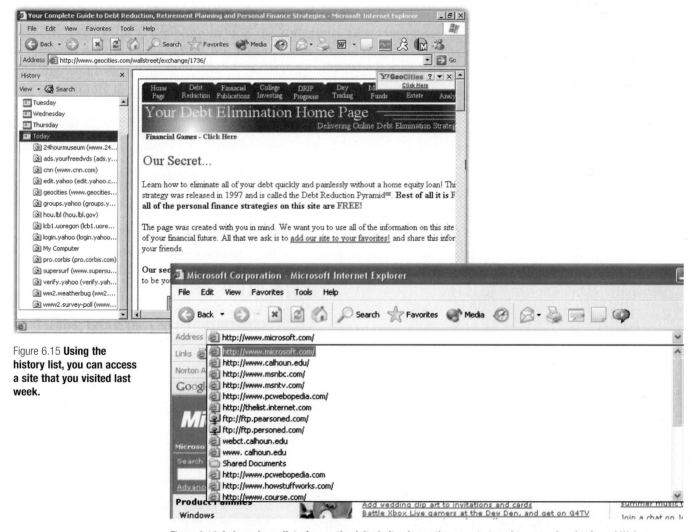

Figure 6.15 **Using the history list, you can access a site that you visited last week.**

Figure 6.16 **A drop-down list of recently visited sites is another way to travel to a previously viewed Web page.**

Understanding Societal Implications

Although the Internet is a wonderful informational tool, there are inherent concerns that you should consider. The very fact that it is so widely accessible leaves the Web open to misuse and hacking. Computer hackers welcome the chance to explore and possibly modify files on other computers, sometimes just for a challenge, but often to gather information that can be used for a profit. Viruses, attached to e-mail messages or downloaded with files, are always a possibility. Viruses infect computers, often destroying files and entire hard disks. Of even more concern to many people is the risk to personal privacy by traveling and conducting business on the Internet. It is a good idea to be aware of security and privacy risks; however, most people agree that the benefits of using the Internet far outweigh any possible problems.

Being aware of privacy and security concerns is a first step toward protecting yourself as much as possible. Antivirus software and firewalls (discussed in Chapter 7) are necessary to prevent damaging viruses that cause you to lose data and to prohibit unauthorized access to your computer. Identity theft, where a third party profits from illegally collecting your private information, is also a common concern. You might worry that businesses keep too much information about you in computer databases, with not enough control over how the information is used. All of those concerns are valid but shouldn't discourage you from using the Internet—simply remain aware of the risks and informed of solutions.

The Internet is full of possibilities and is a revolutionary approach to daily activities, business, and information retrieval. Through your home personal computer, you can easily begin your Internet experience.

In the Know

You can change the number of days that entries are kept on the history list, and you can also remove entries from the history list. In Internet Explorer, click Tools, Internet Options. A dialog box appears, as shown in Figure 6.17. Click the spinner to change the number of days. Click Clear History to remove all items from the history list.

Figure 6.17 **You can remove all entries from the history list and change the number of days or weeks to keep track of visited sites.**

Chapter Summary

DON'T FORGET

- The Internet comprises millions of computers connected globally and in communication with one another.

- The WWW is a component of the Internet, using browsers to share information and multimedia documents.

- Methods of connecting to the Internet include dial-up (using a modem), cable modem, ISDN, DSL, wireless, and Internet TV.

- To connect with an online service company, such as America Online or CompuServe, you can create an account using an installation CD.

- A Web page is a document designed to be displayed on the WWW, possibly containing hyperlinks to other Web pages. A Web site is made up of one or more Web pages.

- A URL identifies every published Web page.

- A typical URL, such as **http://www.sciquest.org/activities**, contains several components, including protocol, domain name, and folder.

- To move among Web pages, type a Web page address in the address bar of your browser.

- A browser is a software tool that allows you to navigate, or "browse," the Web. It is your window to the Web.

- The two most popular browsers are Internet Explorer and Netscape Communicator.

- Web sites include those specializing in online shopping, online banking, news, stock transactions, and government information.

- Searching the Web is an analytical approach to quickly finding information, using search engines, search directories, and keywords.

- Using favorites, you can tag a Web page so that you can visit it later without having to remember the Web page address.

- The history list displays recently visited sites and allows you to access them quickly.

- Societal issues related to the Internet include privacy, security, and communication.

KEY TERMS

America Online	**communications program**	**encryption**
ARPANet	**CompuServe**	**favorites**
Asymmetric DSL	**crawler**	**history list**
Basic Rate Interface	**cybersquatting**	**home page**
bookmark	**dial-up modem**	**HTML**
broadband	**Digital Subscriber Line**	**HTTP (Hypertext Transfer**
browser	**(DSL)**	**Protocol)**
cable modem	**domain name**	**hyperlink**

Integrated Services Digital Net-
work (ISDN)
Internet
Internet access provider (IAP)
Internet Corporation for Assigned
Names and Numbers (ICANN)
Internet Explorer
Internet service provider (ISP)
Internet TV
link
Microsoft Network (MSN)
MSN® TV

Netscape Communicator
NSFNet
online services
password
Primary Rate Interface
protocol
search engine
search tool
Secure Sockets Layer (SSL)
spider
subject directory
top-level domain

Uniform Resource Locator (URL)
user name
Web authoring software
Web page
Web scripting language
Web site
wireless
World Wide Web (WWW)
World Wide Web Consortium
(W3C)
worm

TRUE/FALSE

Circle **T** if the statement is true or **F** if the statement is false.

T F 1. The predecessor of the Internet was ARPANet.

T **F** 2. A keyword area and the address bar are two terms that relate to the same space in a browser.

T **F** 3. A controlled, concise procedure for locating items on the Internet is called "browsing."

T F 4. The Internet is a group of interconnected computers spanning the globe and in communication with one another.

T F 5. A domain name identifies a host computer.

T **F** 6. A browser is another term for a search engine.

T **F** 7. DSL is a high-speed connection available through a television cable.

T F 8. The terms ISP and IAP are interchangeable, referring to the same type of Internet provider.

T F 9. A disadvantage of a dial-up modem, when compared with other connection technologies, is its speed.

T **F** 10. A modem is not required if you contract with a cable company to provide Internet service.

MULTIPLE CHOICE

1. Each published Web page is identified by a unique address, known as a(n)
   a. HTTP
   b. hyperlink
   c. URL
   d. domain name

2. This software tool includes a graphical interface and features that allow you to travel the Internet and customize your Internet environment.
   a. search tool
   b. Hypertext Markup Language
   c. modem
   d. browser

3. A subset of the Internet that makes broad use of hyperlinks and a graphical presentation is the
   a. World Wide Web
   b. ARPANet
   c. ISP
   d. search engine

4. Most dial-up modems are designed to operate at a speed of
   a. 28.8 Kbps
   b. 1.5 Mbps
   c. 56 Kbps
   d. 14.4 Kbps

5. A difference between a search engine and a subject directory is that
   a. a search engine focuses on broad topics, whereas a subject directory is best for narrow topics
   b. a search engine is designed to support online services, whereas a subject directory is a component of an Internet access provider
   c. a search engine searches the Internet, whereas a subject directory searches the World Wide Web
   d. a search engine is best for researching narrow topics, whereas a subject directory provides information on broad topics

6. Which ISDN interface will most home and small business owners find to be appropriate?
   a. BRI
   b. DSL
   c. PRI
   d. wireless

7. To force recognition of search keywords as a phrase, you might
   a. include the keywords in the address bar
   b. enclose the keywords in parentheses
   c. connect the keywords with a plus (+) sign
   d. enclose the keywords in quotation marks (" ")

8. A collection of one or more associated Web pages is called a
   a. Web site
   b. Web location
   c. browser
   d. Web interface

9. A special requirement of DSL is that
   a. you must use existing television cable
   b. you can only contract with an online service, such as America Online
   c. you must be within a certain distance of a telephone switching station (central office)
   d. your computer must have at least 512 MB of RAM

10. The part of a URL that identifies the host computer is the
   a. protocol
   b. directory
   c. top-level domain
   d. domain name

PRACTICAL PROJECTS

1. Search and Find

Using one or more search engines of your choice, find each of the following items and list the URL for each.

   a. Who is the current head football coach of the University of Michigan?
   b. A vexillologist is an expert in what?
   c. Who is the current governor of Arizona?
   d. Where might you go on the Internet to find training materials (or classes) for the MCSE certification?
   e. What is an RCDD?
   f. Give at least one retired hurricane name.
   g. Find the entire text of the U.S. Constitution.
   h. Find a recipe for pumpkin bread.
   i. What is the mascot of the University of New Mexico?
   j. Where might a child go for help with arithmetic homework?

2. Making the Connection

Many people contract with a local cable company for Internet access. Investigate the options in your area, and provide a comparison of cable connection and dial-up connection. In your summary, be sure to list all associated costs, including installation and monthly service. What data transfer speed can you expect from a cable connection? Can you contract with an online service, such as MSN, if you are using a cable service? Provide enough detail so that a computer novice would understand the advantages and disadvantages of cable connection, know its cost and speed, and be able to use that information to select the service.

3. Tutorials and Tips

You can use the Internet to learn about the Internet. There are a great many Internet sites providing tutorials and information on such topics as Internet basics and tips for searching. Help your fellow classmates by providing a list of at least five sites that introduce Internet basics and at least five sites that focus on search engines and tips for searching. For each site, you should include the URL and a brief description of the purpose of the site.

4. Electronic Banking

Most banks offer online banking or plan to do so soon. With online banking, you can access your savings and checking accounts and pay bills online. You can even schedule your payments to occur at a set time, so that you don't have to remember due dates or buy stamps! Although it sounds wonderful, many people are hesitant to trust Internet transfers and worry about privacy. What about you? Write a few paragraphs explaining all that you know about online banking, describing common features and procedures. Provide information on how your bank handles online banking and what is required to work with an online account. Conclude by explaining whether you would use the service and, if not, why not.

5. Just Browsing

Two of the most commonly used browsers are Internet Explorer and Netscape Communicator. Both are available as a free download from the Internet. However, they are not the only choices that you have. Search the Web for browsers, and give a report of your findings. For each browser, including Internet Explorer and Netscape, provide information on how to obtain the browser, as well as any advantages or special features.

Working with the Internet

Working with the Internet is a little like driving a car. You can go places, run errands, and enjoy yourself. Along the way, you might even purchase some items. However, because you are on the road with a lot of other traffic, especially at peak hours of the day, you must understand the rules of travel. The more you drive, the more skilled you become and the more aware you are of favorite destinations and routes. Just as you value your car and would probably never leave it in a crowded parking lot with the windows rolled down and the keys in the ignition, security is a concern on the Internet. Unlike driving a car, working with the Internet doesn't require a license and there are no fatal crashes! Aside from these two things, the analogy aptly describes what you are doing when you work with the Internet—you are traveling along a "highway," making stops along the way, observing rules of the road, and remaining secure.

In this chapter, we will introduce you to different methods of collecting text and pictures from the

Objectives

When you complete this chapter, you will:

- **Understand how to download programs and files from the Internet.**

- **Be able to collect and print items from the Internet.**

- **Understand the concept of the Clipboard and know how to copy and paste items.**

- **Know how to manage plug-ins.**

- **Be able to identify privacy and security risks, including computer viruses.**

- **Be aware of methods used to collect private information, such as cookies and spyware.**

*Internet. Transferring files or software from one computer to another is called **downloading**. Of growing concern are the security and privacy of your personal data, especially given the ever-increasing Internet traffic and the vulnerability of computers without adequate **antivirus** and **firewall** protection. Although an antivirus program scans all incoming and outgoing items for computer viruses, a firewall monitors requests for travel to and from your computer when you are online. It is becoming increasingly important to maintain the privacy of your personal records and to know that you can move among Web sites relatively unobserved and without subsequent advertising appeals. Although some software is available and legislation is in place to protect your privacy online, it is not enough to completely discourage zealous advertisers and unscrupulous people from monitoring your travels and computer records. There are things that you can do to safeguard your privacy and security, as discussed later in this chapter.*

Downloading Software

The Internet contains a wealth of information and resources. As you work with it, you are likely to identify software, games, and other items that you would like to use on your computer. Software manufacturers now offer versions of software for download, enabling you to purchase it online or acquire the software for a trial period before making a purchase decision. You can download screen savers, clip art, games, antivirus software, productivity software, and all sorts of handy gadgets. Although some downloads are available only by purchase, others are free for personal use.

Downloading is the process of getting a file or software application from a distant computer and placing it on your computer's hard disk, a floppy disk, or a CD. Instead of simply viewing the file on a Web page, you are able to keep a copy of the file on your computer system for later use. For example, you might want to have a copy of a lengthy worksheet, prepared by a colleague and offered as a download or included as an e-mail attachment. Friends or family might want to send you a photo of a new baby, or you might identify some computer games you would like to try. Those are all examples of items that you can download and keep on your computer.

Uploading is the process of sending a file from your computer to another computer or server. An instructor might prepare a learning unit at home and then upload it to the campus server for class access. A special type of Internet site, called an **FTP (File Transfer Protocol)** site, makes it easy to transfer files from your computer to an online computer server. Although it is important to understand uploading, it is much more prevalent for people to download files.

Whether you are successful at downloading a file depends upon two things. First, your computer must have enough available disk space. Many downloaded files or programs are large, requiring a great deal of storage space. Second, the file that you want to download might not be available for unrestricted copying. Some files are proprietary or copyrighted; others are housed in password-protected sites. You will learn to identify those items that are available for download, either free or purchased.

There are basically two types of items available for download—programs and data files. Many sites offer *programs*, such as a trial version of an antivirus scanner, as a download. After you download the program, you must install it to make it functional. A *data file* might be your colleague's worksheet or a photograph attached to an e-mail message. You don't have to install data files, but you do need to have appropriate software to open those data files. For example, if the colleague's worksheet that you just downloaded was created with Microsoft Excel, then you must have Microsoft Excel on your system to view the worksheet. Likewise, you must have appropriate software loaded before you are able to view graphic files.

Files to be downloaded are usually found in two places—as e-mail attachments (addressed in Chapter 8) and on Web sites. As you consider downloading a file, it is helpful to know how much disk space the file requires. Often, you will find that information near the download link. If that information is available before you begin the download, you can check your disk to make sure there is enough room for the file.

To download from a Web site:

Web Watch

Some Web sites offer extensive download links. Find extensive download links at **www.download.com**.

1. Create a folder, possibly on the desktop, to hold downloaded files and programs. Although downloading is not complicated, locating the file after it has been downloaded can be time-consuming if you are not careful about where the file is placed on the hard disk. To create a download folder, open Windows Explorer and click to select the desktop in the folders pane. Click File, New, and Folder. Type a name for your folder, and press ⏎Enter. Use the new folder as the location for all downloaded items so that you can easily find them.

2. Locate the item to be downloaded. It might be that you are visiting a Web page and notice an interesting item available for download. Click whatever link on the page appears to initiate the download. Remember that a link is an item, either graphic or text, that you can click to proceed to another page or process. When you move the mouse pointer over a link, it usually becomes either an arrow or a pointing hand. The download link might be as obvious as a *Download Now* designation, but there is no set way for a file or program to be identified. Read the Web page carefully to find any download links. Figure 7.1 shows a Web page with a download link.

3. Follow all prompts to download the item. When asked whether to open the file in its current location or save it to your disk, select the save option, as shown in Figure 7.2. That way, you can scan it for viruses before opening it.

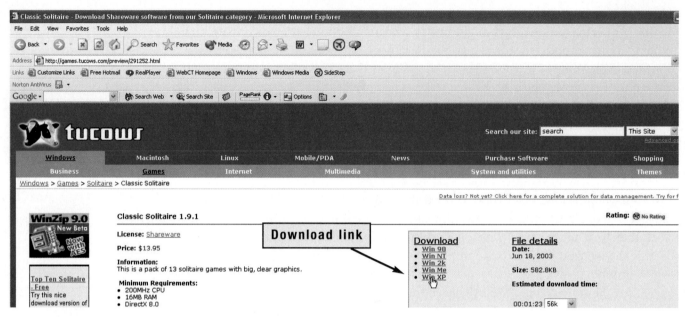

Figure 7.1 **A download link on a Web page begins the download process.**

Figure 7.2 **Choose the Save option when you are downloading so that you can scan the file for viruses.**

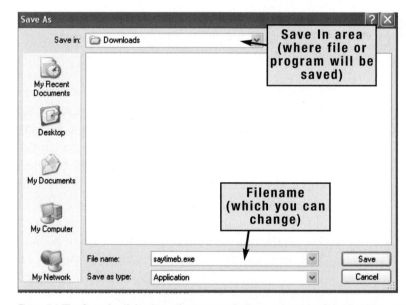

Figure 7.3 **The Save As dialog box allows you to indicate where the file should be saved.**

You will have to specify a location (folder) in which the file should be saved (Figure 7.3). Click the drop-down arrow beside the Save In box, click desktop, and double-click the download folder that you created on your desktop in Step 1. Make note of the filename. Although you can change the filename later, it will be helpful to know the name of the file so that you can identify it later.

4. Scan the downloaded item for viruses, using your antivirus software. Read the documentation or use the Help feature of the antivirus software to learn how to scan files.

5. Install or open the downloaded item. If the download is a program, you must install it before you can use it. If the downloaded item is a file, you can open it. Double-click the download folder on the desktop, and double-click the downloaded item to either open it or install it. During the installation of a program, you will most likely deal with an installation wizard that makes the process as simple as responding to a few prompts. Of course, if the item is a file, and if you have appropriate software on your system, the file will open, displaying its contents.

6. Manage the contents of the download folder. Especially if you download a lot of files and programs, you will want to keep the download folder from becoming too cluttered. When a *program file* is installed, it is placed either as an item on your program list or as an icon on the desktop. At that point, you won't need to keep the downloaded installation file in the download folder, so delete it. The installation program is used only to install the program. A *data file* is not a file that you would install, but you do need to open it to view its contents. If the data file is something that you want to keep, you should move it to a more appropriate folder on your hard disk or CD. Otherwise, you can delete it from the download folder as well.

✓ SANITY CHECK

If you attempt to open a downloaded file but instead of viewing the file contents, you see a dialog box like that shown in Figure 7.4, there is a simple explanation. Either you don't have the software required to open the file or your system doesn't recognize the file type and can't associate it with a specific type of software. Either way, you are not able to view the file. Although the dialog box suggests that you select a program to open, the truth is that unless you are adept at recognizing and manipulating file types, you should accept the fact that you can't view the file. Click Close. If you have saved the downloaded file to your system, perhaps to a folder on the desktop, you should use Windows Explorer or My Computer to delete the file.

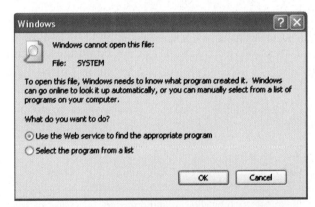

Figure 7.4 **When presented with this dialog box, your system doesn't have the software required to view the downloaded file.**

Collecting and Printing Items from the Internet

You won't need to download complete files or programs if all that you want to do is print or save a section of text from a Web page. Perhaps you want to print a section of an online article or copy a recipe for inclusion in a cookbook that you are creating. You might find an item of clip art (a graphic) that would be perfect for an upcoming newsletter or school report. Collecting or printing those items is easy to do but requires that you understand the concept of copying and pasting.

When you **copy** or **cut** an item, you place it in an area known as the **Clipboard**. The Clipboard is a temporary holding area in RAM where items are placed until you **paste** them into a document or project of some kind. You are probably familiar with the concept of cutting and pasting, where you might physically cut a paragraph from a printed document and paste it on another. The same principle applies to electronic cutting and pasting. Perhaps you are working on a document in a word processor and you decide that you would like a paragraph better on a different page. You can cut the paragraph (placing it on the Clipboard), move to the desired page, and paste the paragraph. Similarly, you can copy a paragraph to another document altogether. Perhaps you have just found some information on the Internet that might be helpful to a friend. By copying that information and pasting it in an e-mail message, you can send it directly to her. Following a few routine steps can simplify the cut, copy, and paste operations. The nice thing is that applications (programs) that are designed to run under Windows contain similar menu and toolbar features, so the cut and copy options are usually found in the same places in each Windows-based program. The table in Figure 7.5 describes several menu selections and shortcut keystrokes that invoke cut, copy, and paste operations.

Collecting Text from the Internet to Save

There will be occasions when you want to copy some text from a Web page to a document that you are creating. Because you cannot cut items from the Internet, copying is your only option. Remember that copyright protection is extended to items posted on a Web page, so you need to use the same caution that you would for printed items when copying anything. Suppose that you have just bought a border collie puppy and need some information on training him. Books are available, but you know that there is probably a lot of information online as well.

Cut	Copy	Paste
Make selection by clicking and dragging. Click Edit, Cut.	Make selection by clicking and dragging. Click Edit, Copy.	Click where you want the selection to be placed. Click Edit, Paste.
Make selection by clicking and dragging. Right-click selection. Click Cut.	Make selection by clicking and dragging. Right-click selection. Click Copy.	Click where you want the selection to be placed. Right-click. Click Paste.
Make selection by clicking and dragging. Press the Ctrl key. While holding it down, press X.	Make selection by clicking and dragging. Press the Ctrl key. While holding it down, press C.	Click where you want the selection to be placed. Press the Ctrl key While holding it down, press V.
Make selection by clicking and dragging. Click the Cut icon on the Standard toolbar.	Make selection by clicking and dragging. Click the Copy icon on the Standard toolbar.	Click where you want the selection to be placed. Click the Paste icon on the Standard toolbar.

Figure 7.5 **There are several different ways to cut, copy, and paste.**

Using a search engine, you can find an article of particular interest and copy a few paragraphs from that article into a document to save and print later. With the article displayed, simply click and drag to select the desired paragraphs, copy them (refer to Figure 7.5 for a method), move to a word processing document, and paste the paragraphs (again, see Figure 7.5 for a pasting method).

✓ SANITY CHECK

Most, but not all, software includes cut, copy, and paste options on the Edit menu or the toolbar. If you are attempting to copy an item but don't see an appropriate menu selection, remember the shortcut key combinations that almost always work—Ctrl-C to copy, Ctrl-X to cut, and Ctrl-V to paste.

Hands On

Activity 7.1—Copying a Recipe from the Internet

In this exercise, you will identify and copy a recipe from the Internet for inclusion in a cookbook that you are creating with a word processor. You are looking for a recipe for beef brisket. Your computer should be at the desktop.

1. Open your word processor. Click Start, All Programs, and select a word processor from the program list. If you don't see a word processor, you can use WordPad by clicking Start, All Programs, Accessories, WordPad.
2. Access the Internet.
3. Go to a search engine site and begin your search for a beef brisket recipe.
4. From the subsequent list of matching sites, click any that look interesting. Remember to click the Back button to return to the listing of sites at any time.
5. When you find a recipe that you want to include in your book, click and drag to select it. *The first step in a successful copy and paste procedure is to select the items or text to be copied.* When an area is shaded, it is selected.
6. Follow one of the suggestions in Figure 7.5 to copy the text.
7. To paste the text, close or minimize the browser window.
8. Return to the word processing document. Because you just opened the word processing document in Step 1, the blinking cursor should be at the top left corner, which is where you want your recipe to be pasted. Follow one of the suggestions in Figure 7.5 to paste the text.
9. Place a floppy disk in the A: drive. To save the document to your disk, click File, Save As. Click the drop-down arrow beside the Save In box and select 3½ Floppy (A:). Type an appropriate filename. Click Save.
10. The document is saved and can be retrieved later for printing or to hold additional information.

■▶Quick Tip

You can also selectively print items from other applications, not just the Internet. Perhaps you have a word processing document on-screen and want to print a couple of paragraphs. Click and drag to select them, click File, Print, and make sure to choose the Selection option. Click Print.

Selectively Printing from the Internet

There are times when you will want to capture items from the Internet for printing but don't necessarily want to save them in a document on your hard drive. All that you want to do is print the selected item. Perhaps an online newspaper includes an article that is of special interest. You might want to print the article but nothing else on the Web page. Because you don't want to save it for later retrieval or editing, you don't need to go through the steps given in the preceding section. Instead, you will simply select the text and print it. The Clipboard is not involved in selective printing, as it is in copying and pasting. By making appropriate selections in the Print dialog box (displayed when you click File, Print), you can print only the selected text.

Capturing Clip Art

Many of the pictures that you see on a typical Web page are considered **clip art** and can be saved to your disk. Clip art images are often used to liven up documents or included in any number of computer projects, such as greeting cards and brochures. Like text, clip art can be copyrighted, so watch for any indication of copyright before saving and using an image. The Web page might post a notice that its clip art images are copyrighted. Also, if the images are available for purchase, they are probably copyrighted. A quick Internet search will identify many Web sites that offer free clip art and photos. Collecting graphics from the Internet is an easy process, as described in the following steps.

To collect a graphic from the Internet:

1. Search the Internet, identifying a Web page with available clip art.
2. Right-click the graphic or clip art that you want to save. A context menu will appear, as shown in Figure 7.6
3. Click Save Picture As.

Hands On

Activity 7.2—Selective Printing

In this exercise, you will print an article from an online newspaper. Your computer should be at the desktop. You should also have access to a printer.

1. Access the Internet.
2. Conduct a search to find the Web site of a local or regional newspaper.
3. Identify an article to print.
4. Select the article by clicking and dragging the text.
5. To print only the selected text, click File, Print. Click the option button beside Selection. Click Print.

4. In the Save As dialog box, note the Save In area. A folder, such as My Pictures, is probably suggested, but you might prefer to save the image in a folder created specifically for graphics, perhaps one that you create on the desktop. If you want to save the image in a folder other than the one suggested, click the drop-down arrow beside the Save In area and navigate to the desired folder.
5. Note the filename, changing it if you like.
6. Click Save.
7. Close all open windows. The clip art image is saved to your computer system for later use.

To view downloaded clip art:

1. Open Windows Explorer.
2. In the folders pane, click to select the folder in which the clip art is saved. The graphic file should appear in the contents pane to the right.
3. You can get a thumbnail view, which is a small image, by clicking View, Thumbnails. To get a larger view, double-click the file to open it.
4. Close all open windows.

Figure 7.6 **Right-clicking an image produces a context menu, from which you can choose to save an image to a disk.**

✔ SANITY CHECK

Sometimes the text that you want to select might extend beyond the viewable area of your screen. Keep holding down the mouse button as you move the pointer to the bottom of the screen to scroll the page. When all text is selected, release the mouse button. If you select more text than you intended, keep holding down the mouse button while you drag back up to highlight only what you need.

Managing Plug-ins

Browsers are well equipped to display most Web pages, but occasionally you will come across an item that won't work unless you get a **plug-in**, which is a specialty program designed to work with multimedia files (requiring special audio, visual, or animation effects). Newer browser versions will have much of what you need to enjoy multimedia formats without plug-ins. However, you will still occasionally be prompted to download a plug-in before a file can be accessed. For example, you might want to watch a news video from a news Web page. If your browser doesn't support video, your system will let you know that you need a plug-in when you click the news video link. Most often, you will agree to download the plug-in because it will be necessary, not only for the current file, but for others that you might access in the future. When you agree to download the plug-in, you will be directed to the Web page containing the download link, or the download will just begin automatically.

⚓ Web Watch

You can find links to common plug-in downloads at **home.netscape.com/ plugins/index.html.**

Common plug-ins include RealPlayer (**www.realplayer.com**), QuickTime (**www.quicktime.com**), Acrobat Reader (**www.adobe.com/acrobat**), and Shockwave (**www.shockwave.com**). Each plug-in specializes in a certain area—audio, video, animation, or the display of forms online. Shockwave facilitates an entire multimedia display, including graphics, animation, and sound. RealPlayer plays audio and video files, often of live events, such as a news broadcast or concert. QuickTime displays movie-type files in a small window on your computer screen. Adobe Reader is a plug-in that allows you to view documents created in Adobe's Portable Document Format (PDF). Although you can try to be well prepared by downloading plug-ins before you need them, it is easier to wait to be alerted to the need for a plug-in when you attempt to access a file or program.

Hands On

Activity 7.3—Working with PDF Files and Adobe Reader

Adobe Acrobat, which is part of a line of software products produced by Adobe, allows documents captured from a variety of word processors and desktop publishing applications to be formatted for appearance on a recipient's monitor or printer. Although you might not be directly involved in the production of such documents, you will often want to read or display those forms on your monitor.

A standard file format, known as Portable Document Format (PDF), is often used by Web developers to display forms online. To view those PDF files, you should have Adobe Reader installed on your system. Most Web pages promoting the PDF format also include a link allowing you to download Adobe Reader if necessary. Although Adobe offers the Acrobat product line at various levels of price and capability, Adobe Reader continues to be a free download, available at **www.adobe.com/products/acrobat/readstep2.html**.

In this exercise, you will view a Portable Document Format (PDF) file.

1. Check your system to see if you have Adobe Reader. Click Start, Control Panel, Add or Remove Programs. A list of all currently installed programs will appear. Check the program list to see if Adobe Acrobat or Adobe Reader is there. Close all open windows. If you don't see the program in the list, you will not be able to complete this exercise.
2. Connect to the Internet. If you are in a computer lab, you will probably need to double-click Internet Explorer at the desktop. Otherwise, connect with your Internet service provider.
3. Click in the address bar of the browser, and type the address **www.calhoun.edu**. Press ⏎Enter or click Go.
4. You will be at the home page of Calhoun Community College. Click Publications and Forms.
5. Click Scholarship Application to view the form. The PDF form will be displayed. Click the close (X) button to close your Internet connection.

Understanding Privacy and Security Concerns

It is no secret that the Internet is a risky place. Computer viruses are rampant, and unscrupulous characters are always looking for opportunities to steal your identity and compromise your personal data. A seemingly innocent downloaded program can bring with it software that tracks your every move and records each transaction that you make online. Targeted advertising banners seem to pop up out of nowhere and, strangely enough, the advertisements are reflective of some sites that you visited recently. Given the obvious privacy and security risks, it is easy to conclude that you have no business online. However, just as you continue to drive a car fully aware of the risks, you will probably decide that the benefits of using the Internet far outweigh the risks. And just as you protect a car with a burglar alarm and locked doors, you can protect your computer by using antivirus scanners, firewalls, and other software designed to counteract security and privacy risks.

Viruses

A computer **virus** is a program that is written to be either annoying or destructive. Computer viruses don't occur naturally; they are maliciously written by individuals intent on challenging networks and demonstrating their computer prowess. Just as human viruses pass from person to person, computer viruses travel among computers, perpetuating a vicious cycle of destruction. They usually infect your system through removable disk media, such as floppy disks and CDs, and through downloaded programs. Some viruses come in through e-mail attachments and, in rare cases, along with a text e-mail message alone. Thankfully, you can count on antivirus software to protect your system against viruses.

Viruses can sabotage your entire computer system, causing you to go to great expense to repair the damage. A virus can alter the behavior of a program or operating system, sometimes waiting for months before wiping out an entire hard disk or otherwise contaminating data. They can affect careers and destroy companies, because data can be wiped out in a second. Imagine the devastation experienced by the loss of all of a company's accounts receivable records. Many companies advise employees to back up all data prior to a Friday the 13th, a popular date for virus mischief. They also make backups of all important files regularly. Once considered merely a nuisance, viruses are costing American companies billions of dollars each year and cause serious aggravation for individual computer users.

An unpleasant type of virus, called a **worm**, is usually sent as an e-mail attachment. When you open the attachment, the worm finds your e-mail address book and sends out the infected attachment to everyone in your address book. In that manner, a worm can replicate itself quickly and bring an e-mail system to a crawl. Some are even capable of scanning your system for such things as passwords, which are then sent back to the originator of the worm. The Kak worm actually hides itself in the signature file of Outlook Express. Outlook Express is an e-mail program installed along with Windows. Although Outlook Express is especially vulnerable to viruses, Microsoft continues to release patches (fixes) for any identified security loopholes in Outlook.

A **macro virus** is one of the most widespread virus types, infecting your system when a data file with an attached virus is opened. Microsoft applications, such as Microsoft Word and Excel, include a **macro language**, which allows certain program processes to be automated. Macro viruses are written in the macro language of an application. When you open a Word or Excel data file, you might have to respond to a dialog box asking whether you want to disable macros. Macros are often used to carry macro viruses, so it is probably a good idea either to disable macros so that there is less chance of a macro virus entering your system through an infected data file or to scan the file for viruses before opening it. Destructive macro viruses can overwrite data, modify the contents of documents, and even send documents by e-mail. Macros do serve a purpose, however, in allowing the automation of certain program activities, such as including some animation in a word processing document.

A **Trojan horse** is a program that appears harmless but really contains instructions to destroy files, programs, or even your file allocation table (whose purpose is to keep track of where files and programs are stored). A Trojan horse might be hidden in a game or utility that you download. Some Trojan horses, called *logic bombs*, execute when a certain logic condition occurs. For example, the virus might change every occurrence of the word "useless" to "useful" in a document. Others are called *time bombs* because they make mischief only on a specific date or time of day.

The newest type of virus is a **Web applet virus**, which can exist in three popular **Web scripting languages**—ActiveX, JavaScript, and Java. A Web scripting language is used by designers of Web pages to create interactive Web sites (sites that respond to input from you and that display animated images). The transfer of a Web applet virus is triggered when you simply access the infected Web page.

Avoiding a Virus

Although there is no foolproof way to avoid a computer virus, there are several things you can do to lessen the chance of getting one. If your computer doesn't already have an antivirus program installed, purchase and install one immediately. You will find a variety of antivirus programs at your local software retailer, or you can download a trial version from the Internet and then purchase it online before the trial period ends.

After the antivirus software is installed, you must be certain to update it often so that it remains current and fully capable of eliminating the newest viruses. The procedure for updating antivirus software varies, but you can usually find and download **virus definitions** (updates to antivirus software that counteract new viruses) at the software vendor's Web site. If your antivirus software is a recent version, you might find that it automatically updates itself without your involvement while you are online. In addition to keeping antivirus software updated, you will want to configure it to automatically scan all incoming and outgoing e-mail, all downloaded programs, and all removable media, such as floppy disks and CDs.

The following activities can also reduce your chances of contracting a virus:

- Install antivirus software and keep it up to date by downloading new virus definitions. You might be able to schedule your antivirus program to update itself when you are online.

- Scan floppy disks and CDs with antivirus software before using them and don't share disks.

- Scan all downloaded programs *before* you install them.

- If you get an attachment, scan it before you open it, even if it is from someone you know.

- Configure your antivirus software to load automatically at startup and to run at all times, scanning all downloaded material, e-mail attachments, and removable media.

- Use the same scanning care whether you are on a company network or at home.

- Make backups of files you can't do without, such as financial information and photographs.

- Run a full system scan (a scan of all components of your computer system) with your antivirus software at least once weekly.

- Don't boot your system from a floppy disk unless you have scanned the floppy disk for viruses. Be sure to remove any floppy disks from your computer when you shut it down. Otherwise, the computer will attempt to read from the floppy the next time you power it on, giving an opportunity for a virus to act.

Virus Symptoms

A virus can affect your computer system in many ways. Some viruses are merely irritating, such as one that causes "Yankee Doodle" to play at 5:00 P.M. every eight days. Others are extremely destructive, perhaps waiting a few days before destroying your entire hard disk. You might become suspicious of virus activity if you experience any of the following:

- Programs take longer to load than normal.

- Your computer's hard drive constantly runs out of free space.

- The floppy disk drive or hard drive runs when you are not using it.

- New files appear on the system and you don't know where they came from.

- Strange sounds or beeping noises come from the computer or keyboard.

- Files have strange names that you don't recognize.

- Program sizes change unexpectedly.

- Programs act erratically.

Removing a Virus

If you have antivirus software installed on your system, it will flag files that contain viruses. When you are notified of a virus, ask the antivirus software to *clean* the file. If the antivirus software lets you know that the file couldn't be cleaned but offers to *quarantine* it, agree. When an item is quarantined, it is sectioned away from the rest of the system components until you decide what to do with it. Check your antivirus software instruction manual for information on how to delete items from quarantine.

Your only protection against viruses is an effective antivirus software package. Antivirus software sales leaders include Norton Antivirus and McAfee VirusScan, but there are other choices, some even free. Carefully choose your software because you will want an effective product that is easy to use and that automates many of the tasks that you are likely to put off or forget, like downloading virus definitions and conducting a full system scan. The table in Figure 7.7 outlines a few of the products on the market.

Antivirus Software	Description	Vendor Web Site
Norton Antivirus	Latest version includes script blocking (Web applet viruses) and worm detection.	www.symantec.com
McAfee VirusScan Home Edition	Latest version stops scripts (Web applet viruses) and mass-mailing worms.	www.mcafee.com
Panda Antivirus Platinum	Combines virus protection and firewall protection. It also includes optional script blocking and attachment filtering combined with daily updates.	www.panda.com
F-Prot for Windows	Includes an easy-to-use interface for computer novices and is very effective.	www.f-prot.com
Norman Virus Control	Allows you to configure e-mail attachment blocking, full system scan, and automatic updates. It was the top pick in 2003 of *PC-World*, a respected industry publication.	www.norman.com
PC-cillin	Features both firewall and antivirus capability, scanning e-mail and all system components automatically. It also works with mobile computing, addressing PDA and wireless security.	www.pc-cillin2003.com
BitDefender Professional	An effective antivirus tool, BitDefender provides comprehensive coverage for all virus types.	www.bitdefender.com
Nod32	Unique in its continued capability to protect older computer systems, Nod32 is barely perceptible on a computer system, yet it includes full virus protection.	www.nod32.com

Figure 7.7 **There are a large number of antivirus software packages available. Most are available for download and purchase online.**

In the Know

For many years, computer viruses have plagued business and home computer users. Through the years, viruses have evolved into a variety of types, categorized by their behavior, the affected operating system, and the type of programming used to create them.

The first type of viruses infected executable files (those with an extension of .exe or .com) by placing their programming instructions inside programs.

Boot sector viruses are transmitted when an infected floppy disk is left in the disk drive and the system is rebooted. They bypass antivirus software by beginning before the operating system is loaded.

Macro viruses were created when software developers like Microsoft began to include programming code in application software so that users could automate commands. The infected data files are run by the applications that support the macros (the programming language included in certain software products).

The worm is probably the most commonly encountered malicious program. It actually replicates itself, usually by e-mail, but doesn't infect other programs. Examples of recent worms are Melissa and ILOVEYOU, both of which caused widespread problems.

Trojan horses trick users into starting them, because they are disguised as harmless software.

Hybrid viruses are able to act in more than one way, such as when a worm, which normally replicates itself only by e-mail, is also capable of infecting program files.

Although new versions of antivirus software are introduced often, you don't need to purchase each new version. Making certain that your software remains current by downloading new virus definitions is usually sufficient. When you purchase antivirus software, you are also purchasing a *subscription*, which entitles you to virus definition updates for at least a year. As your subscription term nears its end, the antivirus software will send you messages to that effect, and you must purchase another subscription to maintain use of the software. Subscription costs are usually in the neighborhood of $15 per year. Eventually, of course, you will find that a new version or different software package offers services and features that make it an attractive replacement for your current antivirus software.

Firewalls

The Internet provides a perfect avenue for computer-savvy individuals to access your computer and personal data. When you are online, your computer is visible and vulnerable, unless it is protected by a software program called a firewall. Once used only by corporate networks, a firewall is now a necessity for home computer security. If your computer is connected to the Internet through a cable

Firewall Software	Vendor Web Site
Outpost Firewall	**www.agnitum.com/products/outpost**
Sygate Personal Firewall	**soho.sygate.com/default.htm**
Deerfield Personal Firewall	**www.deerfield.com/products/personal_firewall**
Norton Personal Firewall	**www.symantec.com/sabu/nis/npf**
Black Ice Defender	**blackice.iss.net**
Tiny Personal Firewall	**tinysoftware.com/home**
Kerio Personal Firewall	**kerio.com/us/kpf_home.html**

Figure 7.8 **Firewall software is designed to place a barrier between your computer and the Internet.**

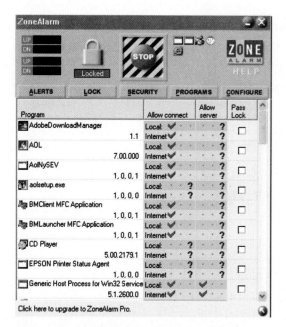

Figure 7.9 **Zone Alarm provides a high level of protection against unauthorized access and is free to download from the Zone Labs Web site.**

modem or DSL, it is even more imperative that you install a firewall because you are online all the time. Home users can find effective firewall software for sale both online and in stores (Figure 7.8). Also, some effective firewalls are available as free downloads.

A firewall acts as a gatekeeper, controlling the Internet traffic leaving from and coming into your computer. A newly installed firewall will ask you for direction each time a program from your system attempts to access the Internet. You will also have to deny or grant permission to entities seeking access to your system. Your responses will be recorded in a table for later reference, so that you are not constantly asked the same questions. A firewall causes your computer to move in stealth mode, which means that it does not broadcast your computer address. Your boot time might increase slightly, as the firewall is loaded each time you power on your computer, but otherwise, you won't need to deal with it much, if at all.

Norton and McAfee both provide reliable firewall packages, as do many other software developers. Zone Labs offers a free version of Zone Alarm, which is a secure firewall product (Figure 7.9). You can download the free product at the Zone Labs site or purchase an enhanced version, which includes such things as e-mail screening and control of Internet advertisements.

Understanding Adware and Spyware

The Internet is a shopper's paradise, which makes it attractive to advertisers who want to promote their products on your computer screen. Because it is so important to those advertisers that they target consumers effectively, many of them produce and send **adware** to your computer, bundled with some freeware that you have downloaded. Ads, which are embedded in the free software, appear when you open the program. Adware often feeds advertising to your screen or directs your browser home page (the page that always appears first when you open your browser) to advertising sites. Sometimes viewing the ads is simply the price you pay for using a free piece of software. (If you prefer no advertisements, you might be able to buy a registered version.) Developers of programs that include adware with their downloads defend the practice, saying that it is necessary to keep development costs down. In effect, adware is much like television commercials that you tolerate because they support the cost of television programming.

However, what bothers most people is an offshoot of adware called **spyware**. Like adware, spyware is often included with freeware, but it does more than just advertise. It reports your online activities to an advertiser's Web site for storage and analysis, so that the advertiser can monitor your interests and send specific marketing your way. Your "record" can even be sold to other parties. Adware might also collect personal information, but it contains a disclosure telling you that it will be collecting your information. Spyware doesn't. Although neither adware nor spyware is illegal, it is disturbing that you have no control over what advertisers do with your information or what they are free to display on your personal computer.

What can you do about adware and spyware? You can install software that removes it from your system. Unlike antivirus software, such software is not configured to scan your system automatically, so you must remember to run it occasionally. Two of the most widely recognized software programs that eliminate adware and spyware are Spybot (**spybot.eon.net.au**) and Adaware (**www. lavasoftusa.com**). Both software programs are free downloads. Spybot, shown in Figure 7.10, is effective and easy to use.

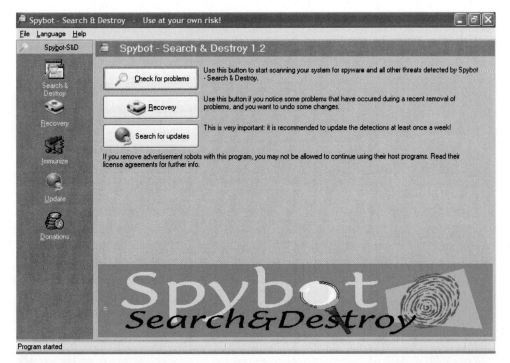

Figure 7.10 **Spybot is available as a free download and is designed to eliminate any occurrences of spyware or adware from your system.**

Cookies

Much like adware, **cookies** can be used to track consumer demographics for advertising agencies. A cookie is a small file written to your hard drive by a Web site that you visit (Figure 7.11). Cookies are used to identify you and to load your personal preferences when you return to the site that distributed the cookie. In that way, cookies can be helpful. However, cookies can also be used to gather data on your shopping and browsing habits so that you can be targeted for advertising. Companies like Double-Click and NetGravity use cookies extensively to distribute consumer information to advertisers. Knowing that your movement and purchases are probably being recorded and distributed as you shop online is a worrisome thought. But that's exactly what cookies allow advertisers to do, and it is not illegal.

Be aware that in some cases cookies are helpful. For example, if you are a frequent shopper at an online store like Lands' End, you probably have an account that is password protected. When you return to the site, you are asked for your password, unless the site can identify you by the cookie on your system. Likewise, if you are enrolled in a distance education class, cookies might be necessary to verify your enrollment each time you log on to the class Web site.

However, if the idea of having cookies stored on your system bothers you, you can remove them. So what can you do about the cookies on your system?

Figure 7.11 **Cookies, small files written on your hard disk, are often used to track your browsing and online shopping habits.**

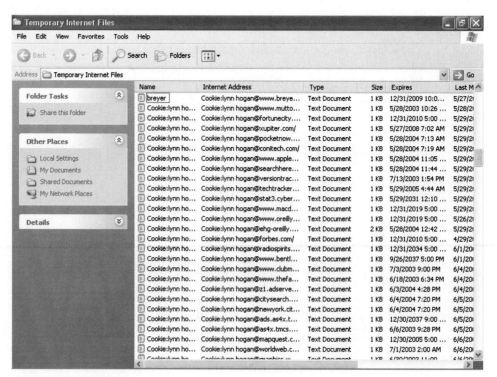

Figure 7.12 **You can work through your browser to view and delete cookies.**

- You can instruct your browser to block all cookies or severely restrict them. To do that in Internet Explorer 6.0, click Tools, Internet Options. Click the Privacy tab. Click and drag the cookie settings slider up or down the scale to select a level of cookie restriction, from complete blocking to wide open access.

- You can also check to see what cookies are currently stored on your system and delete them individually if you like. In Internet Explorer 6.0, click Tools, Internet Options. Click the General tab. Click Settings. Click View Files. A list of temporary files is displayed, as shown in Figure 7.12. You can identify each cookie file by the site that originated the cookie. You will probably recognize some as sites that you recently visited. Delete any or all cookies by clicking to select the file and pressing Del. *Refer to Chapter 5 for instructions on deleting multiple files.* The cookies will be placed in the Recycle Bin, so to rid your system of them permanently, you will need to empty the Recycle Bin.

Digital Signatures

A **digital signature** is used to authenticate the fact that you agree with what is written or promised; it attaches your identity to a transaction, much like your handwritten signature does with paper documents. A digital signature uses cryptography (secret encoding) to create a unique identifier, verifying the identity of the sender. Digital signatures enable us to carry out many transactions

In the **Know** You will find a variety of Internet security products in the software aisle at your local retailer. Many products include antivirus software integrated with a firewall. They can also include management of adware, spyware, pop-up ads, and e-mail spam (unsolicited e-mail). If you are a parent, you might also appreciate the inclusion of kid-friendly controls. The following list is not comprehensive, but it does give a sample of the Internet security products currently available.

McAfee Internet Security (firewall, antivirus, ad blocking, and private information safeguard) **www.mcafee-at-home.com/default.asp**

Norton Internet Security 2003 (firewall, antivirus, cookie manager, ad blocker, privacy, and parental control features) **www.symantec.com/ consumer_products/home-is.html**

Freedom Internet Security and Privacy Suite (firewall, antivirus, privacy block, content filter, management of banner ads, and cookies) **www.freedom.net**

eTrust EZ Armor (antivirus, firewall, and e-mail filter) **http:// my-etrust.com**

online, such as authorizing the transfer of medical records, trading stocks, and applying for mortgages. Businesses also like to use them because they can prove without a doubt the identity of a customer. For example, suppose that Larry bought several books from an online bookseller, but later denies that he bought them and refuses to pay. The bookseller is stuck with the bill because there is no way to prove without a doubt that Larry bought the books. However, if he had used a digital signature, Larry couldn't deny that he was the customer. When former President Clinton signed the Electronic Signatures in Global and National Commerce Act (E-Sign) in 2000, he gave digital signatures the same power as handwritten ones, so they are legally binding.

Digital signatures are not yet in widespread use, but experts believe that they will prove vital to electronic commerce in the future. The U.S. Postal Service is in the process of beginning a program to issue digital signatures, and banks and credit card companies will likely do the same, so digital signatures will be much more prevalent in the near future.

In the Know

With widespread concern over the privacy of computer records, you might wonder if there is anything you can do to cover your online "tracks." Although antivirus software and firewalls are effective at preventing viruses and unauthorized access, they do nothing to remove the trail of your online activities. If that is a concern, one possibility is to download and install a free program produced by Microsoft, called Tweak UI 1.33. Although it is not designed specifically for Windows XP, the program works well in that environment. Tweak UI is found at **www.microsoft.com/ntworkstation/downloads/PowerToys/ Networking/NTTweakUI.asp**.

Download the software to your desktop. Then create a folder in which to store the program files. Open My Computer. Double-click drive C. Click File, New, Folder. Type TweakUI. Press Enter. Close My Computer. To install the software, you should be at the Desktop. Double-click the TweakUI installation file (the one that you downloaded). In the subsequent Unzip dialog box, change the location to C:/TweakUI so that it is saved in your new folder. Click Unzip. Click Close. Open My Computer. Double-click drive C. Double-click TweakUI. Change the view by clicking View, Details. Right-click the tweakui.inf file and choose Install.

After installation is complete, open the Control Panel and click Switch to Classic View (in the left pane.) Double-click the Tweak UI icon and click the Paranoia Tab. A number of options will appear in the Covering your tracks list. If you check any of those options and click OK, Windows will clear them each time you boot your computer. You might not want to select all options, but a few are worth considering. Clearing Document History erases your trail of recently opened documents on your system. Clearing Internet Explorer History erases the list of recently visited URLs in Internet Explorer's address bar. Clearing Run History removes the list of commands that you typed in the Start, Run dialog box.

Chapter Summary

DON'T FORGET

- Downloads of both files and programs are widely available from the Internet. Some downloads are free, whereas others are available for purchase.

- The process of downloading is not difficult, but it does involve several steps, including identifying a download link and specifying where the downloaded item is to be saved on your system.

- The copy and paste technique is used to collect segments of text from a Web page and save them to storage media on your computer system.

- You can select a block of text (one or more characters or paragraphs) from a Web page to print on your printer, without printing the entire Web page.

- Clip art graphics are often available free of charge online. You can save clip art on your computer system for later use in documents or creative projects.

- Viruses are purposely written to be destructive or annoying.

- Antivirus software eliminates known viruses from your computer system.

- A firewall prohibits unauthorized access to your computer while you are online.

- Threats to individual privacy include cookies and spyware, both of which can be managed with software controls.

KEY TERMS

adware	downloading	Trojan horse
antivirus	firewall	uploading
clip art	FTP (File Transfer Protocol)	virus
Clipboard	macro language	virus definitions
cookies	macro virus	Web applet virus
copy	paste	Web scripting language
cut	plug-in	worm
digital signature	spyware	

TRUE/FALSE

Circle **T** if the statement is true or **F** if the statement is false.

T (F)   1. The process of sending a file from your computer to a server is called downloading.

(T) F   2. It is important to scan downloaded files for viruses before installing them.

T (F)   3. Unlike adware, spyware includes a disclosure letting you know that your personal information is being collected.

(T) F   4. A digital signature authenticates your identity online.

CHAPTER 8

E-mail

Objectives

When you complete this chapter, you will:

- **Understand the concept of electronic mail.**

- **Know how to create an e-mail account using a Web-based e-mail service.**

- **Be familiar with Microsoft Outlook Express.**

- **Be able to send and receive an e-mail message.**

- **Understand how to work with e-mail attachments, including sending and receiving attachments.**

- **Be aware of spam and understand how to counteract it.**

- **Be familiar with basic rules of e-mail etiquette.**

O ne of the most often-cited reasons for using the Internet is to communicate with others online. A recent study, conducted by Carnegie Mellon University, found that the most popular reasons for home computer users to access the Internet were to get information relevant to a hobby or personal interest, to communicate with family and friends, and to get enjoyment. The most common way to communicate online is through **electronic mail (e-mail)**.

The fact that you are connected to the Internet through an Internet service provider or through your company network makes it possible for you to send and receive e-mail messages. E-mail has become an indispensable tool for business and home communication, with people of all ages using it to keep in touch with friends and relatives. At this point, some 28 million Americans have an e-mail address, a number that is expected to double every five years. E-mail service is an integral part of online services like America Online. Businesses usually provide e-mail *accounts for their employees, and you can take advantage of free Web-based e-mail accounts. Your options are many, but you will find that however you approach it, working with e-mail is not difficult—you will be sending and receiving e-mail in no time!*

Understanding E-mail

New computer users often wonder why e-mail is any better than or different from messages left on telephone answering machines. If the sole purpose of the message is simply to have someone read it at his or her leisure, there really is no difference in the two methods of messaging. However, e-mail offers several features unavailable in telephone messages. E-mail is often sent to several people at one time by including multiple addresses in the address area. Messages can be forwarded to multiple recipients and responded to immediately. E-mail is actually much more like postal mail, except that it is delivered much faster, usually in just a few seconds. The style of communication in an e-mail message is unique in that messages are usually short and informal. It is perfectly acceptable to send a one-sentence note to someone, without dealing with structure or much content. Finally, you can add attachments to e-mail messages. An attachment is a file that could be anything from a document to a photograph to a software program. The recipient can save and open your attachment.

Given the amount of time that you are likely to spend working with e-mail, it is a good idea to learn to manage it well. After you have settled on an e-mail provider, you will want to learn as much as you can about how to send and receive messages, how to work with attachments, and how to control the type and amount of e-mail that you receive.

E-mail Servers

Fortunately, you certainly don't need to be an expert on e-mail servers and technical procedures to enjoy e-mail. However, it helps to be familiar with some basic terminology and to understand how an e-mail message makes its way from one person to another. Consider the way a letter gets to you through the postal service; it makes several stops along the way at various postal stations. An e-mail message makes several stops as well, but its stops are at **e-mail servers**, which are computers dedicated to the task of managing and passing along e-mail on the Internet. When the postal letter arrives at your mailbox, it stays in the box until you retrieve it. When an e-mail message arrives at the destination mail server, it is held in an electronic mailbox until you retrieve it by connecting to the Internet and accessing your e-mail account. Unlike the postal service, an e-mail service takes just seconds to pass a message from coast to coast, allowing you to communicate quickly with people around the world, any time of the day or night.

To receive and send e-mail, you must have an account on a mail server, just as you have to have an address to receive letters from the postal service. However, you can retrieve postal letters only from your mailbox, whereas you can usually retrieve e-mail from any computer that has access to the Internet. When you connect with your mail server, you can access e-mail messages by downloading them to your computer.

When you send e-mail, you work with what is called **SMTP (Simple Mail Transfer Protocol)**, which is a standard protocol for sending e-mail. A **protocol** is an agreed-upon format for transmitting data between two devices. Although knowing what SMTP stands for and what it does is handy for interpreting some messages that you might see while setting up an e-mail account, you won't have to deal with SMTP at any other level. It is simply a term that relates to the way e-mail is sent from your computer to a mail server. The SMTP mail server looks at the e-mail address on your message (which is similar to the address on an envelope) and forwards it to the recipient's mail server, where it remains until the recipient retrieves it. Because SMTP is limited in its ability to organize e-mail messages on the recipient's mail server, it is used in conjunction with one of two other protocols—**POP3 (Post Office Protocol)** or **IMAP (Internet Message Access Protocol)**. Those protocols help the receiving mail server save messages in a server mailbox and then periodically download them to recipients' individual computers.

Both POP3 and IMAP organize e-mail for later retrieval, but the way that they handle that retrieval differs. A POP3 mail server downloads all e-mail at a user's request, so that the e-mail is no longer stored on the server. It is all saved on the user's hard drive for retrieval at any time. Just as your post office box is empty when you remove all items, your e-mail storage space on a POP3 server is empty when you download all messages. An advantage of the POP3 method is that your mail is always available on your system, even if you are **offline** (not connected to the Internet). POP3 users can download their e-mail, disconnect from the Internet, read messages, and compose their replies. Then they reconnect to the Internet and send their replies. You don't have to worry about how much space you are allotted on the mail server because you download all mail at one time and then it is removed from the server. You can keep it for as long as you like on your computer's hard drive.

An IMAP server, on the other hand, reserves only a certain amount of space on the mail server for e-mail messages that are waiting for you to view. However, that space is usually more than sufficient for typical e-mail correspondence. If your e-mail should exceed the storage space allotted, you might not be able to send or receive messages until you clear some of your e-mail messages from the server. In some cases, the IMAP server automatically deletes the oldest unread messages to make room for more current ones. Likewise, some IMAP servers will save "read" messages for a certain number of days before they are also deleted. With IMAP, you don't download all your messages. You simply view the subject of the e-mail message and the sender, and then determine whether to read the message. Unlike POP3, you can read e-mail only while you are online. A major advantage of IMAP is that you can work with your e-mail from any location. IMAP users can delete, sort, and save messages into multiple folders on the IMAP server.

Most of your e-mail messages will be purely text, or written words. However, it is possible to include photographs, formatted documents, and sound and video files within the body of the e-mail message. That is because of **MIME**

(**Multipurpose Internet Mail Extension**), which is a specification for formatting multimedia messages so they can be sent over the Internet. Most versions of popular e-mail software products are *MIME compliant,* which means that they can support multimedia messages. **S/MIME (Secure/MIME)** is a new version of the MIME protocol that supports encrypted messages. Encryption means that a message is coded so that it can be read only by the intended recipient.

E-mail Clients

To work with e-mail, you must have **e-mail client**, or **e-client**, software installed on your computer. An e-client program is an application that allows you to send, receive, and organize e-mail. Your ISP will usually assign you an e-mail address, and you will probably work with the e-client software that is provided by your ISP. However, depending on how your ISP is configured, you might be able to work with a different e-mail client if you prefer. Most e-client software is free and available as a download. Popular e-client applications include Pegasus Mail, Eudora Mail, and Microsoft Outlook Express.

Creating an E-mail Account

If you contract with an online service provider, like America Online, you won't need to create an e-mail account, because you already have one. The AOL mail server manages your e-mail, letting you know when you have new mail and allowing you to send mail messages. Your e-mail address is your user name (which you created when you installed the service) followed by the @ sign and the mail server identifier (aol.com, in this case).

In some cases, you might want to create an e-mail account even if you already have one. As you work with e-mail, you will find that on the average over 70 percent of the mail you receive is **spam**, which is unsolicited and of

In the Know

In 1972, Ray Tomlinson first used the @ symbol in an e-mail message to indicate the location of the e-mail recipient. He used the symbol because it was not likely to appear in anyone's name, so there would be no confusion. It also represented the word "at," so it was the logical choice to represent a user "at" a particular location.

Linguists are divided as to the origin of the @ symbol. Some suggest that it came from the Latin word ad, *which means at or toward. Latin scribes simplified the amount of strokes required to write it by curving the upstroke of the "d" to the left over the "a." Others suggest that it appeared in the eighteenth century as a symbol of commerce, as in five saddles @ 50 pence. Although the English language recognizes @ as the "at sign," other countries associate the symbol with other things, such as food or animals. Regardless of its true source, the symbol is now universally recognized as an element of an e-mail address.*

Hands On

Activity 8.1—Creating a Web-Based E-mail Account

In this activity, you will create a free e-mail account with Hotmail.com. You can use a fictitious name and information. The e-mail account will be automatically deleted after a period of inactivity.

1. Access the Internet. Go to **www.hotmail.com** (Figure 8.1).
2. Click New Account Signup (Figure 8.2).
3. Complete the registration form, and click I Agree to accept the terms of the license (read it first!). Your account is created, as shown in Figure 8.3.

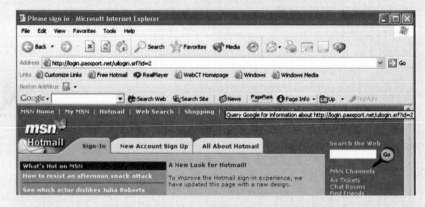

Figure 8.1 **Hotmail is a free Web-based e-mail service sponsored by Microsoft.**

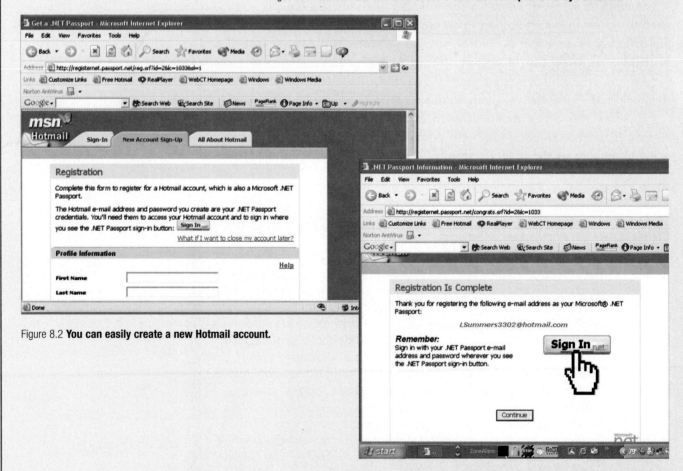

Figure 8.2 **You can easily create a new Hotmail account.**

Figure 8.3 **Hotmail lets you know when your new e-mail account has been created.**

4. Click Continue. The next screen suggests that you subscribe to a Hotmail service in which you get a larger inbox, greater attachment facility, and virus scanning. An account with the paid service doesn't expire, whereas the free service discontinues your account after 10 days of inactivity. For the purposes of this activity, you will subscribe to the free service, so scroll down slightly and click *Free e-mail.*

5. The next page offers several electronic newsletters to which you can subscribe. Scroll down to the bottom of the screen and click Continue.

6. Scroll down to the bottom of the next page and click *Continue.* You are directed to your e-mail account, as shown in Figure 8.4.

7. You will work with e-mail messages in a later activity. At this point, look to the top right corner of the page, as shown in Figure 8.5, to find the Sign Out area. Click Sign Out to leave Hotmail and end your session. It is especially important to sign out appropriately if you are working at a public computer, so that your account is not available to anyone who might work at the computer after you.

8. Close your Internet connection.

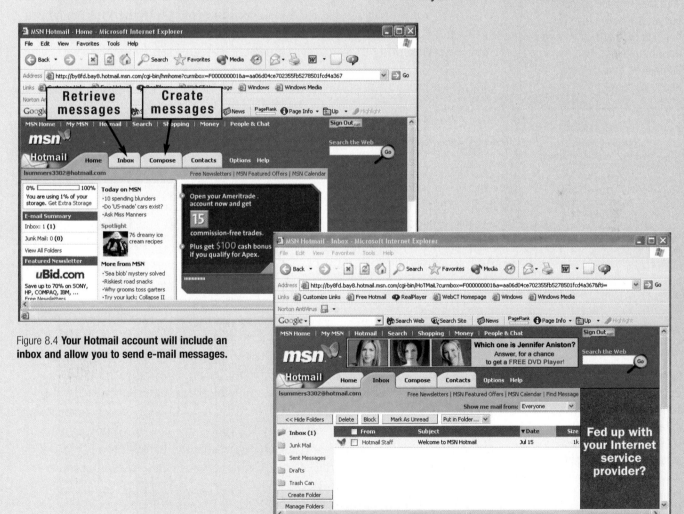

Figure 8.4 **Your Hotmail account will include an inbox and allow you to send e-mail messages.**

Figure 8.5 **It is especially important to sign out of your e-mail account when you have finished working at a public computer.**

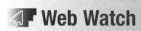
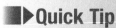
limited interest to most people. To keep spam from making its way into your most-often-used e-mail account, you can create a second address, perhaps with a free Web-based e-mail service, and use that e-mail address for all Internet transactions, purchases, and forms. Several companies offer free Web-based e-mail services, which are usually IMAP servers on which you can create an e-mail account and which you can access from any Internet-connected computer. Some people might want to segment their e-mail in such a way that all work-related messages go to one account and all personal correspondence finds its way to another.

Microsoft offers a free Web-based e-mail service called Hotmail. It is free, easy to work with, and includes features common to other e-mail services, such as an address book, an attachment facility, and filtering. When you filter e-mail, you identify e-mail that should be blocked (not accepted by your e-mail provider). Like most free e-mail services, Hotmail simply requires that you create a user name and a password; little other personal information is required. When you want to access your Hotmail account, sign on to the Internet as you normally do, go to the Hotmail Web site (**www.hotmail.com**), sign in, and read your e-mail. As long as you stay connected, you can send e-mail as well. The only involvement such a process has with your ISP is that you use the ISP to sign on to the Internet. There is no comingling of e-mail messages from the ISP to Hotmail.

Introducing Outlook Express

Outlook Express is an e-mail client program included with the Internet Explorer browser. It is popular due to its widespread availability, ease of use, and cost (it's free!). A full-featured e-mail management system, it allows you to send and receive e-mail, as well as work with address books and attachments. However, Outlook Express is not an ISP or an e-mail server. But, if you have an account with a compatible ISP protocol, you can use Outlook Express to handle your e-mail. Some online services, such as America Online, use a unique proprietary e-mail system that is incompatible with Outlook Express.

Even if you have never worked with e-mail before, Outlook Express makes the process simple by including a setup wizard to get you started. If you have been using another e-mail service, Outlook Express can transfer your address book and messages quickly and easily. Home users often enjoy the creative stationery included with Outlook Express, allowing them to design attractive backgrounds for their messages. Don't be fooled by its simple approach to message management—you will find that Outlook Express packs a lot of power with its support for S/MIME encryption, digital signatures, and multiple POP3, IMAP, and Hotmail accounts. Overall, it is a reliable, easy-to-use e-mail alternative for individual computer users.

On the downside, some find that Outlook Express' filters (e-mail blocking) are difficult to use. Outlook Express has also certainly had more than its share of security problems, due in part to **active scripting**. Programming languages, such as JavaScript and VBScript, are considered active scripting languages because they make Web pages active, or dynamic. An active Web page might update the date and time or create scrolling text. By default, Outlook Express enables active scripting, which means that an HTML-formatted message (one that might include active script from a Web page) can attack your desktop through an e-mail message. Microsoft works diligently to supply patches (programs that correct problems) for Outlook Express, addressing any newly recognized security breaches, including the problem with active scripting.

Selecting Outlook Express as Your E-mail Client

You can use Outlook Express as your e-mail client as long as it supports your ISP mail server protocol. In most cases, there is no problem with using Outlook Express because it supports so many different protocols, such as HTTP (Web-based e-mail servers) and other IMAP and POP3 servers. However, some online services, like America Online, use a unique e-mail protocol that requires specialized e-mail client software. By creating a Hotmail account (an HTTP server account) and then adding the account to your Outlook Express installation, you can get the best of both worlds—the convenience of Web-based e-mail accessible from anywhere and the power and flexibility of Outlook Express.

You can find Outlook Express either as an icon on your desktop or as a selection from within Internet Explorer. You can use Outlook Express to access other e-mail accounts, including those created in Hotmail. Activity 8.2 demonstrates the process of setting up a Hotmail account in Outlook Express.

Sending E-mail

Regardless of the e-mail client that you use, all e-mail messages have two parts—a header and a message body. The header includes the name and e-mail address of the recipient, the name and address of anyone who is being copied,

Web Watch
If you are using Outlook Express, you might want to be sure that you have downloaded the most recent security patch, found at **www.microsoft.com/windows/ie/downloads/critical**.

Hands On

Activity 8.2—Setting Up Outlook Express to Manage a Hotmail Account

In this activity, you will set up Outlook Express to manage the Hotmail account that you created in Activity 8.1. You can then manage all e-mail to and from the Hotmail account using Outlook Express.

1. To open Outlook Express, first open Internet Explorer. Click the Mail button, as shown in Figure 8.6.
2. Click Read Mail. Outlook Express will open, as shown in Figure 8.7.

Figure 8.6 **Outlook Express is included as a component of the Internet Explorer browser.**

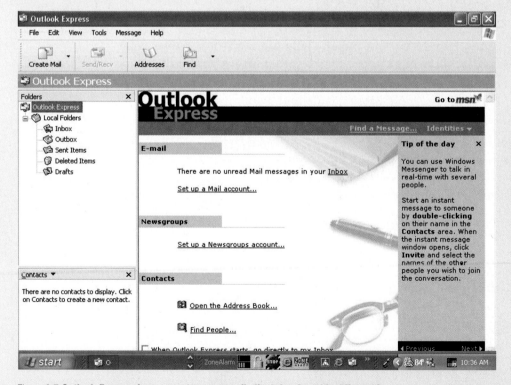

Figure 8.7 **Outlook Express is an easy-to-use e-mail client developed by Microsoft.**

3. Click Tools, Accounts. At the Internet Accounts dialog box, click Add. Click Mail.

4. The Internet Connection wizard appears, as shown in Figure 8.8. Type your name and click Next.

5. Type the address of the Hotmail account that you are bringing into Outlook Express. The e-mail address is the user name that you created in Activity 8.1, followed by @hotmail.com. Click Next.

6. Click the drop-down arrow beside the incoming server type, and select HTTP. Click the drop-down arrow beside the mail service provider, and select Hotmail. Click Next.

7. Click in the password area, and type the password that you supplied in Activity 8.1. Click Next.

8. Click Finish. The Internet Accounts dialog box should appear again, now listing a Hotmail account, as shown in Figure 8.9.

9. Click Close. If prompted to download folders, click Yes. In a few seconds, the Hotmail account and its folders will appear in the left pane, as shown in Figure 8.10.

10. Close Outlook Express.

Figure 8.8 **The Internet Connection wizard assists you in creating an Outlook Express e-mail account.**

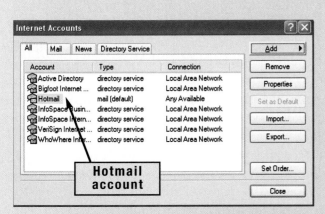

Figure 8.9 **After your Hotmail account has been added, it appears as an entry in Outlook Express.**

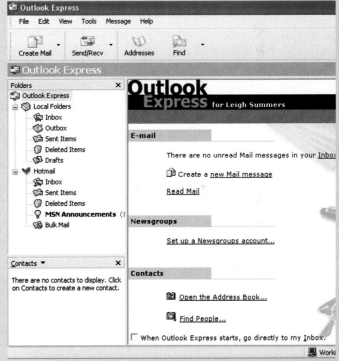

Figure 8.10 **The folders pane of Outlook Express shows all e-mail accounts.**

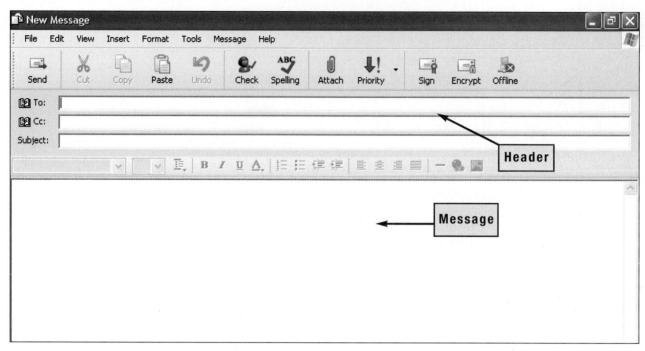

Figure 8.11 **All e-mail messages contain a header area and a message area.**

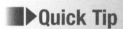
and the message subject. The body contains the message content, as shown in Figure 8.11.

To send an e-mail message, you must know the e-mail address of the recipient. If you use the wrong address or mistype it, the message will either come back to you as undeliverable, a process called *bouncing,* or be sent to the wrong person. Sending e-mail simply means filling in the message form (header information and message), and clicking Send, or Send Now.

You can send e-mail to more than one recipient. Simply list all e-mail addresses, separated by commas or semicolons. Often, you might send a message to one person, with copies going to multiple addresses. In that case, you would list multiple e-mail addresses in the *cc* (*carbon copy*) area, separated by commas or semicolons. Similar to cc, many e-mail clients also provide a *bcc* (*blind carbon copy*) option where you can send a copy to addresses without making it obvious to the recipient. To create a bcc in Outlook Express, click View, All Headers.

As you become proficient with sending and receiving e-mail messages, you will find that it can be time-consuming to type e-mail addresses in the header area, and the more people you correspond with using e-mail, the harder it is to remember each e-mail address. You will probably find an electronic address book helpful, where you can include names and e-mail addresses of your contacts. Although there are many address books on the market, Outlook Express includes an address book feature that is easy to use and will save you time.

An address book is also handy for identifying a group of addresses. For example, imagine Allison is the director of a group of library supporters. She

Hands On

Activity 8.3—Sending E-mail

In this activity, you will use Outlook Express to send an e-mail message to someone. Before beginning, think of an e-mail address to which you can send the message. You might ask a classmate or your instructor for an address, or you might send the message to your home e-mail address, if you have one. The address should be of the form, *user_name@mail_server.xxx*.

1. Open Outlook Express. Refer to steps 1 and 2 in Activity 8.2.
2. Click Create Mail. Be careful to click the button itself, not the drop-down arrow beside the button.
3. An empty e-mail message appears, as shown in Figure 8.12. Maximize the window.
4. Fill in the header, listing the e-mail address to which the message should be sent, and supplying a Subject. Click in the message area and type `I received your reminder of the next class session. I'll certainly be there!`. Click Send. If you are connected to the Internet, click Send/Recv on the main Outlook Express window to make certain all messages in your outbox are delivered and to retrieve any messages waiting in your Hotmail inbox.
5. Close Outlook Express.

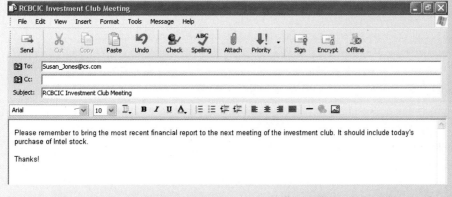

Figure 8.12 **When creating an e-mail message, you must specify a recipient and a subject, and must type a message.**

often sends the same e-mail message to each member of the group. Although she could compose one message, listing each group member's address in the To: area, it would be more efficient to create a group entry in her address book so that she doesn't have to remember or type the multiple e-mail addresses each time.

In the Know

One of the things that most people find appealing about Outlook Express is the use of stationery to brighten up e-mail messages. Stationery is a template (predefined set of selections) that can include a background image, text colors, font types, and custom margins. An example of stationery is shown in Figure 8.13. You can apply stationery to all outgoing messages or only to individual ones.

To apply a stationery pattern to all outgoing messages:

Open Outlook Express. Click Tools, Options, and select the Compose tab. Under Stationery, select Mail. Click Select. From the list of files, click any one to see its preview to the right. When you find one that you like, click OK. Click OK again. From that point forward, the stationery will be applied to all messages that you send. You can change the selection anytime.

To apply a stationery pattern to an individual message before you begin the message:

Open Outlook Express. Click Message, New Message Using, and then select a stationery style. Compose the message and send it as usual.

To apply a stationery pattern to a message after you have already begun the message:

Open Outlook Express. Begin a new e-mail message. Click Format, Apply Stationery, and then select a stationery style.

✓ SANITY CHECK

Stationery settings can be applied to messages only if HTML formatting is on. If you try unsuccessfully to apply stationery, check the format. Simply begin a new e-mail message and click Format. Check to be sure Rich Text (HTML) is selected.

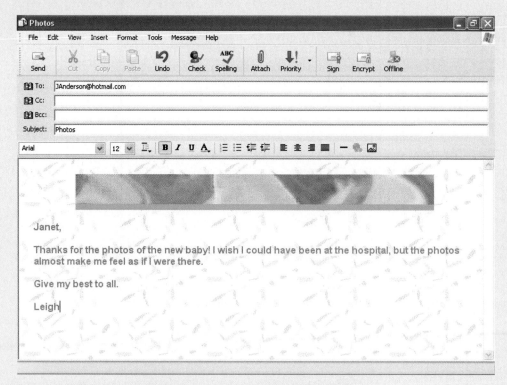

Figure 8.13 **Outlook Express allows you to create e-mail messages on stationery.**

Hands On

Activity 8.4—Using an Address Book

In this activity, you will create several address book entries and then use Outlook Express to send e-mail to someone in your address book.

1. Open Outlook Express.
2. Click Addresses in the menu bar. An address window opens, as shown in Figure 8.14.
3. Click New. Click New Contact.
4. A dialog box appears, as shown in Figure 8.15.
5. Type contact information in the boxes. If you don't know anyone to include as an e-mail contact, type **Leigh** in the First Name area, **Summers** as a Last Name, and **LSummers@ hotmail.com** for an e-mail address. Click Add. Click OK. Your new contact appears in the Address list.
6. Click the close button (X) to close the address book. You should be back at the Outlook Express window.
7. To send a message to your new contact, click Create Mail. Click the To button (not the text box beside the word "To:," but the button itself).
8. Your address book opens, as shown in Figure 8.16. Click to select the contact name to which you want to send the message. Click the To button beside the contact list. You would do the same for any contacts that should receive carbon copies or blind carbon copies. Click OK.
9. The contact name appears in the To: area of a new e-mail message. You might find that instead of the contact's e-mail address his or her name is displayed. Don't worry—the e-mail address is linked to the contact name, so the e-mail message will be routed appropriately. Continue by completing the remaining header and message areas. Click Send.
10. Close Outlook Express.

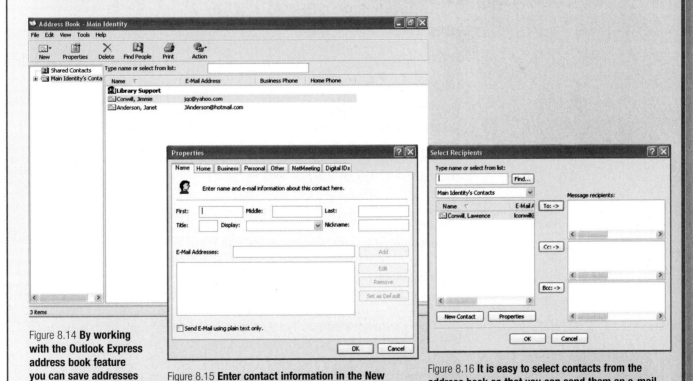

Figure 8.14 **By working with the Outlook Express address book feature you can save addresses of your e-mail contacts.**

Figure 8.15 **Enter contact information in the New Contact Properties dialog box.**

Figure 8.16 **It is easy to select contacts from the address book so that you can send them an e-mail message.**

■▶**Quick Tip**

To remove stationery, open Outlook Express. Click Tools Options, and click the Compose tab. To the right of the Mail area, click Select. Click Blank.htm. Click OK. Click OK again.

To create a group:

1. Open Outlook Express, and click Addresses.
2. Click New.
3. Click New Group. Type a name for the new group.
4. If you are adding members who are already in your address book, click Select Members. Click a member's name, and click Select. Click OK. In like fashion, add any other members to the group.
5. If you are adding members for which you have *not* already created an individual Contact, click New Contact. Fill in all information, including the e-mail address, and click OK. Click OK when all members have been added to the group.
6. Close the Address book.

To send a message to an entire group:

1. Make sure Outlook Express is open. Click Create Mail.
2. Click the To: button.
3. Click the group name, and click To. Click OK.
4. Complete the message, and click Send. Each member of the group will receive the e-mail message.

In the Know

A bounced e-mail is one that has been returned to you as undeliverable, usually with an error message indicating why the communication was unsuccessful. E-mails are bounced for several reasons; the most common of which is that the recipient's e-mail address is incorrect or no longer valid, perhaps because the recipient has discontinued connection with the ISP. The recipient's e-mail server might also have rejected the e-mail because the recipient's e-mail is filtered or blocked. Sometimes a mail server is just busy and can't handle the request at that time. The e-mail account to which the message is directed might be full, which means that there is not enough allotted disk space to accept the message. Some mail systems predetermine a maximum message size and reject any messages that exceed that size. Finally, a glitch in the network at either the sender's or the recipient's end will cause an e-mail message to bounce back to the sender.

If you suspect that you typed the e-mail address incorrectly, or that the recipient's e-mail account was temporarily full, you can recreate the e-mail message and send it again. Of course, if the recipient has discontinued the e-mail service or if your e-mail is blocked by a filter, it will do no good to resend the message.

Reading E-mail

Reading e-mail is much simpler than sending e-mail because there are fewer steps involved. Most e-mail clients allow you simply to double-click the message listed in the inbox. The message then opens for you to read. Single-clicking a message allows you to preview it before reading it. You might want to preview messages so that you can determine whether to open them. If the e-mail message is from someone you don't know, or if you have any other reason to be suspicious of it (possibly a virus threat), you can preview it without opening it, thereby avoiding a possible virus attack.

After reading an e-mail message, you can easily print it or reply to the sender using the icons that appear in the toolbar at the top of the message window, as shown in Figure 8.17. The toolbar icons are available only while a message is selected, so if they appear gray and inaccessible, select a message from your inbox. The toolbar icons should brighten and become available.

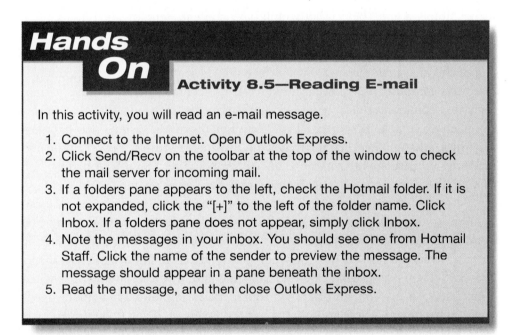

Hands On

Activity 8.5—Reading E-mail

In this activity, you will read an e-mail message.

1. Connect to the Internet. Open Outlook Express.
2. Click Send/Recv on the toolbar at the top of the window to check the mail server for incoming mail.
3. If a folders pane appears to the left, check the Hotmail folder. If it is not expanded, click the "[+]" to the left of the folder name. Click Inbox. If a folders pane does not appear, simply click Inbox.
4. Note the messages in your inbox. You should see one from Hotmail Staff. Click the name of the sender to preview the message. The message should appear in a pane beneath the inbox.
5. Read the message, and then close Outlook Express.

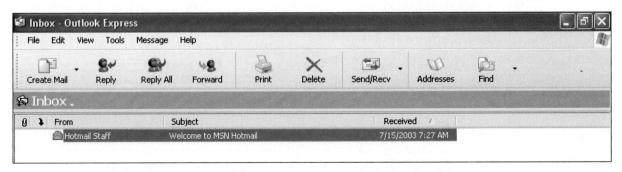

Figure 8.17 **A typical e-mail toolbar includes icons for replying to, forwarding, and printing e-mail.**

The Outlook Express toolbar includes the following buttons:

- **Print**—Click the Print button to print the e-mail message.

- **Reply**—Click the Reply button to send a message back to the person who sent you the selected message. Type your response in the message window that appears, and click Send.

- **Forward**—Click the Forward button to send the selected e-mail message to another recipient. Type the address of the recipient, and click Send.

- **Delete**—Click the Delete button to move the selected e-mail message to the Deleted Items folder.

Working with Attachments

E-mail is a convenient way of sharing ideas and passing along messages to friends, family, and coworkers. Sometimes the item that you want to pass along is not simply a note, but a photograph or document. Sending such items along with an e-mail message is called adding an **attachment**, and it is one of the things that makes e-mail such a powerful tool. An attachment is simply any file that you append to an e-mail message. When the e-mail is sent, so is the attachment.

Most computer users have learned to view attachments with caution because they are a common vehicle for viruses. In the last chapter, you learned that viruses are often executable files, or programs. Attachments can be disguised as harmless data files, when in fact they might contain executable viruses. Downloading and opening an attachment can cause an associated virus to go into action. You should, therefore, scan all attachments for viruses before opening them.

Although there is no way to ensure that a virus will never affect you, you can minimize your risk by working with attachments sparingly. Avoid using and sending attachments if possible. Of course, part of the fun of e-mail is sharing items, so you will need to use your judgment in determining which attachments are worth the risk and which aren't. That being said, if you receive an unsolicited e-mail attachment from an unknown source, delete the message without opening the attachment. These are simply too risky. Likewise, if you open the message itself and find an empty message body, close and delete it. If the attached file was created in a Microsoft Office product, and you get a message asking whether you want to disable macros, always respond affirmatively to forestall the possibility of damage by a macro virus.

Creating and Adding an Attachment to an E-mail Message

An attachment is simply a file. It can be created in any application, perhaps using a word processor or some graphics software. Although you can attach any file to an e-mail message, remember that the recipient of the attachment must have the same software to open the attachment. For example, if the graphics software that you used has its own proprietary file type, then a file created with that software

Hands On

Activity 8.6—Attaching a File to an E-mail Message

In this activity, you will create and attach a file to an e-mail message.

1. Open Word (or WordPad). To open Word, click Start, All Programs, Microsoft Word. To open WordPad, click Start, All Programs, Accessories, WordPad.
2. A student in your woodworking class has asked for the supply list that you plan to distribute when the class begins. You decide to create the list early and send it to him as an attachment. Click in the white document area if necessary, and type a supply list. Include as many items as you like, such as 1 pkg. nails, 1 set safety glasses, work gloves, and 5 pkg. sandpaper.
3. Place a blank floppy disk in the A: drive. To save the supply list, click File, Save As. Click the drop-down arrow beside the Save In box and select 3½ Floppy (A:). Choose a filename to reflect the project, perhaps *Woodworking Supply List.* Click Save. Close Word or WordPad.
4. Open Outlook Express.
5. Click Create Mail. Maximize the New Message window.
6. Compose an e-mail message to a friend or to your instructor, making sure to include a subject and a message.

7. In the toolbar, click Attach. The dialog box shown in Figure 8.18 appears.
8. Click the drop-down arrow beside the Look In area, and select 3½ Floppy (A:) Double-click the supply list. An additional line appears in the header, showing the attached file.
9. Click Send to send the message, along with the attachment.

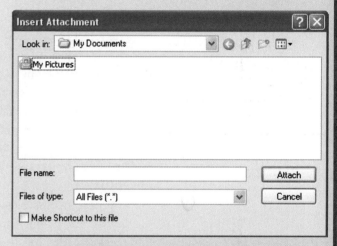

Figure 8.18 **When adding an attachment to an e-mail message, you must indicate where the file to be attached is found.**

and attached to an e-mail message can be opened only by the same software on the recipient's computer. Consequently, there are times when you will receive an attachment that you can't open—you don't have the required software installed on your computer.

Suppose that Allison wants to create and send a list of recent library acquisitions to members of her group of library supporters. Using Microsoft Word, she creates the list and saves it to the library folder on her hard disk. She then accesses her e-mail account and composes a message to the library group. Near the body of the message, perhaps on the toolbar, she will find a button or icon titled *Attach* or *Add Files.* After clicking the button, she indicates where the file to be attached is currently stored on her system. When she sends the message, the attachment will accompany it.

Understanding File Compression Software

There will be times when you want to send photographs, graphics, or large text files by e-mail. Successfully sending those files is dependent upon several variables, among them connection speed, Internet traffic, and file size. Connection speed can bring file transfer to a crawl—or stop it altogether—especially if you are working with a dial-up modem. You are more likely to be successful if Internet traffic is light, perhaps late at night or early in the morning. Some files are so large that it is just not reasonable to send them as attachments due to the time it takes to upload them to your mail server and the time it takes the recipient to download them. What you might want to consider is using **file compression software**, which stores data in a format that requires much less space than usual. It enables communication devices to transmit the same amount of data in fewer bits, thereby speeding up the file transfer.

Fortunately, file compression is not as technical as it sounds. In fact, a typical computer user can download and begin to use such software in a matter of a few minutes. Although there are several choices of free file compression software, the one most often used by individual computers users is WinZip, available at **www.winzip.com**. Another choice is PKZip, found at **www.pkzip.com**. Both programs allow you to compress files, creating new files with a .zip extension, indicating that the files are reduced in size and associated with file compression software. You can also decompress, or restore files to their original size, with WinZip and PKZip. If you choose to use a file compression program, you can learn to use the software by checking the Help site.

Recent versions of online services, such as AOL 9.0, automatically compress and decompress files without your having to download a file compression program. If you attach more than one file to e-mail that you send, AOL will compress the files together in one .zip file. When you sign off AOL, it will decompress any files that you have downloaded.

Retrieving, Saving, and Opening Attachments

When you receive an e-mail message with an attachment, you will need to download the attached file before you can view it. Downloading the file is not difficult, although each e-mail client handles the task differently. The difficulty is more often in finding the file that has been downloaded and saved!

Take your time and watch carefully as an attached file downloads so that you know where your e-mail client saved it on your system. It might be a good idea to go ahead and create a folder on your desktop where you can save attachments until you scan them for viruses.

To create a folder for your attachments on the desktop:

1. Access the desktop.
2. Right-click an empty area of the desktop.
3. Click New. Click Folder.
4. Type a name for the new folder, perhaps **Attachments**, and press (↵Enter).

✓SANITY CHECK

In the process of creating a folder on the desktop, something went wrong. You accidentally named the folder *New Folder.* How do you correct it? Right-click the folder name, and click Rename. Type the correct name, and press ⏎Enter.

E-mail messages with attachments are usually designated with a special icon, such as a paper clip or disk, which you can click to download the attachment. In some cases, you might see a Download button instead. You will have to indicate a disk location in which to save the downloaded file. If you have created an *Attachments* folder on the desktop, you could select that folder. Figure 8.19 shows an e-mail message with an attachment.

✓SANITY CHECK

The security settings on your installation of Outlook Express might be so high that they deny attachments. If you have difficulty opening an attachment, click Tools, Options, and click the Security tab. Deselect *Do not allow attachments to be saved or opened that could potentially carry a virus.* Of course, you should ensure that your virus scanning software is configured to automatically scan all incoming e-mail and attachments.

If you plan to retrieve the attached file later, you will need to save it to your computer system. Opening an e-mail message allows you to access the attachment. Figure 8.20 shows an opened e-mail message that contains an attachment

To open or save an attachment, double-click the filename of the attachment. Some e-mail services include, instead, a Download button that you can click. You will be asked whether you want to open or save the file. You will probably want to save most attachments so you can refer to them later. You can always delete

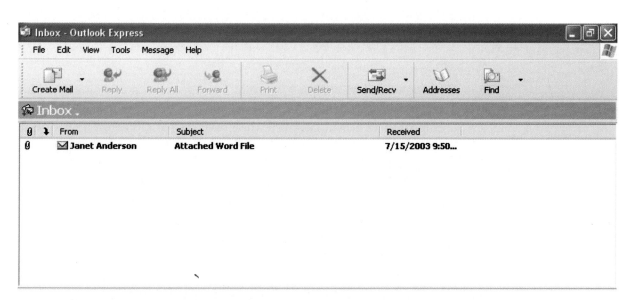

Figure 8.19 **E-mail attachments are usually designated with a special icon, like a disk or a paper clip.**

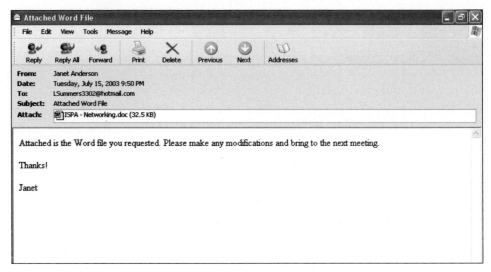

Figure 8.20 **An attachment is usually listed by name somewhere near the e-mail message, in this case on a separate "attach" line.**

the files later. Be sure to carefully specify where you want to save the file. It is at this point that many people lose track of where the file is saved, so it is not a good time to hurry! If you are using an *Attachments* folder on your desktop, direct the save to occur there by clicking the drop-down arrow beside the Save In area, selecting desktop, and double-clicking *Attachments*. The file is saved in the desktop folder.

After the file has been saved, you can open it if you have the required software. Open the *Attachments* folder by double-clicking it. Double-click any of the listed files to open them. If a file doesn't open but instead you are presented an Open With dialog box, you might not have the required software. Although you can attempt to identify a software program that would open the attachment, you probably don't have the necessary software, so you should just close the Open With dialog box. Attachments are files and can be deleted just as you would delete any file—by clicking once to select the file, and pressing the (Del) key.

Spam

E-mail is a wonderful convenience, opening new avenues of communication that everyone can enjoy. However, it is not without its problems. Earlier in this chapter, we compared an e-mail system to the postal system. To continue that analogy, consider the amount of junk mail that you receive each week. Now triple that number, and you have some idea of how much electronic junk mail will land in your e-mail inbox each day. **Spam**, the electronic equivalent of junk mail, is unsolicited, and usually unwanted, e-mail. To make matters worse, spam can potentially be offensive, sometimes including pornographic material. The reason you receive spam is the same reason you receive junk mail. Advertisers hope to convince you to purchase a product. Because most spam goes unanswered, advertisers must send it out in great volume, hoping to attract a few buyers. The result can be an inbox that contains a few personal messages but is monopolized by unwanted e-mail. Figure 8.21 shows a typical e-mail inbox, filled with unsolicited e-mail.

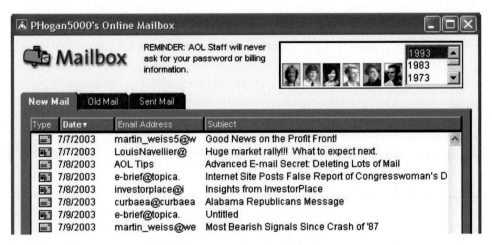

Figure 8.21 **Most e-mail inboxes quickly become filled with unsolicited and unwanted e-mail, called spam.**

What can you do about spam? You can do exactly what you do with some junk mail—you can delete it without reading it. Although it does take time and might be annoying to have to select and delete multiple messages, it is one sure way to remove them from your e-mail account. However, similar mail will just reappear the next day! If the same spam comes regularly, you can set filters to automatically delete it or block it from your inbox. Check with your ISP for directions on filtering. Software products that attempt to control spam are available, but some might require more management than you are likely to want to deal with. Antispam software is often included in Internet security packages, including Norton Internet Security and McAfee Internet Security. One thing that you should never do is to respond to unwanted e-mail or send a note asking to be removed from the mailing list. That just confirms that your e-mail address is valid, possibly adding you to even more spam mailing lists.

Although it is virtually impossible to stop spam after it has started, here are a few things that you might consider in an attempt to minimize spam:

- If subscribing to anything on the Web, always indicate, if asked, that you don't want your e-mail address or personal information shared with anyone else.

- Never reply to any junk e-mail or visit any Web site suggested in the mail.

- Never reply to a request to let a mailer know if you want to be removed from the mailing list.

- Disable cookies, as described in the preceding chapter. You might also consider deleting any cookies that are already on your system. However, remember that not all cookies are harmful, so use your best judgment.

- Be aware of your ISP's suggestions for dealing with unwanted mail. Some ISPs ask that you forward unwanted e-mail to a special account so that they can help filter future e-mails from the sender.

- Create a separate e-mail account, and use that address for those situations when you must provide a valid e-mail address.

- Install an Internet security software package or antispam software.

Web Watch

A highly rated software product, SpamBuster, captures most junk e-mail before it is downloaded to your inbox. Check **www.contactplus.com/products/spam/spam.htm** for more information on SpamBuster.

Practicing E-mail Etiquette

In many cases, e-mail is your first, and only, point of contact with other people. It is important that your words accurately convey your message. Because e-mail messages use casual conversation, it is easy for the tone of the message to be misunderstood. It is easy to forget how much effect friendly body language and a joking tone of voice have on the way a spoken message is perceived. Keep in mind that at the end of every e-mail message is a person, not a computer. Treat that person with the same respect that you would give in a personal conversation, making every effort to be polite and articulate and to avoid expressing unbridled anger or frustration.

Netiquette is a term coined for the practice of proper etiquette on the Internet, especially concerning online communication. Although there is no comprehensive list of do's and don'ts, here are a few suggestions that will put you well on your way to being an effective online communicator.

- *Watch your spelling.* Take the same care with an e-mail message that you would take with a written document. The immediacy and the informal nature of e-mail encourage a lack of attention to proper grammar and spelling. Don't fall into that trap. Always read an e-mail message carefully before sending it. Once it's gone, it's gone!

- *Avoid writing e-mail messages in all caps.* Most people interpret that as shouting.

- *Keep e-mail to the point.* It is not the place for lengthy summaries or discussions. Many people pay for Internet connection by the hour, so you don't want to take up too much of their time with wordiness.

- *Never put anything in an e-mail message that you would mind seeing on the evening news.* E-mail messages are not private. Therefore, they should not contain any inflammatory or confidential information.

- *Clearly identify the subject of your e-mail.* The subject line of an e-mail message gives an idea of the contents, so the recipient knows a little about the topic before opening the e-mail message. The subject can also serve to identify you as the sender of the e-mail, making the recipient less wary of a virus.

- *Avoid flaming.* **Flaming** is the airing of a disagreement publicly in an e-mail correspondence. Always keep in mind that e-mail is a written form of communication, which is susceptible to mass reproduction and forwarding. As such, it might come back to haunt you.

- *Keep e-mail addresses confidential.* Your friends probably don't mind if you have their e-mail address, but they might not appreciate your giving their address to others. That is exactly what happens when you list several addresses as recipients or carbon copies. When a person receives the e-mail, he can see the addresses of all others to whom you sent the message. Instead, place addresses in the blind carbon copies area so that each recipient sees only his or her own e-mail address.

Web Watch

Look at some basic rules of netiquette at **www.albion. com/netiquette/corerules. html**.

- *Avoid excessive humor and sarcasm.* Those sentiments are difficult to convey with the written word.

- *Always include your name and e-mail address in the message body.*   The person receiving the e-mail message needs to know that the message is from you, but your user name in the header might not be all that descriptive of who you are.

- *Don't use emoticons for formal messages.*   Emoticons are symbols that add humor and personality to e-mail but might be interpreted as too informal for some communications.

- *Avoid the urge to forward chain letters.*   They are annoying to many people who see them as a waste of time and computer resources. Chain letters are messages that instruct receivers to redistribute the message to a larger group of people. Most workplaces discourage or prohibit chain letter activity.

In the Know

Emoticons, sometimes called smileys, add humor and personality to your informal e-mail messages. They are expressions that you can create using characters on your keyboard. An Internet search will reveal a multitude of emoticons. Some of the more popular ones are listed below.

:-)	Happy		:-e	Disappointed
:-(	Sad		:-<	Mad
:-o	Surprised		:-D	Laughing
:-@	Screaming		;-)	Winking
:-l	Indifferent			

Abbreviations of common phrases are often included in e-mail, as well. Listed below are a few abbreviations.

BTW	By the way
IMHO	In my humble opinion
ROFL	Rolling on the floor laughing
LOL	Lots of love, or Laugh out loud

Chapter Summary

DON'T FORGET

- Most people cite e-mail as a primary reason for using the Internet.

- E-mail servers manage e-mail messages. POP3 servers download all messages from the server to a user's computer, whereas IMAP servers maintain e-mail messages on the server, allowing users to read them from there. SMTP servers accept outgoing e-mail.

- An e-mail client is application software that allows you to read, send, and organize e-mail.

- Web-based e-mail services allow you to create and manage an e-mail account on the Internet.

- Microsoft Outlook Express is a popular e-mail client because it is easy to work with and free. It is included with some versions of Windows and the Internet Explorer browser.

- The process of sending e-mail is similar in all e-mail clients. An e-mail message always has two parts—a header and a message.

- To read e-mail, access your inbox and double-click a message title or sender to display a message.

- Attachments are files that are sent along with e-mail messages.

- File compression software can be used to reduce the size of attachments before they are sent.

- Spam is unwanted, unsolicited e-mail. Software is available to minimize spam, and there are some things you can do, such as filtering your e-mail, that might help avoid some spam.

- E-mail etiquette, or netiquette, is suggested rules of online communication.

KEY TERMS

active scripting	file compression software	PIM (personal information manager)
attachment	flaming	POP3
e-client	IMAP	protocol
electronic mail (e-mail)	MIME	S/MIME (Secure/MIME)
e-mail client	netiquette	SMTP protocol
e-mail server	offline	Spam

TRUE/FALSE

Circle **T** if the statement is true or **F** if the statement is false.

T F 1. Microsoft offers a free Web-based e-mail service called Hotmail.

T F 2. To remove yourself from an advertiser's electronic mailing list, it is recommended that you send a note asking that your address be deleted from the list.

T F 3. Outlook Express allows you to include stationery (backgrounds and text colors) in your e-mail messages.

T F 4. Reading e-mail involves many more steps than sending e-mail.

T F 5. A problem with attachments is that they tend to become disconnected from the e-mail message to which they were originally attached.

T F 6. The two parts of a typical e-mail message are the header and the message.

T F 7. An advantage of Web-based e-mail is that you can access your e-mail from any Internet-connected computer.

T F 8. You can include names and e-mail addresses of your contacts in the address book.

T F 9. WinZip and PKZip are examples of e-mail client software.

T F 10. You should never leave the subject area of an e-mail message blank.

MULTIPLE CHOICE

Circle the correct choice for each of the following.

1. A specification for formatting multimedia messages so they can be sent over the Internet is
   a. POP3
   b. MIME
   c. IMAP
   d. SMTP

2. A difference between junk mail and spam is that
   a. you receive much more junk mail than you do spam
   b. spam is not as effective as junk mail in attracting new customers
   c. spam is sometimes offensive, possibly including pornographic material
   d. spam cannot be sent by e-mail

3. Active scripting
   a. makes Web pages dynamic
   b. scans attachments for viruses
   c. blocks spam
   d. includes an e-mail client

4. To send a copy of an e-mail message to someone, without the knowledge of the message's primary recipient, you would use a
   a. carbon copy (cc)
   b. attachment
   c. blind carbon copy (bcc)
   d. address book

5. You can find Outlook Express as a(n)
   a. icon on the status bar
   b. component of Internet Explorer
   c. selection in My Computer's File menu
   d. icon on the Word standard toolbar

6. If you want to include multiple e-mail addresses under one heading in your address book, so that you can send a message to all members of the group at one time, you would create a
   a. group
   b. subset
   c. category
   d. club

7. A file that you create and append to an e-mail message is a(n)
   a. appendage
   b. folder
   c. subunit
   d. attachment

8. A tool that blocks unwanted e-mail is called a(n)
   a. blocker
   b. terminator
   c. filter
   d. separator

9. To send an e-mail message to more than one person, include the e-mail addresses of all recipients in the To: area, separated by
   a. slashes
   b. asterisks
   c. dollar signs
   d. commas

10. A protocol that supports encrypted multimedia e-mail messages is
    a. S/MIME
    b. MIME
    c. R/MIME
    d. SMTP

PRACTICAL PROJECTS

1. A Flying Horse?

Pegasus Mail is a popular e-mail client used by many businesses to support e-mail functions. It has been in use for over 10 years, garnering accolades from the business community for its reliability and comprehensive features. Take a closer look at Pegasus Mail by researching it online, and provide a complete summary of the product, including its history, its features, and its ability to support e-mail processing on individual computers. Who developed Pegasus, and when? Where can you get a copy of the product? How much does it cost? Is it available only for the Windows operating system? Is it possible for you to use it at home? You might find that reviews of the product contain helpful information.

2. Some Things in Life Are Free

In this chapter, you worked with Hotmail, a free Web-based e-mail service. As you are probably aware, there are many choices of Web-based e-mail services. Consider whether you would want to use a Web-based e-mail service in addition to your regular e-mail account. What advantages are there? What disadvantages? What are your choices? Why is it free? Prepare a report, giving a description of Web-based e-mail, including information on features and availability. In your report, be sure to include Web addresses for Web-based e-mail services and instructions for their use. If you were going to use a free e-mail service, which would you select and why?

3. Fighting Spam

As soon as you begin to work with e-mail, you will be faced with spam, usually from advertisers intent on making a sale. Unless you have a high level of tolerance and a great deal of time, spam can become annoying. Although it is not a security risk for your system, you might want to explore software options for controlling spam. Conduct some research to identify antispam software. You might use the Internet and visit retail stores to gather information. Prepare a table listing at least five software products that include some facility for eliminating or avoiding spam. Be sure to include a description of each software package, including its cost, availability, and features.

4. Messaging in an Instant

Although it is not considered a form of e-mail, instant messaging is a popular form of online communication. By using an instant messaging client, you can tell if friends are online and you can send them an "instant message" to which they can respond. Because the messages are sent back and forth in real time (without delay), you can actually carry on a conversation. Employees find instant messaging a convenient way to communicate—somewhere between a telephone call and an e-mail message. However, privacy groups point out that such communication is not secure, as employers can, and often do, monitor instant messages. Prepare a report on the use of instant messaging in the workplace. Include information on any privacy and security risks associated with instant messaging at work. Also provide information on corporate use of instant messaging, including Web conferencing, screen sharing, and simultaneous collaboration.

5. Security Breaches

Due to Outlook and Outlook Express's immense popularity, they have become targets for computer hackers' mischief. Because they initially allowed active scripting, Outlook products were easy targets for Web-scripting viruses, which caused a great deal of havoc. Microsoft was quick to address those security breaches with patches, available as downloads from the Microsoft Web site. Give a summary of past security problems with both Outlook and Outlook Express. Be sure to indicate what caused those security problems and how Microsoft responded. What viruses or worms specifically targeted Outlook installations? What did they do? Do you think it is safer to use Outlook now than it was in the past? Why or why not?

CHAPTER 9

Creating Documents (Using Microsoft Word 2002)

I f you use your computer for only one task, it is likely to be **word processing**. Many people find it hard to imagine writing an entire manuscript with pen and ink, or even using a typewriter for a lengthy document. Those people have discovered the powerful software tool that makes it easy to create, edit, format, and print documents—the word processor. Word processing software allows you to type a letter, write and edit a research paper, create a flyer, print a brochure, publish a newsletter, and print labels. Anyone who writes can take advantage of the speed and ease of use of a word processor.

Learning to create simple documents using a word processor is not a complicated task. In fact, in a matter of a few minutes, you can be typing, editing, and printing documents. Of course, it takes a little longer to become a proficient user of such a powerful word processor as Microsoft Word. This chapter introduces you to the basics of Microsoft Word 2002, providing direction on how to create, format, edit, and print documents.

Objectives

When you complete this chapter, you will:

- **Be familiar with the concept of word processing and how a word processor can be used to create, edit, and print documents.**
- **Be able to use Word 2002 for basic word processing tasks.**
- **Understand the Word 2002 software interface.**
- **Know how to create a document, both from a blank document and from a general template.**
- **Be able to edit and save documents.**
- **Know how to close documents, as well as how to reopen and edit them.**
- **Be able to preview and print documents.**
- **Be able to change the format of characters, paragraphs, and documents.**

Introducing Word Processing

By definition, word processing software is designed to create, edit, and print documents. It enables you to save your documents and edit, or update, them later. Although it is tempting to compare a word processor to a typewriter, they actually have little in common, except that both began as text processing devices. Unlike a typewriter, a word processor gives you an opportunity to make corrections and to change the appearance of a document before it is printed. A word processor also includes a full range of options for working with graphics and animation, allowing you to create vivid documents with pictures, borders, backgrounds, tables, and many other formatting features. The dividing line between word processing and **desktop publishing** (using a personal computer to create documents for publication) is blurring, as word processors now include a full range of graphic design features, making it possible to create high-quality printed documents.

Not all word processing software is the same. Some, like Microsoft Word and Corel WordPerfect, include everything you need to create just about any kind of document. They feature spelling and grammar checkers, predesigned document formats, many different fonts and document styles, and even an art component, from which you can choose text designs. Others are more basic, with limited formatting capability and no spelling checker. However, most word processing software does share one common feature: a **WYSIWYG** interface. WYSIWYG—pronounced *WIZ-ee-wig* and short for *what you see is what you get*—means that you see on the display screen exactly what will appear when the document is printed. All font settings, graphics, and page breaks are evident as you type and will look exactly the same printed as they do on-screen.

Although word processing software is sometimes sold by itself, you will often find it included as part of an office suite. An office suite is a bundled group of software that shares common resources and provides assistance with typical office applications. Word processing is, without fail, included in all office suites. Perhaps the most recognizable office suite is Microsoft Office, but there are others, including Corel WordPerfect Office, Lotus SmartSuite, and StarOffice. Microsoft Works is a Microsoft product that includes several components, including spreadsheet, word processing, and database programs. It is called an *integrated software package* because, unlike an office suite, its software components cannot be purchased separately. It is often included on new computer systems because it costs less than Microsoft Office and because it is capable of working with most home computer applications. When you purchase word processing software or an office suite, check the system specifications to make sure you buy the correct version for your system. Some are designed for Windows, others for Linux or Macintosh.

Creating and Managing Documents

At first, you might think creating a document using word processing software is much like creating a document using a typewriter, except that you type on a blank area of the screen instead of on paper. From that point, however, the paths

◢▰ Web Watch

Microsoft sponsors a Web page with the latest information on Microsoft Office XP, including tips and supporting materials. Find the page at **www.microsoft.com/office**.

In the Know

Word processing did not grow from computer technology. Rather, it evolved from the needs of writers and secretaries. It was actually a gradual automation of the physical aspects of editing and writing, progressing from the typewriter, to a dedicated word processing system, and finally to the microcomputer. The term "word processing" was coined by IBM in 1964 to market its Selectric typewriter, which recorded text on tape. Magnetic tape was the first reusable storage medium for typewriters, allowing typed material to be edited without having to retype the whole text.

In 1969, IBM introduced MagCards, which were inserted into a typewriterlike device, recording text as it was typed on paper. The cards were then used to recall and reprint text. Companies that sent out large numbers of form letters found the MagCards particularly useful. However, only about one page of text could be recorded on each card. Dedicated word processing systems were prevalent in the 1970s and early 1980s. Unlike today's microcomputer, those systems were designed for only one function—word processing. Also, they were bulky and expensive.

The floppy disk, developed by IBM in the 1970s, brought word processing to the desktop. Early disks, capable of holding 80 to 100 pages, permitted the creation and editing of multipage documents without having to change storage media. Probably the first word processing program designed for the PC was the Electric Pencil, in 1976. Soon after, John Draper designed Easy-Writer for the Apple II, and in 1981 he revised EasyWriter for IBM.

Released in 1979, WordStar was the first commercially successful word processing software program. Developed by MicroPro International, it was quickly adopted by many businesses and home computer users. By today's standards, it was rudimentary, requiring keyboard commands for every activity and producing a document on-screen that was hard to read, appearing disjointed with all the special codes that were required. It was not at all WYSIWYG! Its success continued for several years until competitors, such as Microsoft, brought out new word processors for the Windows GUI.

diverge. Word processing software includes a comprehensive menu and toolbar structure including selections that help you design, save, and print documents. As you type, you can make changes to and rearrange text. You can even preview the document to see exactly how it will look when it is printed.

Regardless of which word processing software you use, creating and managing documents is handled in the same manner. Therefore, you can easily transfer skills that you learn using one word processing program to others. Because you are likely to encounter it in the workplace and in college and public computer labs, and because it is such a comprehensive, well-designed software package, we will use Microsoft Word 2002 in this chapter. It enables you to type, edit, format (change the appearance of), print, and save text. It also corrects spelling and grammatical errors. With special tools that allow you to add graphics, pictures, tables, and sounds to documents, Word is definitely a complete word processing system for both home and corporate users. You can find Word 2002 as an individual software item or included in Microsoft Office XP, which is Microsoft's office suite.

In the
Know
Windows XP and Office XP are not the same, although people often confuse the two. Windows XP is a version of the Windows operating system, and Office XP is a software suite that includes commonly used office components. Windows XP provides an environment in which application software packages, such as Office XP, can work. Another common misconception is that you must have Windows XP installed to run Office XP. The truth is that Office XP can run with a number of different versions of the Windows operating system, not just Windows XP. Check the system specifications listed on the Office XP packaging to determine whether you have an appropriate operating system.

The Word Interface

If Word is installed on your system, you will find it by clicking Start, All Programs, Microsoft Word. The Word application window will open, as shown in Figure 9.1. Your window might appear slightly different, because Word allows users to customize the appearance of window elements. However, you should see a menu, at least one toolbar, and a large white document area. Other window components are diagrammed in Figure 9.1.

Document Views

You can customize the view of the document so that it is appropriate for the task in which you are involved. Your choices are Normal view, Web Layout view, Print Layout view, and Outline view. You might use the Outline view to check the document's structure and flow of thoughts, and then switch to other views for editing and printing. Four view buttons, found at the bottom left of the document area, allow you to quickly shift between views. Those view buttons are shown in Figure 9.1. As you create a document, you will probably prefer to work with Normal view because it gives the most typing space, while still clearly showing such items as tabs and indents. To display a document in a different view, just click the corresponding view button.

- Normal view — Used for typing, editing, and formatting text
- Web Layout view — Used for creating and viewing documents to be posted as Web pages
- Print Layout view — Used for seeing how the page will appear when printed
- Outline view — Used for organizing contents of documents, based on headings and subheadings

Title Bar

In all Windows-based applications, the **title bar** always appears at the top of the window, indicating both the application name (in this case, Microsoft Word) and the filename. Because you have not yet created or saved a document, the filename

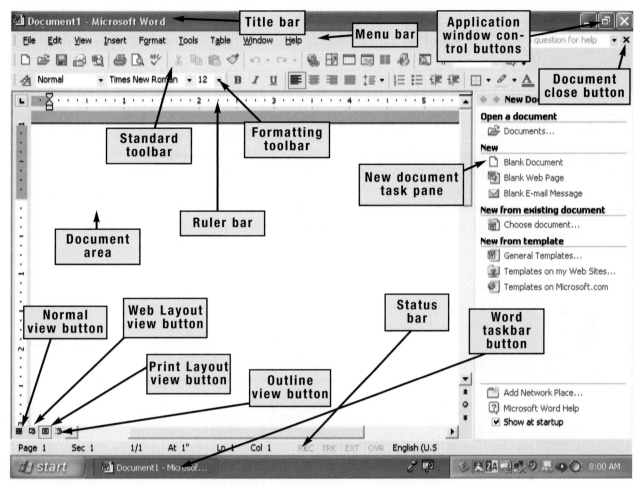

Figure 9.1 **Microsoft Word opens as a window, containing a menu, toolbars, and a document area.**

appears as *Document 1*. To the right of the title bar are the three familiar application control buttons: *minimize, restore,* and *close.* Word allows you to have multiple documents open at one time. Although you typically view only one document on-screen at a time, you can get to any other open documents by clicking the Word button on the taskbar and selecting the document name from the list that appears. When you want to close a document, click the *document close* button found at the right side of the menu bar.

✓SANITY CHECK

Clicking the close button is a quick way to close either a document or the Word program. Perhaps you intended to close a document, but when you clicked the close button, Word asked if you wanted to save the document, and upon your response, closed the entire application (Word). What happened? Instead of clicking the document close button (the lower "x"), you clicked the upper close button. The upper close button closes not only the document, but Word as well. Thankfully, Word doesn't close without asking whether you want to save any open documents, so you are not likely to lose any text. To get back to your document, you must open Word and then open the document (as described later in this chapter).

Menu Bar, Toolbars, and the Ruler Bar

The **menu bar** appears directly below the title bar. It includes options for issuing commands related to creating, editing, formatting, saving, and printing documents. Many menu commands are also available as selections from a **toolbar**. Toolbars make it easier to access commonly used menu commands by shortening the number of mouse clicks necessary to invoke a command. By default (unless directed otherwise), two toolbars should appear when you first open Word—the *Standard toolbar* and the *Formatting toolbar.* To determine what each toolbar button does, move the mouse pointer over a toolbar button and hold it steady. A **screen tip** pops up beneath the button, identifying the associated command.

✓ SANITY CHECK

Toolbars are normally displayed on separate lines near the top of the application window. Although you work primarily with the Standard and Formatting toolbars, you can open others and close those that you don't need. To control the display of toolbars, click View, Toolbars, and then select (or deselect) any that you want to display or remove from view.

The ruler bar can also be helpful, but what if it is not displayed? Click View, Ruler, to toggle the ruler on or off.

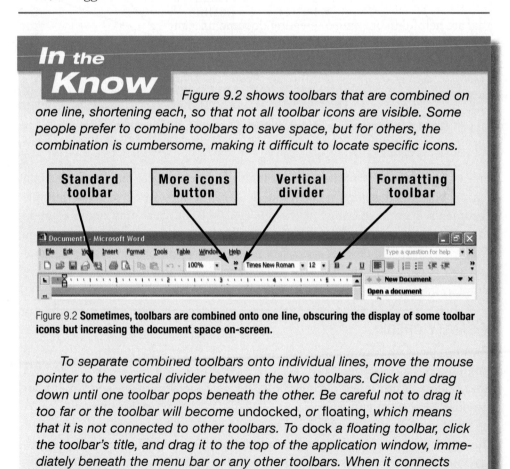

In the Know

Figure 9.2 shows toolbars that are combined on one line, shortening each, so that not all toolbar icons are visible. Some people prefer to combine toolbars to save space, but for others, the combination is cumbersome, making it difficult to locate specific icons.

Figure 9.2 **Sometimes, toolbars are combined onto one line, obscuring the display of some toolbar icons but increasing the document space on-screen.**

To separate combined toolbars onto individual lines, move the mouse pointer to the vertical divider between the two toolbars. Click and drag down until one toolbar pops beneath the other. Be careful not to drag it too far or the toolbar will become undocked, *or* floating, *which means that it is not connected to other toolbars. To* dock *a floating toolbar, click the toolbar's title, and drag it to the top of the application window, immediately beneath the menu bar or any other toolbars. When it connects seamlessly with the others, release the mouse button.*

Beneath the toolbars, you will see a **ruler bar**. The ruler bar is a handy way to set tabs, as you will find out later in this chapter. It is measured in inches, with the left and right margins clearly denoted by a change in color. If your document is in Print Layout view, the ruler bar appears to the top and left of the document area. In Normal view, it is displayed only at the top of the document area.

✓ SANITY CHECK

When you place the mouse pointer over a toolbar button, a screen tip should appear, giving information about the button. However, if a screen tip doesn't appear, you can click Tools, Customize and click the Options tab. Make sure *Show Screen Tips on Toolbars* is checked. Click Close.

Task Pane

The **task pane** appears on the right side of the application window. The task pane is a window that provides quick access to commands relevant to a task in which you are involved. Although the exact heading of the task pane varies depending upon the task initiated, its view and commands are similar. When you first open Word, the task pane is titled "New Document" and includes features that are helpful in opening or creating documents. Colored options in a task pane are called *hyperlinks*. When you click a hyperlink in Word, much like on the Internet, it invokes a particular command or feature. For example, if you click General Templates, a dialog box will appear, allowing you to choose from some predesigned document layouts.

Task panes are sometimes opened because of menu selections. When you click Edit, Office Clipboard, the task pane changes to the Clipboard pane. Similarly, when you click File, New, the New Document task pane appears. You can close any task pane by clicking the close button in the top right corner of the task pane. The task pane does not appear when you open a previously saved document.

Status Bar

The horizontal bar that appears at the bottom of the application window is called the **status bar**. The left side of the status bar indicates the current page, line, column, and number of inches from the top of the page. In the middle is information about features or keys that are active. For example, you can tell from the status bar whether you are in *overwrite* or *insert* mode, indicating whether characters that you type will overwrite existing characters or whether they will be inserted between existing text. The language your computer is using is identified on the right.

Creating a Document

When you open Microsoft Word, you will find yourself at a blank document. A blinking vertical line at the top left corner of the document area—called an **insertion point**—indicates the position where text will appear when you begin typing. As you type, the insertion point moves with you. Make it a point to always be aware of this bar so that you will know where text will appear when you type.

As you move the mouse over the document, you can see that the mouse pointer moves. You can click anywhere within existing text to reposition the insertion point.

There will be occasions when you have been working in Word and have closed all open documents so that there is no document with which to work. Instead, you will see an empty gray area, as shown in Figure 9.3. If you want to create a document, you must first open a blank one. Click the New Blank Document button on the Standard toolbar to open a new document.

✓ SANITY CHECK

Let's say that you've typed a paragraph of a new document and want to continue typing in the lower part of the white document area. You know that you can click to reposition the insertion point, so you move to an empty part of the document and click. Instead of moving to the empty area, however, the insertion point remains at the end of the last paragraph. Why didn't it move? You should know that, although you can see an entire document page on-screen, the current document includes only the area in which you have already typed some text or pressed a key (⏎Enter), for example. Therefore, the empty part of the white area is not yet included in your document and is not accessible. To begin a new paragraph, or to move to an empty area, position the insertion point at the end of the last paragraph, and press ⏎Enter repeatedly. You can also double-click anywhere in the empty document area to move the insertion point. When you double-click an empty area, Word places multiple hard returns in the empty area, just as if you had pressed ⏎Enter repeatedly. The insertion point will progress down the page to the intended location.

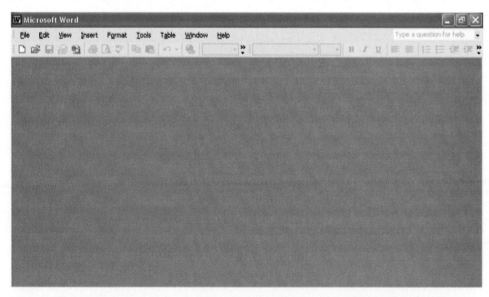

Figure 9.3 **When all open documents are closed, a gray area appears in the Word application window.**

Word Wrap

If you have ever used a typewriter to create a document, you remember listening for the bell as you approached the right margin and then pressing Return to proceed to the next line. With a word processor, however, there is no bell and you don't need to press Return at the end of each line! As you reach the right margin, the text automatically moves to the next line. This action is called **word wrap**. The only time you need to press ⏎Enter is at the end of a paragraph or an individual line that doesn't wrap, such as a heading, address, salutation, or date. In word processing, pressing ⏎Enter is called a **hard return** because you are forcing a return where there wouldn't normally be one. When text wraps automatically, it is called a **soft return**.

Correcting Mistakes

As you type, you are likely to make mistakes. Of course, the ease with which you can correct errors is one of the features that makes word processors so appealing. Simply click to place the insertion point where you want to make the correction. Then, press Del to remove characters to the right of the insertion point, or ⌫Backspace to remove characters to the left. With the error removed, type the correct text. As you type the correction, it will be inserted between existing text.

By default, you should be in *insert mode*, which means that as you type, the text is placed between any existing text. For example, if you have mistyped the word *together* as *togethr*, you can click to place the insertion point after the *h*. Then type the letter **e**, and it will be placed between the *h* and *r* to correctly spell the word. However, sometimes you can best make a correction by typing over existing text. When this happens, you need to switch to *overwrite mode*, where typed text replaces existing characters. To toggle between insert and overwrite mode, press Insert on the keyboard. If the *OVR* indicator on the status bar is bold, you are in overwrite mode.

Checking Spelling and Grammar

Word checks your spelling as you type. If a word is not recognized, you will see a red wavy line appear underneath it. It is important to remember that this doesn't necessarily mean the word is misspelled, only that it is not included in Word's dictionary. Right-click the underlined word to check spelling options. If the word is actually spelled correctly—perhaps it is a person's last name—you might want to add it to the dictionary by selecting *Add to Dictionary*. However, if the word is misspelled, you should correct it. If the correct spelling is on the context menu, click it to correct the spelling. If you don't see the correct spelling listed, click outside the menu to remove it from view, and then manually correct the word. The red wavy lines are not printed, so if a word is spelled correctly but Word identifies it as misspelled (by underlining it), you can simply continue typing.

Green wavy underlines indicate a possible problem with grammar. Right-click an underlined area to see Word's suggestions. Sometimes the question is simply a matter of style. Perhaps Word interprets your style as too informal and suggests that you refrain from using contractions (using "does not," instead of "doesn't," for example). Other times, the problem might be a sentence fragment

▶ Quick Tip

To return to the top of a document, press Ctrl + Home (hold down Ctrl while pressing Home). To move to the end, press Ctrl + End.

▶ Quick Tip

You will find one of the most useful toolbar selections to be the *Undo* icon. No matter how careful you are, you will inevitably make mistakes. You might delete an entire paragraph and then realize that it was the wrong paragraph! You can recover quickly by clicking the Undo button ↺, which looks like a counter-clockwise-turning arrow. Pressing it repeatedly will undo previous actions as well, in reverse order of occurrence. However, you cannot undo some actions, such as a save or a print. The button just to the right of Undo is Redo ↻, which reverses the action of an "undo." If you deleted the word "playing" and then clicked Undo, the word would be displayed again. Then, if you clicked Redo, the word would once again be deleted.

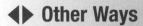

◄► **Other Ways**

You can spell-check a document by clicking the Spelling and Grammar button ✓ on the Standard toolbar. You will then be prompted to either correct or ignore each occurrence of a spelling or grammatical error. Before beginning a check, you should place the insertion point at the beginning of the document.

or use of the passive voice. If you like the phrasing as you have it, ignore Word's suggestions and proceed. The green wavy underlines will not be printed.

Perhaps you don't want Word to check your spelling as you type, or you prefer that the grammar check be a little less formal. You might not even want Word to check your grammar at all. You can specify your preferences in the Spelling and Grammar dialog box. You can modify Spelling and Grammar Check settings by clicking Tools, Options and selecting the Spelling and Grammar tab.

Saving a Document

Saving a document means placing it on disk for later retrieval. RAM holds documents only while you are working with them. As you type a document, it appears on-screen and is stored in RAM. However, RAM is active only when there is a constant supply of electricity. To avoid losing your document due to a power outage or power surge, you should periodically save it to your disk. To save a document, click File, Save. Click the drop-down arrow beside the Save In box and select the location where you want to save your file. Change the filename, if desired, and click Save. A filename can be up to 255 characters in length and can include spaces. The following list of special characters cannot be included in filenames.

Forward slash (/)	Back Slash (\)
Greater than sign (>)	Less than sign (<)
Colon (:)	Semicolon (;)

Saving a Document in a Different File Format

Word saves files with the extension .doc. If you use Word to save a file called *Book List*, it is actually named *Book List.doc*. A file extension associates a file with a spe-

In the
Know

Don't wait until you have completed a document to save it! Every few minutes, save the document in the same location with the same filename. That way, if you experience a power outage, you can retrieve it from your disk, losing only what you might have typed after the most recent save operation.

If you are a not as vigilant as you should be in saving files, Word will automatically save your document at specified intervals. To check the AutoRecover settings, click Tools, Options, and click the Save tab. Select the Save AutoRecover info every check box, and then indicate the preferred interval of time (in minutes) that you want Word to wait between automatic saves. However, don't use the AutoRecover as a substitute for regular saves using menu options or the Standard toolbar. It is only designed as a safety net in the case of a loss of power or system shutdown.

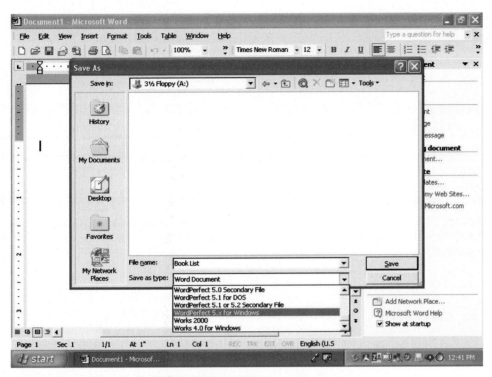

Figure 9.4 **Using Word, you can save files in several different software formats.**

cific software package, which means that to open the file, you must use the same software. When you save a file, you can choose to save it as a different file type. For example, if you are working in a computer lab on a Word document but want to save it so that you can open it at home using WordPerfect, you can save it as a WordPerfect document. If this is not your first save and you want to make changes to the file type, filename, or save location, you must click File, Save As to begin the save operation. (If it is the first time you are saving the file, you can select either File, Save or File, Save As.) When saving the document, you would click the drop-down arrow beside *Save as Type*, as shown in Figure 9.4, and scroll down to find your version of WordPerfect. Click to select the version, and continue with the save operation. If you saved the file on a floppy disk or CD, you could then take it home and open it in WordPerfect to continue your work.

Closing a Document

When you have finished working with a document and have saved it, you are ready to close it. When you close a document, it is removed from memory but not from the disk on which it is saved. To close a document only, click the document close button, as shown in Figure 9.1 (in the upper right corner of the application window, just beneath the title bar). You can also click File, Close. Both methods close a file (document) but leave the Word application open so that you can work with other files. When you close Word, by clicking the uppermost close button (or File, Exit), Word is closed, along with all open documents. If you have made any changes to documents since the time of the last save, you will be prompted to save them before Word is closed.

> ### ■▶Quick Tip
> Some file types are proprietary, which means that a file can be opened only with the same type of software in which it was saved. Others are more commonly recognized, such as rtf (Rich Text Format). When you are saving a document to send as an e-mail attachment, you might consider saving it as an rtf document. That way, it is more likely that the recipient of your e-mail will be able to read the document.

Hands On

Activity 9.1—Creating and Saving a Document

In this activity, you will create and save a document. Your computer should be at the desktop.

1. Open Word (Click Start, All Programs, Microsoft Word).
2. Type the following text. (Remember not to press ⏎Enter until you reach the end of the first paragraph. To indent each paragraph, press Tab⇆ once. Press ⏎Enter twice after the word "problems," to begin a new paragraph.)

> As easy as it is to use e-mail, you might someday find your e-mail messages increasing in number to the point that the service becomes almost a nuisance. You might find yourself on multiple mailing lists that offer you online deals or newsletters. Given the ease of forwarding messages, your friends might flood you with them. Working people find it difficult to leave work-related issues at work, because they can (and often feel obligated to) retrieve and respond to e-mail messages at home. The

> workday can easily extend into the home environment, contributing to stress-related problems.
>
> Understanding your options makes it easier to control the technology, instead of letting it control you. E-mail is truly a marvelous convenience when managed appropriately so that it does not dominate your leisure time.

3. Correct any spelling errors that you might have made. (To correct an error, click in the location of the mistake, and either delete or backspace to remove the text. Then, type it as it should appear.)
4. Place a blank floppy disk in the A: drive.
5. Save the document to the disk. Click File, Save. Click the drop-down arrow beside the Save In area, and select 3½ Floppy (A:). Change the filename to *E-mail Tips*. Click Save.
6. Leave your disk in the A: drive because you will continue working with the document in Activity 9.2. Don't close Word.

▶Quick Tip

If you have saved all open documents and are ready to end the Word session, you don't have to close all documents before exiting Word. Just closing Word automatically closes all open documents as it closes the application.

Opening and Editing an Existing Document

When you first open Word, the task pane will appear. If you want to open a document that you have viewed recently, you can reopen that file by clicking the filename in the list that appears in the *Open* area of the task pane, as shown in Figure 9.5.

If the file is not listed in the task pane, you can still open it by clicking File, Open, or by clicking the Open button found on the Standard toolbar. From the Open dialog box, shown in Figure 9.6, click the drop-down arrow beside the Look In area to select the disk drive on which the file is saved. If the file is saved in a folder on the disk, double-click the folder to access it. Finally, double-click the filename to open it.

Printing a Document

Most people rarely create documents that they don't intend to print. Therefore, it is important to have an idea of the way a document will look when printed and be

In the Know

You might have noticed that when you begin a save operation, there are two "save" choices on the File menu—Save and Save As. What is the difference? The first time you save a file, there is no difference. Choosing either option causes a dialog box to appear, allowing you to identify the save location, the filename, and the file type.

However, suppose that you later open the document, make some changes, and want to save it again. This time, there is a difference between the two methods. If you click File, Save, the file is saved in the same location, with the same filename and file type. It is a quick way to save a file when you don't want to make any changes to the location or filename. You can even click the Save button, which is a shortcut for the File, Save menu selection.

If you click File, Save As instead, you are presented with the same dialog box that you saw during the initial save, asking for confirmation of a save location, filename, and file type. If you want to make a backup copy of the file, possibly on another storage medium, the File, Save As menu selection is the best choice.

able to manage printing options. Word includes a feature whereby you can preview documents before printing. That way, you can make corrections and adjustments so you don't waste paper on something that does not look the way you want it. Print settings allow you to specify how many copies of a document to print, which pages to print, and even which text (perhaps just one paragraph!) to print.

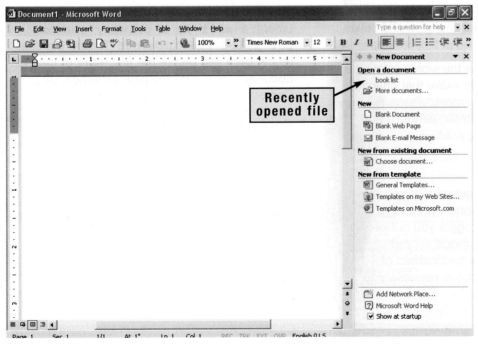

Figure 9.5 **Recently opened files are displayed in the task pane.**

Selecting Text

You can change the format of text either before or after you type it. If you know ahead of time that you want to right align a document, for example, you can click the right align button on the Formatting toolbar, and then type the document. If you decide after the fact to make text changes, you must first select the text that you want to change and then apply formatting.

Although you can always select text by clicking and dragging, there are more convenient methods, as summarized in Figure 9.11.

Changing the Appearance of Characters

An effective way to make a document more appealing and to draw attention to specific text is to modify some character attributes. You can select a new **font** (character design, also called **typeface**) or change font size. Changing font color, italicizing text, or adding boldface can make your document more attractive. Perhaps you'd like to highlight a heading or add a border. There are numerous possibilities for changing text or for formatting before you type. Commonly used formatting options are available on the Formatting toolbar, as shown in Figure 9.12.

To select a character attribute *before* typing text, you must set the attribute on, type the text, and then set the attribute off again. If you select a character attribute *after* typing text, you must first select the text to be affected, and then select the new attribute. Although you can make most text formatting changes by clicking icons on the Formatting toolbar, you can also make changes by clicking Format, Font and choosing options from the Format dialog box.

Formatting Paragraphs

When working with a document, you might want to change the alignment of the text, set tabs, change line indents, or change line spacing. All of those activities are possible when you format paragraphs using Word.

◀▶ Other Ways

Shortcut keyboard commands are handy ways to format text without moving your hands from the keyboard. You can make text boldface by pressing Ctrl + B. To underline, press Ctrl + U, and to italicize, press Ctrl + I. You should press the same key sequence when you have finished typing formatted text to end the formatting effect.

To Select	Do This
A word	Double-click the word
A sentence	Press Ctrl and click anywhere within the sentence
A line of text	Point to the line and click in the selection bar (the area between the left edge of the document and the left side of the page)
A paragraph	Triple-click anywhere within the paragraph
A document	Click Edit, Select All (or type Ctrl+A)

Figure 9.11 **You can select words, sentences, lines, paragraphs, and even entire documents before applying formatting changes.**

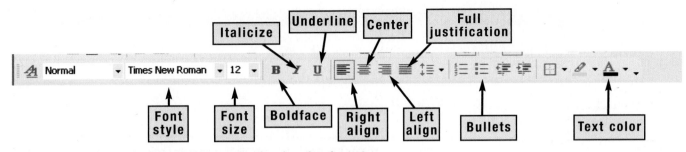

Figure 9.12 **The Formatting toolbar includes several options for enhancing text.**

By default, text is lined up on the left margin (left aligned). However, you can align text on the right, center it, or make it fully justified, like what you see in newspapers. All of those options are available on the Formatting toolbar, as shown in Figure 9.12. If you have already typed text, and then decide to change the alignment, you must first select the text to be realigned.

Indentation refers to variations in the left and right margins of text in a paragraph. You have probably seen documents containing lengthy quotes in which the quotes were indented equally on the left and right to denote them properly. Perhaps you have worked with a bibliography, where you had to create a *hanging indent,* in which the first line was placed at the left margin, with following lines indented to the right. To change indents, click Format, Paragraph, and make selections from the dialog box, as shown in Figure 9.13. Before you make any changes, the insertion point should be in the paragraph to be indented.

◀▶ Other Ways

Some people find it easier to set tabs using the ruler bar, which is found at the top of the document area. If the ruler is not displayed, click View, Ruler. To the left of the ruler bar, you will find a symbol indicating the active tab type. Hold the mouse pointer steady over the tab symbol to get a screen tip defining the tab type. To change to another type, click the corresponding tab symbol. Then click anywhere on the ruler bar to set a tab of that type. A tab symbol will appear on the ruler bar. Press (Tab↹) to move the beginning of the text to the new tab stop. To remove any tab stop, click and drag the tab symbol from the ruler bar.

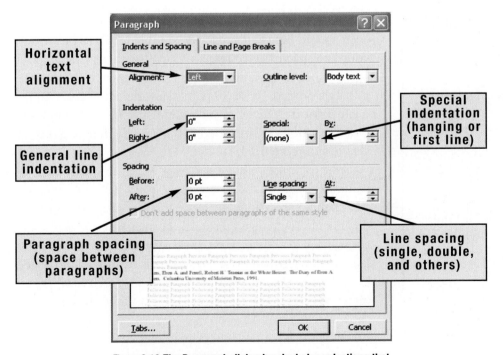

Figure 9.13 **The Paragraph dialog box includes selections that allow you to change indents.**

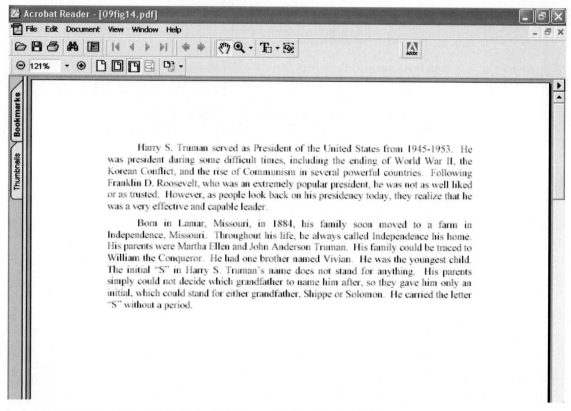

Figure 9.14 **This text is single-spaced, with 6 points of space after each paragraph.**

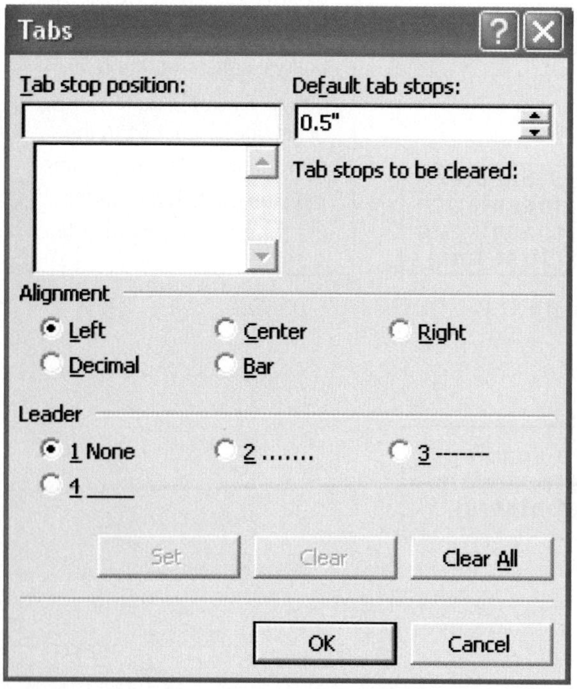

Figure 9.15 **The Tabs dialog box contains options that let you set and clear tabs.**

Documents can be single-spaced, double-spaced, or even spaced between single and double (1.5). Regardless of your line spacing selection, you can also choose the amount of space between paragraphs. The text shown in Figure 9.14 is single-spaced, with 6 point spacing after paragraphs. Each point is 1/72 of an inch. Line spacing and paragraph spacing options are included in the Paragraph dialog box, as shown in Figure 9.13.

You can use tabs when you want to place text in columns. By default, tabs are set at every half inch, but you can change tab settings to make them appropriate for your document. To change tabs, click Format, Tabs, type the tab stop (in inches), and select from available tab types (right, left, center, decimal, or bar). A leader is the dotted or dashed line that can appear between tabbed items, such as what you might see on a restaurant menu. The Tabs dialog box is shown in Figure 9.15.

When you set tabs, they apply only to any text that you type *after* setting the tab or to text that you *select* before setting the tab. Therefore, different parts of a document can have different tab settings.

Formatting Documents

In Normal view, a faint, dotted line indicates a page break. In Page Layout view, a page break is more obviously indicated as a gray bar. Word automatically sets page breaks so when you reach the bottom margin, the text wraps to the next page, but sometimes you might want to force a page break where one would not normally be required. Perhaps you have typed a title page and are now ready to move to the body of a report. You can break the page after the title information by clicking Insert, Break, selecting Page Break, and clicking OK.

Word wraps your text to fit within top, bottom, right, and left margins, all of which can be changed by clicking File, Page Setup to open the Page Setup dialog box, shown in Figure 9.16. Make sure the Margins tab is selected, and then change any margin. Click OK when you are finished. The new margins apply to the entire document. If you want the margins to apply only to a section of a document, select the text included in the section, and then set the margins. In the *Apply to* box, click Selected text. The new margins will be applied only to the text that you selected.

A document can be aligned vertically by using the *top aligned, centered,* or *bottom aligned* option. When a document is created, it is automatically aligned from the top, which means that text begins at the top margin and continues downward. Often, however, you might want the document centered, as in the case of a title page. To change vertical alignment, click File, Page Setup. Click the Layout tab. In the Page area, click the drop-down arrow to select a different vertical alignment.

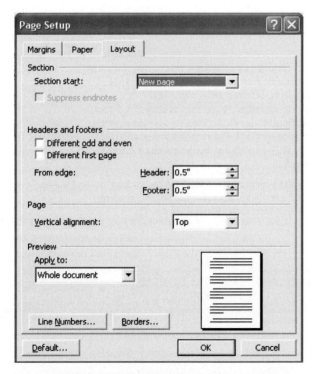

Figure 9.16 **Using the Page Setup dialog box, you can change the margins and layout of a document.**

Hands On

Activity 9.5—Formatting a Document

In this activity, you will format a document. Your computer should be at the desktop.

1. Place the disk that you used in Activity 9.4 in the A: drive.
2. Open the *E-mail Tips* file. It should appear as shown in Figure 9.17.
3. Include a heading on the first line of the document. If the insertion point is not at the beginning of the document, press ⌘+Home. Press ↵Enter twice to open a blank line and some space. Press ⌘+Home to place the insertion at the new beginning of the document. Click the Center button ≣ on the Formatting toolbar. Type **E-mail Tips**. As you type, the words should be centered on the line.
4. Change the left and right margins. Click File, Page Setup. Click the Margins tab. Either type **2** in the boxes for the left and right margins or click the spinner for each setting to increase the margin size to 2. Click OK. The document should be realigned with the new margins.

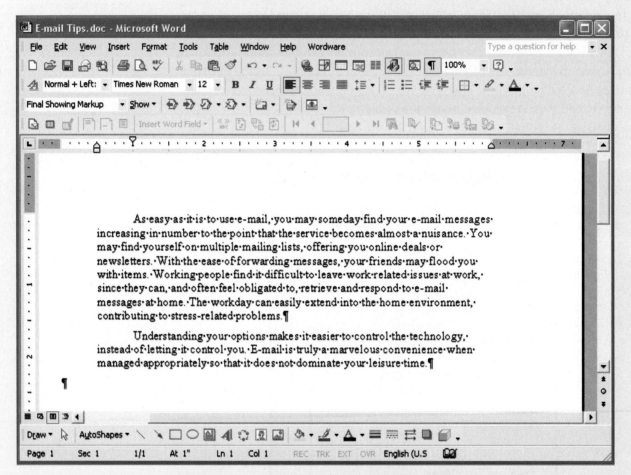

Figure 9.17 **The *E-mail Tips* file is shown here.**

5. Change the line spacing. Press `Ctrl`+`A` to select the entire document. Click Format, Paragraph. Click the drop-down arrow in the Line Spacing area, and click Double. Click OK. Except for some extra space between the heading and the body of the report and between paragraphs, it looks evenly spaced. Click the Show/Hide button on the Standard toolbar. The document now reveals some non-printing characters that indicate the position of keystrokes, such as the hard return (which looks like a backward "P") and a space (a small gray dot). The extra space after the heading ("E-mail Tips") is caused by the extra hard return, which you can now delete. Click to place the insertion point just before the hard return. Press `Del`. You have deleted a hard return, causing the extra space to disappear. Do the same with the hard return appearing between the two paragraphs.

6. Make the heading boldface. Move the mouse pointer to the selection area beside the heading "E-mail Tips." (The selection area is the white space between the left edge of the text and the left edge of the document space.) Click once to select the heading line. If a line other than the heading is selected, try the selection again. Click the Bold button on the Formatting toolbar. Click anywhere outside the heading to see the change.

7. Center the document vertically. Click Page, Setup. Click the Layout tab. In the Page area, click the drop-down arrow and select Center. Click OK.

8. View the document as it will be printed; click File, Print Preview. It should appear centered on the page. Click Close.

9. Move to the end of the document (press `Ctrl`+`End`). Press `↵Enter`. Set a left tab at the .5" mark and another one at the 2" mark. Click Format, Tabs. Click in the Tab Stop Position box, and type **.5**. Make sure the selected tab is *Left,* and click Set. Click in the Tab Stop Position box again, and type **2**. Click Set. The tabs that you have selected should appear as shown in Figure 9.18. Click OK.

10. Before typing any more text, set the line spacing back to Single. (Work with the Format, Paragraph dialog box.)

11. Press `Tab` once. Click the Bold button on the Formatting toolbar. Type **Topic**. Press `Tab` again. Type **Source**. Click the Bold button once more to toggle off the Bold setting. Press `↵Enter`.

12. Press `Tab`. Type **E-mail Definition**. Press `Tab`. Type **www.webopedia.com**. Press `↵Enter`. Notice that Word automatically makes the text a Web link. Anyone reading the document can move to the indicated Web site by holding down `Ctrl` while clicking the link (if they are already connected to the Internet).

13. Press `Tab`. Type **Societal Concerns**. Press `Tab`. Type **www.albion.net**. Press `↵Enter`.

14. Save the document. (Click the Save button on the Standard toolbar.)

15. Close Word.

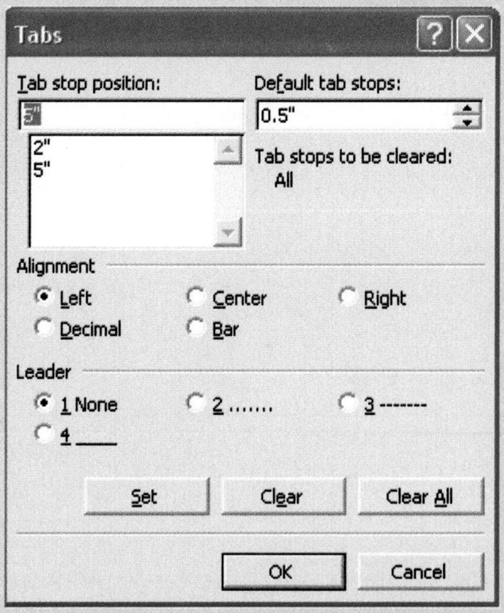

Figure 9.18 **Tabs can be set by making selections in the Tab dialog box.**

Chapter Summary

DON'T FORGET

- Word processing is one of the most commonly used computer applications, allowing you to create, edit, format, and print documents.

- Word 2002, included in the Microsoft Office XP software suite, is a popular word processing package.

- The Word interface includes a menu bar, toolbars, a document area, and a status bar.

- As you create a document, you can make changes to correct any errors.

- A document can be saved in a different file format so that you can use other word processing software to open it.

- You can save a document to a disk, CD, or hard drive.

- After a document is saved, you can reopen it at any time.

- You can preview a document to see how it will look when printed so that you can make any necessary changes before printing.

- Formatting can be applied to characters, paragraphs, or entire documents.

KEY TERMS

desktop publishing	**screen tip**	**toolbar**
font	**soft return**	**typeface**
hard return	**status bar**	**word processing**
insertion point	**task pane**	**word wrap**
menu bar	**template**	**WYSIWYG**
ruler bar	**title bar**	

TRUE/FALSE

Circle **T** if the statement is true or **F** if the statement is false.

T F 1. Word allows you to have several documents open at one time.

T F 2. Web Layout view displays pages as they will appear when posted as Web pages.

T F 3. WYSIWYG stands for "Where you Send is Where you Go."

T F 4. The status bar always appears at the top of the Word window.

T F 5. The task panes that appear to the right of the document area cannot be closed.

T (F) 6. Pressing Del removes characters to the left of the cursor.

(T) F 7. The process of automatically continuing text on another line is called word wrap.

(T) F 8. Word won't print the red wavy lines that indicate that a word is misspelled.

T F 9. A filename cannot contain spaces.

T F 10. By default, Word saves all documents with an .rtf extension.

MULTIPLE CHOICE

Circle the correct choice for each of the following.

1. When you close a document
   a. it is removed from memory and from the disk
   b. it is removed from the disk but not from memory
   c. it is removed from memory but not from the disk
   d. it is removed from RAM but not from memory

2. If you want to view the organization of a document, choose this view:
   a. Web Layout
   b. Outline
   c. Print Layout
   d. Normal

3. To print pages 2 through 4 and page 5 of a document, indicate the page range as:
   a. 2–4, 5
   b. 2:4, 5
   c. 2, 4, 5
   d. 2–4 and 5

4. A preformatted document is called a
   a. model
   b. pattern
   c. design
   d. template

5. To select a paragraph,
   a. click anywhere in the paragraph and double-click
   b. click anywhere in the paragraph and triple-click
   c. click anywhere in the selection bar
   d. press Ctrl and click anywhere in the document

6. Variations in the left and right margins of text in a paragraph are called
   a. indents
   b. text alignment
   c. line spacing
   d. paragraph spacing

7. When a document is created, it is automatically aligned vertically
   a. from the bottom of the page
   b. in the center of the page
   c. from the top of the page
   d. on the right margin of the page

8. To bold text after it has been typed,
   a. click in the selection bar and click the Bold button
   b. select the text to be formatted and click the Bold button
   c. click just before the text to be formatted and click the Bold button
   d. triple click anywhere in the sentence and click the Bold button

9. Which of the following is an office suite?
   a. Microsoft First Office
   b. Sun Office
   c. Corel SmartSuite
   d. Microsoft Office

10. The two toolbars that are normally displayed when Word is started are the
    a. Drawing toolbar and Formatting toolbar
    b. Standard toolbar and Formatting toolbar
    c. Standard toolbar and Help toolbar
    d. Menu toolbar and Query toolbar

PRACTICAL PROJECTS

1. Sun and Star

Sun Microsystems has developed a product called StarOffice, which includes a word processor comparable to Word. Many computer users, especially those working with the Linux operating system, enjoy using StarOffice. StarOffice is capable of opening and saving files in the Microsoft Word format, so even loyal Word users can migrate to StarOffice with the assurance that they can still access their Word files. Look into StarOffice, and provide a report of your findings, answering the following questions:

a. How can you obtain a copy of StarOffice? If it is available for purchase, where do you purchase it, and how much does it cost? How does its cost compare with that of Microsoft Word?

b. What features are included? How do those features compare with Microsoft Word?

c. With which operating systems does StarOffice work?

d. StarOffice is open source. What does that mean? When did it become open source?

e. What is the current version of StarOffice?

f. How does Sun's software philosophy differ from that of Microsoft?

2. A Recipe for Success (with Word Processing)

a. Label a blank formatted disk with your name. Place it in the A: drive.

b. Open Word. Set a left tab at $3^1/2$".

c. Type the following recipe. Center the heading and make it boldface, then use the tab stop to place the ingredients in two columns.

```
          Fresh Apple Cake

1¹/₂ cup salad oil    2 cups sugar
2 large eggs,         1 tsp. salt
  beaten
1 tsp. baking soda    2 tsp. baking
                        powder
1 tsp. vanilla        2¹/₂ cups all-
                        purpose flour
3 cups chopped        1 cup chopped
  apples                pecans
```

   Beat salad oil and sugar at low speed until creamy; add eggs which have been beaten. Sift flour, salt, baking soda, and baking powder. Add to sugar mixture. Add vanilla. Beat until smooth. Mix in nuts and apples. Pour in tube pan and bake 55–60 minutes at 350 degrees. Let cool before removing from pan.

d. Correct any errors. If you see any grammatical mistakes, as indicated by a green wavy underline, right-click the underlined area to check on the problem. If necessary, correct it.

e. Save the recipe on your disk in the A: drive as Apple Cake Recipe.

f. Close Word.

3. Cover Up

a. Place a disk labeled with your name in the A: drive.

b. Open Word.

c. You will type a cover page for a report on Harry Truman, as shown in Figure 9.19.

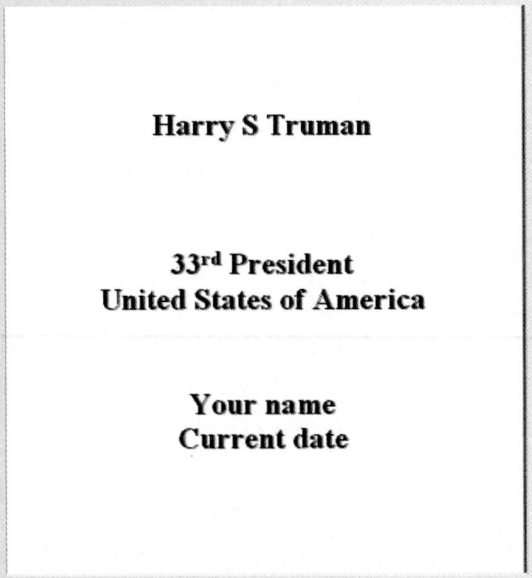

Harry S Truman

33rd President
United States of America

Your name
Current date

Figure 9.19 **Using Word, you can create report title pages.**

d. Set the font to Arial, with a size of 36.

e. Press ↵Enter twice.

f. Click the Center Align button, and type the first line.

g. Press ↵Enter three times.

h. Type the second line. Press ↵Enter, and type the third line.

i. Press ↵Enter three times.

j. Type your name. Press ↵Enter, and type the current date.

k. Center the page vertically. (Click File, Page Setup. Click Layout. Change the vertical alignment to Center.)

l. Preview the page (File, Print Preview). Is it centered correctly?

m. Click Close.

n. Save the document on your disk as *Cover Page*.

o. Close Word.

4. Spell It Out

a. Place a disk labeled with your name in the A: drive.

b. Open Word.

c. Set paragraph spacing to 6 pt. after. Line spacing should be single. Type the following paragraphs exactly as they appear, with all errors. Bold all text as it appears.

A Perfect Union

The church was aglow with candllight. Magnolias and ivy cascaded from the windowsills and the the floors glistened with fresh polish. The women of the church had worked tirelessly to transform the litle chaple into a work of art for this wedding. This was no ordinary wedding; it was one that the congragation had encouraged for quite a while! Their rector, a lifelong bachelor, was marrying the woman who had moved into the little town only six months earlier. Althought a newcomer, she had won the hearts of the townspeople with her charm, wit, and open nature. Sam Stribling thought he was the happiest man on earth!

The Wedding

It was the winter of 1859, a dreadfuly hold time for a wedding. The snow that began to fall that Morning had fallen ceaselessly through the day. By the afternoon, drifts piled against the little chapel, giving it a bereft appearanc, but only adding to the wonder of the day.

d. Place the insertion point at the beginning of the document. Click the Spelling and Grammar button on the Standard toolbar. As each misspelled word is presented, make a decision to ignore it or to correct it.

e. When the spelling check is complete, proofread the document yourself. Are there any words that are used incorrectly or spelled wrong? If so, correct them.

f. Save the document on your disk as *The Wedding*.

g. Close Word.

5. Check the Calendar

Word includes templates, not only for typical business documents, but for other items, such as calendars. In this project, you will create a calendar from one of Word's templates.

a. Place a disk labeled with your name in the A: drive.

b. Open Word.

c. Click File, New. Click General Templates in the Task pane. Click the Other Documents tab. Click Calendar Wizard. Click OK.

d. The Calendar Wizard begins. Click Next.

e. Select the Banner option. Click Next.

f. Select Landscape. Click Next.

g. Set the start and end dates for the current month. Click Next.

h. Click Finish.

i. If the Office Assistant offers help, click Cancel.

j. Save the document on your disk as Calendar.

k. Close Word.

CHAPTER 10

Creating Spreadsheets (Using Microsoft Excel 2002)

Objectives

When you complete this chapter, you will:

- **Understand the concept of spreadsheet software.**

- **Be able to create and edit a worksheet.**

- **Know how to select, copy, and move worksheet components.**

- **Be able to create formulas and work with functions.**

- **Know how to format a worksheet, making changes to the font, alignment, and column width.**

I magine that you are working with an antiques auction, responsible for keeping record of each item's selling price. If all you had were a pencil and a piece of paper, how would you organize that data? Most likely, you would list items in one column and respective prices in the next column. Possibly, at the bottom of the price column, you would include a total sales amount. What you have just envisioned is a spreadsheet. You could keep the antiques auction records on paper, adding and changing data by erasing and rewriting, or you could use computer software to record the data so you could more easily change and rearrange data.

A spreadsheet is simply a list of data arranged in a grid of columns and rows. If you have ever worked with an accounting worksheet or a teacher's grade book, then you are familiar with the spreadsheet format. Spreadsheet software makes it easy to organize numbers in a table format and to express the relationships between them. Accountants have embraced the use of spreadsheet software, many *discarding or minimizing paper methods of recording transactions. Businesses use spreadsheets extensively for maintaining records and for exploring the effect of changes in business variables. Schools and families monitor expenses and keep track of budgets using spreadsheet software. You will find that one of the most practical reasons to use a home computer is for maintaining records of financial data and transactions— tasks made possible by spreadsheet software.*

Introducing Spreadsheet Software

From an early age, we learn to organize our thoughts in written form. We have no problem creating sentences and organizing them into paragraphs, sections, and chapters. Similarly, you can simplify the complex relationships between sets of numerical data in spreadsheet format. The price of a new home depends on many variables, including lumber, brick, and workers' wages. By expressing those relationships in a column-and-row format, it is easy to see how they interact and how they affect total cost. Even something as simple as a checkbook register shows the relationship between variables that can be organized in spreadsheet form. As you write checks, the bank balance is reduced, whereas deposits increase the balance. Although spreadsheet software is not magic and does not free you from the responsibility of organizing your data, it is well worth the effort to learn.

Just as a word processor simplifies the task of organizing words, a spreadsheet makes it easy to organize numbers. A spreadsheet program, such as Microsoft Excel, records the numeric and text information electronically, so that you can retrieve, print, and change it later. Before you decide that a spreadsheet program is just an oversized calculator, look at what it can do for you!

- After you indicate which variables should be included in a calculation, it does the arithmetic quickly and accurately. You don't need to be a mathematician. You only need to be able to organize your numbers and to understand the dependencies among them, such as how deposits and withdrawals effect the ending balance in a checkbook spreadsheet.

- It answers questions, allowing you to model situations. You might ask, "What will the payment be on that new car if I borrow $15,000 over three years at a 5.9 percent interest rate?" or "How will my sales be affected if the state raises the tax rate by one percent?" or even "How much clear income will I have if my rent goes up by $100?" To ask those questions, you will change numeric data. For example, to determine what happens if your rent goes up, you should be able to change the rent amount in the spreadsheet. Because the net income is based, in part, on the rent expense, the final net income figure will reflect the updated amount.

- It is a one-time investment of effort. A harried instructor will quickly attest to the benefit of recording grades in a spreadsheet that automatically calculates

In the Know

Introduced in 1979, VisiCalc was the first computer spreadsheet program. It was immensely successful. Companies that invested time and money in recording financial information on manually calculated spreadsheets jumped at the chance to automate that information. One of the developers of VisiCalc, Dan Bricklin, estimated that VisiCalc took work that had required 20 hours per week and turned it into only 15 minutes of effort.

Dan Bricklin and Bob Frankston teamed up to develop VisiCalc. Shortly thereafter, they started their own company, Software Arts, to develop and market the product. Initially produced for the Apple II, versions were quickly developed for the Tandy TRS-80, the Commodore PET, and the Atari 800. By October 1979, VisiCalc was a top seller at $100. Lotus Development Corporation purchased VisiCalc in 1983 and developed it into the Lotus 1-2-3 program.

final student averages. Although setting up the spreadsheet and indicating the necessary calculations might take a little time, after it's done, it's done. All that is necessary to continue enjoying the benefit of the spreadsheet is to change variable data, such as student names and exam scores.

You can use numbers, words, or formulas as you work. The budget worksheet shown in Figure 10.1 includes all of these elements. However, it is important to remember that a worksheet is not simply a place to type information that you want to print later. If that is all you want to do, creating a table in a word processing program is a better choice. Spreadsheet software is a "what-if" tool, where you can tie formulas to data so that if the data changes, the result of the formula reflects that change. Excel is called a "what-if" tool because you can ask questions, such as "what if my rent goes up by $100?" Increase the rent figure by $100 and you will immediately see the resulting change in net income. Of course, for you to use it in that manner, the worksheet must be set up correctly, which you will learn to do later in this chapter.

	Monthly Budget					
1	Monthly Budget					
2	Text	Numbers				
3						
4	Salary	$2,000				
5						
6	Expenses					
7	Rent	300				
8	Groceries	150				
9	Car Payment	185				
10	Gasoline	100				
11	Entertainment	125				
12	Utilities	150				
13	Phone	30				
14	Cable	50	Formula			
15	Total Expenses	1090				
16						
17	Net Income	$910				
18						

Figure 10.1 **A worksheet can include text, numbers, and formulas.**

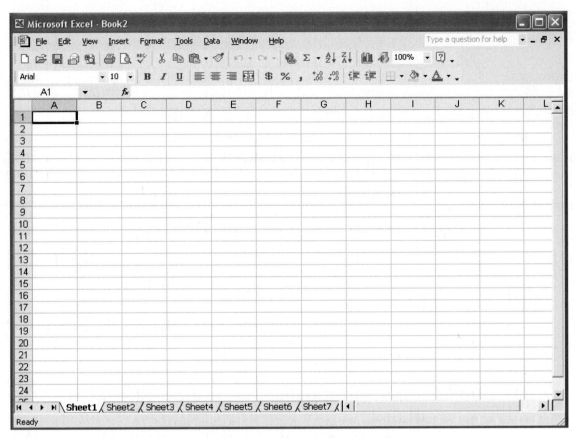

Figure 10.2 **An Excel worksheet begins as a blank grid of columns and rows in which you record data.**

The Excel Interface

This chapter introduces Microsoft Excel 2002, which can be purchased separately or is a component of Microsoft Office XP. Excel is a powerful spreadsheet program, capable of manipulating data in a variety of ways, including presenting it as a chart. Excel is widely used in business and educational settings, so if you learn to use only one spreadsheet software package, it is a good choice. Features found in Excel are also present in comparable spreadsheet software, such as Lotus and Microsoft Works, so you can easily transfer spreadsheet concepts from one to another.

If Excel is installed on your system, you will find it by clicking Start, All Programs, Microsoft Excel. The Excel application window will open, as shown in Figure 10.2. However, your window might appear slightly different, because Excel allows users to customize the appearance of window elements. Regardless of any variations, you should see a menu bar, at least one toolbar, and a worksheet area arranged in a grid of columns and rows. Because Excel is Windows-based software, the title bar, task pane, menu bar, and toolbars serve the same purposes as described in the preceding chapter. However, some menu selections and toolbar icons are a little different, because they provide options that are unique to Excel.

Web Watch

An excellent Excel tutorial, introducing basic spreadsheet concepts, is found at **www.lfc.edu/getwired/ tutorials/excel_tutorial**.

Creating and Managing Workbooks

Just as a book is made up of a series of pages, a **workbook** is made up of one or more **worksheets**. Each worksheet is an electronic grid of columns and rows in which you can enter data. When you save an Excel file, you are actually saving a workbook. A worksheet might be only one "page" within the workbook. You can easily move to other worksheets within the workbook. For example, if your workbook is actually a summary of sales information of various branches of your company, you can place each branch site's information on a worksheet, label it accordingly, and move among worksheets, comparing sales data. The workbook that you save will include several worksheets, each summarizing a branch's performance.

After you have created a worksheet, you can customize its appearance by adding formatting features, much like those available with a word processor. You can center items and make them boldface, change the appearance of numbers by adding dollar signs or commas, and include bordering and shading.

You can also print worksheets or entire workbooks. You have several options to consider when printing: whether to print the gridlines (bordering around cells), which selections of a worksheet to print, and how to include column headings. Similar to word processing, you can indicate how many copies to print, as well as include header and footer information.

Workbook Elements

The grid of columns and rows is the **worksheet area**. The gray area at the top of the worksheet area includes column headings (identified by letters), whereas gray area to the left lists row headings (identified by numbers). Columns are identified by letters, whereas rows are numbered. The rectangle at the intersection of every column and row is a **cell**. Each cell is uniquely identified by a **cell reference** (also called a **cell address**), which is a conjunction of the column letter and row number that meet to form the cell. For example, the cell at the intersection of column B and row 5 is cell B5. The active cell, which is

In the Know

A workbook and a worksheet are not the same thing! A workbook is an Excel file that can include multiple worksheets. You can open and close workbooks, but you cannot open and close worksheets individually. A worksheet is closed only when the workbook in which it is included is closed. Just as you could have several books on a table, with each book including many pages, you can have several Excel workbooks open in memory at one time, each including many worksheets. To move among open workbooks, click the Excel icon on the taskbar, and select from the subsequent list of open workbooks.

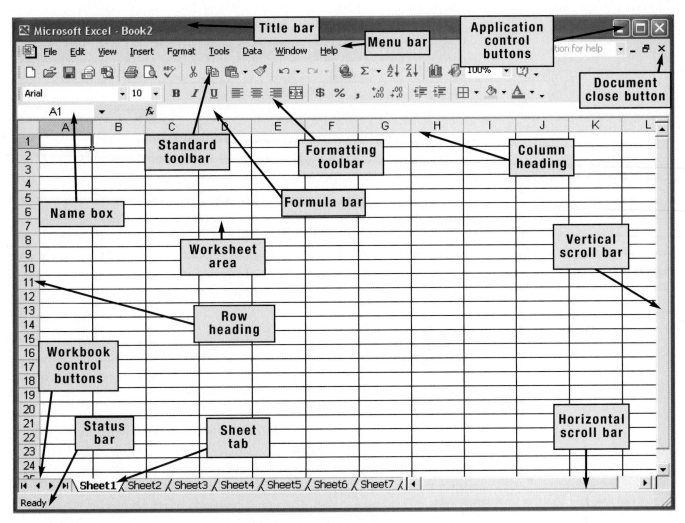

Figure 10.3 **Microsoft Excel opens as a window containing several screen elements.**

surrounded by a dark border, is the cell into which you can currently enter data. The active cell shown in Figure 10.3 is cell A1. The lines separating cells are called **gridlines**.

What you see on-screen is actually only a small portion of the entire worksheet area. A worksheet can easily extend beyond the visible workspace area; portions that are off-screen are accessible by scrolling with the vertical or horizontal scrollbar. There are 256 columns and 65,536 rows. Columns are labeled from A to Z, and then AA, AB, and so forth, ending at column IV.

Just below the toolbars are the Name box and the Formula bar. The **Name box** indicates the position of the active cell. The Name box in Figure 10.3 shows cell A1 as the active cell. Next to the Name box is the **Formula bar**, which displays the contents of the active cell. Because the active cell in Figure 10.3 is empty, the Formula bar contains no information. Later in this chapter, you will learn to use the Formula bar to change cell contents, correct data entry mistakes, and adjust formulas.

Each workbook can include several worksheets. The number of worksheets in a workbook is limited only by available computer memory. Each worksheet is identified by a sheet tab, as shown in Figure 10.3. You can rename sheet tabs to better represent worksheet contents. You can also delete, insert, and move sheets to other locations within the workbook.

Navigating within a Worksheet

Moving among cells in the worksheet area is as simple as clicking where you want to go. If you move the mouse pointer in the worksheet area, it looks like a large white plus (+) sign. Remember that the active cell is the cell into which you can place data, so if you want to enter data in cell B8, for example, you could click cell B8 and then type the data. Although clicking cells is a convenient way to move among closely situated cells (those displayed on one screen of the worksheet area), there are other methods of moving among cells anywhere on the worksheet, as shown in Figure 10.4.

Creating a Workbook

When you first open Excel, you will be at a blank worksheet, with the active cell at A1, as shown in Figure 10.3. If workbook doesn't appear for some reason, you can open one by clicking the New button on the Standard toolbar.

Entering data is as easy as selecting a cell, typing the data, and pressing ↵Enter (or clicking the Enter button on the Formula bar). Remember that you can enter three types of data—text (also called labels), numbers (values), and formulas. Characters that you type in a cell determine the data type. If the first character is a letter, the entry is considered to be text. If all characters in a cell are numeric, the entry is identified as a value, and if the first character is an equal

Web Watch

Learn more about Excel, including any upcoming versions, at www.microsoft.com/office/excel/default.asp.

Action	Mouse Command	Keyboard Command
Move to a cell	Click the cell	Use the arrow keys (directional keys on the right side of the keyboard)
Move to cell A1	Click the cell	Press Ctrl + Home
Move up one screen	Click in the vertical scroll bar above the scroll box	Press PgUp
Move down one screen	Click in the vertical scroll bar below the scroll box	Press PgDn
Move to a specific cell, even if it's off-screen	Click Edit, Go To. Type the cell address in the reference area, and click OK.	Press Ctrl + G, or press F5. Enter the cell reference, and click OK.

Figure 10.4 **There are several ways to navigate within a worksheet.**

sign, the data is assumed to be a formula. If the entry is a combination of letters and numbers, Excel defines it as a text entry.

If you type data into a cell and press ⏎Enter, the **cell pointer** (dark border surrounding the active cell) moves to the next cell down in that column. If, however, you are typing in cells along a row, you might prefer that the cell pointer move one cell to the right on the same row. In that case, press ➔ instead of ⏎Enter when you finish typing data in the cell. Similarly, you can use the other arrow keys to direct movement up, down, or left.

Working with Multiple Worksheets

A workbook can include multiple worksheets, each summarizing data related to a particular situation. For example, a college instructor could create one workbook for each semester, with individual worksheets summarizing the performance of each class. Worksheets are identified by sheet tabs, which can be renamed according to their purpose.

Elaine has just been hired to teach science classes at a local community college. She is teaching four classes this term and has decided to use Excel to maintain her class records. She creates a workbook containing four worksheets, one for each class. On each worksheet, she records the class roll and identifies space for student grades. She saves the workbook, including all four class worksheets, as *Summer 2004*.

She realizes that the sheet tabs (*Sheet 1, Sheet 2, . . .*) are not descriptive enough for her to remember which class is represented where, so she renames them, as shown in Figure 10.5. To rename a sheet tab, Elaine can right-click the first sheet tab and select Rename from the context menu. Without clicking anywhere, she types the new sheet tab name, and presses ⏎Enter. The sheet is renamed. When Elaine is ready to work with the astronomy class, she can simply click the Astronomy sheet tab. Moving back to the biology sheet is as easy as clicking the Biology sheet tab.

Being highly organized, Elaine wants the sheet tabs to be in the correct order alphabetically. To move the Astronomy sheet to the first position, she can click the sheet tab and drag it to the left. As the mouse pointer moves, a small black triangle pops up with it to indicate a new position. When the triangle appears just to the left of the Biology sheet tab, she can release the mouse button, repositioning the Astronomy sheet.

Now that she has her classes organized, Elaine can begin to use the *Summer 2004* workbook. In a single workbook, she can work with all of her class sheets.

> **▶ Quick Tip**
>
> You might prefer that the cell pointer remain in the current cell, even after you press ⏎Enter. To make that change, click Tools, Options, and click the Edit tab. Click to remove the check mark from *Move Selection after Enter*. The next time you type data into a cell and press ⏎Enter, the cell pointer will remain in the current cell. However, if you press a directional (arrow) key, it will advance one cell in the direction indicated.

	A	B	C	D	E	F
1	**Introduction to Biology**					
2	BIO 103					
3						
4	Instructor: Elaine Vallette					
5						
6	Student	Exam 1	Exam 2	Final Average		
7	Anderson, Andrea					
8	Blalock, Richard					
9	Cheatham, Susan					
10	Hallmark, Karen					
11	Haghighi, Mike					
12	Hannah, Blake					
13	Mitchell, Sharon					
14						
15						
16						
17						
18						
19						
20						
21						
22						
23						
24						

◄ ◄ ► ►◄ \ **Biology** ∕ Physical Science ∕ Astronomy ∕ Geology ∕ Sheet5 ∕ Shee

Ready

Figure 10.5 **Sheet tabs can be renamed to reflect worksheet contents.**

Hands On

Activity 10.1—Creating and Saving a Workbook

In this activity, you will create a workbook and save it to a floppy disk. Your computer should be at the desktop.

1. Place a blank, labeled floppy disk in the A: drive.
2. Open Excel (Start, All Programs, Microsoft Excel).
3. The active cell should be A1. Check the Name box to be sure the cell pointer is at cell A1. Type **Sunny Days Garden Center** and press (↵Enter). The cell pointer should move to cell A2. Press (↵Enter) once again to move the cell pointer to cell A3.
4. Type **Plant/Seeds** and press (↵Enter).
5. Complete the column, as shown in Figure 10.6, pressing (↵Enter) after each entry.
6. Click in cell B3. Type **Price**. Press (↵Enter).
7. Complete column B, as shown in Figure 10.7, pressing (↵Enter) after each entry. As you type the numbers in column B, notice that they are positioned to the right side of the cell (right justified). By default, text entries are left justified, whereas numeric entries are right justified. You will learn later how to change that orientation.
8. Complete columns C and D, as shown in Figure 10.8.
9. Save the workbook on the disk in the A: drive. Click File, Save. Click the drop-down arrow beside the Save In area and select 3½ Floppy (A:). Change the filename to *Garden Center.* Click Save.
10. Close Excel.

	A	B	C	D
1	Sunny Days Garden Center			
2				
3	Plant/Seed			
4	Tomato			
5	Radishes			
6	Cucumber			
7	Corn			
8				

Figure 10.6 **Type the text as it appears above.**

	A	B	C	D	E
1	Sunny Days Garden Center				
2					
3	Plant/Seed	Price			
4	Tomato	1.38			
5	Radishes	1.21			
6	Cucumber	2.44			
7	Corn	1.5			
8					
9					
10					
11					

Figure 10.7 **The numeric entries in column B are positioned to the right side of the cell.**

	A	B	C	D	E
1	Sunny Days Garden Center				
2					
3	Plant/Seed	Price	Cost	Profit	
4	Tomato	1.38	0.56		
5	Radishes	1.21	0.43		
6	Cucumber	2.44	1.09		
7	Corn	1.5	0.74		
8					
9					
10					
11					

Figure 10.8 **Complete the worksheet, as shown above.**

Hands On

On

In this activity, you will op
10.1 and make a few cha
desktop.

1. Place the floppy disk t
2. Open Excel.
3. If the task pane is ope
   Open, and then naviga
   click the filename.
4. Change the garden ce
   click just before the w
   delete the word. Now
5. The *Tomato Cost* is in
   ing cost. Type **.54**. Pr
6. Add another product i
   and press →. In cell B
   type **.67**. Press ↵Ente
   Figure 10.10.
7. Save the workbook ag
   dard toolbar.
8. Close Excel.

	A	B	C
1	Sunny Days Garden Shop		
2			
3	Plant/Seed	Price	Cost
4	Tomato	1.38	0.54
5	Radishes	1.21	0.43
6	Cucumber	2.44	1.09
7	Corn	1.5	0.74
8	Green Bea	1.48	0.67
9			
10			
11			

Figure 10.10 **The Garden Center wo**

The Margins tab includes
margins. You can also choose
the Header/Footer area, you c
taining your name or the curr
are not part of the worksheet
Finally, the Sheet tab allows y
as gridlines and row and colu

After creating her workbook, Elaine learns that she will be released from teaching the astronomy class to pursue some additional training. After having transferred her student records to another instructor, she wants to delete the Astronomy sheet. She can right-click the Astronomy sheet tab, and select Delete from the context menu. This is a great way to keep your workbook up-to-date with your latest information. However, you need to be careful because you can't bring back a deleted worksheet by clicking the Undo button on the Standard toolbar.

Saving a Workbook

An Excel workbook, including all of its worksheets, is essentially a file. Therefore, when you save a workbook file, all worksheets are saved under one filename. Windows gives an Excel workbook an extension of .xls. An Excel file that you name *Business Transactions* is actually titled *Business Transactions.xls*. The same rules that you used for naming Word files, which you learned in the last chapter, apply to the naming of Excel files. If you know you want to open your workbook in another program, you can save an Excel file as another format, just as you learned that you could save a word processing document in another format. For example, you might save an Excel file in a format that allows you to open it with database software, so that you can use specific record-handling features found in the database program.

Closing a Workbook

Excel allows you to have multiple workbooks open at one time. The number of open workbooks is limited only by the amount of available RAM. Before closing a workbook, make sure that you have saved it to disk if you intend to work with it or print it later. To close a workbook, click File, Close, or click the document close button found just beneath the application control buttons on the title bar. Remember that closing a workbook only removes it from memory—not from the disk (if you have previously saved it).

Opening and Editing an Existing Workbook

There are a couple of ways to open an existing Excel workbook. The task pane, which appears to the right of the application window when you first open Excel, contains the names of recently opened Excel files. Click a filename in the task pane to open it. If the file that you want to open is not listed on the task pane or if the task pane is not open, click File, Open. If necessary, select the disk drive and folder where the file is saved, and double-click the filename to open it.

You will often want to make changes to a worksheet. This process is called *editing*. Some items might be misspelled, or you might want to delete some cell contents. The table in Figure 10.9 gives several methods of making changes to cell contents.

Changing Page Setup Options

The procedures for printing a worksheet are similar to the procedures you used to print a document in the preceding chapter. However, before printing you will

◀▶ Other Ways

You can rename a sheet tab by double-clicking the sheet tab, typing the new name, and pressing ↵Enter.

▶ Quick Tip

Just as folders in a filing cabinet might be colored, you can add color to sheet tabs. Right-click a sheet tab, and select Tab Color. Make a color choice, and click OK. To see the full effect of the change, click another sheet tab.

▶ Quick Tip

To open a new workbook, click the New button on the Standard toolbar. Alternatively, you can click the Blank Workbook link on the task pane.

◀▶ Other Ways

Clicking the Open button on the Standard toolbar is another way to open a file.

To

Completely change cell contents

Make minor corrections to cell conte

Delete cell contents

Figure 10.9 **There are several ways to mak**

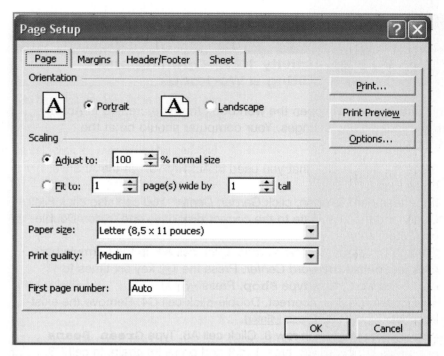

Figure 10.11 **The Page Setup dialog box includes options for changing many aspects of the worksheet before printing.**

Printing a Workbook

When you're satisfied with the way the worksheet looks and with the print selections that you have made, you are ready to print the worksheet. You can click the Print button on the Standard toolbar to send the worksheet directly to the default printer. However, if you first want to make some changes to the default print setup (such as the number of copies to print) click File, Print to display the Print dialog box, as shown in Figure 10.12.

Selecting, Copying, and Moving Workbook Contents

It is often more efficient to work with a group of cells rather than one at a time. For example, you might want to delete a group of cells or print them. Perhaps you want to change the way the data in a group of cells looks—maybe adding a dollar sign and commas to all the numbers in the group. A selected group of one or more cells is called a **range**. Most ranges include adjacent cells; however, you can also create a range that is made up of nonadjacent cells.

There will be times when you decide that a range of cells should be moved, or possibly copied, to another location within the worksheet, or even to another worksheet. When ranges are copied or moved, they are actually placed temporarily on the Clipboard. The Clipboard is a location in RAM where text can be held until you indicate where it should be placed. After you select the location to which you want the data copied, you can paste it.

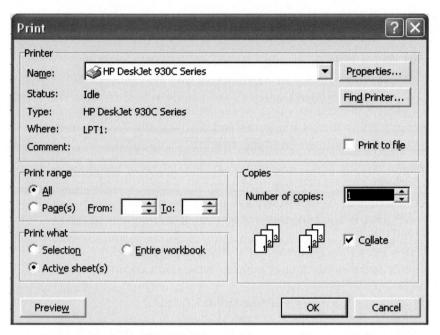

Figure 10.12 **By making selections in the Print dialog box, you can set the number of copies and indicate which worksheets to print.**

You can also insert and delete entire rows and columns. For example, perhaps you meant to include a title for a worksheet (in row 1) but forgot to do so. Now that the worksheet is complete, there is no space remaining at the top for the title. You can easily insert a row at the top and type the title.

Selecting Ranges, Columns, and Rows

When working with any Windows application, such as Excel, you must keep an important rule in mind: *Select before you change*. What that means is that when

In the Know

Occasionally, you might want to print only a section of a worksheet. You must first click and drag to select the cells you want to print. Be sure to click and drag in the worksheet area, not the gray border that includes column and row headings. If you want to include column or row headings in the selection area, you need to select entire rows and columns, not just a section of cells. As you know, a row extends across 256 columns, whereas a column includes more than 65,000 rows! That is likely to be much more than what you want to include in a selected print area.

After the selection to be printed is shaded, click File, Print. In the Print What area, choose Selection. Click OK. Only the shaded cells will be printed.

Hands On

Activity 10.3—Changing Page Setup Options and Printing a Workbook

In this activity, you will print the worksheet that you created in Activity 10.2. Your computer should be at the desktop.

1. Place the disk that you used in Activity 10.2 in the A: drive.
2. Open Excel.
3. Open the *Garden Center* workbook. (Click the filename in the task pane, or click File, Open, select the A: drive, and double-click the filename.)
4. Click the Print Preview button on the Standard toolbar.
5. Click the Zoom button to get a closer look. Click Zoom again.
6. Click Setup.
7. Click the Page tab. Select Landscape orientation.
8. Click the Margins tab. Click to select *Center on page Horizontally*.
9. Click the Header/Footer tab. Click Custom Header. Click in the Center section, and type your name. Click OK.
10. Click the Sheet tab. Gridlines (the lines separating columns and rows) are not normally printed with a worksheet. To cause them to print, click to select *Gridlines*.
11. Click OK, and then click Close to close the Print Preview window.
12. To print the worksheet, make sure that your computer is connected or networked to a printer and that the printer is on. Click File, Print.
13. Change the number of copies to 2, either by clicking in the number box and typing the new value or by clicking the spinner control to the right of the box.
14. Click OK. Two copies of the worksheet will be printed. Your name will appear centered above the worksheet.
15. Close Excel. Save the workbook, if prompted.

▶ Quick Tip

To select a range of nonadjacent cells, click or click and drag the first section of the range. Then hold down the Ctrl key while you click and drag other sections. When you release the mouse button, all sections are shaded as one range.

you want to change, delete, move, or copy one or more items, you must first *select* them. For example, if you want to change the format of a column of numbers to display a dollar sign (a format called currency), you must select the column before changing the format. If you want to delete a range of cells, select the cells first, and then delete them.

To select a range of adjacent cells, click and drag over them. Release the mouse button when all cells to be included are shaded. When you select multiple cells, they will all appear highlighted, except for the first one that you clicked, which will remain white. The white cell is included in the range; the lack of shading just indicates that it is the active cell. Just as a cell is identified by a cell address (cell reference), a range of cells is identified by a **range reference**. A range is a rectangular block of cells, whose cell reference includes two cells in opposite corners of the range, separated by a colon. For example, the range of cells shown in Figure 10.13 is identified by the range reference *A7:D12*.

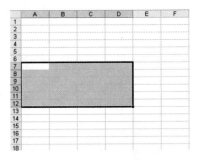

Figure 10.13 **This range of cells is identified by the range reference A7:D12.**

✓ SANITY CHECK

Be careful when selecting a range of cells—before clicking and dragging, make sure the mouse pointer looks like a large white plus sign! If you click when the mouse pointer is, instead, a small black plus or an arrow, you will move or copy data when all that you wanted to do was to select it. If you mistakenly move or copy data, click the Undo button.

You might want to affect every item in a particular column or row. A column might include data that you want to display differently, perhaps changing the orientation or including commas in numbers. By selecting the entire column and then changing the format, all items in that column are immediately changed. To select a column, click the column heading (in the gray border above the worksheet area). Similarly, to select a row, click the row heading. You can select multiple columns and rows by clicking and dragging several column or row headings.

✓ SANITY CHECK

Remember that columns and rows extend far beyond the viewable worksheet space, so if you select a row and then format the contents differently, even those items that you cannot see in that row will be formatted. If you are unsure of what might be included that's currently off-screen, it is probably safer to select cells by clicking and dragging only those you want changed, and then applying the format.

Inserting and Deleting Columns and Rows

In a perfect world, you would plan a worksheet completely before creating it. You would make no mistakes, and you would not leave out any data. Realistically, though, you are likely to decide, after a worksheet is well underway, that

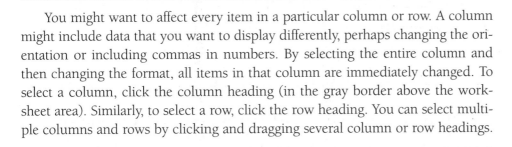

In the **Know** Deleting a row or column is not the same as deleting cell contents. You can remove cell contents by clicking the cell (or selecting the range of cells) whose data is to be deleted, and pressing Del. The column or row remains intact, but the selected cell's contents are erased. When you remove a row or column, the entire row or column is removed, along with any cell contents.

you intended to include a heading or that another column of data would be helpful. In that case, you must insert columns and rows. Similarly, you might decide that a row of information is no longer necessary and you will want to delete it. The table in Figure 10.14 outlines methods of inserting and deleting rows and columns.

Columns are inserted *before* the selected columns, shifting all columns to the right and relettering them. For example, if you select column C and insert a column, the new column will be inserted as column C, whereas the original column C shifts right and becomes column D. Similarly, rows are inserted *above* selected rows. You indicate how many rows or columns you want to insert by selecting that many rows or columns as the first step.

✓ SANITY CHECK

To select rows and columns, be sure to click in the gray border area, when the mouse pointer is a small black arrow.

Cutting, Copying, and Pasting Cell Contents

If some worksheet data is not in the right location or if you want to make a copy of it in another location, you can easily place the data where you want it to go. Moving data is called *cutting;* copying data is understandably called *copying.* You were introduced earlier to the concept of the *Clipboard*, which is a temporary

To	Do This	Or This
Insert a column or columns	1. Click the column heading (or click and drag multiple column headings). 2. Click Insert, Columns.	1. Click the column heading (or click and drag multiple column headings). 2. Right-click in the shaded area. 3. Click Insert.
Insert a row or rows	1. Click the row heading (or click and drag multiple row headings). 2. Click Insert, Rows.	1. Click the row heading (or click and drag multiple row headings). 2. Right-click in the shaded area. 3. Click Insert.
Delete a column or columns	1. Click the column heading (or click and drag multiple column headings). 2. Click Edit, Delete.	1. Click the column heading (or click and drag multiple column headings). 2. Right-click in the shaded area. 3. Click Delete.
Delete a row or rows	1. Click the row heading (or click and drag multiple row headings). 2. Click Edit, Delete.	1. Click the row heading (or click and drag multiple row headings). 2. Right-click in the shaded area. 3. Click Delete.

Figure 10.14 **You can insert and delete rows and columns in several ways.**

Hands On

Activity 10.4—Inserting and Removing Rows and Columns

In this activity, you will insert and delete rows and columns. Your computer should be at the desktop.

1. Place the disk that you used in Activity 10.3 in the A: drive.
2. Open Excel.
3. Open the *Garden Center* workbook.
4. You no longer sell Radish seed, so you want to delete the row. Click the row 5 heading (in the gray border area, when the mouse pointer is a small black arrow). Click Edit, Delete. The row is removed. You will still see a row 5, but look carefully—what was row 6 has been moved up and renumbered. The Radishes row is gone.
5. You want to include numbers for your garden items in the worksheet, just to the left of the price column. Remember that when you insert columns, new columns are placed to the *left* of selected columns. Because you want the new column to be to the left of what is currently column B, select column B. (Select the column by clicking the column heading in the gray border area.)
6. Right-click in the shaded column, and select Insert from the context menu.
7. What was once column B is now column C, and a blank column appears just to the left of the price column. Click cell B3. Type **Item Number**. Press `⏎Enter`.
8. In cells B4 through B7, make up and enter an item number for each plant.
9. Save the workbook again as *Garden Center*.
10. Close Excel.

holding location for text or cell contents that have been cut or copied. The Clipboard holds data until you *paste* it to a new location.

Sometimes you want to copy an item from one cell, or range, to adjacent cells. Suppose that you are creating a worksheet for a science class in which you keep record of daily rainfall. You have created a worksheet area with column headings for each day of the week, beneath which you will record rainfall statistics. Because you will repeat that information for each week of the month, you might want to copy the day-of-the-week column headings to other worksheet areas. In that case, you can use a feature known as the **fill handle**. When you move the mouse pointer to the bottom right corner of a cell or selected range containing the data to be copied, the mouse pointer becomes a small black plus, which is called the fill handle. At that point, click and drag, shading all the cells to which the data should be copied. Release the mouse pointer when all cells are bordered. The cell contents will be copied.

In the Know

When you copy data to adjacent cells, Excel attempts to recognize a pattern. If it does, as in the case of month names or days of the week, it will copy them according to the pattern. For example, suppose cell D3 contains the word April. You plan to record data for May and June, as well. Instead of typing the month titles in cells E3 and F3, you can copy them! Just click in cell D3, and then click the fill handle at the lower right corner of the cell and drag it across to cells E3 and F3. When you release the mouse button, the words May and June will occupy cells E3 and F3. Similarly, Excel recognizes days of the week, and any obvious series, such as Quarter 1, Quarter 2, . . . , so that when you copy such data using the click and drag method, the series are adjusted accordingly.

✓ SANITY CHECK

When moving or copying data, use caution in selecting the area to paste your selection. If there is any data already in the area to which you plan to copy data, it will be replaced. If you accidentally replace data that you meant to keep, click the Undo button.

◀▶ Other Ways

There are several ways to copy and paste data. With a cell or range selected, you can right-click the selected area and select Cut (or Copy) from the context menu. You can also press Ctrl + C to copy or Ctrl + X to cut a selected area. To paste the selection, press Ctrl + V.

If you want to copy a cell's contents to one or more cells that are not adjacent to it, you can use a different approach. The copy and paste method, in which you copy a selection to the Clipboard and then paste it to a receiving area, works in Excel, as it does in other Windows applications. Click to select the cell contents to be copied. Click Edit, Copy. Now click the cell to which the selected contents should be copied. Click Edit, Paste.

When you want to move data from one cell or range to another, you can cut and paste. Unlike copying, when you cut a selection, it is removed from the original location and placed in another. First, click to select the data to be moved. Click Edit, Cut. Next, click the cell where you want to move the selected data. Click Edit, Paste.

Working with Formulas

Excel's real strength lies in its ability to work with formulas. Totaling columns of numbers, calculating averages, and determining monthly payments are just a few of the things Excel does in a snap! To perform calculations like these, you need to know how to build formulas. A **formula** is a group of instructions that tells Excel how to perform a calculation. You can either build formulas from scratch or use one of the many formulas that are built into Excel.

Hands On

Activity 10.5—Cutting, Copying, and Pasting

In this activity, you will practice cutting, copying, and pasting text. Your computer should be at the desktop.

1. Place the disk that you used for Activity 10.4 in the A: drive.
2. Open Excel.
3. Create the worksheet shown in Figure 10.15, exactly as it appears.
4. Insert a column before the August column. Name the new column Member. Enter data as shown in Figure 10.16.
5. Rename Sheet 1. To rename the sheet, double-click the sheet tab, type **August–October**, and press ⏎Enter.
6. Rename Sheet 2 **November–January**.
7. Click the August–October sheet tab. Copy cells A1:A3 from the *August–October* sheet to the *November–January* sheet. Click and drag to select cells A1:A3. Click Edit, Copy. Click to select the *November–January* sheet. Click in cell A1. Click Edit, Paste.
8. Similarly, copy the member names and numbers from *August–October* to *November–January*. Click the *August–October* sheet tab. Click and drag to select cells A5:B10. Click Edit, Copy. Click the *November–January* sheet tab. Click in cell A5. Click Edit, Paste.
9. In the *November–January* sheet, click cell C5. Type **November**. In cells D5 and E5, type **December** and **January,** respectively.
10. Mr. McDonald walked 35 miles in November, December, and January. Type **35** in cell C6 and press ⏎Enter. Click cell C6 again, and then move the mouse pointer to the lower right corner of the cell. When the mouse pointer becomes a small black plus sign, click and drag the mouse pointer over to cell E6. Release the mouse button.
11. Still in the *November–January* sheet, move the words "(Miles Walked)" from cell A3 to cell A4. Click in cell A3. Click Edit, Cut. Click in cell A4. Click Edit, Paste.
12. Click to select the *August–October* sheet. Move the words "(Miles Walked)" from cell A3 to cell A4.
13. Save the worksheet on your disk as *Walking Program*.
14. Close Excel.

	A	B	C	D	E
1	Summerlane Fitness Academy				
2	Walking Program				
3	(Miles Walked)				
4					
5		August	September	October	
6	McDonald	30	36.8	37	
7	Hale	20.5	28	32	
8	Matthews	34	33	35	
9	Martin	47	50.5	56.2	
10	Smith	22.6	30	38	
11					

Figure 10.15 **This worksheet includes data for a fictitious walking program.**

	A	B	C	D	E	F	G
1	Summerlane Fitness Academy						
2	Walking Program						
3	(Miles Walked)						
4							
5		Member	August	September	October		
6	McDonald	894	30	36.8	37		
7	Hale	366	20.5	28	32		
8	Matthews	946	34	33	35		
9	Martin	380	47	50.5	56.2		
10	Smith	223	22.6	30	38		
11							
12							
13							
14							

Figure 10.16 **Column B, which was inserted, includes member number.**

Creating Formulas

A major strength of Excel is the ability to calculate formulas and display results. A formula should begin with an equal sign, so that Excel knows the entry is a formula. When typing a formula in a cell, you will work with a predefined group

In the Know

At times, you might want to copy or move an entire range of data from one area to another. To copy a range, click and drag the group of cells. If you want to copy the range to adjacent cells, click the fill handle at the bottom right corner of the selected range and drag to highlight the receiving cells. When you release the mouse button, the data is copied.

To copy the selected range to a nonadjacent area, click Edit, Copy. Next, click the cell that will serve as the upper left corner of the receiving range. You don't have to select the entire receiving area, as the cells to be copied will fill in the space beneath the selected cell, as necessary. Click Edit, Paste.

To move a range of cells to another location (regardless of whether the receiving range is adjacent or nonadjacent), follow the same steps given in the preceding paragraph for copying cells, except that you should click Edit, Cut instead of Edit, Copy.

▶ Quick Tip

When typing formulas, you don't have to capitalize cell references: *b7* works just as well as *B7*.

of arithmetic operators, such as the plus sign and minus sign. Figure 10.17 lists the set of arithmetic operators from which you can choose.

When typing a formula, refer to cell addresses wherever possible. That way, if the contents of the cells change, the formula won't have to be rewritten. The following scenario illustrates the use of a simple formula. Mike has created the worksheet shown in Figure 10.18. He is now ready to calculate the difference between his sales goal and the actual sales amount. The formula that he will place in cell C7 should subtract the actual sales amount (B7) from the sales goal (A7). The formula in cell C7 should read *=A7−B7*, which subtracts the contents of cell B7 from the contents of cell A7. If he had used the formula *=50000−49527.34*

Operation	Symbol
Addition	+
Subtraction	−
Multiplication	*
Division	/
Exponentiation	^
Percent	%

Figure 10.17 **Arithmetic operators are used in Excel formulas.**

and either the sales quota or actual sales amount changed, he would have to go back and retype the formula.

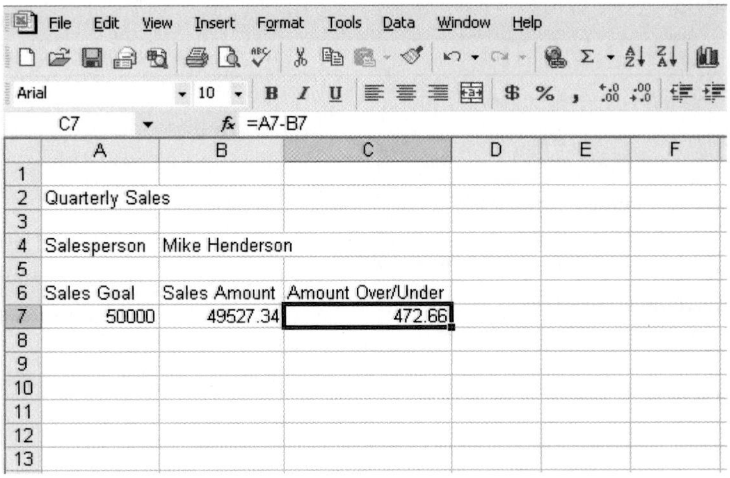

Understanding the Order of Precedence

Many formulas include more than one operator. For example, the formula *=A8+B8/C8* includes two operators, + and /. Will Excel divide B8 by C8 first, or will it first add A8 to B8? It all hinges on the **order of precedence**, which is a set of rules that Excel uses to determine the order in which mathematical operations are to be calculated. The standard order of precedence is:

Figure 10.18 **Formulas are often included in Excel worksheets.**

- Any exponentiation operation is done first. Exponentiation is raising numbers to a power. For example, the number 10 raised to the tenth power is 100.

- Next comes any multiplication and division. If both operators are present, the order is determined from left to right.

- Finally, any addition and subtraction is calculated—from left to right if more than one operator is present.

Using Functions

Formulas can become quite complex. Figure 10.19 is a sample grade book, showing a few quiz scores. The instructor plans to calculate an average, beginning in cell F6. The formula in cell F6 would read *=(B6+C6+D6+E6)/4*. Because the teacher wants the four grades to be averaged, the parentheses are necessary to force the addition to be done before the division. Because there are only a few quizzes, this formula will work well. But what if the instructor gives 25 quizzes during the semester? She could still use the same process to create her formula, and it would work just fine, but it would be extremely long. Alternatively, she could use a **function**—a predefined formula that simplifies complex or lengthy calculations. In this case, the instructor could use an Average function (*=Average(B6:E6)*) to simplify the original formula.

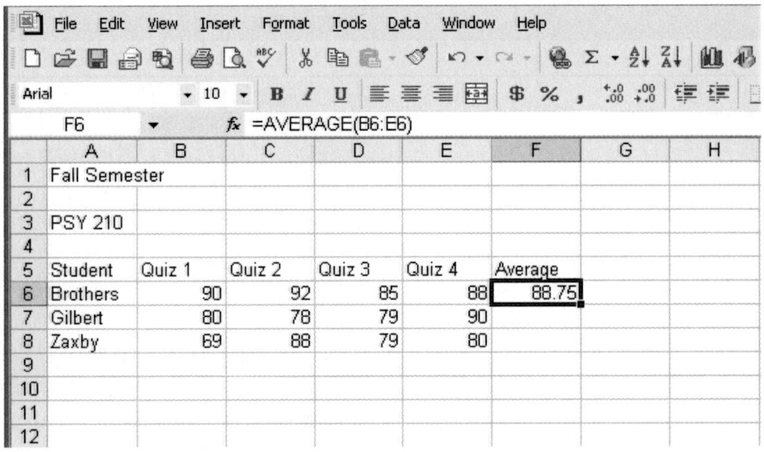

All functions include at least one argument, within parentheses, that includes variable information. For example, the function

> **▮▶Quick Tip**
>
> You can override the order of precedence by including part of a formula in parentheses, such as =(A7+A3)/B12. Operations included in parentheses are always calculated first.

Figure 10.19 **Some formulas, such as calculating a quiz average, can be simplified by using functions.**

▮▶Quick Tip

When typing a function, if you forget to type the final parenthesis, Excel will assume that you intended to close the parentheses, and will do so for you. For example, if you type the function
=Average(C5:C10, Excel will interpret it as
=Average(C5:C10).

=Average(B6:E6) includes an argument indicating the range of cell addresses to include in the average calculation. Some functions, such as the Average function, are considered statistical functions, because they perform analysis on a range of data. Others are financial functions, such as the PMT function, which calculates payment on a loan. Other categories of functions include logical and database.

Because it is nearly impossible to remember the format of all functions, you can use the *Insert function* button, found on the Formula bar. When you click the *Insert function* button, a dialog box appears, from which you can choose a function category. Excel will display a description of the function and will guide you through the process of creating the function formula. However, a few of the commonly used functions, like Sum and Average, are easy to remember so you probably won't need to use the *Insert function* feature for them.

Working with Absolute and Relative Cell References

When a formula is copied, its cell references normally adjust according to the copy location. For example, if you copied the formula *=B5+B6* from cell B7 to cell C7, the formula would be adjusted to read *=C5+C6*. Most often, you want the formula to be adjusted, but there are occasions when one or more of the cell references should remain unadjusted. The following scenario describes both forms of copying formulas—adjusted (relative) and unadjusted (absolute). Ruth's fifth-grade class is involved in a reading program. The children must keep a record of how many pages they read each week. Ruth creates a worksheet, shown in Figure 10.20, to keep up with the children's reading progress.

In the
Know
    You can enter formulas by simply pointing at the cells to include. For example, if you are in cell C4, and want to enter a formula to add cells A4 and B4, you could type **=A4+B4**. *Alternatively, you could type* **=** *and then move the mouse pointer to cell A4 and click. The formula begins =A4. Type a plus sign to cause the formula to read =A4+. Move to cell B4 and click. The formula is now =A4+B4. Press* [↵Enter] *to accept the formula. You created a formula without typing a single cell address!*

    You will develop a preference as to how you like to create formulas. Some people like to point and click to select cells for formulas because they feel they are less likely to make mistakes that way. After you practice the method, you might also prefer it.

    You can even click and drag to select ranges for inclusion in a function. If you are building a Sum function to be =Sum(C6:C10), place the cell pointer in the cell to hold the result, and type **=Sum(**. *Then click and drag cells C6:C10. The formula reads =Sum(C6:C10. Press* [↵Enter].

Activity 10.6—Creating Formulas and Functions

In this activity, you will use the worksheet that you worked with in Activity 10.4 (*Garden Center*). Your computer should be at the desktop.

1. Place the disk containing the *Garden Center* workbook in the A: drive.
2. Open Excel.
3. Open the *Garden Center* workbook.
4. Click cell E4, which is where you will put a formula to calculate Profit. Type **=C4−D4**. Press ⏎Enter. The result will be displayed in cell E4. To check the formula, click cell E4. Look at the Formula bar, where the formula that you typed is displayed. If a formula is incorrect, you can click in the Formula bar and change the formula.
5. Copy the formula in cell E4 to cells E5:E7. Click cell E4. Move the mouse pointer to the lower right corner of the cell until it becomes a small black plus. Click and drag down to cell E7. Release the mouse button. The formula should be copied.
6. Click in cell A8. Because you plan to enter a total in this row, type the word **Total**. Press ⏎Enter.
7. Click in cell E8. You want to add the entries in the column above. The Sum function is a quick way to add entries in adjacent cells. Type **=Sum(E4:E7)**. Press ⏎Enter. Click back in cell E8 to check the formula.
8. Click in cell A9. Type **Average** and press ⏎Enter.
9. Click in cell E9. Create a function that will average the profit for all garden items. Type **=Average(E4:E7)**. Press ⏎Enter. Check the formula.
10. Save the worksheet again as *Garden Center.*
11. Close Excel.

Ruth needs to put a formula in cell B12 to calculate to number of pages the first student has read. She types **=Sum(B7:B10)** and presses ⏎Enter. Ruth realizes that the formula is relatively the same for each student. In fact, what the formula really says is "sum the occupied cells immediately above this location," which would be the same for all children. She wonders if she can just copy the formula over to the other children. She clicks in cell B12, which contains the original formula. Then, moving the mouse pointer to the lower right corner of

	A	B	C	D	E	F	G	H	I
1	Brookhaven Elementary School								
2	Fall Reading Program								
3									
4	Number of Pages Read								
5									
6	Week	Sandra Holland	Elizabeth Jenkins	Martha Smith	Robert James	Daniel Harding			
7	10/14/2004	125	229	108	73	209			
8	10/21/2004	113	143	76	149	287			
9	10/28/2004	156	200	89	113	255			
10	11/4/2004	132	214	103	210	241			
11									
12	Total								

Figure 10.20 **You can use a worksheet to keep a record of many activities, in this case, a school reading program.**

■▶**Quick Tip**

The AutoSum button shortens the task of typing an *=Sum* function. For example, if the cell pointer is at cell D10 and you plan to sum entries in the column above, click the AutoSum button. The cell will display a suggested *=Sum* function, including as an argument the occupied cells adjacent to the cell pointer. Press ↵Enter to accept the suggested function.

the cell, she clicks the fill handle (the location where the mouse pointer becomes a small black plus sign) and drags to copy the formula to the other columns. It works! The formula accurately sums each child's total pages, adjusting cell references as it is copied. The formula in cell B12 reads *=Sum(B7:B10)*. Clicking in cell C12, Ruth finds that the formula reads *=Sum(C7:C10)*. Copying a formula where the cell references adjust *relative* to the new location, is called a **relative reference**. To continue the worksheet, Ruth adds a column to sum each week's total pages, as shown in Figure 10.21.

Next, she wants to determine each week's percentage of the total pages read. In cell H7, she types **=G7/G12** and presses ↵Enter. She finds that approximately 23 percent of the total pages read were completed in the first week of the program. To save time, she decides to copy the formula from cell H7 to the remaining weeks in the column. Instead of finding correct percentages, the data appears as shown in Figure 10.22. What happened?

Taking a closer look at the formula as it was copied, Ruth finds that, although the formula was correct in cell H7, it was adjusted as it was copied to cell H8 to read *=G8/G13*. Although the first cell reference (G8) adjusted correctly to reflect the next week's total, the item to be divided needed to remain referenced as cell G12 (total pages read for the month), not adjusted to G13. When it was adjusted to cell G13, a division by 0 error occurred, because there is no entry in cell G13

	A	B	C	D	E	F	G	H
1	Brookhaven Elementary School							
2	Fall Reading Program							
3								
4	Number of Pages Read							
5								
6	Week	Sandra Holland	Elizabeth Jenkins	Martha Smith	Robert James	Daniel Harding	Total Pages	Percent of Total
7	10/14/2004	125	229	108	73	209	744	
8	10/21/2004	113	143	76	149	287	768	
9	10/28/2004	156	200	89	113	255	813	
10	11/4/2004	132	214	103	210	241	900	
11								
12	Total	526	786	376	545	992	3225	
13								

Figure 10.21 **Column G includes the total pages read each week.**

	A	B	C	D	E	F	G	H
1	Brookhaven Elementary School							
2	Fall Reading Program							
3								
4	Number of Pages Read							
5								
6	Week	Sandra Holland	Elizabeth Jenkins	Martha Smith	Robert James	Daniel Harding	Total Pages	Percent of Total
7	10/14/2004	125	229	108	73	209	744	0.230697674
8	10/21/2004	113	143	76	149	287	768	#DIV/0!
9	10/28/2004	156	200	89	113	255	813	#DIV/0!
10	11/4/2004	132	214	103	210	241	900	#DIV/0!
11								
12	Total	526	786	376	545	992	3225	
13								
14								
15								
16								

Figure 10.22 **The percentages in column H are incorrect.**

	A	B	C	D	E	F	G	H
1	Brookhaven Elementary School							
2	Fall Reading Program							
3								
4	Number of Pages Read							
5								
6	Week	Sandra Holland	Elizabeth Jenkins	Martha Smith	Robert James	Daniel Harding	Total Pages	Percent of Total
7	10/14/2004	125	229	108	73	209	744	0.230697674
8	10/21/2004	113	143	76	149	287	768	0.238139535
9	10/28/2004	156	200	89	113	255	813	0.252093023
10	11/4/2004	132	214	103	210	241	900	0.279069767
11								
12	Total	526	786	376	545	992	3225	
13								

Figure 10.23 **The formula in the Percent of Total column is copied correctly when an absolute reference is included.**

(it is null, or zero). The G12 reference in the original formula should have remained absolute, or constant. It should not have been adjusted relative to its copy location. To cause the cell reference to remain absolute, Ruth must retype the formula in cell H7. It should be *=G7/G12*. The dollar signs included in the cell reference cause Excel to interpret it as an **absolute reference**, so that it will not be adjusted as it is copied to another location. Now, when Ruth copies the formula down the column, the correct percentages appear, as shown in Figure 10.23. Because the G12 cell is absolute, each percentage is divided correctly by the total shown in cell G12.

Formatting a Workbook

You can improve the appearance of a worksheet by applying formatting changes, which means altering the way numbers and text look. The Formatting toolbar includes icons that allow you to make boldface, italicize, underline, change font type and size, and change the alignment of cell contents. The Format menu provides another way to apply formatting changes. Columns are often too narrow to display cell contents fully. You can easily expand or reduce column (and row) size. With the bordering and shading options, a worksheet can take on the appearance of a colorful, well-designed document. After a worksheet is printed, it might even be difficult to determine whether it was created in Excel or Word!

Using Spelling Check and AutoCorrect

Excel includes some helpful proofing tools—Spelling and Grammar, and Auto-Correct. The Spelling and Grammar button is found on the Standard toolbar. To check spelling and grammar in a worksheet, make cell A1 the active cell, and click the Spelling and Grammar button. Words that aren't in Excel's dictionary are highlighted and displayed in a dialog box. You can choose to Ignore one occurrence or to Ignore All occurrences (throughout the worksheet) of the mis-spelling, or you can accept one of the suggested corrections. If the correct spelling is not included in the dialog box, you must correct the word yourself.

Although the function of the Spelling and Grammar tool is obvious, you might not be familiar with the AutoCorrect feature. As we hurriedly type, we are bound to make mistakes, some more frequently than others. How many times

**Quick Tip**

Remember the Undo button! Especially when centering a heading across the width of a worksheet, things can go wrong. Instead of worrying about exactly what happened, just click Undo and try it again!

Hands On

Activity 10.7—Using Absolute References

In this activity, you will create a worksheet using formulas and absolute references. Your computer should be at the desktop.

1. Place a disk in the A: drive.
2. Open Excel.
3. Create the worksheet shown in Figure 10.24.
4. Click cell C5. To calculate the Bonus, you must multiply the Sales amount by the Bonus percent (3%). You might think that the formula should be =B5*B12, which is a step in the right direction, but consider what will happen when the formula is copied to other employees. Brown's formula will be =B6*B13. It is true that Brown's Sales amount is found in cell B6, but what is in cell B13? Nothing, which means that the Bonus for Brown will be 0, which is incorrect. Cell B12 should be listed as an absolute reference, so that it is not adjusted as it is copied. Therefore, the correct formula to type in cell C5 is **=B5*B12**.

	A	B	C	D	E	F	
1	Home Supply Central						
2	Sales and Commission						
3							
4	Employee	Sales	Bonus	Total			
5	Anders	4095					
6	Brown	3444					
7	Connors	3474					
8	Dupree	2009					
9	Huggins	3881					
10	Terry	2222					
11							
12	Bonus %	3%					
13							

Figure 10.24 **This worksheet summarizes employee data.**

5. Click cell C5 once again. To copy the formula down the column, move the mouse pointer to the lower right corner of the cell. The pointer becomes a small black plus sign. Click and drag down to cell C10. Release the mouse button. The formula is copied correctly.
6. Click cell D5. Type the formula **=B5+C5**. Copy the formula down the column.
7. Click cell A11. Type the word **Total**. Press ⏎Enter.
8. Click cell B11. Click the AutoSum button. The suggested formula should sum cells B5:B10. Press ⏎Enter to accept the suggestion.
9. Click back in cell B11. Copy the formula across, ending at cell D11.
10. Save the worksheet on your floppy disk as *Bonus*.
11. Close Excel.

have you typed the word "the" as "teh"? The AutoCorrect tool is quick to correct that misspelling without even flagging it as misspelled. AutoCorrect is designed to correct not only common misspellings, but also to capitalize the first letter of a sentence, to capitalize the names of days, and to correct two initial capital letters by changing the second letter to lowercase. If you frequently misspell certain words, you can add them to the AutoCorrect dictionary. Click Tools, AutoCorrect Options, and type the word that you often misspell in the Replace area. Then type the correct spelling in the Replace With box. Click OK to accept the new word.

Aligning Data

Excel automatically aligns text data to the left side of a cell and numbers to the right. However, you can easily change that alignment. You might decide that a column heading would look better right aligned over a column of numbers.

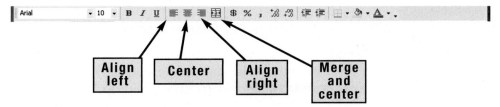

Figure 10.25 **You can align data to the right, left, or center of a cell.**

Before changing alignment, remember the rule to *select before you change.* The alignment icons are found on the Formatting toolbar, as shown in Figure 10.25.

Often, you will want to center a title or heading over the width of the worksheet, not just within one cell. Don't go to the trouble of manually centering the title, because Excel makes it easy to automate that task. Just type the title in a single cell above the left edge of the worksheet data. Complete the worksheet. To center the title, click and drag the title and the width of the worksheet. Then click the *Merge and Center* button, as shown in Figure 10.25.

Formatting Numbers

When you enter numbers in an unformatted worksheet, they appear without dollar signs, commas, or leading or trailing zeros. To improve the appearance of numbers, you can apply numeric formats. Perhaps you want a total row to display as currency (dollars and cents). Another column might look better when expressed as a percentage. Still another cell should include a comma, no decimal places, and no dollar sign. All of those formats are easy to apply and can make a dramatic difference in the appearance of worksheet data, making it easier to read and understand.

As always, the first step is to select the range of cells that you want to format. If all the cells in a column are to be affected, you can select the entire column. If only one cell should be changed, click the single cell. Some formatting options (such as currency, comma, and percent) are found on the Formatting toolbar, as shown in Figure 10.26. You can use the Format Cells dialog box (click Format, Cells, Numbers) to make more precise settings.

Adjusting Column Width

If your data is too wide to fit into a cell, it will "spill over" into the next cell. If the next cell is vacant, then that's no problem. However, if the next cell is occupied, the data will be truncated, or cut off. Even if it is truncated, the data is still

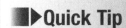**Quick Tip**

You can increase or decrease row height the same way that you increase or decrease column width. If you are using the Format menu, select Rows instead of Columns.

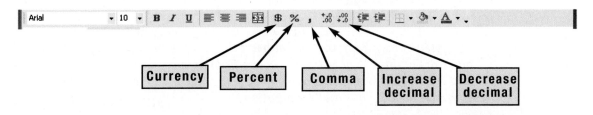

Figure 10.26 **You can quickly change the numeric format of a cell by making selections from the Formatting toolbar.**

in the cell—it is just not all displayed. To cause the data to appear, you can expand the column width. There are a few ways to do that:

- Click and drag the boundary (small black line) in the gray area following the cell that is too narrow. You can increase or decrease column width this way.

- Double-click the boundary (small black line) in the gray area following the cell that is too narrow to automatically apply the width necessary to display the longest entry in the column.

- Select the column (or columns) to be widened. Click Format, Column. Choose Width (which allows you to enter a specific point size for column width) or AutoFit Selection (which automatically expands the column to accommodate the longest entry).

✓ SANITY CHECK

If the result of a calculation is too long to fit in the column, you might see a series of pound signs (#####) in the cell. Don't panic—the value is still in the cell, you just can't see it because the cell is not wide enough. To correct the problem, expand the column width.

Hands On

Activity 10.8—Formatting a Worksheet

In this activity, you will create and format a worksheet. Your computer should be at the desktop.

1. Place a disk in the A: drive.
2. Open Excel.
3. Create the worksheet shown in Figure 10.27. Some of your columns will not be wide enough to display all data. You will widen them later, so don't worry if the data is truncated.
4. Expand column A to accommodate the longest entry by double-clicking the boundary between columns A and B (in the gray border area). Similarly, expand any other columns necessary.
5. Make the column headings in row 3 boldface. Click the row 3 heading (in the gray border area), and click the Bold button.
6. Make the title in cell A1 boldface. Change the font size by clicking the drop-down arrow beside font size on the Formatting toolbar. Select a size of 16.
7. Enter a formula in cell C10 to sum the values in the column above.
8. Change the alignment of the word "Customer" in cell A3. Click cell A3, and click the Center Align button.
9. Change the alignment for column C. Select column C by clicking the heading in the gray border area. Click the Center Align button. Click anywhere outside the selected area.
10. Format the numbers in column C. Click and drag to select cells C4:C8. Click Format, Cells, and click the Number tab. In the Category area, click Number. If necessary, set the Decimal positions setting to 2, which means that two numbers will be displayed to the right of the decimal point. Click OK.
11. Format the total in cell C10 as currency, with two decimal places. Click cell C10. Click the Currency button on the Formatting toolbar.
12. Center the label in cell A1 across the width of the worksheet. Click and drag from cell A1 to cell C1. Click the Merge and Center button. The label should be centered across the worksheet.
13. Save the workbook on your disk as *Stanhope Florist*.
14. Close Excel.

	A	B	C	D	E	F
1	Stanhope Florist					
2						
3	Customer	Arrangement	Charge			
4	Owens, Max	Lily	38.95			
5	Landers, Marie	Spring Flowers	25.5			
6	Hagood, Lyle	Roses	52			
7	Cook, Brad	Daisy/Balloon	18.95			
8	Henderson, Susan	Roses	52			
9						
10	Total.					
11						
12						
13						

Figure 10.27 **The columns in this worksheet have been widened to accommodate lengthy entries.**

Chapter Summary

DON'T FORGET

- Spreadsheet software simplifies the task of organizing numeric data on an electronic grid of columns and rows.

- A workbook includes one or more worksheets.

- Microsoft Excel is a spreadsheet program included in the Microsoft Office suite.

- Data can be typed in a worksheet as labels, values, or formulas.

- Before making any changes to worksheet data, you must first select the cells to be affected.

- A range is a group of one or more cells.

- You can select ranges, columns, and rows.

- A formula is a set of instructions that tells Excel how to perform a calculation.

- Functions are predefined formulas that simplify complex operations.

- Absolute cell references in a formula don't change as the formula is copied to another location, whereas relative cell references change relative to the position they are copied from.

- When you make changes to a worksheet, such as aligning data, formatting numbers, or changing the appearance of worksheet data, you are formatting it.

KEY TERMS

absolute reference	Formula bar	range
cell address	function	range reference
cell pointer	gridlines	relative reference
cell reference	landscape orientation	row headings
column headings	Name box	workbook
fill handle	order of precedence	worksheet
formula	portrait orientation	worksheet area

TRUE/FALSE

Circle **T** if the statement is true or **F** if the statement is false.

T F   1. Each worksheet can include several workbooks.

T F   2. The dark border surrounding the active cell is called the cell pointer.

T F   3. A selected group of one or more cells is called a range.

T F   4. You can enter three types of data in cells—labels, values, and formulas.

T F   5. The Name box indicates the position of the active cell.

T F   6. Worksheet columns are identified by numbers, and rows by letters.

T F   7. A worksheet is normally printed in landscape orientation.

T F   8. You can have only eight workbooks open at one time.

T F   9. A cell reference in a formula that is not adjusted as it is copied is an absolute reference.

T F   10. If a cell entry begins with a plus sign, Excel interprets the entry as a formula.

MULTIPLE CHOICE

Circle the correct choice for each of the following.

1. The intersection of each column and row is called a
   a. Name box
   b. cell
   c. Formula bar
   d. reference

2. Excel saves files with the extension
   a. .exl
   b. .ftp
   c. .mse
   d. .xls

3. A quick way to get to cell A1 is to press
   a. Ctrl + Home
   b. PgUp
   c. π
   d. Shift + Tab

4. Predefined formulas that simplify complex calculations are called
   a. ranges
   b. arguments
   c. functions
   d. clipboards

5. Text is automatically aligned to the
   a. center
   b. right
   c. left
   d. merge and center

6. Formatting options that are found on the Formatting toolbar are
   a. Currency, Number, and Accounting
   b. Currency, Percent, and Comma
   c. Percent, Date, and Text
   d. Currency, Percent, and Decimal

7. Which function key places a selected cell in edit mode?
   a. F2
   b. F1
   c. F8
   d. F5

8. To print gridlines, select this tab in the Page Setup dialog box.
   a. Margins
   b. Page
   c. Sheet
   d. Header/Footer

9. Before clicking and dragging to make a selection, you should be sure the mouse pointer looks like a(n)
   a. small black plus sign in the lower right corner of the first cell in the range
   b. arrow
   c. small box with a grid diagram inside
   d. large white plus sign

10. The number of columns included in an Excel worksheet is
    a. 65,536
    b. 128
    c. 256
    d. dependent on the amount of RAM

PRACTICAL PROJECTS

1. Troop Projects

As leader of a Cub Scout troop, you want to record the dollar amount spent for supplies for weekly meetings. Place a disk, labeled with your name, in the A: drive. Create an Excel worksheet, as shown in Figure 10.28.

a. Make the title in cell A1 boldface.
b. Expand any columns necessary to let cell contents fully appear.
c. In cell A15, type the word Total.
d. Include a formula in cell B15 to sum all expenses.
e. Format the total as Currency, with two decimal places.
f. Format all other numbers as Number, with two decimal places.
g. Save the worksheet on your disk as Cub Scouts.
h. Close Excel.

	A	B	C	D	E
1	Grove City Cub Scout Troop #116				
2					
3					
4		Spent			
5	15-Jan	8.97			
6	22-Jan	22.67			
7	29-Jan	5.43			
8	5-Feb	11.5			
9	12-Feb	9.36			
10	19-Feb	0			
11	26-Feb	6.64			
12	5-Mar	7.59			
13	12-Mar	5.5			
14					
15					
16					

Figure 10.28 **An Excel worksheet is a convenient way to record expenses.**

2. Balancing Act

Excel includes templates, which are predesigned workbooks for common tasks, such as sales invoices and balance sheets. Although a balance sheet is normally used by businesses, you can use the template to keep up with checking account records. Place a disk, labeled with your name, in the A: drive.

a. Open Excel.
b. If the task pane is not open, click View, Task Pane.
c. Under New From Template, click General Templates.
d. Click Spreadsheet Solutions.
e. Click Balance Sheet.
f. Click OK.
g. Complete the worksheet, as shown in Figure 10.29. The beginning balance represents your beginning checking account balance, with checks and deposits recorded in the area below. After the worksheet is complete, scroll to the right to see the running balance.
h. Save the worksheet on your disk as Checking Account.
i. Close Excel.

3. Raising Funds

You are involved with a fundraising event for your daughter's seventh-grade class. The kids are selling school jackets. To maintain records of items sold and to quickly calculate the class's markup, you will use Excel. Place a disk, labeled with your name, in the A: drive. Create the worksheet shown in Figure 10.30. Expand all columns necessary to display complete cell entries.

	A	B	C	D	E	F	G	H
1	Caplan Trading Post							
2	River Heights, Maryland							
3								
4		January	February	March	April	May	June	
5	Sales	48000	39800.27	45287.64	42567.22	40500	42675.9	
6	Cost of Goods Sold							
7	Net Sales							
8								
9	Expenses							
10	Operating	4509.31	4671	4500.08	4239.36	4891.88	3999.25	
11	Insurance	3090	3090	3090	3090	3090	3090	
12	Wages	8922	8922	8922	8922	8922	8922	
13	Other	7222.87	8646.11	7409.78	7620.61	8330.1	7407.01	
14	Total Expenses							
15								
16	Gross Income							
17	Tax							

Figure 10.29 **The Balance Sheet template includes areas for recording receipts and payments.**

	A	B	C	D	E	F
1	Fairfield Middle School Fundraiser					
2						
3	April, 2004					
4						
5	Item	Cost	Markup	Price		
6	Quilted Jacket	19.5				
7	Nylon Jacket	12				
8	Fleece-lined Jacket	22.95				
9						
10	Markup Percentage	75%				
11						
12						
13						

Figure 10.30 **This worksheet will determine price, based on markup.**

a. Format the numbers in column B as Number, with two decimal places. Do not, however, format the markup percentage in cell B10.

b. Center all entries in columns B, C, and D.

c. Enter a formula to calculate markup. Markup is *Cost * Markup Percentage*. Because you will copy the markup formula down to other items in column C, be sure to make Markup Percentage an absolute reference. Copy the Markup formula to cells C7 and C8.

d. Enter a formula for Price. Price is *Cost + Markup*.

e. Copy the Price formula to cells D7 and D8.

f. Format all numbers in columns C and D as Number, with two decimal places.

g. Apply an AutoFormat to the worksheet. First click and drag to select cells A1:D10. Then click Format,

AutoFormat. Select Classic 3 style. Click OK. Click outside the selected area to see the format.

h. Save the worksheet to your disk as *Fundraiser*.

i. Close Excel.

4. Keeping Score

You have been hired as a part-time college instructor to teach one section of American history. Having given two exams, you want to prepare an Excel worksheet to summarize exam scores and to calculate each student's final average. Place a disk, labeled with your name, in the A: drive. Create the worksheet shown in Figure 10.31.

a. Expand any columns necessary to fully display cell contents.

b. Enter a formula in cell E7 to calculate Final Average. The formula should be =*Average(B7:D7)*. Although students have not yet taken the third exam, you can include it in the Average formula ahead of time. That way, it will automatically be averaged with the other two exams when you type a score. Copy the formula in cell E7 down to cells E8 through E11.

c. Click cell A13. Type the words **Class Average**. Expand column A, if necessary.

d. Enter a formula in cell B13 to get a class average for the first exam. Use the =Average function. Copy the formula across to cells C13, D13, and E13. Ignore the

	A	B	C	D	E	F	G
1	American History						
2	T/Th 5:30-7:30						
3							
4	Fall, 2004						
5							
6	Student	Exam 1	Exam 2	Exam 3	Final Average		
7	Adams	98	92				
8	James	87	78				
9	Lawson	59	70				
10	Monroe	98	89				
11	Whitten	76	90				
12							
13							
14							
15							

Figure 10.31 **Excel is a wonderful tool for keeping class records.**

division by zero error that you get in cell D13. When you enter exam scores, the error will be corrected.

e. Make the column headings in row 6 boldface.

f. Make the entry in cell A1 boldface, and change the font size of that cell to 16.

g. Center the entry in cell A1 across the width of the worksheet.

h. Rename the sheet tab *American History*.

i. Type scores for the third exam. Make up a score for each student. The final average should reflect the new exam score.

j. Format all numbers in the worksheet as Number, with one decimal place.

k. Center all column data in cells B6 through E13. Expand column E to accommodate the longest entry.

l. Delete row 2. (Delete the entire row, not just the row contents.)

m. Save the worksheet to your disk as *Class Average*.

n. Close Excel.

5. Chart a Course

a. Using Excel, create the spreadsheet shown in Figure 10.32.

b. Expand any columns necessary to display cell contents.

c. Change the font of cells A1 and A2 to Century Schoolbook. Change the font size to 18.

d. Bold the items in cells A1 and A2.

e. Center cells A1 and A2 over the width of the worksheet.

f. Enter formulas for the following items:

Cost of Goods Sold = 25% * Sales

Net Sales = Sales − Cost of Goods Sold

Total Expenses = Sum of all expenses

Tax = Gross Income * Tax Rate

Net Income = Gross Income − Tax

g. Format all numbers as Number with two decimal places.

h. Select and apply an AutoFormat for the worksheet.

i. Name the sheet tab *Caplan Trading Post*.

j. Save the worksheet on a floppy disk as *Caplan Trading Post*.

	A	B	C	D	E	F	G	H
1	Caplan Trading Post							
2	River Heights, Maryland							
3								
4		January	February	March	April	May	June	
5	Sales	48000	39800.27	45207.64	42567.22	40500	42675.9	
6	Cost of Goods Sold							
7	Net Sales							
8								
9	Expenses							
10	Operating	4509.31	4671	4500.08	4239.36	4891.88	3999.25	
11	Insurance	3090	3090	3090	3090	3090	3090	
12	Wages	8922	8922	8922	8922	8922	8922	
13	Other	7222.87	8646.11	7409.78	7620.61	8330.1	7407.01	
14	Total Expenses							
15								
16	Gross Income							

Figure 10.32 **This worksheet data summarizes hours worked by volunteers.**

Appendix
Checklist for Purchasing
a Home Computer

Have you ever considered purchasing a home computer, only to become quickly intimidated by the sheer number of choices? Perhaps you have scanned newspaper ads and industry publications, only to find yourself confused by the technical specifications. What exactly is SDRAM? What size hard drive is large enough, and what does a sound card have to do with anything? Although it is easy to become overwhelmed by the choices, it is just as easy to follow a few simple guidelines and do a little research so that you more fully understand computer technical descriptions. Then you will more likely make the right choice for your computing needs.

When you examine a computer advertisement, you will probably find a listing of components and software included on the computer. That list is called the computer specifications, and it is important in your quest for a home computer. As you learn to interpret computer specifications, you will understand exactly what you are buying and can determine whether the computer configuration is appropriate for you. As you narrow down the choices, you will finally have to decide whether to purchase your computer from an online source or a local retail store.

Interpreting Computer Advertisements

One of the most challenging tasks for people new to the field of computers is interpreting computer advertisements. When you begin a search for a new computer, you will be on the lookout for computer ads and appealing offers. But when you find an interesting ad, do you understand what the computer specifications in the advertisement describe? Although the major categories, such as RAM, hard drive, and monitor, are relatively easy to understand, there will always be additional levels of detail that can be confusing. Without further study, it is impossible to understand every computer specification in every advertisement. However, the more specifications that you find and study, the better you will become at interpreting what they are saying about the computers that they are advertising.

The computer specifications given in Figure 1 describe a typical home computer configuration. Each specification is described in detail so that you can better understand what you are likely to see in other ads.

DIMENSION XPS DETAILS

Figure 3 Computer companies, such as Dell, allow you to customize a computer, specifying the configuration that you want to buy.

Whether you buy online or in a store depends on your level of computer confidence. If you have a firm foundation in computer basics and know what you want from a computer system, you might find online purchasing to be the quickest, most foolproof approach to purchasing a computer. If, however, you feel uncomfortable evaluating computer specifications and don't feel sure of yourself when comparing the computer models that are available for purchase online, you will probably be more comfortable working with a salesperson at an electronics or computer store to identify the best system for you.

However you choose to purchase a computer, keep in mind the need to include a service plan and to explore customer support. Make sure that you will be able to talk with a technical support representative in fairly short order if you have any problems. Be sure that you thoroughly understand the service plan, including parts, labor, and on-site repairs.

Glossary

A

A Drive—The A: drive—also called the floppy drive—is a device that reads from a reusable magnetic storage medium called a floppy disk. Because the capacity of a floppy disk is often insufficient for many files and projects, floppy disks are becoming outmoded and are often not included as a standard component of new computer systems.

absolute reference—An absolute reference is a cell address that does not change, even if it is included in a formula that is copied elsewhere.

access time—The access time is the average time lapsing between initiating a request to retrieve a data file from disk and obtaining the first character of the file. It includes the time it takes to move the read/write head to the required disk track, and the time it takes the disk to rotate to the required sector.

active scripting—Active scripting languages make web pages active, or dynamic. An active web page might update the date and time or create scrolling text.

adware—Much like spyware, adware is software that gathers information about a computer user's Internet travels without the person's knowledge. Adware sometimes accompanies downloaded software, usually with some written acknowledgment of the adware's presence.

America Online—America Online (AOL) is the world's largest online information service, with more than 35 million customers. It provides access to the Internet, e-mail, chat rooms, and a variety of databases and online services.

antivirus—An antivirus program scans computer systems and files for evidence of known viruses that have attached themselves to executable programs. Computer users must periodically download new virus definitions to maintain effective virus protection.

antivirus software—Antivirus software searches a computer system for computer viruses, removing any that are found.

applet—An applet is a program that is executed from within another application.

ARPAnet—ARPAnet (Advanced Research Projects Agency Network) began in 1969 as a computer network advancing communication between government and scientific organizations. After several transitions in name and purpose, the network is now managed by commercial Internet service providers. ARPAnet was the forerunner of the current Internet.

asymmetric DSL—ADSL (Asymmetric Digital Subscriber Line) is a type of DSL usage that provides fast downloading, but slower uploading.

attachment—An attachment is a file that has been linked to an e-mail message so that they travel together to their destination. Any type of file can be attached, such as a document, photograph, or spreadsheet.

B

background—The background is the base color, or image, displayed on the desktop (behind the icons). The background only appears on the desktop, not on open windows.

backup—A backup file is a copied file on a different storage media. The backup file can be used to restore a file if the original copy becomes damaged or unusable.

backup utility—A backup utility is a program that copies files to another storage medium so that they can be recovered if the original storage device fails.

backward compatible—Software is backward compatible if it can use files created with an older version of the same program.

Basic Rate Interface—Basic Rate Interface (BRI) is Integrated Services Digital Network's basic service, which is comprised of several data communication channels. When all channels are combined into one, the total data rate is 128 Kbps, which is four and one-half times faster than a 28.8 Kbps dial-up modem.

bit—Short for binary digit, a bit is the smallest unit of information that a computer can represent. Each bit can hold one of two possible values—1 or 0.

bookmark—A bookmark—sometimes called a favorite—is a stored URL address for quick retrieval at a later date. As you visit web pages, and find favorites that you would like to visit later, you can save the URL as a bookmark. To get to the page later, select the URL from the list of bookmarks.

booting—Booting is the process of starting a computer. The name comes from the phrase, "to pull yourself up by your bootstraps."

broadband—Broadband is high-speed data transmission, approximating that of a T1 line. Internet access through cable modems and DSL is often referred to as broadband.

browser—Short for web browser, a browser is software that displays the Internet on your computer. To move to other web sites, you can type the URL (address) of any web site in the browser's address bar. The two most popular browsers are Internet Explorer and Netscape Navigator. Some online service providers, such as AOL, incorporate a browser into the interface, so that you don't need a separate browser.

byte—A byte is a unit of measurement based on the binary system, representing one character. The capacity of memory and storage devices is measured in bytes.

C

cable modem—A cable modem connects a computer to a cable TV service that provides Internet access. Cable modems provide an always-online Internet connection that is much faster than dialup access. Data communication speed varies, depending on how many customers share a cable segment.

cascade—When more than one window is open, the windows can be displayed in a cascade format, with open windows overlapping each other in an orderly arrangement.

CD-ROM—A CD-ROM (Compact Disk-Read Only Memory) disk is a form of optical storage, capable of holding up to 1 GB. A CD-ROM can be read from, but not written to.

CD-R—A CD-R (Compact Disk-Recordable) disk is a form of optical storage that can be written to one time and read from many times. Once data is written to a CD-R, it cannot be erased.

CD-RW—A CD-RW (Compact Disk-ReWritable) disk is a form of optical storage that can be read from and written to many times.

Cell—A cell is the intersection of a column and row in a spreadsheet. Data is entered in a cell.

cell address—A cell address refers to the location of a cell within a spreadsheet. The column and row indicators, such as A1 or D15, designate the address.

cell pointer—The cell pointer is the dark border surrounding the active cell in a spreadsheet.

cell reference—See cell address

clip art—Clip art is images, saved as graphic files that can be used to illustrate documents or projects. Clip art is available either as shareware or for purchase.

clipboard—The clipboard is a reserved section of computer memory that temporarily holds items or sections of text until they are transferred to other applications. You can use cut, copy, and paste functions to move data into and out of the clipboard.

closing a window—To close a window, click the close button—it has a picture of an X on it—found at the upper right side of a window. When you close a window it is removed from memory as well as from the screen.

column headings—Column headings are the letters found in the gray area at the top of a worksheet.

commercial software—Commercial software is software that is available for sale to the general public.

communications program—A communications program is software that manages the transmission of data between computers.

CompuServe—CompuServe is an online information service that provides Internet access as well as e-mail and instant messaging. AOL acquired CompuServe in 1998. Whereas AOL targets the home computer user, CompuServe includes features attractive to the professional business user.

computer virus—A computer virus is software that is purposely written to damage computer files or to annoy computer users. Viruses are often disguised within other programs.

contents pane—The contents pane is displayed on the right side of the Windows Explorer window, showing all the subfolders and files contained in the currently selected folder.

context menu—A context menu appears when you right-click an on-screen object or area. The options displayed on a context menu are completely dependent upon the object or area of the screen that a user right-clicks.

control menu—The control menu is a list of options that appear when you click the control menu icon, found at the far left side of all title bars. The menu contains options for restoring, closing, maximizing, resizing, moving, and minimizing a window.

control menu icon—The control menu icon is the small icon found at the far left side of all title bars. Clicking the control menu icon causes a control menu to appear.

cookies—A cookie is a data file that is stored on a user's computer either temporarily or permanently. Cookies are created by Web servers and serve to identify users and keep track of their preferences. Cookies sometimes remember passwords so that a user doesn't have to reenter them when he or she returns to the Web sites later.

copy—Items or text can be copied to the clipboard, where they remain until they are pasted or until other copied items replace them.

copyleft—A copyleft is a license that accompanies some types of software giving the right to use and modify the software and requiring that the same licensing stipulation is available to anyone who obtains the software.

copyright—Based on the Constitution, a copyright is the legal protection granted to literary works, music, and computer programs, making it illegal to reproduce them without permission.

CP/M—CP/M is an operating system created by Gary Kildall of Digital Research in the early 1980's.

CPU—The central processing unit (CPU) is the controller of a computer system, interpreting and acting on program instructions. It is sometimes simply called the processor.

crawler—A crawler is a program that searches for information on the Internet. It follows links from server to server and indexes information based on a search criteria specified by a computer user. Crawlers are also known as spiders, ants, robots (bots), and intelligent agents.

crippleware—Crippleware is a variation of shareware in which software is available free of charge, but the software becomes inactive after a specified number of days. Some advanced features may not be available at all until you pay a fee to the author.

cut—Selected data or items can be cut from an original document or project and placed in the clipboard, where the items will remain until pasted to another application or until another set of data replaces them. The difference between a copy and a cut is that a copy retains the duplicated data in the original location whereas a cut removes the original data when it is placed in the clipboard.

cybersquatting—Cybersquatting is registering an Internet domain name for the purpose of reselling it for a profit. The Anti-Cybersquatting Consumer Protection Act enables trademark holders to obtain civil damages up to $100,000 from cybersquatters that register their trade names as domain names.

D: drive—The D: drive is usually the disk drive that reads from a CD or DVD.

database software—Database software serves as an electronic filing cabinet, making it possible to record, update, and retrieve records.

data file—A data file is created by a user when working with an application program. A data file can contain just about any type of information, such as documents, spreadsheets, or photographs.

desktop—The desktop is the on-screen background with icons, found with graphical user interfaces that are included in such operating systems as Windows and Macintosh.

desktop computer—A desktop computer is a microcomputer in which all components, including the keyboard, mouse, monitor, and system unit, easily fit on or under a desk.

desktop publishing—Desktop publishing is using a personal computer to produce high quality or camera-ready printed output. Desktop publishing software, a microcomputer, and a high-quality printer are all components of a desktop publishing system.

dial-up modem—New computers typically come equipped with a dial-up modem, which is a device that allows a computer to transmit data over a standard telephone line. A dial-up modem (simply called a modem) converts digital computer information to analog signals that a telephone is equipped to transmit. At the receiving end, a modem converts analog signals to digital.

dialog box—A dialog box is a special-purpose window that is displayed in response to a user selecting a menu option. A dialog box is designed to provide the current status of a program or operation and to accept input or directions from a user.

digital camera—A digital camera is a device that records images digitally so that you can download them to a computer and use a graphics program to manipulate and print them.

digital signature—A digital signature is an electronic encryption that ensures that the file originated with the entity signing it and that it was not tampered with after the signature was applied.

Digital Subscriber Line (DSL)—DSL (Digital Subscriber Line) is a technology that increases the digital capacity of telephone lines. DSL is only available to those people within a certain distance of a telephone switching station.

Disk Cleanup—Disk Cleanup is a utility program that removes files from the Recycle Bin (the temporary holding area for deleted files), deletes temporary Internet files, and compresses old files.

disk drive—A disk drive is a device that reads data from and writes data to a disk, such as a floppy disk, hard disk, CD, or DVD.

Diskette—Also known as a floppy disk, a diskette is a 3 1/2" removable magnetic disk on which data and programs can be stored.

disk scanner—A disk scanner is an error-checking utility that examines a disk, determining whether the disk is reliable and identifying any areas that are becoming unusable.

docking station—A docking station is a hardware unit into which a portable computer can be plugged, providing access to such devices as a printer, mouse, and additional disk drives.

domain—A domain name is the address of an Internet site. A domain name always has at least two parts, separated by a dot.

dot pitch—The dot pitch is a measurement of the diagonal distance between picture elements on a display screen. It is a primary factor in the determination of display quality, with the lower the number, the clearer the image.

downloading—Downloading a file means to receive a file transmitted over a network. Files and programs are often downloaded from Web sites.

driver—A device driver is a program that manages the functioning of a peripheral device, such as a printer or scanner. When a new hardware device is connected to a computer, its driver must be installed before the device can operate.

DVD—A DVD is similar to a CD, but with a much higher storage capacity. A DVD can hold a minimum of 4.7 GB, enough for a full-length movie. Other forms of DVDs include DVD-R and DVD-RW.

E

electronic mail (e-mail)—Electronic mail (e-mail) is the transmission of messages over a computer network, such as the Internet. Users can send e-mail messages to a single recipient or to multiple e-mail addresses. A user can also attach files, such as documents or photographs, to e-mail messages.

e-mail client—An e-mail client is software housed on the user's computer that can access e-mail servers on a network. The e-mail client makes it possible to send and receive e-mail messages and attachments.

e-mail server—An e-mail server is a computer that stores incoming mail for distribution and forwards outgoing e-mail.

embedded—An embedded object is an Object Linking and Embedding object that is not modified if the original object changes. An Excel chart could be included in a Word document as an embedded object, but when the chart is changed in the original Excel workbook, it is not changed in the Word document.

Encryption—Encryption is a method of coding data so that it is unreadable during data transmission.

end user license agreement (EULA)—A license, often called an End User License Agreement (EULA), accompanies software and specifies the terms of usage.

ergonomics—Ergonomics is the science concerned with the coordination of the workplace to the human body, assuring a high level of comfort and avoidance of certain health hazards.

error checking—Error Checking is a utility program that examines a disk for data storage errors, from physical defects on the disk surface to weakened areas that might cause that space to be unreliable. It corrects any errors that it can.

executable files—Also called program files, executable files are files that contain program instructions. Executable files are those files that cause programs, or applications, to run on your computer.

extension—Files are identified as specific types by an extension that is added to the end of the file name. Although most extensions continue to be three-letter lengths, such as doc and ppt, file formats now allow extensions to exceed the three-letter limit. An extension is separated from the file name by a dot (period).

F

favorites—See bookmark

file—A file is any item created by a user while working with an application program or by a programmer in creating an application program. A file is a collection of bytes saved as an individual entity.

All files are identified by a unique file name assigned by the user or programmer.

File Allocation Table (FAT)—Each disk storage medium contains a file allocation table (FAT), which is a file system used in the Windows environment that keeps track of where data are stored on the disk.

file compression—A file compression utility compresses files so that they require less space for storage or data transmission over the Internet.

file defragmentation—A file defragmentation utility rearranges bytes on a disk to rejoin pieces of files, placing them in adjacent locations and improving disk performance.

fill handle—A fill handle is a feature of a cell, which when clicked and dragged, causes cell or range data to be copied. In Excel, the fill handle is found at the lower right corner of a cell, as evidenced by a small black plus sign when the mouse pointer rests on it.

firewall—A firewall is hardware or software designed to give users secure access to the Internet or a company network. Firewalls are designed to prohibit unauthorized access to computer resources and files.

flaming—Flaming is the act of sending angry messages, usually by e-mail.

flash memory—Flash memory is often found in digital cellular phones, digital cameras, and notebook computers. It is a type of constantly powered nonvolatile memory with no moving parts.

floppy disk—A floppy disk is a soft magnetic disk encased in a rigid plastic cover. You can read from and write to a floppy disk multiple times. A floppy disk is portable, but has less storage capacity than most other forms of storage. The disk drive that reads a floppy disk is usually the A-drive.

folder—A folder is a holding area on a disk storage medium, designed to organize data, applications, and other folders. Sometimes referred to as a directory, or subdirectory, a folder is represented by a folder icon in a graphical user interface (GUI).

folders pane—The folders pane is displayed on the left side of the Windows Explorer window, showing drives, folders, and other resources on a computer system. It does not display files.

font—A font is a particular typeface design, size, and particular implementation. Fonts can be changed in many application programs, such as word processing. Examples of fonts include Times New Roman, Arial, and Helvetica.

formula—A formula is a combination of cell references and arithmetic operators that identifies how the data in a specific cell is to be calculated. The formula =A8+C9 means that the contents of cell A8 are to be added to the contents of cell C9, with the result placed in the cell where the formula is located.

formula bar—The formula bar is found just below the toolbars in an Excel window. The formula bar displays the contents of the active cell. If the active cell contains a formula, the formula bar displays the formula, whereas the cell itself displays the result of the formula. Changes to formulas or cell contents can be made on the formula bar.

fragmented—A fragmented file is one that is broken apart as it is saved, with pieces of the file being stored in any available free disk space. Fragmented files require extra disk head movement, slowing file access time.

freeware—Freeware is software that is available at no cost. Because freeware is copyrighted, you can redistribute the software, but not modify it.

FTP (file transfer protocol)—FTP (file transfer protocol) is used to transfer files to and from a Web server. It includes functions to log onto the network, list directories, and copy files.

full version—A full version of a software product contains all of the features and capabilities of the software.

function—A function is a predefined formula that simplifies a lengthy or complicated formula. Examples of functions include =SUM and =AVERAGE.

GIF—A graphic file format, GIF (Graphics Interchange Format) is a popular bitmapped graphics file format that is widely used on the Web because it compresses files well and is capable of displaying animated screen effects.

gigabyte—A gigabyte (GB) is equivalent to 1,024 megabytes, or approximately one billion bytes.

gigahertz—A gigahertz (GHz) is used as a measurement of processor speed, and is equivalent to 1 billion cycles per second.

graphical user interface (GUI)—A graphical user interface (GUI) is a screen display that incorporates windows and icons. Using a mouse, you can make selections from a GUI.

graphics—The term *computer graphics* encompasses creating, saving, and manipulating picture images on a computer.

graphics software—Graphics software is used to create or modify pictures and drawings. Some graphics programs are referred to as image editors, which accept digitized photographs and provide editing and enhancement features

gridlines—The horizontal and vertical borders separating cells are called gridlines.

handheld computer—Sometimes called a personal digital assistant, a handheld computer is small enough to fit in a hand. It is capable of supporting software similar to that found on a personal computer, but is most often used to manage personal information.

hard disk—A hard disk is a magnetic disk capable of storing much more data than most other data storage media. It is usually a fixed media, which means that it is not removed from the computer. The disk drive that reads a hard disk is usually the C-drive.

hard return—When you press the Enter key while typing a document, you insert a code, called a hard return. A hard return can be inserted and deleted just as you would any other character in the document.

hardware—Hardware is any piece of computer equipment that can be touched, such as the keyboard, monitor, and mouse.

history list—A history list is maintained by a Web browser, listing Web pages visited during a specified interval of time. From the history list, you can click a Web page to revisit it. You can set the history list to maintain history for a designated period of time (one month, two weeks, and so forth).

home page—A home page is the first page displayed when accessing a Web site. It contains general information and usually acts as a table of contents for other pages on the same site.

HTML—HTML (HyperText Markup Language) is the document format used to display Web pages. Pages are built with HTML tags (codes) which are embedded in the text and which describe a page's layout, font, graphic elements, and links to other documents.

HTTP—HTTP (HyperText Transfer Protocol) is the communications protocol used to connect to servers on the World Wide Web. It establishes a connection to a server and then transfers HTML pages to the computer user's browser. Most Web addresses begin with http://. However, if you leave off the http section of a Web address, the browser usually defaults to the http protocol.

hyperlink—A hyperlink connects one object or Web page with another. A link on a Web page is displayed either as text or as a graphic. A text hyperlink is usually underlined, while a graphic hyperlink is a picture of any size or shape. When you move the mouse pointer over a link, the pointer usually becomes a pointing hand.

I

icon—An icon is a small onscreen picture representing an object, such as a document, program, folder, or disk drive.

IMAP—IMAP (Internet Message Access Protocol) is a mail server protocol that holds incoming e-mail messages until an e-mail user logs on and reads the mail. To read e-mail from an IMAP server, a user must be online.

ink jet printer—An ink jet printer is a non-impact printer capable of producing high-quality text and graphics. It is the most popular choice for home computer users.

input—Input is data that is entered into the computer. Common input devices include the keyboard and mouse.

install—Before software can be used, it must be installed, or copied, onto a computer hard disk.

integrated program—An integrated program combines multiple functions, or activities, in one unit. Individual software components included in an integrated program are not sold separately.

Integrated Services Digital Network (ISDN)—ISDN (Integrated Services Digital Network) is a standard for providing digital communications from a computer user to a telephone network. ISDN separates an existing telephone cable into channels for the delivery of voice, data, or video. A dedicated ISDN modem is required for ISDN access.

Internet—The Internet is a huge network of networks made up of computers in more than 100 countries, providing access to commercial, academic, and government information. Sometimes referred to as the "information superhighway," the Internet provides information on just every subject imaginable.

Internet access provider (IAP)—Often called an ISP, an IAP (Internet Access Provider) is actually a subset of an ISP, offering only Internet access, with no additional services.

Internet Corporation for Assigned Names and Numbers (ICANN)—The Internet Corporation for Assigned Names and Numbers (ICANN) is a non-profit international association that manages Internet address and domain names.

Internet Explorer—Also known as IE, Microsoft Internet Explorer is a Web browser that is available as part of the Windows installation or as a free download. As the current market leader, Internet Explorer is also included in AOL's online software.

Internet service provider (ISP)—An ISP (Internet Service Provider) is an organization that provides consumers and businesses with access to the Internet. Customers pay a fee for usage of the ISP services. An ISP can include leased lines and web page development services.

Internet TV—Internet TV is an Internet service that uses a set-top box to connect a TV to a modem and telephone line. The first Internet TV service was WebTV (later called MSN TV).

insertion point—The insertion point is a blinking vertical line that indicates the position where text will begin. On a blank document, the insertion point is located at the top left corner of the document area.

keyboard—The keyboard is the primary input device for a microcomputer. It consists of a grid of keys that are very similar to a typewriter, but contain additional keys as well.

kilobyte—A kilobyte is 1,024 bytes, most often approximated as 1,000 bytes.

landscape orientation—Landscape orientation is printing a document across the wider side of the paper. Landscape orientation is wider than it is tall.

laptop computer—Sometimes called a notebook computer, a laptop computer is a small portable computer sized to fit in a lap. It utilizes a flat panel display and includes all computer components in a small, relatively lightweight, package.

laser printer—A laser printer is a non-impact printer using the same technology as a photocopier.

link—A Web page link (hyperlink) is a text or graphic area within a Web page that, when clicked, directs movement to another Web page or location.

linked—A linked object is an Object Linking and Embedding object in which changes to the original object are reflected in the linked object. For example, an Excel chart can be linked and displayed in a Word document. If the original chart is changed in the Excel worksheet, it is automatically changed in the Word document, as well.

Linux—Linux is an open-source operating system found on a variety of hardware platforms. It is readily available from such vendors as Red Hat Software and the SCO Group.

liteware—See crippleware.

lossless—A lossless compression method compresses an image without losing any of the data. GIF is an example of lossless compression.

lossy—A lossy compression method achieves a high degree of compression by removing some of the image when it is compressed. JPEG is an example of lossy compression.

M

magnetic disk storage—Data is recorded on a magnetic disk as microscopic magnetized areas on the disk surface. Data can be recorded and read any number of times. Magnetic disk formats include floppy disk, hard disk, and zip disk.

Mac OS—The Macintosh Operating System (Mac OS) supports Apple computers.

Mac OS X—The newest version of Mac OS is Mac OS X, which runs legacy Mac applications written for Mac OS 9 and earlier, as well as those applications specifically written for Mac OS X.

macro language—Applications, such as spreadsheet software and word processors, include a special purpose command language called a macro language. Although it is not a full-blown programming language, it is used to automate sequences within the application.

macro virus—A macro virus is code written in a macro language that is placed within a document or data file. When the document is opened, the program is run, causing whatever destruction or annoyance it is designed to accomplish.

maximizing a window—A window that is maximized fills the entire screen. To maximize a window, click the maximize button found at the upper right side of a typical window.

megahertz—A megahertz (MHz) is used as a measurement of processor speed, and is equivalent to 1 million cycles per second.

memory—Memory is temporary internal storage in a computer, holding programs and data currently in use. It is volatile, which means that contents are lost with any interruption in power supply. Random access memory (RAM) is a form of memory.

menu bar—Windows applications, such as Word and Excel, include a menu bar, which is a row of menu titles displayed across the top of the application window. Click any menu title to open the menu and select from subsequent options.

microcomputer—Sometimes called a personal computer, a microcomputer is designed to be used by an individual.

microprocessor—The microprocessor is a hardware unit that houses the CPU. The terms microprocessor and CPU are often used interchangeably.

Microsoft Network (MSN)—MSN (Microsoft Network) is Microsoft's ISP service, competing directly with AOL. With more than nine million customers, MSN is one of the largest Internet Service Providers in the United States.

Microsoft Windows—Microsoft Windows is the most widely used operating system for desktop and laptop computers. Available in various versions, Windows provides a graphical user interface utilizing movable onscreen windows.

MIME—MIME (Multipurpose Internet Mail Extension) is a method for transmitting non-text files by e-mail.

minimizing a window—A window that is minimized does not appear on-screen, but is listed as a button on the taskbar, and is still resident in memory. To minimize a window, click the minimize button found at the upper right side of a typical window.

monitor—A monitor is the primary form of output for a microcomputer. It is a television-like unit, sometimes called a CRT (cathode ray tube). Another form of monitor is the flat panel display, prevalent with laptop computers.

mouse—A mouse is a small input device that is used to control the onscreen movement of a mouse pointer, which moves in the same direction that the mouse is moved. It derives its name from its mouse-like shape, with the connecting cable resembling a mouse tail.

MS-DOS—Often simply called DOS, MS-DOS (Microsoft Disk Operating System) is a single user operating system produced by Microsoft in the 1980s. Unlike Windows, MS-DOS is a command-driven operating system that does not include a GUI.

MSN® TV—MSN® TV was developed in 1996 by Web TV and acquired in 1997 by Microsoft. It is an Internet TV service that uses a modem and telephone line to deliver Web content to a television set.

multifunction device—A device that includes such functions as a printer, fax machine, scanner, and copier in one unit.

N

name box—The name box is found just below the toolbars in an Excel window. It indicates the position of the active cell.

netiquette—Netiquette (network etiquette) is the set of rules dictating proper manners when communicating over the Internet.

Netscape—Netscape Navigator is Netscape's Web browser, a direct competitor to Microsoft Internet Explorer. It is available as a free download.

notebook computer—A notebook computer is a lightweight computer that is small enough to fit in a briefcase. It usually weighs less than six pounds.

NSFnet—The National Science Foundation Network (NSFnet) began during the 1980s as a computer network for academic information sharing. It served as the primary Internet backbone (passage) until the Internet became commercialized in the 1990s.

O

object—An object is an item, such as a picture, table, or chart, that is included in a document, spreadsheet, presentation slide show, or other application data file.

object-based graphics software—Object-based graphics software is a blending of features of both bitmap graphics software and drawing programs. Examples of object-based graphics software include Adobe Photoshop and CorelDRAW.

object linking and embedding (OLE)—Microsoft includes an Object Linking and Embedding (OLE) component in many Microsoft applications, which allows an object such as a graphic, video clip, or table to be duplicated (either by linking or embedding) in a file. When an object is embedded it is simply copied in the new location. However, when an object is linked, it is not only copied, but retains connection with the original item, so that any changes made to the original are also reflected in the copy.

office suite—An office suite is a combination of office productivity software components, each of which can be sold as a separate software package. The combination of software products into a suite provides a complete package at lesser cost than purchasing each component individually.

Online services—An online service is an organization that provides access to the Internet as well as special services and proprietary content. Examples of online services include America Online and CompuServe.

open source software—Open source software is software whose source code is free and available to anyone. The intent here is that a broader group of reviewers will produce a more useful and error-free software product.

operating system (OS)—The operating system is system software that coordinates system resources with application software, controls internal operations, saves documents and projects to disk, and manages memory.

operating system platform—An operating system platform is the environment in which hardware and software coordinate with a particular operating system. An operating system platform is categorized by operating system, such as a Windows platform or a Mac OS platform.

optical disk storage—Data is recorded on an optical disk by burning microscopic holes in the disk surface with a laser. Optical disk formats include CD and DVD.

order of precedence—The order of precedence is a set of rules that Excel uses to determine the order in which mathematical operations are to be calculated. Exponentiation is done first, followed by multiplication and division, and then addition and subtraction.

output—Output is information that comes out of a computer. Common output devices include the monitor and printer.

P

path—A path is the route to a file or folder on a disk. For example, the path to a folder titled "Curriculum Info," which is stored within the "College Info," folder on the hard drive (drive C:) is C:\College Info\Curriculum Info.

password—A password is a code that serves to secure data or equipment from unauthorized access. Passwords are often required to access Web sites, to sign on to a user account, or to access data.

paste—Items that have been cut or copied to the clipboard can be pasted to a document by making appropriate menu selections.

PC-DOS—PC-DOS is the original operating system developed by Microsoft for the IBM PC in the early 1980s. PC-DOS and MS-DOS were almost identical until the advent of MS-DOS version 6.

personal computer (PC)—A personal computer is a computer designed for use by an individual.

personal digital assistant (PDA)—A PDA is a handheld or palm-sized computer that allows you to record information, keep track of appointments, and manage your life much as a daily planner might. A typical PDA uses a touch screen and handwriting recognition software.

PIM (personal information manager)—A PIM (personal information manager) is a software application that provides organization of names and addresses, notes, calendar entries, and a scheduler. Microsoft Outlook is an example of a PIM.

pixel (picture element)—A pixel is a single dot on a graphic display. Because pixels are so close together they appear connected.

plug-in—A plug-in is a program that assists a browser with multimedia effects, such as audio, video, and animation on web pages. Examples of plug-ins include Shockwave, RealPlayer, and QuickTime.

PNG—PNG (Portable Network Graphics)—is a bitmapped graphics file format endorsed by the World Wide Web Consortium (W3C). It may eventually replace the GIF format.

POP3—POP3 (Post Office Protocol 3) is an e-mail server protocol that holds incoming e-mail messages until a user logs on and downloads them. All messages and attachments are downloaded together to the user's computer, and removed from the mail server.

portrait orientation—Portrait orientation is printing a document across the narrow side of the paper. Portrait orientation is taller than it is wide.

POST (power-on self test)—A POST is a self-diagnostic procedure that occurs when you start a computer. It verifies that all system components are operational.

presentation software—Presentation software is used to prepare computer slide shows, which are consecutively displayed screens of information. Businesses use presentation software to produce slide shows.

Primary Rate Interface—PRI (Primary Rate Interface) is high-speed ISDN service. It provides multiple channels for voice, data, and video transfer. ISDN is often used to support high-quality videoconferencing.

printer—The printer is a common output device for microcomputers. It is a device that prints text or graphics on paper. Common printers for home computers include ink jet printers and laser printers.

processor—See CPU

program—A program is another term for software or application. It is a collection of instructions that tells the computer what to do. Examples of application software include word processing and spreadsheet software.

program files—See executable files.

Progressive JPEG—A Progressive JPEG is a JPEG image that first appears as a low-quality, blurred picture, slowly coming into focus as it is displayed. Such image display gives the illusion that the picture appears faster, even though it takes the same time to fully display a progresseive JPEG image as it does to display a regular JPEG image.

protocol—A protocol is a hardware or software standard that coordinates data transmission between computers. TCP/IP is the fundamental transport protocol for the Internet, whereas HTTP, FTP, SMTP, and others are also used for Internet communication.

public domain software—Public domain software is not copyrighted and has no terms of usage or conditions attached.

Q

QDOS—QDOS (Quick and Dirty Operating System) was developed by Seattle Computer Products and purchased by Microsoft as the basis for PC-DOS and MS-DOS.

R

RAM—An abbreviation for random access memory, RAM is the most common type of memory found in computers. It holds data and programs currently in use. Because it is volatile its contents are lost with an interruption in power.

range—A range is one or more cells in a rectangular fashion that can be referred to as a group. It is defined by one corner and its diagonally opposite corner.

range reference—A range reference defines a range by two cells in opposite corners of the range, separated by a colon. A range extending from cell A1 in the top left corner to cell D25 in the lower right corner is identified by the range reference A1:D25.

refresh rate—The vertical refresh rate is the rate at which the monitor is redrawn. It is measured in hertz (Hz).

relative reference—A relative reference is an address that changes when the formula in which it is included is moved to a new location. The reference changes relative to the location of the move.

resolution—Resolution is a term that refers to the sharpness of an image on a printer or monitor. Screen resolution is simply the number of pixels on the screen, while printer resolution is the number of dots printed per inch.

restoring a window—A window can be restored to its original size (the size in which it displayed when it was first opened) by clicking the restore button found at the upper right side of a typical window.

root folder—The root folder is the starting point in a disk file hierarchy. The root folder is typically a disk drive, such as C:\ or A:\. Access to folders on the disk file hierarchy begins with the root directory, such as C:\Documents\October Memos.

row headings—Row headings are the numbers found in the gray area at the left side of a worksheet.

ruler bar—A ruler bar is a representation of a ruler that is displayed across the top of some Windows applications, such as Word. In a word processor, the ruler bar is used to set indents and tabs.

scaling—Scaling is an option in the Print dialog box, which enables you to fit a worksheet to a page, without manually changing font sizes.

scanner—A scanner is a device that converts text or graphics into a digital image. A scanner has an optical resolution as well as a digital resolution, which is computed by software.

Scheduled Task Wizard—The Scheduled Task Wizard is an automated process whereby you can schedule tasks to occur without your involvement. The Scheduled Task Wizard is a component of Windows XP.

screen saver—A screen saver is a constantly moving image that prevents a monitor from being permanently etched by a non-moving image. You can designate a specified duration of time without keyboard or mouse input after which a screen saver will begin. Pressing a key or moving the mouse restores the screen.

screen tip—A screen tip is a short description of a toolbar button. It appears when you hold the mouse pointer steady over any toolbar button.

search engine—A search engine is software that searches the Internet for data based on search criteria specified by the user. Search sites, such as Google and Excite use search engines to display sites matching some search criteria.

search tool—A search tool is a subject directory or search engine that simplifies the task of searching for information on the Internet.

sector—A sector is the smallest unit of storage read or written on a disk. It is a pie-piece shaped area of storage in which data can be stored for later retrieval.

server—A server is a computer that is designed to support other computer systems and to provide access to resources.

server license—A company can purchase a server license, which permits users connected to a server to access a single copy of software installed on the server.

shareware—Shareware is copyrighted software that is usually free only for a limited time.

shortcut—A shortcut is a pointer to a program or data file. Shortcuts are represented as desktop icons, which when double-clicked, open the associated file or program.

Site license—A site license allows an organization to make copies of a software product on several computers.

shortcut menu—See context menu.

S/MIME—S/MIME (Secure MIME) is a MIME version that supports encryption for secure transmission of multimedia e-mail messages.

SMTP—SMTP (Simple Mail Transfer Protocol) is the standard e-mail protocol for e-mail messages on the Internet. It defines the message format and includes facility for storing and forwarding mail.

soft return—As a document is typed using a word processor, the typist doesn't press the Enter key at the end of each line, but instead allows the text to automatically wrap at the right margin. The word processor inserts a code into the text to mark the end of the line, called a soft return. Unlike a hard return, the position of a soft return changes when margins are changed.

software—Software is the set of instructions that tells the computer how to accomplish a particular task.

software License—A software license describes the rights granted to a purchaser of software. Software is typically licensed, not sold,

so that a software purchaser can use the software without a time limit, but never owns the software itself and cannot make copies beyond what is specified by the license.

software piracy—Copying and distribution of software beyond the terms of a software license is called software piracy.

software suite—See Office Suite.

source code—Programming instructions that are written by a programmer are called source code. Source code is not directly executable by the computer, but must be converted into machine language by compilers, assemblers, or interpreters.

Spam—Spam is electronic junk mail that is unsolicited by computer users. Spam is usually advertisement that is indiscriminately sent to a large number of people.

spider—See crawler.

spreadsheet software—Software that provides a grid of columns and rows as the workspace is called spreadsheet software. It is often used for budgets and plans.

spyware—Spyware is software that is often built into free downloads. Its purpose is to send information about your Internet travel back to the computer from which it originated. Most computer users are not aware that spyware has been loaded onto their computer system.

SSL (Secure Sockets Layer)—SSL is a protocol designed to provide secure Internet communications.

standalone program—A standalone program is a software package that addresses only one application, such as a personal finance program or image editing software.

Start menu—The Start menu is launched from the Start button, usually found at the left side of the taskbar. It is the route to follow to run programs as well as to shut down a computer system.

status bar—The status bar is the horizontal bar that appears at the bottom of an application window giving information on document features, position, and language.

subfolder—A subfolder is an additional folder found within another folder. Each folder can include multiple subfolders, each of which can also contain subfolders.

subject directory—Very similar to a search engine, a subject directory offers links that are organized into subject categories. A subject directory is best used when you have a broad topic or idea to research.

surge protector—A surge protector is a device that provides protection from electrical power surges that could damage a computer.

system software—System software includes operating systems and utility programs. It is designed to control computer operations, assist with machine-level tasks, and run application programs.

system unit—Sometimes called the main unit, the system unit includes memory, disk drives, and ports. It is the main part of a personal computer.

system utilities—System utilities are programs that address such tasks as backing up disk files, scanning disk drives for errors, and eliminating computer viruses.

T

taskbar—The taskbar is the horizontal bar usually found at the base of the Windows desktop. It displays active applications (tasks), as well as the Start button and selected toolbars.

task pane—The task pane is a rectangular area that provides quick access to commands relevant to a task in which you are involved.

template—A template is a pre-designed document formatted for common purposes, such as a memo, calendar, or business letter. Templates are included in a standard Word installation.

tile—When more than one window is open, all windows can be displayed in a tile fashion, where parts of all open windows appear in a horizontal or vertical arrangement on-screen.

title bar—A title bar is the horizontal bar displayed at the top of a window, containing the name of the application or file.

toolbar—A toolbar is a row or column of on-screen icons that provide shortcuts to many menu selections. Some toolbars are customizable.

top-level domain—The top-level domain is found at the end of the domain name, and represents the purpose of the organization sponsoring the web site. The top-level domain of the address http://www.roundabout.com is ".com," which means that the organization is a commercial (for profit) entity.

track—A track is a storage channel on a disk or tape. On magnetic disks, a track is a concentric circle. CD and DVD tracks have one continuous, spiral-shaped channel starting at the center and moving outward. Magnetic tapes have tracks that are parallel lines along the length of the tape.

trackball—A trackball works much like an upside-down mouse, with the ball on the top. To move the onscreen pointer, you rotate the ball.

Trojan horse—A trojan horse is a program that appears to be harmless, but performs some destructive activity when it is run. Although similar to a virus, a Trojan horse does not replicate itself.

typeface—The typeface is the design of a set of printed characters. Although the terms *font* and *typeface* are often used interchangeably, the typeface is the primary design, while the font is the particular implementation and variation of the typeface, such as bold or italics.

U

Uniform Resource Locator (URL)—A URL (Uniform Resource Locator) is the address of a Web page. The URL, which defines the route to a file on the Web, is typed into the browser address area to direct travel to that file or page.

uninstall—Uninstalling is the process of removed unwanted programs from a computer.

UNIX—UNIX is a multi-user operating system widely used with workstations and servers. Written in the C programming language, it was developed by AT&T.

uploading—A file can be uploaded, or transmitted, from a personal computer across the Internet to a Web server.

upgrade—A software upgrade is a change to a newer version of existing software.

user account—a user account is a set of permissions associated with a user name and password

user name—A user name is the name by which you identify yourself when logging onto a computer or online service. Both a user name and a password are usually required in order to use an online service or to access protected data.

utility software—Utility software assists with computer tasks, such as file management, performing diagnostic routines, and antivirus scanning.

V

virus definitions—As new viruses are discovered, antivirus software developers create virus definitions, which identify and eliminate specific viruses. Computer users must download updated virus definitions often to maintain antivirus effectiveness.

W

Web applet virus—A web applet virus is coded in a web scripting language and is invoked when you access an infected web page

web authoring software—Web pages can be developed with web authoring software, which enables pages to be created visually and which produces underlying HTML code. Web authoring software does not require that the web developer be skilled in HTML coding.

web page—A web page is a web document that is identified by a particular URL. Several Web pages can make up a Web site.

web scripting language—A web scripting language is a programming language specifically oriented toward the production of web pages. JavaScript is often used to develop web pages, including forms controls, drop-down menus, and other flashy menu and graphics actions.

Web Site—A Web site is a server containing Web pages that are online 24 hours a day. A Web site is also considered a collection of one or more Web pages.

windowing environment—A windowing environment is an operating system configuration that makes use of windows, which are scrollable viewing areas on screen.

Windows Explorer—Windows Explorer is a Windows feature that allows you to view and manage all the folders on your system

Windows XP—Windows XP is the newest Windows version, introduced in 2001. It provides a new user interface, with an updated Start menu, taskbar, and control panels. It is available in two editions: Home and Professional.

wireless—Wireless data transmission uses various methods of communication including infrared, cellular, microwave, and satellite. A wireless network communicates without the assistance of cabling.

wizard—A wizard is a series of guided screens that simplifies a task by asking questions and allowing you to modify settings, typically in a question and answer format.

word processor—Software used to create text documents is called a word processor. It is also used for basic desktop publishing, in which graphics and enhanced text and typesetting can be incorporated into document tasks.

word wrap—Word wrap is a word processing feature that automatically moves words to the next line as text meets the right margin.

workbook—An Excel workbook is made up of one or more worksheets. When you save an Excel file, you are actually saving a workbook.

worksheet—An Excel worksheet is an electronic grid of columns and rows in which you can enter data.

World Wide Web—The World Wide Web (WWW) is an Internet service that connects documents or Web pages for display on browsers. The WWW is a subset of the Internet. The Internet is the physical network over which WWW communication travels.

World Wide Web Consortium (W3C)—W3C is a volunteer organization that creates standards for the World Wide Web. It is based at the Massachusetts Institute of Technology (MIT).

worm—A worm is a destructive program that replicates itself, using up computer resources, possibly bringing the computer system down.

WYSIWYG—A feature of word processing software, WYSIWYG (What You See Is What You Get) is the display of text and graphics on screen in the way that they will appear when printed. It is impossible to display text on screen exactly as it will print, however, because screen and printer resolutions differ. However, WYSIWYG is a very close approximation.

Z

zip disk—A zip disk is a high-capacity floppy disk that is slightly larger physically than a normal floppy disk and at least twice as thick. It can hold at least 100 times more data than a floppy disk.

Credits

fig #

1.12b	Courtesy of International Business Machines Corporation. Unauthorized use not permitted.
1.14	Courtesy of Canon USA. The Canon logo is a trademark of Canon Inc. All rights reserved.
1.18	Copyright © 2003 Iomega Corporation. All Rights Reserved. Zip is a registered trademark in the United States and/or other countries. Iomega, the stylized "i" logo and product images are property of Iomega Corporation in the United States and/or other countries.
1.19	© Royalty-Free/CORBIS
2.10	© 2003 Symantec Corporation
2.24	Courtesy of the Software & Information Industry Association
6.3	© TOUHIG SION/CORBIS SYGMA
6.5	© Intel
6.10	© 2003 by Consumers Union of U.S., Inc., Yonkers, NY 10703. Used by permission. Log on to www.ConsumerReports.org.
6.10	© 2003 WebMD Inc
6.11	Reproduced with permission of Yahoo! Inc. © 2003 by Yahoo! Inc. YAHOO! and the YAHOO! logo are trademarks of Yahoo! Inc.
6.12	© 2003 Lycos, Inc.
6.13	© 2003 Google
6.15	Debt Elimination Homepage
7.1	© 2003 Tucows Inc.
7.9	©1999-2003 Zone Labs, Inc. All rights reserved.
7.10	PepiMK Software
7.11	© Ralph A. Clevenger/Corbis
8.21	AOL screenshots © 2003 America Online, Inc. Used with permission.
A.3	Copyright 1999-2003 Dell Computer Corporation

Index